D1204350

UNIVERSITY OF WINNIPEG
LIBRARY
515 Portage Avenue
Winnipeg, Manitoba, R3B 2E9

apor

upor

THE INDEPENDENT THEATRE
IN EUROPE

1887 TO THE PRESENT

PN
2570
.M5
1966

THE
INDEPENDENT THEATRE
IN EUROPE

1887 TO THE PRESENT

By

ANNA IRENE MILLER, PH.D.

Associate Professor of English in Goucher College;
Lecturer in the College for Teachers,
The Johns Hopkins University

BENJAMIN BLOM  New York/London

First Published New York 1931
Reissued 1966, by Benjamin Blom, Inc., New York 10452
Library of Congress Catalog Card No. 65-27914

Printed in U.S.A. by
NOBLE OFFSET PRINTERS, INC.
NEW YORK 3, N. Y.

To the Memory

of

MY FATHER AND MY MOTHER

PREFACE

THIS book, the author hopes, will interest three groups, students who are taking courses in modern drama and wish a novel approach; little theatre directors, clubwomen, and teachers who are seeking unusual plays for reading or production; and the general reader. Though it has not seemed best to cumber this volume with full lists of the plays given at even the more famous little theatres, the bibliography includes the titles of several books which would form the basis for more detailed study.

A census of the theatre world at a given moment cannot be exact any more than that of a state, and even if it were possible to catalogue all European independent theatres, one book could not hold their history. This volume is a chronicle of some of the more important organizations of this type in the five countries in which there has really been a movement of significance,—France, Germany, Russia, Ireland, England, including Scotland and Wales. There have been a few isolated or sporadic theatres with many of the characteristics of the free theatre among other nations, as Olë Bull's National Theatre at Bergen in Ibsen's day and Strindberg's Intimate Theatre at Stockholm, which is still doing unusual work. A few years ago in Italy there was a radical group under the early futurist, Marinetti; now Bragaglia's Teatro degli Indipendenti has its small auditorium in the ruined baths of Septimus Severus at Rome. There are also several producing groups in Vienna and Prague, too new for an estimate of their importance.

Any book, the history of a movement in particular, must depend upon many others beside the writer. Most of all I wish to acknowledge my great debt to Professor George Pierce Baker of the Yale School of the Drama, who suggested the subject to me, directed my preliminary studies for it, and whose interest has been an inspiration throughout the writing. I am grateful also to Mr. Sheldon Cheney, who as leader of a Drama League Tour of Europe gave richly of his knowledge of the theatre and its art; to Professor Eunice R. Goddard of the Department of Romance Languages, Goucher College, for her generous assistance in the English rendering of selections from Antoine's journal of the Théâtre Libre and other source material in Chapter III; and to Professor Joseph Dunn of the Department of Celtic, of the Catholic University of America and the School of Linguistics of the Linguistic Society of America, for unusual information upon the background of the Irish literary renascence and upon the native theatre of Brittany.

The books and periodicals which I have used the bibliography records. I wish to express my appreciation for the large amount of material sent me by the directors and secretaries of many of the little theatres: without this, the accounts of the English, Scottish, and Ulster theatre groups could not have been written. Among the distinguished men and women who have taken time to send me personal letters, programs, leaflets, printed addresses, and newspaper clippings are Miss A. E. F. Horniman of the Gaiety Theatre, Manchester; Mr. William Poel, The Elizabethan Stage Society; Dr. Glen MacKemmie, Honorary Secretary, The Scottish National Theatre Society; Miss Gwladys Williams, The Portmadoc Players; Miss Mary Kelly, The Village Drama League Society; The Secretary, His Majesty's Stationery Office, London; Mr. W. Matthew Norgate, Secretary, The Incorporated Stage Society; Miss Lilian Bayles, The Old Vic; Miss Ana M. Berry and Miss Eleanor M. Elder, Honorary Organizing Secretaries, The Arts League of Service; Mr. Harold Gibson, Managing Director and

Acting Secretary, The Lena Ashwell Players; Miss Lilian Locke, The Play Actors; Miss Gertrude Bibby, The Fellowship of Players; Mr. Walter V. Tobias, The Repertory Players; Miss Kitty Willoughby, The International Theatre Society; Sir Nigel Playfair, The Lyric, Hammersmith; Mr. Norman Macdermott, The Everyman Theatre; Mr. Paul Jewitt, The Play and Pageant Union, London; Mr. G. Marston Haddock, The Little Theatre, Leeds College of Music; Mr. William Armstrong, The Playhouse, Liverpool; Mr. Nugent Monck, The Maddermarket Theatre, Norwich; Miss Ruth Goddard, Brighton and Hove Repertory Company; Mr. Edward R. Lingard, Honorary General Secretary, Stockport Garrick Society; Miss Dorothy A. Crosse, The Unnamed Society, Manchester; Miss E. C. Gilmore, Honorary Secretary, The Huddersfield Thespians; Mr. Harold Downs, Bath; Miss D. Viola Barker and Mr. Arnold Freeman, The Sheffield Educational Settlement; Mr. E. Montague Spurrier, Bristol's Little Theatre; Miss Mary Ibberson, The Settlement, Letchworth; Mr. Bache Matthews, The Birmingham Repertory Theatre; Miss Dorothy Tompkins and D. Amiel Roberts, The Cotswold Players; Mr. Rutland Boughton, Glastonbury Festival School; Mrs. Eleanor Rawnsley, Allan Bank, Grasmere; Mrs. Godwin King, Stonelands, West Hoathly, Sussex; Mr. H. R. Barbor, Shoreham (Kent) Village Players; the late Mr. Edward Martyn, The Irish Literary Theatre, Dublin; The Secretary of the Gaelic Dramatic League; Mr. Lennox Robinson, The Abbey Theatre; Mr. Gerald Macnamara, The Ulster Players; and Mr. Parker K. Lynch, the Munster Players. Many of these have extended to me the hospitality of their theatres, which I have accepted whenever possible. I deeply appreciate their graciousness.

I also wish to make grateful acknowledgement for permission to use copyrighted material to André Antoine, for allowing me to translate several passages from *"Mes Sou-*

venirs" Sur Le Théâtre Libre; to Sir Owen Seaman, for his
verses, *When We Sleeping Beauties Awaken;* to Professor
Louise Delpit of Smith College for allowing translation of
several paragraphs of *Paris—Théâtre Contemporain;* and
to the following publishers and authors for the use of quota-
tions from the books mentioned: Somerset Folk Press, London (S. R. Littlewood and Others, *Somerset and the Drama*);
Little, Brown, and Company, (Constantin Stanislavsky, *My
Life in Art;* Oliver M. Sayler, *The Russian Theatre under
the Revolution;* Leo Wiener, *The Contemporary Drama
of Russia*); Professor Archibald Henderson (*George Ber-
nard Shaw, his life and works,* Hurst and Blackett, Lon-
don); Brentano's, (Oliver M. Sayler, *Inside the Moscow
Art Theatre, Moscow Art Theatre Series of Russian Plays,
Max Reinhardt and His Theatre;* George Bernard Shaw,
Introduction to Plays Pleasant and Unpleasant); Cuala
Press, Dublin, (William Butler Yeats, *The Bounty of
Sweden*); W. Heinemann, Limited, London, and J. T. Grein,
(*The World of the Theatre; Impressions and Memoirs*);
The Macmillan Company (George William Russell, "On
Behalf of Some Irishmen Not Followers of Tradition" in
Collected Poems; John Masefield, *Introduction* to *Tragedy
of Nan;* William Butler Yeats, *Collected Works;* Sean
O'Casey, *The Silver Tassie*); Doubleday, Doran and Com-
pany, (Huntly Carter, *The New Spirit in the European
Theatre,* Ernst Toller, *Man and the Masses,* translated by
Louis Untermeyer); Mercure de France, Paris, (Adolphe
Thalasso, *Le Théâtre Libre*); Gustav Brauns, Leipzig,
(M. G. Conrad, *Von Zola bis Hauptmann*); Jonathan Cape,
Limited, London, (Cicely Mary Hamilton and Lilian Bayles,
The Old Vic); Charles Scribner's Sons, (George Moore,
Impressions and Opinions); G. P. Putnam's Sons (Lady
Gregory, *Our Irish Theatre*); Hodges, Figgis and Company,
Dublin, (Lady Gregory, *Poets and Dreamers*); D. Appleton
and Company, (Archibald Henderson, *European Dramatists*

and George Moore, *Hail and Farewell*); Dodd, Mead and Company, (G. K. Chesterton, *Irish Impressions;* Maurice Maeterlinck, *The Treasure of the Humble*); Harvard University Press, (Norreys Jephson O'Conor, *Changing Ireland*); Henry Holt and Company, (Kuno Francke, *Social Forces in German Literature*); The Viking Press, (Herman George Scheffauer, *The New Vision in the German Arts*); Houghton Mifflin Company (Havelock Ellis, *Affirmations,* Otto Heller, *Henrik Ibsen*); The Frank A. Munsey Company, (Eden Greville, "Bernard Shaw and His Plays"); the *Boston Evening Transcript,* (an article by George Moore on the Irish Theatre and an account of an address by W. B. Yeats); *Fortnightly Review,* (William Archer, "The Free Stage and the New Drama," Stephen Gwynn, "The Irish Literary Theatre and its Affinities" and "An Uncommercial Theatre," Granville Barker, "Two German Theatres"); the *Forum,* (Barrett Clark, "New Trends in the Theatre").

The staffs of all the libraries at which I have worked have been untiring in their helpfulness and courtesy. These are the libraries of Harvard University, Yale, Columbia, and the Johns Hopkins; of Radcliffe College and Goucher; the Boston and the New York public libraries; the Peabody Institute, the Enoch Pratt Library, and the Congressional Library.

This book will be justified if it brings to the reader a deepening of interest in an art which looks with irony and pity upon all humanity and by its understanding makes "the too much loved earth more lovely."

ANNA IRENE MILLER

Department of English
Goucher College
Baltimore, Maryland

CONTENTS

THE INDEPENDENT THEATRE
IN EUROPE

1887 TO THE PRESENT

I

WHAT IS AN INDEPENDENT THEATRE?

The function of the theatre is to stir people, to make them think, to make them suffer.

My plays have only one subject: life; and only one attitude: interest in life.

George Bernard Shaw

In the last years of the nineteenth century, scarcely more than a generation ago, this art form, into which the Greeks, Shakespeare, Molière had poured their genius, had very nearly ceased to present any aspects of human life or any true criticism of it. Except for an occasional echo of the masters, pallid, attenuated, lacking in vitality, the contemporary drama of Europe at the hands of its most brilliant practitioners was a marvellous product of versatility and cleverness, but held within its unfaltering technique no thought and no desire for it. Today the plays of Shaw, Galsworthy, Masefield, Brieux, Curel, Hauptmann, Chekhov, and of the Americans Eugene O'Neill and Paul Green, to choose only a few names, suggest at least (to many people they prove) that any theme of sincerity and profound thought or exalted imagination can be made effective in the theatre.

On what magic carpet did the drama soar from one continent, a dark continent of the unreal, the trivial, the nonessential, to another chaotic, indeed, both horrible and beautiful, with the burden and the glory of actuality, of dreams, of desires, and of longings?

Revolutions may begin within or without an institution.

The movement which includes the reform of the modern theatre and the revival of the drama in five European countries—and more recently in America—found its origin outside the established commercial playhouses. The salvation of the drama did not come through managers, actors, playwrights of the old régime, imbued with its conventions and prejudices, but through outsiders, *amateurs*, in the derivative sense of the word, men and women who through other paths have been led to a delight in the play and its production until their avocation has dominated their lives. One of the early independent theatres was founded by a clerk on a small salary whose leisure was devoted to acting and to reading realistic novels, another by a group of young journalists many of whom were socialists, and a third by a poet, a novelist, and a writer of plays which did not hit the fancy of the managers of the regular theatres. Ideally, the leaders of the reform have put behind them all mercenary considerations; actually, their consecration to their purpose has been notable. They have worshipped only the twin deities of freedom and truth.

Several terms have been applied to the theatre of revolt. The names *free theatre* and *independent theatre* are both used of the entire movement, and in a more limited meaning of the dramatic society with advanced tendencies which defies both conservatism and official interference by opening its performances to subscribing members only. In the eyes of the law, since no money is received at the box-office, such an organization is not a theatre at all. This kind of group is sometimes called a *Sunday society* because of its favorite hour for meeting. The *théâtre à côté*, the theatre which stands apart from the public theatres, may be a true free theatre or it may be simply a means of recreation, repeating successes of the popular stages.

Little theatre, which, particularly in America, has given one general name to the movement, is also used in a limited sense. Plays before small audiences in castle or hall have existed from the middle ages; the public theatres of Shakespeare's London had a much smaller and more homogeneous audience than do many of our own day; and the theatre of Marie Antoinette at Versailles architecturally is a charming little theatre. While a group which plays in a small auditorium may not forward the contemporary dramatic movement, the tiny, intimate playhouse is in its very nature adapted to some moods of contemporary drama, realism and phantasy particularly, and has housed many of its most characteristic expressions from Moscow to Dublin and Dublin to Los Angeles. The *repertory theatre* also has existed at least from the time of Molière. It is the playhouse which changes its program frequently, often two or three times a week, and with a company of capable actors and actresses keeps ready a large number of plays which after their original production require comparatively few rehearsals. The Comédie-Française and many municipal theatres of Germany presenting the classics are repertory theatres, though not experimental. Here again there is nothing in the nature of the organization which requires an advanced theatre, but for experimenters the repertory plan does have marked advantages. First a group of talented men and women may be far more conscientious and successful in their interpretation of a play—and the modern play of significant content should be more than a field in which actors may disport themselves—in a repertory company than an equal number would be under the "star-system," where the inflated ego and inflated salary of one individual tend to reduce the efficiency of the others. Second, the long run is injurious to the members of the cast themselves because it cramps their abilities into one mould for many months. Third, the repertory theatre gives the public an opportunity to see many plays well presented rather than a few. Conditions in this kind of theatre are also favorable for the significant play which makes a deep appeal to a limited audience,—the play which could never hope for "a long run" except perhaps in a great city, London or New York, but may be revived from time to time. Several famous "little theatres" have been repertory houses. In contrast, the enormous New People's Theatre of Berlin, controlled by a hundred thousand socialists, one of the striking manifestations of the spirit of our generation, is organized on the repertory plan.

Originating in the experimental theatre movement, the *art theatre* is not entirely of it. Though few of the more prominent theatres of amateurs have been oblivious to the need for reform in scenic art as well as in acting and play writing, only a limited number have had the means for much experiment of this sort. Several of the theatres mentioned as dedicated to the possibilities of the new art of stage design are borderline theatres as far as this account is concerned, close both to the professional and to the amateur stage. Since the directors of several important art theatres have been nurtured in the little theatre and have passed from acting or management in it to the theatre of the more general audience, there is some reason for including their history. An art theatre may present old or new; it may give inspired beauty of production to a play of daring innovation in theme or treatment or a fresh loveliness to something already hallowed by the years.

The development of acting throughout this dramatic revival in two of the five countries which are studied in this book,—the countries in which experiment has been continuous and significant—has amounted to a revolution; in a third, actors and actresses of genius have appeared where hitherto there had been no distinguished native acting and no native drama. The influence of the little theatre upon play writing and upon producing, as well as upon acting, in the regular theatre has been enormous. During this period the drama has very nearly caught up with life instead of lagging hopelessly behind. Great minds have again turned to the drama as among the Greeks and the Elizabethans: a list of European playwrights of the free stages includes Shaw, Masefield, Galsworthy, Hauptmann, Brieux, Curel, Chekhov, Gorky. The Irish drama from Edward Martyn to Sean O'Casey is the creation of the Irish little theatre movement. In England for many years the only distinguished writers for the stage who had not entered by the door of the little theatre were Henry Arthur Jones and Sir Arthur Wing Pinero, veteran playwrights before Grein's Independent Theatre was born, and Sir James Barrie, beloved of all audiences. In America, the first dramatist of international fame, Eugene O'Neill, saw his early work at the Provincetown Theatre and his later at the New York Theatre Guild. It is not necessary, here, to comment upon the achievement of these playwrights, for many of them are among the dominating minds of our time.

In the hands of these revolutionists and countless others, the play has suffered many a sea-change. It has rejected old conventions, the necessity of the noble hero, the romantic love story, the happy ending. It has refused to worship Aristotle or any other interpreter of dramatic form. Like modern painting, modern sculpture, modern music, the drama believes that there is no so-called law which cannot be broken with impunity, provided always that a genius is the breaker.

"Will the little theatre endure?" is a question asked often, sometimes in the jesting form, "When is a little theatre not a little theatre?" with the answer, "When it is a success."

As this history shows, there is a tendency for the little theatre, in origin the theatre of amateurs, to pass into some kindred form,—semi-professional, or professional,—the community theatre, the municipal theatre, or even the state or national theatre. But what if the little theatre should cease to exist? If the next generation should find another tool better fitted for its task? The little theatre has been the means of expression for a whole generation of creative spirits. Many of them fortunately are still writing, but even when that ceases to be true, they will be among us, part of our very thinking and of the fabric of our dreams. As Maeterlinck says, "We know that the dead do not die. We know that it is not in our churches that they are to be found, but in the houses, the habits of us all."

II

"GIANTS OF THE NORTH"

What is really wanted is a revolution of the spirit of
man.
Letter of Henrik Ibsen to Georg Brandes,
December 20, 1870.

Not from the old homeland of European drama, the land
of Aeschylus, or from its Latin neighbor, did the impetus to
the modern dramatic revolution come, but from the far
north, Norway, the more remote and the younger in national development of the sister countries of Scandinavia.
The land of fjords, of snow-covered mountains, of winter
storms, no longer sent its pillaging vikings but adventurers
of the spirit, questing far seas of thought and the bounds of
knowledge. Their traits were the old heroic traits of the Ger-
manic peoples, an unflinching courage, a respect for woman
translated now into a troubled awareness of her needs, her
wrongs, and her potentialities for both evil and good, and
a reverence, grown somewhat wistful, for truth and freedom, elusive and Protean things.

Ibsen, the foremost of the giant figures of Scandinavian
drama, has been rightly called "the father of the little
theatre movement." *Ghosts*, "the harbinger of the whole
modern dramatic movement" as William Archer calls it, is
the play which opened three great revolutionary theatres
and was an early program at a fourth. It has been given on
many advanced stages. The founders of the earliest little
theatres in four countries were familiar with the work of

7

Ibsen before they began their ventures, and Antoine in France, where Ibsen was at first almost unknown, became absorbed in the possibilities of his dramas a few months after the birth of the Théâtre Libre. In technique or theme, Ibsen has influenced minds as diverse as Shaw, Galsworthy, Brieux, Hauptmann, Maeterlinck, Yeats.

Today Ibsen's position is almost unchallenged. "Henrik Ibsen has attained to supreme eminence and authority in the drama of our time. . . . No extravagance lurks in the statement that Henrik Ibsen is the greatest Teutonic dramatist since Shakspere, and the greatest dramatist of any race or clime, of our modern era," says Archibald Henderson.[1] "In this or that respect he was unquestionably outranked by many of his contemporaries in Germany, France, Russia, Italy, and Belgium, but what other writer of the nineteenth century has become to the same extent a European influence? While still living, his historic importance was recognized, as the chief expositor of ideas which specifically distinguish our age from the past, and as the discoverer of a new vehicle for their expression," writes Professor Heller, and adds: "the new conception to which he [Ibsen] turned instead was indeed not slow to conquer the resistance of Scandinavia, Europe, eventually the whole world. It has revolutionized the art of the actor as well as of the dramatist. Far more than this, it has been one of the prime levers of the social revolution which is sweeping over us."[2]

If Ibsen started the whole ball rolling, the little theatres certainly had much to do with bringing him before a widening public. In 1868, when Georg Brandes began his championship, Ibsen, who had already written *The Pretenders, Brand,* and *Peer Gynt,* was unknown beyond Scandinavia

---

[1] From *European Dramatists,* by Archibald Henderson, p. 92. Courtesy of D. Appleton and Company, Publishers, New York.

[2] From *Henrik Ibsen, Plays and Problems,* by Otto Heller, pp. xx, 87. Courtesy of Houghton Mifflin Company, Publishers, Boston.

and even there his position was not established. By 1882
The Pillars of Society and *A Doll's House* were played
occasionally in Germany, and there were in print German
versions of several of the earlier plays. In 1892, after the
founding of the Théâtre Libre, the Freie Bühne, and the
Independent Theatre, *The Master Builder* was published in
Norwegian, English, French, German, Russian, Dutch,
Hungarian, Bohemian, Polish. That was the year in which
Havelock Ellis called Ibsen "the chief figure of European
significance that has appeared in the Teutonic world of art
since Goethe."

What Ibsen taught the playwrights of the new drama can
be barely mentioned here: it has been discussed in more
than one brilliant study. He flung the doors of drama open
to the daylight of actuality with its piteous glare and its
amazing shadows; he faced the moods and problems of the
modern world as developing science and a deeper feeling of
social responsibility complicated its issues; he found again in
terms of contemporary life all the mystery, the beauty, and
the terror of the eternal soul at war with forces both within
and beyond itself. He turned also to folklore and legend
with its people of "personal, eventful, really vital existence"
and its natural magic joining mountain, plain, and forest
with human life by some mystic nexus before the beginning
of history. Yeats has acknowledged the debt of the Irish
theatre to Norway; the seed, wind-borne across a second
ocean, has likewise flowered in our Carolina folk-move-
ment. Ibsen's ideals became truly "procreative" as he believed that all ideals should be, quickening others not to
imitation but to original conception. Something of the cold
gleam of Brand's Ice Church falls upon the mountain top
of *The Sunken Bell,* and Shaw's plays from *Widowers'
Houses* to *The Apple Cart* are inspired by Ibsen's "Muse of
Distrust."

Ibsen stood for realism, for the elimination of the artificial, the unessential, and also, in the work of his first and of his last periods, for poetry and symbolism. Though he often followed the three unities of Aristotle, he put above them a greater unity, what the Germans call "Stimmung," atmosphere, the harmony of mood. In the broad canvas of *Peer Gynt* with its mingling of actuality and phantasm, and in an emphasis upon the individuality of the creative artist and his right to freedom of every kind, the Norwegian was a prophet of attitudes beyond his time. In 1874, before a group of university students, he said of poetry, by which he meant great imaginative literature:

Not till late in life have my eyes been opened to the fact that to be a poet means as much as to be a seer; but, mark well, to see in such a way that the things seen are shown to the public as the poet has seen them. Now it is a fact that only those things can be thus seen and assimilated which are a part of our experience. And this experience is the secret of modern poetry. All I have written during the past decade is part of my spiritual experience.

And later:

Do you really attach much value to categories? I, for my part, believe that the dramatic categories are elastic and that they must accommodate themselves to the literary facts—not vice versa.

Again:

I gave up universal standards long ago, because I ceased believing in the justice of applying them.

Björnstjerne Björnson, the other great Norwegian, has influenced modern drama in the same way as Ibsen, though not to the same degree. A strongly individual dramatist, the author of many plays of originality and beauty and in *Beyond Our Power* of one superb drama, he is, like Ibsen, alert to the problems of modern life, which he, however, viewed emotionally without Ibsen's genius for incisive analysis. His friendship for Ibsen, in spite of serious disagreements, was a lifelong one, and the geniality of his nature and the variety of his literary and political interests reinforced in the mind of Norway the work of her other genius, austere, aloof, and for many years in self-imposed exile. Many European little theatres have been interested in Björnson's plays.

Ibsen is said once to have shown a guest a photograph of Strindberg with the remark, "Here is a greater than I." August Strindberg, an intellectual giant, the creator of Swedish drama, as Ibsen and Björnson were of Norwegian, was a violent individualist, an arch rebel. The number and variety of his plays, ranging from sheer naturalism to mysticism and fairy-drama, have baffled many of his readers, and his attitude toward women, whether viewed as misogyny or an attempt to free a controversial subject from age-long sentimentality, has rendered much of his work distasteful to the American mind. But his influence upon both the thought and technique of recent playwrights has been enormous. His introduction to *Countess Julie* advanced a new theory of the one-act play. He was more directly interested in the experimental theatres than was either Ibsen or Björnson. Edward Martyn, Shaw, and Eugene O'Neill are his admirers. Curiously, Strindberg's influence at the present time is increasing very noticeably. He has indeed been credited with the discovery of the methods of expressionism long before that term came into existence. "He belongs," says a recent critic, "simply as a man of the theatre, perhaps more to the present, and even to the future, than either Ibsen or Björnson." [3]

[3] Tucker, S. Marion, *Modern Continental Plays,* p. 699.

III

ANTOINE AND THE THÉÂTRE LIBRE; OTHER REVOLUTIONARY FRENCH THEATRES

THE experimental theatre movement of the late eighties, which was to revolutionize modern French drama and to provide a model for the revitalizing of much of the drama of Europe and America, was the child of the French realistic novel, the novel of Balzac, of Flaubert, of Huysmans, the Goncourts, above all of Zola. It was also the child of earlier drama, that of Augier, of Dumas fils, of Musset, of Becque. At the beginning of the movement Ibsen was unknown in France either on the stage or in the study.

The influences which were quickening the imagination of young Frenchmen of 1887 and making them turn from the conventional and outworn drama of the great theatres were the freedom and largeness of vision of the naturalistic novelists, particularly Zola, and an awareness of the new forces in human thought, strange provinces for the eye and soul: the discoveries of science, Darwinism, determinism, experimental psychology, an awakening social consciousness, a deeper yearning for truth and a more scientific pursuit of it. What Havelock Ellis says of the effect of Zola upon other novelists applies to his influence upon playwrights:

The chief service which Zola has rendered to his fellow-artists and successors, the reason of the immense stimulus he supplies, seems to lie in the proofs he has brought of the latent artistic uses of the rough, neglected details of life. The Rougon-Macquart series has been to his weaker brethren like that great sheet knit at the four corners, let down from Heaven full of four-footed beasts

12

I am attempting no justification of my own cause, [he writes]
I am merely expressing my profound conviction—upon which I
particularly insist—that the experimental and scientific spirit of
the century will enter the domain of the drama, and that in it lies
its only possible salvation.

Unlike the playwright, the novelist may interest a number
of individuals, his own choice spirits, at ease in their studies,
without having to reckon with the whimsical and baffling
psychology of the audience, which adds a gambler's risks to
play writing and play production. Again, the novelist is
almost unhampered by time and space: his tale may take
many hours to read, his analysis of character run to many
pages; he may indulge in long descriptions or have his men
and women speak their hearts out in long confessions or in
broken phrases. Can the writer for the stage do the same?
Most of the nineteenth century playwrights had denied this.
He can, according to Zola, and if the stage is to endure he
must. Cannot stage settings take the place of long descriptions, dialogue carry the accent of individuality? "A word,
a cry, in Balzac's works is often sufficient to present the entire character. This cry belongs essentially to the stage."

I am waiting [Zola says] for them, in the first place, to put a
man of flesh and bones on the stage, taken from reality, scien-
tifically analyzed, without one lie. I am waiting for them to rid
us of fictitious characters, of conventional symbols of virtue and
vice, which possess no value as human data. I am waiting for the
surroundings to determine the characters, and for characters to
act according to the logic of facts, combined with the logic of their
own temperament. I am waiting until there is no more jugglery of
any kind, no more strokes of a magical wand, changing in one
minute persons and things. I am waiting for the time to come
when they will tell us no more incredible stories, when they will
no longer spoil the effects of just observations by romantic incidents, the result being to destroy even the good parts of a play. I
am waiting for them to abandon the cut and dried rules, the

worked-out formulas, the tears and cheap laughs. I am waiting until a dramatic work free from declamations, big words, and grand sentiments has the high morality of truth, teaches the terrible lesson that belongs to all sincere inquiry. I am waiting, finally, until the evolution accomplished in the novel takes place on the stage; until they return to the source of science and modern arts, to the study of nature, to the anatomy of man, to the painting of life, in an exact reproduction, more original and powerful than anyone has so far dared to place upon the boards.[2]

When Zola published this essay in 1881, an enthusiastic young admirer of his was in Africa, bored and homesick, only half through his years of military training. To this young man of twenty-two who remembered the serial publication of *L'Assommoir* in the newly founded *La République des lettres* as one of the outstanding events of boyhood and each successive novel as marking an epoch, to a young man who had an unquenchable delight in all innovations, exile from Paris was vexatious. But all things end, even military service, and in 1883, he returned quietly to Paris to his former position in the employ of the Gas Company, without suspecting that in four years he was to be the most discussed person in the literary circles of Paris and that he was to have a more profound influence upon the drama of modern Europe than any other except the great Scandinavian. Ibsen brought life again to the drama; it is a question how far his influence would have penetrated without the help of adventurous and disinterested producers. A host of writers, among them many of the greatest of modern Europe, might have besieged the stage in vain without the experimental theatre as a rallying ground.

André Antoine recounts the events of his childhood and early manhood in his delightful journal, *"Mes Souvenirs" sur le Théâtre Libre.* A mysterious destiny, he thinks, pre-

[2] Zola, Emile, *The Experimental Novel and Other Essays*, pp. 142, 143.

pared him for being hurled like a bomb into the Parisian theatres of 1887. This destiny was scarcely apparent in his heredity or early environment, for he was born into a family without unusual background or culture, a family of *petits employés,* as he calls them, at Limoges, January 31, 1858. When he was a child of eight, the family moved to Paris. There was no money to give the eldest of four more than an ordinary education; accordingly, just at the close of the War of 1870, André, thirteen, began to earn his own living, first as errand-boy and then clerk at the publishing house of Hachette, and finally with the Gas Company. Thirteen or fourteen hours a day, with the munificent salary of one hundred and fifty francs a month eked out by clerical work far into the night, would seem the very formula for destroying individuality and initiative. Yet Antoine survived; not only survived, he triumphed. He discovered his own university: the easily accessible and often forgotten treasuries of the great city, its libraries, its art galleries, its special exhibits. He devoured everything,—Dumas père, Eugène Sue, George Sand. Antoine's very poverty enlarged his education, for since money spent for books and journals restricted his luncheons, noon hours gave enough time for hurried visits to the École des Beaux-Arts, the exhibit hall of the Prix de Rome, and an acquaintance with Manet, Regnault, the classics. Classic art naturally led him to the study of mythology and of Greek and Roman history. Taine's *Histoire de l'Art* brought him in contact with one of the most stimulating precursors of the modern. A fellow-workman, a little older, who prided himself on being an intellectual, led Antoine to the world of modern thought, to the work of the realistic school, to contemporary poetry.

This myriad-sided culture which he was classifying represented, as Antoine later realized, a much greater knowledge than most boys carry from the classroom: he was able to synthesize as few are. The battle which he was later to wage in the theatre he recognized as already won by the naturalists in the novel, the impressionists in painting, and the Wagnerians in music. This vision of the essential unity of truth inspired Antoine in many a perplexing hour.

His training for the stage was also self-acquired. From childhood it was his ruling passion; most delightful of early memories were those of the matinées to which his mother took him and at which the green ticket for fifteen centimes included both the delight of a little comedy or operetta and a tiny package of confections. Later he worshipped the great actor Taillade, who starred in melodramas. Another experience long remembered was an evening when a neighbor, a young girl who acted little parts at the Gaîté, slipped him into the prompter's box to watch a performance of *La Chatte blanche*. There were many tableaux, much fairy machinery, and almost countless metamorphoses. André watched the performance with the wonder of a child and an unchildlike absorption in discovering the sources of the fantastic effects.

Later *Les Dix Degrés du crime, La Dame de Saint-Tropez, Atar Gull ou la Vengeance d'un nègre,* made André long for acting as they did another lad, the young Gémier, who was to be one of Antoine's actors at the Théâtre Libre, and his assistant at the Théâtre Antoine.

Spasmodic theatre-going changed to regular attendance when the lad became self-supporting, particularly when he had discovered the possibility of reducing the admission fee by becoming a "claqueur." As a hired applauder, he clapped at many a great evening for romanticists or for classicists, and for many of the celebrated actors and actresses, Sarah Bernhardt, Mounet-Sully, Got, Coquelin the elder. (A few years later Père Boutin, the leader of the "claqueurs" of the Odéon, nearly dropped his velvet skull-cap when his erstwhile assistant seated himself in the director's armchair.) Then, growing bolder, Antoine became a "figurant," a "super," walking on at many of the important theatres, following the great performers like their shadows, and secretly learning their parts. He studied Got's methods especially, later acknowledging more than once his debt to this precursor of realism.

But these nights at the theatre made Antoine realize his limitations and long for training. Though free only certain evenings, he enrolled himself in a little school of declamation under a Marius Laisné in the rue de Seine. Here he learned all the famous rôles of the repertoire and in 1878 distinguished himself at this "Gymnase de la Parole" in *L'Ami Fritz,* one of Got's favorite dramas, playing the part of David Sichel, created at the Théâtre-Français by Got himself. Antoine was also the director and the artist of the *mise en scène* for this evening. Emboldened by this success, he presented himself for admission to the Conservatoire, but this stronghold of tradition promptly refused him as it did all young men without special influence. With too much good sense to attempt a second time what seemed impossible, he quietly gave up all hope of the stage as a profession and at twenty-eight seemed to the officials of the Gas Company that exemplary being "un excellent employé sans aucune velléité, sans le moindre rêve d'aventure" (an excellent employee without the least dream of adventure).

There are, however, certain men for whom indifferent opportunities become fateful; one of them held horses before a theatre door only to find himself shortly after collaborating with some of the most gifted university men of his age and writing lines remembered long after theirs. We call this group geniuses; Antoine is of their number.

The mark of genius in Antoine is, probably, the union in a high degree of the sympathetic, almost instinctive, knowledge of books and people with the courage and resolution to be independent of them. In reading the journal of the seven years of the Théâtre Libre though one is impressed by Antoine's kindness and fairness, one is even more impressed by his aloofness and his self-confidence. His rehearsals become the meeting place of the young literati and some of the older, but the times when he asks advice are few. He selects his own programs. He refuses a play if, in his own judgment, it is too bad or too good, that is, if it fails to come up to the standard to which a laboratory theatre should be held, or if it is so excellent and by so well-known a playwright that it should not consume the energies of a pioneering group. He refuses to be influenced by the desires of the interfering; he is untouched by the jibes of enemies; and most difficult of all, he is not swayed from his own orbit by the advice of friends, withheld, perhaps, by affection but to be had for the asking. Not even Zola swayed the policies of Antoine's theatre.

Of course, Antoine, at least in the Théâtre Libre days, was an autocrat. His enemies charged him with the fact, and his friends admitted it. Yet his theatre in number of playwrights presented, in variety of types, and in the spirit of the whole endeavor, is the most democratic of the entire European experimental movement. (This fact leads to the interesting conjecture whether the arts, at least in their organization and management, can be thoroughly democratic.)

Into the monotony of Antoine's life opportunity came in a most unspectacular way—by membership in an amateur dramatic association. Paris in the eighties was filled with groups of young people who turned to acting for relaxation: acting was a craze then, Antoine avers, as dancing is now. Aderer gives an account of several of these little theatre-societies which, in our accepted meaning of the term, were not "little theatres" at all as they were in no real sense experimental. (A few of them later caught the breath of the time and did become the true laboratory theatres for which their organization fitted them.) The Cercle Gaulois,

to which a friend brought Antoine, was neither more nor
less ambitious than many others. It was composed of working men and women under the directorship of "Père
Krauss," who had founded it in 1874. He was an elderly
retired officer, late in life seized with a passion for the
theatre. He had built with his own hands the wooden hall
and stage, a pocket handkerchief affair, called by the name
of the little street at the end of which it stood,—"number
thirty-seven Passage de l'Elysée des Beaux-Arts." Père
Krauss, though kind and enthusiastic, was conservative and
routine-bound, fond of the successes of the great stages and
with a special leaning toward Scribe and his disciples. To
him the new member, Antoine, seemed distressingly radical.
The young man pleaded for stronger and more varied
theatrical fare, and urged the society to produce some original play and thereby equal its rival, the Cercle Pigalle,
whose members, of somewhat higher social rank, had recently given an original review—honored by the presence
of the great Sarcey and his good-natured compliments in
le Temps. Antoine was obsessed with the idea of experiment. Becoming one of the leading actors in his circle, he
talked of the *"inédit,"* "the unproduced" work of young
writers, in season and out of season. He felt that the real
value of the Cercle Gaulois lay in its power to discover the
new.

To the delight of Père Krauss, new plays were not at
once forthcoming, for Antoine was unknown to literary people, and had no influence in reaching them. Finally one
night, a young man, Arthur Byl, stayed to congratulate
Antoine on his acting. When Antoine began to speak on
his favorite theme, Byl surprised him by saying that he had
in his possession a play, *Le Préfet,* as yet unacted, which
he would be glad to contribute. This little play seemed at
the moment a godsend, though Antoine shortly discovered
it to be a work of naïve violence. Byl also offered to intro-

duce Antoine to Jules Vidal, a friend of Goncourt, who in turn arranged an introduction to Paul Alexis, of the inner circle of Zola. Alexis was able to get from Léon Hennique, another of the naturalistic group, a one-act play, an adaptation of an incident from a novel of Zola's, which had been recently refused by Porel, director of the Odéon. Antoine saw at once the value of Zola's much loved and much hated name.

The program was now complete, including four one-act plays: *Mademoiselle Pomme,* a farce comedy adapted from Duranty, an early naturalistic writer; *Le Préfet* by Arthur Byl; *La Cocarde,* comedy by Jules Vidal; and *Jacques Damour,* adapted from Zola by Hennique. *Mademoiselle Pomme* was already in rehearsal for one of the regular meetings of a group of artists who discussed literature, art, and politics, calling themselves the Cercle de la Butte. They were a heterogeneous group, by a slight majority representing the symbolistic camp and an abhorrence of Zola, but there were enough revolutionists among them to sympathize with Antoine's venture and to promise to send their own actors. Antoine distrusted the ability of these amateurs, but thought best to accept the offer. The other parts were assigned to members of the Cercle Gaulois.

Here Antoine had an experience of a peculiarly disconcerting kind. He crossed an important bridge in his personal adventure and, as he thought, in the artistic life of the Cercle Gaulois, and looked back to find his fellow-members, at least, most of them,—particularly those who had not been given parts—still safely if ingloriously on the other bank. That is, the Cercle Gaulois had taken to flight at the name of Zola and had not been rallied by the yet more alarmed Krauss. As their spokesman, he conveyed to Antoine the decision that while he might rent his little theatre for one night, rehearsals could not take place there, the program could not bear the name of the organization, and, logically, the treasury of the society could not defray the expenses. This decision was expected to deal a death blow to the new movement. Antoine was indeed nonplussed, but for only a short time. A solution came to him: why not give the performance on the Gas Company's pay day and leave to the gods such problems of the future as the lodging and food required by even a revolutionary director?

The force of this decision was so stimulating that Antoine went soon after to Jules Prével, who wrote advance notices of plays for *le Figaro,* and asked that the great journal announce the program of his little group. A strange figure, Antoine pictures himself: stammering with embarrassment, all too apparently the underpaid clerk, he addressed the elegant frequenter of Parisian boulevards. Monsieur Prével shook his head; then at Antoine's impassioned appeal, said only "We shall see"—and proceeded to give in *le Figaro* a longer account than Antoine had dared to hope. The announcement concluded thus:

If this attempt is successful—and the organizer Monsieur Antoine, a young leading man, is giving himself enough trouble in order to succeed—similar attempts will be made which may inaugurate a charming fashion for young writers to get an idea of what they have done and to present their pieces to the directors no longer on a manuscript of Leduc, but as a living experiment.

Antoine's attempt to outdistance the Cercle Pigalle had outgrown its immediate purpose: the first laboratory theatre was to be born.

The manager, almost penniless, except for what Paz, another enthusiast of Cercle Gaulois, was able to contribute, was meeting all sorts of difficulties with ingenuity and good nature. Without money to hire a hall for rehearsals, he secured the permission of the owner of a little wine shop, close to the Elysée des Beaux-Arts, to use an adjoining billiard room each evening on condition that all the performers should taste and pay for the host's wine. Antoine would have been glad to omit this expenditure. Another irritation was as real though more amusing. A billiard hall, naturally, had a billiard table, this one the largest that anyone had ever seen, a kind of cosmic billiard table around which all lesser luminaries like free theatres had to revolve. The table was difficult enough to forget when the actors were alone, but impossible, the director felt, when Alexis wished to bring Hennique to a rehearsal of his own play. Père Krauss, relenting somewhat, allowed the use of his theatre for the last two rehearsals. Here Alexis brought Hennique, and Hennique brought Zola.

This meeting of the master and his young follower was dramatic. At the end of the rehearsal of *Jacques Damour,* Zola climbed to the stage and, drawing the young actor under a gas jet, scrutinized his face. Antoine, almost fainting at the earnest gaze and the abrupt words, "Who are you, you?" hesitated and stammered; the older man went on, "It is very good, very beautiful! Hennique, isn't it beautiful! We will come again tomorrow."

Besides rehearsals there were other troublesome matters, for a director who had only his evenings free. The programs and invitations were printed, and, to economize postage, were delivered largely by hand. A name for the new theatre was essential. Antoine thought long for a designation which should be something more than a title. "Le Théâtre en liberté," "the theatre in freedom," borrowed from Victor Hugo, suggested itself, but seemed to smack of romanticism. "Le Théâtre Libre," "the free theatre," Byl cried out, and the name exactly fitted the requirement. Byl also contributed a prologue in the form of an occasional poem. This was certainly not "genial," as Antoine admitted in his diary while accepting it for want of a better. *The Bears* (Les Ours), a "prologue scientifique," represented the speaker as visiting a menagerie and finding the four plays of Antoine's

program among the animals, Zola, the keeper, and other
attendants, representative of naturalism, cultivating "the
human document." Indeed the verses implied that the
Théâtre Libre was bound hand and foot to naturalism. Antoine could not afford to antagonize Byl by any hostile
criticism.

The great evening came, announced by half a dozen
journals. Promptly at five, Antoine received his monthly
salary and was freed from one anxiety. Otherwise, the evening opened inauspiciously: the hall did not fill with noted
critics, for the première of a much heralded comic opera
was the same night. Sarcey, most renowned of dramatic
critics, was out of Paris on business, as he later explained
when Antoine took him to task for failing to encourage the
work of new authors. There were more serious accidents.
When the curtain rose, the young Conservatory student, a
member of Cercle Pigalle, who was to speak the prologue,
forgot his lines, hesitated, finally gave up. The stage settings were not complete even though Antoine had moved
much of his mother's furniture by wheelbarrow through the
streets of Montmartre. Of the plays themselves, *Mademoiselle Pomme* awakened slight interest, *La Cocarde* fared little better, and *Le Préfet* was almost hissed off the stage.
But *Jacques Damour* was a triumph. Antoine felt the power
of the little play as he was acting Jacques, felt it again more
strongly in the following days when the few critics who
had been in the audience recorded their impressions. The
comments were distinctly favorable. Henry Fouquier of
le Figaro wrote that he was sure that he was speaking for
many of his colleagues when he declared that "the new"
for which they were looking was the ideal which inspired
Antoine and his comrades. Denayrouze of *la République
française* added of the Zola adaptation:

Surely, if the naturalistic theatre includes many acts like that,
people need not worry about its future.

The plot of this quickly famous playlet is built upon an Enoch Arden situation handled with a lack of Tennysonian idealism, but with a directness in itself appealing. Jacques Damour—the part was wonderfully acted by Antoine—is an ex-soldier who has gone to America, has made and lost a fortune, and has now returned to claim his wife, who, supposing him dead, has married a prosperous tradesman. A little daughter of the second marriage is of the age at which Damour remembers his own little girl,—no longer living. Damour does not renounce the wife whom he still loves; instead he forces her to choose between him and her present husband. Damour, defeated, accepts cheerily his rival's invitation to drink with him before passing out of his life forever.

Two days later, Porel, who had originally refused *Jacques Damour,* for the Odéon, informed Hennique that he would accept the little play. This success of *Jacques Damour* and the praise of the critic Fouquier decided Antoine to continue the life of the Théâtre Libre,—a gallant, if not reckless, decision for one burdened with a debt of three or four hundred francs and with, so far as he knew, the earning power of little over one hundred and fifty francs a month. Now followed eight years of almost superhuman work, of a constant meeting of vexing problems, of an ever-present anxiety over money, and yet, of success. Antoine had now entered upon that long struggle to which he has devoted his life, the championship of the art of the theatre for its own sake and for its effect upon the spirit of man.

Of this life drama, the Théâtre Libre is only the opening act, if the most startling, the most revolutionary. Antoine divides his warfare into three campaigns: "from 1887 to 1895, at the Théâtre Libre against the upholders of the theatre of the past; from 1896 to 1906, at the Théâtre Antoine for the conquest of the general public; and from 1906

to 1914, at the Odéon, the last fight against official traditions and administrative routine."

The enthusiasm of Antoine and his helpers in the little
theatre was almost apostolic: as though the sacred coal of
fire had been laid upon his tongue, the director, the "petit-
employé," as he calls himself, whose youth had been passed
among the undistinguished, now approached some of the
foremost literary men of Paris with an eloquence which
surprised himself. Now he interpreted his ideals, seeking
criticism and publicity in the leading journals; now he persuaded some noted writer to lend his play and his name—
to help the unknown young men of the Théâtre Libre.
Friendships rushed to him: within a few months he was an
intimate friend of Alphonse Daudet, of Becque, of Zola,
Villiers de l'Isle-Adam, Edmond de Goncourt. Countless
tributes from dramatists and critics show his ardor and that
which he awakened in others. Jean Jullien, an early member
of the Théâtre Libre group, later for a considerable period
estranged from Antoine, wrote long afterwards of the
"feverish impatiences, the enthusiastic joys, the generous
angers, the immense confidence in the future," in "the hours
of exaltation of these heroic times." Antoine himself has
said: "I think, in reality, we were all well intentioned people and that neither the survivors nor those who have dis-
appeared will be diminished on emerging from a splendid
epoch burning with literary passion."

The history of the Théâtre Libre falls into three periods:
first, the beginning of its activities, that is, the two programs of the spring of 1887 and those of the following
theatre season; second, the years of its triumph, October,
1888, through June, 1893; and third, those of its decadence,
November, 1893, through April, 1896, during a little over
a year of which period, Antoine was no longer director. Like
most divisions, these are somewhat arbitrary: an occasional early program made the pessimistic shake their heads

over the approaching dissolution of the house, while even during its last years there were great evenings, among them the beautiful production of *Hannele*. Indeed terms, as well as divisions, are misleading: seen from another angle, the period of decadence might even be called that of fulfilment; for the comparative slightness of the programs was largely a result of the exodus of successful playwrights and actors to the regular stages of Paris.

The historian of any experimental theatre should examine several phases of its activity: its organization as a group of actors and spectators; its methods of production, including both acting and stage decoration; and its plays, both for their own importance and for the emergence of literary types, new and old.

The organization of the Théâtre Libre was unique, for the accidental nature of its beginning gave Antoine unusual freedom. Since the venture, disowned by the Cercle Gaulois, had now become his personal responsibility, he had to devise some plan to meet the problem of financing. Emile Paz, remembering his experiences in another dramatic club, suggested a voluntary assessment of those most interested. From this suggestion came gradually the plan of the subscription audience, or more exactly, the membership audience, a group held together, at least during the early days of the theatre, by a close community of interests. This plan was also an ideal arrangement for evading the government censorship of plays, since a playhouse which takes no money at the door is not in the legal sense a theatre at all. (This plan of subscription audience has been followed widely in Europe and America.) In other ways, Antoine's plan of invitation membership was excellent: it increased the sense of intimacy of the audience and gave each subscriber a realization of his part in the fortunes of the house. However, this method had one great disadvantage, which will be discussed later.

The invitations to the performances emphasized the spirit of comradeship. For example, the announcement of the second program read like a social invitation:

The Théâtre Libre, 37, passage de l'Elysêe des Beaux-Arts. Monsieur Emile Bergerat, Monsieur Oscar Méténier, and the charter members of the Théâtre Libre have the honor to invite you to the performance of two dramatic experiments:
First, a realistic piece in one act and in prose, entitled,
                    En Famille.
Second, a tragi-comedy (in the older taste), three acts, in verse, entitled,
                La Nuit Bergamasque.
And they hope that this double attempt, one of light-hearted verse and the other of the naturalistic theatre, will for an hour or two draw you away from the cares of every day life.
Performance the thirtieth of May, 1887.[3]

This second performance, a happy combination of the work of a well-known literary man and a newcomer to the stage, brought to the little hall in Montmartre writers, artists, producers, and the leading critics of Paris. Got, the actor, noticing the faces in the audience, declared that the great days of the French stage had returned. Sarcey—the great Sarcey—disagreed: though he praised the acting, especially its perfection of detail, he declared that if *En Famille* represented the play of the future, he hoped to have the good fortune not to see that future. But approving or not, the critics were already giving the same consideration to a "little" theatre as to a "greater." In three months the Théâtre Libre had "arrived."

During the spring and summer of 1887, Antoine, still tied to the Gas Company, was wrestling with the problems of the next season, particularly the programs. He now dared to ask established writers for new work as well as to issue

[3] Thalasso, Adolphe, *Le Théâtre Libre*, p. 40.

a general invitation to young volunteers. With the older
literary men, he was usually successful. When he sought
an interview with Théodore de Banville, the distinguished
poet's heart was won by his beautiful reading of verse and
Le Baiser, written especially for the Théâtre Libre, was the
result. At Antoine's suggestion, other literary men were
glad to undertake translations and adaptations. Sarcey, kind
if sceptical, published in *le Temps* Antoine's challenge to
youthful playwrights:

June 25, 1887

Monsieur:

Do you know that it is no sinecure, this being a director even
for one's own amusement? I am organizing for the Free Theatre,
six or eight performances, a whole series, for next season. I shall
have some Zola, Goncourt, Richepin, Catulle Mendès, Coppée,
etc., all the well known men. The older generation are answering
my appeal with the utmost kindliness; but the younger and less
well known men? Well, I do not see any coming, although I in-
quire everywhere, in studios, and literary circles, cabarets, and
cafés. So far I have had responses only from provincial old gentlemen and old ladies who bring me things in verse the like of which
I had never imagined.

What is the cause of this? Can it be perhaps that directors
are less "mufles" than they are painted? I entreat you, Monsieur,
save the Free Theatre, which is going to become a gallery of illus-
trious people instead of a refuge for the younger authors, as I had
hoped, and a laboratory. Have you nothing on hand? I am sure
that you must receive manuscripts by the dozen.

Send me the works and the authors, I beg you.

Most cordially yours,
A. ANTOINE.

Answers came quickly; by late summer, Antoine was able
to announce a tentative program. Meanwhile he was laboring far into the night on another problem—that of securing
enough subscribers to insure a season. He wrote thirteen

hundred personal letters, each to accompany a leaflet describing the aims of the theatre, expecting to deliver them himself. After days at the Gas Company, such efforts were fatiguing: once, just before dawn, making his last call for that night, Antoine had to fumble for several minutes before he could discover the letter box. This is his statement of his ideals:

The organizer of the Free Theatre is stating nothing new when he points out the extreme difficulties experienced by dramatic authors in general, and by beginners in particular, in finding a theatre in which to present their works to the public.

It must be admitted, moreover, that directors of large theatres, being obliged to safeguard material interests of consequence, can scarcely expose their capital (and often that of their associates) to the hazards of purely literary ventures. Consequently, a theatrical enterprise is almost always a financial affair.

The great subsidized theatres are no more accessible. Like everything which concerns the administration, the higher officials must deal with conditions entirely foreign to art.

So it is a piece of extraordinary good luck for a young man to have something received by a real theatre. . . . Celebrated persons themselves sometimes experience no less difficulties there. Have there not been during these last years ten examples like that of Théodore de Banville, with a position in the literary world beyond question, waiting fifteen years to have a play presented at the Comédie-Française, where, however, one of his works, "Gringoire," has been for twenty years in the repertory.[4]

During this summer of 1887, the wildest dream of Antoine's boyhood came true. Porel, the director of the Odéon, one of the two French state theatres, called him to become one of his permanent company with the opportunity to star at once in the revival of Augier's *La Contagion* with a part originally created by Got. But Antoine's destiny was al-

[4] Quoted from a rare brochure of 1887 which was partly reprinted in 1890.

ready too deeply entwined with the Théâtre Libre for him to be drawn aside. To Porel's prophecy that the Théâtre Libre, a "studio theatre for a little group of Parisians" (Sarcey's phrase) would close in a year, Antoine replied that if this came to pass, he would then be available for the Odéon. A few days later, in July, he took his courage in his hands and resigned from the Gas Company to give all his time to the Théâtre Libre.

That autumn the Théâtre Libre reopened with sufficient plays for a season, a little studio for rehearsals, in which the director slept to reduce expenses, a debt of several thousand francs, nearly forty subscribing members. Season prices ranged from seventy-five francs for a gallery seat to five hundred francs for a box.

The first evening of the season was propitious. *Sœur Philomène,* an adaptation of a novel by the brothers Goncourt, was received with respect. *L'Évasion,* a one-act drama by the poet-mystic Villiers de l'Isle-Adam, in spite of some inconsistencies, was carried by the brilliant acting of Mévisto as the main figure, Paguol, and the unusual mingling of brutality and sentiment in this part. An escaped convict who has just murdered an aged woman, he plans to kill a newly married couple for the sake of the bride's dowry. The two are very young and very beautiful. Standing before them as they sleep, Paguol finds his heart weaken and experiences a sudden conversion: "This is not a man, this is not a woman. These are godlings." The enthusiasm of the audience was enough to delight any director's heart. Success, nevertheless, had a curious result. Père Krauss was alarmed not only for the sensibilities of the members of the original Cercle Gaulois who were present, but for their lives and limbs endangered by the weakening of the floor under heavy applause. Accordingly, permission to use the building was withdrawn; the Théâtre Libre was forced from its early home.

Demolished long ago to fit the changing needs of Montmartre, this small playhouse—it seated less than three hundred and fifty—has a memorial in the charming account in
which Jules Lemaître of *les Débats* chronicled his first
visit:

The card of invitation read: 37, passage of l'Elysée-des-Beaux-
Arts, Place Pigalle. So, last Tuesday, at about half past eight in
the evening, you might have seen ghostly figures slipping along
between the street-booths of Montmartre, carefully picking their
way among the puddles of water in the road, around the Place
Pigalle, scrutinizing through their eyeglasses the signs at the
street corners. No passage; no theatre! Finally, we have recourse
to a lighted wine shop, and then we enter a steep, tortuous, ill-
lighted alleyway. A row of cabs is going up slowly in the same
direction. We follow them. On each side, dim hovels and dirty
walls; quite at the end a dim stairway. We seemed so many
"great-coated Magi," seeking a hidden and glorious manger. Is
this the manger where the Drama, that decrepit old man, that
dotard, will be reborn?

The plays, largely one-act, given in November and December, created so much discussion that Antoine's theatre became at once the most talked-of playhouse in France.
Esther Brandès, in particular, tantalized the spectator by the
drawing of a woman about whom all the action centers and
whose motives even in the gravest situations are never made
clear. This play contained also one of Antoine's famous
parts in Morel, a dying man, whose presence touches each
scene with ghastliness. (Within the next few months, as he
gave to the public the work of the realistic school, Antoine
was to die so often that one of the excitements of his theatre
was the opportunity to study his latest method.) *Tout pour
l'Honneur* was to prove one of the most effective adaptations from Zola in the history of the Théâtre Libre. Perhaps no plays could be in greater contrast than Jean Jullien's *La Sérénade* and Théodore de Banville's *Le Baiser*

on a program of the early winter. *La Femme de Tabarin* by Catulle Mendès soon became part of the repertory of the Comédie-Française.

Jullien, whose book of dramatic theory was later to help popularize the theories of Ibsen and Strindberg in France, thinks that *La Sérénade* established the *genre théâtre libre*. The *genre théâtre libre* is a direct and more brutal descendant of the *comédie rosse* of Becque and other early realists. *Rosse,* a Spanish word, meaning originally "jade," a worn-out horse, passing into the vocabulary of criticism, became more and more ill-favored. Of the *comédie rosse,* Filon writes:

It is a sort of childlike and heavenly repose in an atmosphere of corruption, which suggests a travesty of the Golden Age—a world in which all our principles of morality are reversed, and where, in the words of Milton's Satan, evil has become good. . . . Imagine a society which retains the Decalogue as its moral code and guides its actions by the Seven Deadly Sins.

In basic situation this play of French naturalism is not unlike a Greek tragedy, but the treatment is without poetry, nobility, beauty. It has as compensation a great deal of humor, a disconcertingly pleasant humor, which makes the spectator wonder whether there is any event of life which cannot be glozed over smilingly. A prosperous shop-keeper discovers that the tutor whom he has recently engaged for his son has become his wife's lover. Wishing to avoid unpleasantness, he is willing to let the lovers go. At this moment, he learns from his daughter that she too has been the tutor's mistress, and that she is to have a child. As head of the family, he decides that forgetfulness of the past is the best procedure, and allows the tutor to marry the younger woman. In spite of these unsavory entanglements the betrothal dinner is a genial affair.

After a play of this mood, the joy of the audience in Banville's verse-fantasy can be imagined. Exquisite in finish and mingling naïvete and sophistication, it divides with Housman and Barker's *Prunella* the honor of being the most delightful of modern Pierrot plays. To the woods in which dwells the fairy Urgèle, by enchantment changed to an ugly old woman, comes Pierrot with his little hamper of good things for a day of picnicking. He is young and very innocent and white, "white as the blossom of the hawthorn," white as the little white boy of a Dutch garden. In his loneliness he prays for a companion, even the devil himself, and is answered by the appearance of the crone. Cheerfully leading the ugly creature to a pleasant nook he prepares to make the best of the odd companionship, even promising her, in answer to her request, that she shall have anything within his power. A kiss seems to him an unpleasant duty; nevertheless he summons his courage and presses his boy's lips to the old face. Of course, the miracle happens: Pierrot finds himself looking into the loveliest face in the world. His heart is hers at once; he finds her scarcely less enamoured. They plan their future in woods and meadows with nothing to disturb the magic of their pastoral life. Suddenly the voices of Urgèle's sisters call to her in a compelling song. She struggles a little in a weak, bird-like way, then flits to her fairy kindred. Pierrot is overwhelmed: indeed he questions seriously whether his life should be allowed to continue. Soon a gentle joy, tinged with melancholy, falls upon him as made wise by the first kiss, he reflects that there must be many charming lips in Paris. As he turns toward the city, Urgèle appears to him for a moment to sing of its delights.

The Théâtre Libre reopened in November at the Théâtre Montparnasse, 31, rue de la Gaîté, on "the wrong bank of the Seine," as pessimists among Antoine's friends remarked. With Tolstoy's *Power of Darkness*, on February tenth, began Antoine's custom of giving once a season a play by a great foreign dramatist. Political exiles from Russia, friends of the young translator, Pawlowsky, lent many authentic costumes and accessories for the stage setting. Antoine, taking the part of Akim, led a remarkable group. Except for Mévisto, the creator of Nikita, who had had some slight professional experience, the cast was entirely of amateurs: clerks, business men, a dressmaker, a telegraph operator. To the interpretation these young people gave their best, acting the terrible story with simplicity and truth. Before the performance there had been much head-shaking: indeed, the leading playwrights, Dumas fils, Sardou, Augier, had been against the production: "impossible on the French stage," "too sombre," "without sympathetic personages," "a novel in dialogue," "cruelly true and very beautiful, but to be read not acted," were some of the comments. The first evening won the journalists completely. The admiration of *la Revue des Deux Mondes* was typical:

It was Austerlitz; when the curtain fell on the final scene, during a tempest of acclamations, the public was transported; . . . I have not noticed an instant of delay or hesitation during the four hours. . . .

Each time that I have had any doubt about the intelligence of our French young people, about their rapidity in comprehending works [of literature] diametrically opposed to our own taste I have made a serious mistake.

Here were seen, for the first time on a French stage, a setting and costumes borrowed from the daily habits of Russian life without the enlivenments of comic opera and without that taste for the meretricious and the false which seem inherent in the atmosphere of the theatre.

The success of the first performance and of a revival in response to popular demand was enormous.

Such praise Antoine must have needed, for all was not smooth sailing for the Théâtre Libre even in the spring of

1888. No atmosphere is so favorable for the inflation of the ego as that of a dramatic association. Antoine with benevolent autocracy ruled his players, who were constantly under the influence of his enthusiasm; but the playwrights, less constantly with him, were not always in accord. Byl and Vidal had been early deserters, leaving Antoine when, realizing the failure of their first plays, he refused to bind himself to later productions. (They had, however, been won back by his offer to allow them to adapt the *Sœur Philomène* of Edmond and Jules de Goncourt.) A more serious defection was that of Paul Bonnetain, Lucien Descaves, Paul Margueritte, Gustave Guiches, and Henri Lavedan, who objected to what they considered the Zolaistic realism in vogue at the Théâtre Libre. At Zola's suggestion, the five were offered an evening to prove their mettle. *Les Quarts d'heure,*—two playlets by Guiches and Lavedan,—were the significant part of the evening. A novelty in their brevity and in their "cruel and incisive irony," they received from the critics the epithet, "slices of life," a term somewhat less hackneyed forty years ago.

Other controversial programs of this first season were *Matapan,* a verse play by Moreau; *Le Pain du Péché,* Paul Arène's adaptation of an old Provençal legend that food given by an unfaithful wife and her lover will poison her children, and *La Fin de Lucie Pellegrin* by Paul Alexis. This last, a study of scenes in the life of a prostitute, was so naturalistic that the more conservative journals recommended a fumigation of the theatre, and Felicia Mallet, the leading actress, wrote to the papers excusing herself for taking her rôle. Antoine, who had accepted the piece because of its high literary quality, began to wonder whether there are themes before which even a revolutionary director should hesitate. *Monsieur Lamblin* by Georges Ancey, an ironic comedy, and *La Prose* by Salandri, a drab and pessimistic play in which a young girl chooses between two suitors neither of whom brings her much possibility of happiness, completed the important dramas of the year. The season was on the whole representative of three of the dominating moods of Antoine's theatre; sophisticated comedy as immoral—or unmoral—as that of the English Restoration, domestic drama of unrelieved realism, and the play of the sensational and shocking.

Quite aside from his influence upon the actor's and the producer's art—to be discussed later—Antoine had an enviable record. In fifteen months, he had presented twenty-three plays new to the French public. Of this list, nine—one an adaptation, *Sœur Philomène,* and one, a translation from the Russian—were in two or more acts. Of the fourteen one-act plays, eleven were original, not adaptations. All of the great successes, except Tolstoy's play, received their first production at the Théâtre Libre; most of them, including the much discussed *En Famille, Sœur Philomène, Le Baiser, Monsieur Lamblin,* were written for it. Antoine had produced several times as many new plays as either of the state-endowed houses. One of his plays had already reached the Odéon, and one, the Comédie-Française.

As he thought over the completed season, Antoine felt some justice in the recurring charge of naturalism: though the popularity of *La Nuit Bergamasque* showed his interest in poetic drama, the naturalists had furnished "the best and the most significant" part of the experiment with *Esther Brandès, La Sérénade, Sœur Philomène, Monsieur Lamblin, La Pelote;* even *Les Quarts d'heure* though its collaborators were opposed in theory. The *Power of Darkness,* which many critics classed with these revolutionary dramas, had in Antoine's opinion far more affiliation with Greek tragedy. In his journal, Antoine reaffirmed the creed of an experimental theatre and warned himself against carrying naturalism too far.

Thus the year closed, outwardly with success, inwardly

UNIVERSITY OF WINNIPEG
LIBRARY
515 Portage Avenue
Winnipeg, Manitoba R3B 2E9

with anxiety, for by the stage entrance stood a wolf whose howling, inaudible to the audience of the little playhouse, constantly assailed the actor-manager's ear. Now the creature would be propitiated by the receipts from the public performance of the Russian drama, by some ingenious stage-setting which required almost no expenditure, or by tours to other countries. (Twice during 1887-1888 Antoine went to Brussels, unwillingly enough.) "Déjà les honneurs: on m'annonce que je recevrai les palmes académiques au 1er janvier. Hélas! j'aimerais mieux un peu d'argent, car je me sens embarqué dans quelque chose d'effroyable et qui me mènera Dieu sait où." ("Honors already! I am informed that I am to receive the palms of the Academy at New Year's. Alas! I would prefer a little money, for I feel that I am embarked on something dreadful which will lead me God knows where.")

The next season opened with some elements of security: a group of two hundred regular subscribers, soon greatly increased, and a permanent theatre. That the Parisians who had braved the journey to unfashionable Montparnasse during the season of '87 and '88 might not be willing to face the same discomfort during another season had been Antoine's worry and particularly that of his more pessimistic friends. Through Frantz Jourdain, friend of Daudet, Goncourt, and Zola, Antoine was introduced to Derenbourg, manager and architect of the Théâtre des Menus-Plaisirs in the Boulevard de Strasbourg. In business this gentleman had amassed a considerable fortune, which in his theatre venture he was losing slowly but steadily. He was discovered to be most enthusiastic over Antoine's experiment, ready to lease his theatre for the performances each month and for two or three days of preparation for a small fixed amount and a percentage on the subscriptions. For his headquarters and hall for the earlier rehearsals, Antoine retained the studio in the rue Blanche. The arrangement with Derenbourg was so satisfactory that the Théâtre Libre never again changed quarters; indeed when the experimental days had passed and Antoine began his campaign to capture the general public, the Théâtre des Menus-Plaisirs became the Théâtre-Antoine.

At this new home Antoine opened his season in mid-October with a varied program: Icres' *Les Bouchers,* a study of violence and brutality among humble people, rather surprisingly, in verse; *La Chevalerie Rustique,* translated from the Italian by Paul Solanges (the story is better known in the opera *Cavalleria Rusticana*); and Rodolphe Darzens' *L'Amante du Christ,* a poetic drama, inspired by the medieval mysteries and prophetic of many later plays in similar vein, as *The Servant in the House.* This prominence given to verse, recalling the early months of the theatre, was typical neither of this season, nor of the later years of the Théâtre Libre: after the spring of 1889, Antoine produced only a few brief plays and one long drama in verse.

Probably the most important evening of the season was December first with the premières of *Le Cor Fleuri* by Ephraïm Mikhaël, a slight but graceful fairy drama reminiscent of Shakespeare; *La Mort du Duc d'Enghien,* in which Léon Hennique brought the new realism to the service of the chronicle history play; and *La Chance de Françoise,* in which Georges de Porto-Riche, forsaking the vein of poetic drama in which he had written ten years before, enshrined at the Théâtre Libre if not a new form, at least a new mood of delicate psychological analysis. Antoine, though tracing the spiritual ancestry of this play to Dumas fils rather than to Becque, acknowledged "a sensibility, an agitation, a fever which the writers of the romantic drama of the preceding generation had not possessed." The success of the play, which soon reached the Théâtre du Gymnase, encouraged its author to write *L'Infidèle, L'Amoureuse,* and other dramas which have established him as one of the chief "laureates of love" in the contemporary French theatre. Analysis of passion, some variation of the three-cornered plot, and expert handling of intrigue are all dear to the Gallic theatregoer.

Unfortunately for Antoine's ideal of catholicity, the season's most ambitious excursion into romanticism, *La Reine Fiammette*, by Catulle Mendès, failed in spite of its beautiful and elaborate staging, because of the audience's amusement at the Provençal accent of the young man playing the hero, on whose appointment the author had insisted. Because of its slightness, *Le Cœur Révélateur*, *The Telltale Heart*, adapted from Baudelaire's translation of Poe's story failed to represent any great victory for romanticism. Realism fared better. *Madeleine*, drawn from an early novel of Zola's, was his only drama contributed directly to the free theatre. A play called *La Patrie en Danger*, an adaptation of a novel by Edmond and Jules de Goncourt, was produced in loyalty to these pioneers of French realism soon after the public of the Odéon had almost hissed off the stage *Germinie Lacerteux*, in spite of Réjane's interpreting the central figure. Ancey's *Les Inséparables*, Jullien's *L'Echéance*, and Céard's *Les Resignés*, notable programs, were realistic.

Yet hospitality to many forms and moods was still Antoine's longing. He appended an "important notice" to the last program of the year:

The liberal eclecticism which, with equal respect for all literary schools, has presented, one after another, works which are very varied, *La Nuit Bergamasque* as well as *En Famille*, and *La Fin de Lucie Pellegrin* as well as *Le Baiser*, now leads the Théâtre Libre to play *La Casserole*, product of a very violent realism, which puts on the stage a cruel picture of the underworld of Paris.

By many tokens, though the Théâtre Libre was to last for six years longer, the next season, 1889-1890, was the most momentous of the theatre: the year which witnessed the début of two of the notable dramatists of contemporary France,—one of them to attain international fame,—the first production of an Ibsen play in France, and an extraordinary widening of the influence of the theatre at home and abroad.

Realism at first was the genre. Pierre Wolff, whose première, *Jacques Bouchard*, was given by Antoine in the spring of 1890, later when the days of realism were waning, was to follow his early themes of crime and violence with plays of marked sentiment and become a well-known playwright. The other and greater dramatist discovered during this season was Eugène Brieux. Two slight plays written almost ten years before in collaboration with Salandri and never given in Paris had not encouraged Brieux in the life of a dramatic author; Antoine's interest in him alone encouraged the energetic young journalist and editor of a provincial journal to turn again to plays. "This varied labor," writes Antoine of Brieux's journalism, "will have the most beneficent influence in the development of this young man in giving him a sense of actuality, a 'flair' for the public, very precious in his career as dramatic author." Though *Ménage d'artistes*, the first of Brieux's plays at the Théâtre Libre, has never been so well received as *Blanchette*, produced there two years later, the actor-manager discerned in it something unusual and promising:

There is, in this drama, *Ménage d'artistes*, played today in our theatre as the début of Eugène Brieux, much declamation, much triteness of plot, but an extraordinary quarrel scene in the third act between Sylviac and me which has produced, as I expected, a sensational effect through a dialogue possessing a truth, an accent, a movement which make understandable why I have given a play which on the surface is not so strong and less audacious than we have been accustomed to give.

With the possible exception of *Ménage d'artistes,* the production of *Ghosts,* under the title of *Les Revenants,* was the most influential play of the year. This was undertaken with all the care which Ibsen's importance demanded. Antoine, who, as has been said, did not know the work of Ibsen at the founding of the Théâtre Libre, had his attention first drawn to *Ghosts* during the summer of 1888 when in Brussels he became acquainted with the work of the Duke of Meiningen and his company. He learned that this "subversive" play of Ibsen's, forbidden in the public theatres, had been given on the Duke's own estate before an invited audience which included the author and a group of German critics. Antoine procured a translation, but circumstances prevented his staging the play early the following autumn, as he hoped to do. More than a year later, Zola called his attention to an article by Jacques Saint-Cère on a recent production of *Ghosts* in Germany and the position of Ibsen among modern dramatists. Zola continued to urge the production of this play at the Théâtre Libre, and volunteered to find a French translator. He felt that this study of heredity in both theme and literary energy equalled *The Power of Darkness:*

I have read *Les Revenants.* [Antoine wrote soon after the French translation had reached him.] It resembles nothing in our theatre; a study on heredity of which the third act has the sombre grandeur of Greek tragedy. However, it seems to me long, which is natural enough in a French translation of a German text adapted from the Norwegian; evidently it is this which slackens and obscures the dialogue, but all the same, I don't hesitate.

Later Antoine did have moments of doubt. In perplexity he decided to consult three of his Théâtre Libre playwrights; his account of their reactions is an interesting document in the history of early Ibsen criticism:

I am still very much perplexed about *Les Revenants*. I fear long speeches for an audience so quickly impatient as that of the Théâtre Libre. Last evening, at the close of the rehearsal in the rue Blanche, I asked Mendès, Céard, and Ancey to stay after the departure of the others, to listen to the reading of it and give me advice. I told them that, in my opinion, there is something tremendous here which I would not wish to injure by any clumsiness of presentation. Cuttings are perhaps necessary; it seems to me that this work ought to be done by a man of letters, one of our dramatic authors, who would take the responsibility and also be recognized, receive the honor of a fellow-workman. I did not myself wish to meddle with a work of this importance. After the reading, all three are moved by the new accent and power of this drama. In this little silence which ensues, I beg their sincere opinion.

Mendès, who speaks first, and whose reaction is of prime importance for me, throws himself back in his chair with his habitual gesture of tossing back his locks, saying, "Dear friend, this piece is impossible with us."

Céard, no less positive, gives as his opinion: "Yes, it is very beautiful, but it is not clear to our Latin minds. I should like a prologue, in which the spectators should see Oswald's father and Regina's mother surprised by young Mrs. Alving. This, practically, would put into action what the wife of the chamberlain tells the pastor. After this exposition, the French audience could enter into the play with all necessary security."

As for Ancey, he said to me simply: "It is magnificent, it does not need to be touched. If you are afraid of the long speeches, and there are some in fact, perhaps because of the translation, make the cuts yourself in the parts of the dialogue which might cause your players difficulty."

In a word, all three are struck differently, according to their temperaments and their minds, but I feel that no one of them cares to assume the responsibility of the revision.

Their variety of opinion made Antoine even more eager to obtain as exact a French translation as possible. While he was waiting for the text, another sharpening of curiosity came in the English reviews of the London production of the play. "Revolting obscenity," "the world of the lugubrious," "the malodorous Ibsen" are phrases from this tirade, collected by George Bernard Shaw in the *Quintessence of Ibsenism*. About the same time, Céard wrote an open letter to *Gil Blas* in which he explained why "after reflection it has not seemed possible to adapt *Les Revenants* and the necessity of not interfering with the essentially local psychology of the work." As Antoine had never thought of adaptation, but, at the most, the shortening of a few speeches, this unfavorable publicity was not merited. However, Ibsen's interest helped Antoine. The dramatist approved a more literal translation than the one which he had previously authorized, and expressed his faith in the Théâtre Libre, which he had watched from its foundation. For a time, Antoine even had hopes of welcoming him to Paris on the opening night—hopes which his temperamental aloofness disappointed.

The Théâtre Libre shone on this historic night. The cast was the strongest the little theatre could muster: Arquillière as pastor Manders; Janvier, Engstrand; Mademoiselle Barny, Mrs. Alving; Mademoiselle Lucie Colas, Regina; and Antoine himself, Oswald, "the finest rôle which an actor could play." The success of the performance may be judged from Antoine's comment:

May 30, 1890—We played *Les Revenants* last evening. I believe that on some the effect was profound; for the majority of the spectators, boredom followed astonishment; however, during the last scenes, a veritable anguish gripped the house. I can speak of it then only in the briefest words, for I underwent an experience new to me, the almost complete loss of my own personality; from the second act I remember nothing, neither the audience, nor the effect of the scene, and after the fall of the curtain I found myself trembling, unnerved and incapable of getting hold of myself for some time.

George Moore, a young man familiar with the literary life of both London and Dublin, was present at one of the rehearsals and has left an account of his impressions:

Céard, with whom I discussed the question, whether plays acted as they read, while waiting for *Ghosts* to begin, said that he did not think it would act as well as *Nora*. *Ghosts* had seemed to him vague and undetermined in the reading, but when the third act was over I heard his voice in the tumult of praise congratulating Antoine. He confessed that he had misjudged the play; the dimness and vagueness that he feared in the reading had, in the representation been changed into firmest outline.

Antoine was wonderful in the part of Osvalt. The nervous irritation of the sick man was faultlessly rendered. When he tells his mother of the warnings of the French doctor, at the moment he loses his temper at her interruptions—she seeks not to hear the fearful tale—Antoine identifying himself with the simple truth sought by Ibsen, by voice and gesture, casts upon the scene so terrible a light, so strange an air of truth, that the drama seemed to be passing not before our eyes, but deep down in our hearts in a way we had never felt before. . . .

Paris artistic and literary was in the stalls and boxes, and since the memorable night when Tolstoi's *Puissance des Ténèbres* was given, the Théâtre Libre has not won a triumph either so deep or so pronounced.[5]

This was the year, also, of a Senate investigation of Antoine's theatre, precipitated by those who viewed as a subsidy the subscription for four seats which Antoine had received from Monsieur Larroumet, the Minister of Public Instruction and the Fine Arts. Against violent opposition he praised Antoine for the service which he was rendering, and defined the Théâtre Libre as a "kind of dramatic organization in which lovers of the art of the theatre come to hear, in accordance with their personal taste and on their own

[5] From *Impressions and Opinions,* by George Moore, pp. 163, 167. Courtesy of Charles Scribner's Sons, Publishers, New York.

responsibility, plays which only in exceptional cases are given before a general public." He commended particularly Antoine's readiness to give young and unknown playwrights a hearing and referred to their original and powerful ideas "of which the influence has already made itself felt in dramatic literature."

A few months later, Antoine again found the official searchlight turned upon him; the occasion was the production of *La Fille Elisa,* an adaptation of a novel of Edmond de Goncourt. A debate in the Chamber of Deputies continued intermittently for a year and a half, passing from consideration of this play to the general subject of censorship. Hither were summoned several prominent literary men and playwrights, and, to his surprise, Antoine. Many were thorough-going in their opposition to the censorship; others favored it in theory, but condemned a practice which almost invariably forbade a serious treatment of a sex theme, while allowing a suggestive farce or review. Goncourt, in his plea, traced through the ages the gradual development of modern realism:

Virtually, the interest of the public has passed successively from Agamemnon and the kings of antiquity to the marquises of the seventeenth and eighteenth centuries, then from the marquises to the bourgeois of the nineteenth century, . . .

They do not suspect, these gentlemen, [the censors] that a hundred and fifty years ago, at the moment when Marivaux was publishing the novel of *Marianne,* that he was being attacked with the taunt that the adventures of the nobility could alone interest the public, and that Marivaux was obliged to write a preface in which he proclaimed the interest which he found in what public opinion denominated as ignoble middle-class happenings, affirming that people who were somewhat philosophical and not dupes of social distinctions would not be grieved to learn something of the life of the wife of a great cloth-merchant.

Alas, a hundred and fifty years later—here, I am speaking for myself—it may perhaps be permitted a philosophical spirit of

Marivaux's kind, to descend to a maid of all work, to a low prostitute.

In January, 1892, the special commission recommended the omission from the budget of any provision for a censorship. "What a victory," cried Antoine, "if, as everything permits us to hope, the government ratifies this!"

The following season opened with *L'Honneur* by Henry Fèvre, "a bourgeois study of implacable ferocity," as Antoine calls it, which, nevertheless, disarmed criticism by the sanity and balance of its treatment. Among dramatic innovations were *La Belle Opération* by Julien Sermet, an almost plotless scene of a group of physicians in consultation; Auguste Linert's *Conte de Noël,* a strange mingling of naturalistic horror and mysticism; *Nell Horn* by Rosny anticipating *Major Barbara* in the portrayal of Salvation Army life; and Eugène Bourgeois' *Le Pendu,* said to foreshadow faintly the Synge mingling of satiric humor and tragedy. The performance of Ibsen's *Wild Duck* was intrinsically the greatest of this year. An audience at first puzzled and hostile was completely transported by the truth and pathos of the last act. Of the critics, Sarcey expended the ammunition of his rather heavy fieldpiece upon the duck,—symbol or actual fowl. Jules Lemaître answered in *Débats,* by a brilliant interpretation ending with the query, "What is so obscure or strange in the *Wild Duck?*"

The next summer, there came to Antoine one of the curious experiences of his life. He was living quietly in a little fishing village, Camaret, to save expense, for the season had closed with a debt. Almost five hundred plays had followed him. As he was attacking this mass, he happened upon a three-act play, *L'Envers d'une sainte,* signed "Charles Watterneau." The power of this drama haunted him for a sleepless night; he wrote at once accepting the play and offering to produce it soon. Two days later fortune smiled upon him

again in the pages of *L'Amour brode* by a playwright named
"Weindel," who gave his address as Vienna. This manuscript, like the other, announced to Antoine "a true dramatic
author." Just as Antoine was writing to this second genius
there came a delighted letter from the author of *L'Envers
d'une sainte,* giving his true name, François de Curel,
acknowledging also the authorship of *L'Amour brode,* and
informing the astounded producer that if he would explore
more deeply the mountain of manuscript he would find a
third play, *La Figurante.* This was the explanation: Curel
had received so many rebuffs from the commercial theatres
that finally, to acquit himself of any charge of easy discouragement, rather than with any real hope, since rumor had
for some time been maligning the Théâtre Libre as a "petite
chapelle," strictly realistic in its sympathies, he had turned
to Antoine. The three pseudonyms were devised to assure
each play as impartial a judgment as possible. Antoine
offered to produce any one of the three plays early in the
season. His choice and Curel's were the same, *L'Envers
d'une sainte.* During the fall and the beginning of winter,
Antoine looked forward to this production as a proof of his
eclecticism. "François de Curel has the quality which is going, I believe, to take us out of what Jules Lemaître and
others begin to call the *poncif* of the Théâtre Libre."

L'Envers d'une sainte is an intense and powerful character study of Julie Renaudin, who has been a nun for eighteen
years since she attempted to kill Jeanne, the young wife of
her cousin Henri, who had first loved Julie herself and then
deserted her. Now after Henri's death, Julie returns to the
world and continues her vengeance by trying to lure the
young daughter, Christine, to the cloisters. She is softened
only when she learns that Henri throughout his married life
had thought of her with tenderness. The other play of the
evening, Brieux's *Blanchette,* is the story of a young girl of
a bourgeois family, educated beyond her station by the

wish of her doting father and then, when she can find no employment suited to this education, cast upon the streets. This drama was beautifully acted, for Antoine's little group had often impersonated characters of the same genre. Curel's play taxed its actors to the utmost and then lost delicate over-tones and subtleties of interpretation. "Weakly enough acted," was the verdict of Antoine's diary. Yet the evening but deepened Antoine's first impression of Curel's talent. It departed from old formulas: "un théâtre tellement neuf, tout intérieur," "a theatre new in a certain way, a theatre of the moods of the soul."

For once the major critics were in agreement with the producer, except Sarcey, to whom this play seemed enveloped in an atmosphere of obscurity, through which emerged words with "certain qualities of style, austere and firm, which mark a writer, but a dramatic writer never." "If the text were only signed Ibsen!" sighed Lemaître. Doumic wrote enthusiastically:

L'Envers d'une sainte recommends itself by the rarest qualities; the very elevated conception, a fine curiosity regarding the secrets of the interior life, a daring in continuing to its outcome the study of a psychological case, a vigor of analysis pushed to the very foundation, and finally the gift which consists in giving life to a being of imagination.

No other summer brought any such influx of plays or any native writer of equal power. Difficulties increased. Harassed by the need of money, for his innovations in stage setting and production continued to be very expensive, forced to undertake tours when he coveted leisure for his Paris season, Antoine began to lose heart. Even the triumph of his old associates, playwrights and actors, on other stages —each individual success is applauded in his journal— weakened his organization and increased his problems. While Paris was ringing with praise—and vituperation—

Antoine's dejection grew deeper. In May, 1893, he confided to his diary:

> Although I have almost decided to give up the attempt and no one has any suspicions of it, this evening I have a bitter regret for what we might have been able to do in the future. My energy alone and my courage are no longer sufficient for holding out. I have, up to the present, drawn everything from myself and my friends, authors and actors, everything that we had in us, but money, I can't manufacture that. Finally, I have threatened too many interests, irritated too many people to hope for anything except a general satisfaction in finally seeing me defeated. If I had not promised to undertake another season, I would end everything with this last play which we have in preparation.

Again in the early autumn:

> I am returning from touring across all France and along the coast, exhausted but content with the increasingly sympathetic reception of the great public, which gives me confidence for the future, when I shall be forced to become a professional actor to earn my living and pay the debts of the Théâtre Libre.

But the great days were not yet over. Three successes marked the year of 1892-1893; it is significant that of their authors, only one was a native playwright. Georges Courteline in *Boubouroche* enveloped in gay cynicism a group of thoroughly unmoral people caught in an amorous intrigue. *Mademoiselle Julie* by Strindberg, chosen both for its original and powerful delineation of abnormal psychology and its novelty of form, introduced to Paris a genius second only to Ibsen's. Antoine, who considered Strindberg very important, reprinted his revolutionary introduction to *Mademoiselle Julie* and distributed it among the subscribers of the Théâtre Libre. The third great play was *The Weavers,* or as it stands in the French translation, *Les Tisserands.*

Upon this Antoine lavished especial care, incurring a heavy debt. *The Weavers* was to be memorable, if not actually the swan-song of his little theatre, at least one perfect thing wrested from evil days. For the Théâtre Libre it had a special interest since Hauptmann was the discovery of the Freie Bühne, the first German independent theatre. *The Weavers* is the first and perhaps the noblest of the plays which present not the struggle of individual antagonists, but great masses of frenzied humanity locked in industrial conflict. The evening was worthy of the play. Antoine wrote:

Les Tisserands is an immense success. It must be recognized that no dramatist of France is capable of painting a canvas of this amplitude and this power. The play, created at the Théâtre Libre of Berlin, had had a tremendous effect. Hauptmann, behind whom was ranged all the literary world of Young Germany, had obtained the raising of the imperial edict. Here in our theatre, contrary to what I expected, this play of revolt rang first of all as a cry of despair and of misery; from act to act, the rapt audience never ceased applauding. It is the masterpiece of a social theatre which is rough-hewing itself, and Jaurès, filled with enthusiasm, has told me that such a play accomplishes more than all campaigns and political discussions.

Moreover, as I feel strongly that it is one of the last plays which I am putting on and that the end of my effort begins to appear on the horizon, I have consecrated to it all that I have left of force, of resources, and of energy, and I can say that the interpretation has been admirable. Gémier, as Father Baumert, has revealed himself as what I have known him to be for a long time, a great actor, and Arquillière has been splendid. [Antoine himself was Hilse.] All the second act with the chant of the weavers, which serves as a *leitmotiv*, and the cannonading, which rumbles continually off stage, has made a prodigious effect. In the fourth, in the storming of the manufacturer's house, the effect of terror was so intense that every one in the orchestra stood up. The last scene, with the death of old Hilse during the fusillade and the uproar of the crowd, ended in the midst of applause.

As French plays became more difficult to obtain, Antoine turned again to foreign dramatists,—to Björnson, whose work was little known in France, and again to Hauptmann. *En Faillite* (*The Bankruptcy*) seemed to Antoine "the most pathetic tragedy on money that has ever been put on the stage." Besides, he found a melancholy and ironic pleasure in the appropriateness of the title to his own affairs, now that he knew that the days of the Théâtre Libre were numbered. In November, with several members of his group, he journeyed to Berlin to see the première of Hauptmann's *Hannele*. (Here Hauptmann and Sudermann, Germany's two leading dramatists, representing the capital city, paid Antoine every honor.) Soon after returning to France, Antoine gave his own interpretation of the play. *Hannele* did not have the sensational success of *The Weavers,* but it delighted those who loved fantasy and vision, and contained some of the most beautiful stage pictures which Antoine had presented. "It has cost the very eyes out of my head; in the state of affairs where I am now, I might as well do one or two beautiful things before going on the rocks."

Even this last winter of Antoine's included the première of a French playwright of considerable originality, Maurice Barrès, in *Une Journée Parlementaire,* the study of an official whose political ambitions are frustrated by his own dishonesty. Originality also marked the last play of the season, *Le Missionnaire* by Luguet. This was a series of five scenes linked by the commentaries of a reader placed before the curtain. After the reading of each fragment, the scene unrolled itself on the stage. An incident connected with this program decided Antoine to end the long struggle at once:

I took the difficult part of the reader and all the evening I was exposed to the pleasantries of the crowd. It even happened once in the midst of the noise that a handful of sous hit me in the face; it is extremely symbolic. This brutal gesture decided me, on the spot, to abandon the Théâtre Libre. These wretches don't know, and if I had dared to interrupt the performance and reveal to them suddenly the real situation, it is probable that they would have been ashamed.

This was in May. In June, Antoine ceded the Théâtre Libre to Larochelle, the son of an old director and actor, who for several months had been eager for a part in the management. No money passed in exchange. Larochelle promised to give the three programs still due the subscribers and to include in his productions *L'Argent,* by Emile Fabre, and *La Fumée puis la flamme,* by Caraguel. To the new director Antoine turned over all the belongings of the theatre, including eighty complete stage decorations, the furniture of the hall in the rue Blanche, and the use of the name Théâtre Libre. He promised that after his tour had closed he would become one of Larochelle's actors. The past with its weight of debt belonged to Antoine.

This, the first chapter in the drama of Antoine's life, is the only one which falls within the scope of this book, and a brief summary of his later activities must suffice.

To reduce the debt of the Théâtre Libre as quickly as possible, Antoine accepted an offer for an extended tour through Europe with a company composed of some of his finest actors and actresses. The season in Germany was a success, but in Italy when the risks of the venture grew greater, the impresario under whom Antoine and his friends were acting alleged slight breaches of contract to extricate himself from an awkward situation. "Here," wrote Antoine, "the odyssey of the Théâtre Libre comes to a close; seven years ago I left my garret in the rue de Dunkerque with fourteen sous in my pocket to go to rehearse our first play in the house of the little wine merchant in the rue des

Abbesses, and now I find myself in Rome, with nearly the same sum in my purse, surrounded by fifteen comrades as much discomforted as I, with a hundred thousand francs of debts awaiting me in Paris, and no knowledge of what the next day will bring."

A reversal of fortune came quickly. After his tour, Antoine played in the company of his successor, meanwhile appearing in *L'Age difficile* of Jules Lemaître at the Gymnase; his acting at the Théâtre Libre over, he signed with the Renaissance Theatre for the production of *La Figurante* of François de Curel. June 4, 1896, with Ginisty he shared the honor of appointment to the directorship of the Odéon, a partnership from which Antoine, not accustomed to a divided authority, resigned seventeen days later. In October, he was offered the stage-managership of the same theatre, and acceptance was followed by a resignation almost as prompt. In the autumn of 1897, after a tour to South America, he decided to risk that in which his great interest lay, a commercial theatre for the larger public, which in so far as financial integrity allowed should continue the ideals of the Théâtre Libre. September 30, this theatre, the Théâtre Antoine, opened with *Blanchette* and *Boubouroche,* two of the successes of the pioneer theatre. For nine years, Antoine and Gémier, his director, continued in this larger arena their struggle for sincere dramatic art. In 1906 Antoine was again called to the Odéon, this time as sole director. He accepted and gave as daring plays as are possible in a state-controlled theatre, adding enormously both to its fame and its debts. Since his resignation in 1914, he has divided his time between a sojourn in Constantinople and life in Paris, where, as a dramatic critic, he has influenced the French theatre again and again.

To return to the history of the Théâtre Libre, a brief chronicle—Larochelle was devoted to his work, tenacious of will, ardent in his appeals, but entirely powerless to arrest the inevitable decline. Even the inauguration of musical drama aroused little interest. With the exception of the plays which Antoine had chosen, only two evenings, *Le Cuivre* by Paul Adam and an adaptation of Maupassant's *Mademoiselle Fifi,* recalled the great days. April 27, 1896, saw the last performance of the theatre.

The first cause of this disbandment of the Théâtre Libre was its failure to solve its financial problem. In founding the theatre, Antoine was unassisted by wealthy patron or municipal aid. The initial difficulties did not lessen, for as Antoine identified himself entirely with the theatre, his standards in stage-setting, in accuracy of costuming, and in the number of supernumeraries advanced, though he was not extravagant—indeed the director of Fine Arts was asked to discover why a state-endowed theatre should require large subsidies when Antoine's productions sometimes cost but five hundred francs. But the great stages of Paris had their large audiences and several performances of each play; the Théâtre Libre, at the height of its popularity, offered only three performances of each play including an invitation evening for critics and friends. The season of Antoine's spectacular success, 1889-1890, closed with a deficit of 12,778 francs.

The tours of the Théâtre Libre were another reason for its decline. Except for the first, a challenge to the infant theatre, each tour was undertaken reluctantly for financial reasons. The occasional public performances at home had the same lure and danger. Of them the director writes:

I am not fond of these public performances, however lucrative they may be, for they warp the character of our undertaking. The day when the great public is freely admitted to see these spectacles reserved for a select group, we shall no longer be anything but an ordinary theatre and we fall into the claws of the censor.

And of the tours:

Once engaged in this system of public performances we run the risk of taking away from our evenings a great deal of their individuality.

Success beckoned from Holland, Belgium, England, Germany, Italy. Some of the largest profits came from the French provinces: Rouen, home of Brieux, supported *Blanchette* to the extent of 40,000 francs. In three years, Antoine had lost so many of his prominent actors and actresses that occasional distributions of money were necessary to hold the others. Besides, the tours had an educational value for they carried the banner of the new movement to the stages of other countries. The tour to England influenced those who were later to support Grein's Independent Theatre, and the fame of the Théâtre Libre led to the early establishment of the Freie Bühne. Yet for the organization itself there was a strong element of danger.

A kindred reason for the waning popularity of the theatre was the type of play frequently given on the regular program. In the latter days, the *genre Théâtre Libre* appeared more and more frequently. In the hands of minor playwrights—many of Antoine's greatest were now writing for the commercial stages—these plays were without the leaven of brilliant satire and were sometimes revolting. Two other adverse criticisms were levelled against the programs, one, the almost complete absence of poetic plays, the other, too great admiration for the foreign. The first charge may be admitted. The other criticism was not justified as the theatre, in its nine years, included only eleven foreign plays, —four of them, one-act plays. The feeling of abuse may be accounted for by the failure on the part of any later play to surpass *Ghosts* and *The Power of Darkness* in interest, by the confusion which *The Wild Duck* and *Mademoiselle Julie* brought to the average mind, and by the dearth of unusual native talent in the final seasons, which gave the foreign plays an unintentional and unfortunate prominence.

Another danger to the theatre lay in the audience. As early as the beginning of his second season, Antoine discovered that its qualities were changing; there was no longer the loyalty to true art of every kind, the eagerness to understand the purpose of playwright and manager, and there was an easily aroused and disconcerting levity:

This tendency to find amusement in the plays does not nonplus me; I am not of the humor to let it slip by unnoticed and we shall certainly have to find a way to secure the respect and attention of these new spectators.

Antoine was aggressive, decisive, not easy to influence, perhaps failing to grasp the really objectionable features of some of the plays of his theatre: indeed his certainty and independence made enemies and were in a small degree a contributing cause in his undermining. But impartial observers felt the unfairness and even brutality of the audience, or rather of the wealthy bourgeoisie always on the watch for the sensational and the suggestive. Yet the subscriptions of these scandal-mongers were needed.

Again, the exodus of actors and actresses to the professional stage inevitably brought a lowering of standards; after the first three years, the theatre became virtually a training school for the new realistic acting. Unable to fill his broken ranks with outstanding artists, Antoine gave some inferior performances. No one recognized this more clearly than himself.

In the final analysis, then, the Théâtre Libre closed its doors because of the natural forces of development, the evolution of a new form, and the stretching toward wider boundaries. It had proved its thesis: it no longer needed to experiment. New methods of organization, which Antoine had originated, were already the model for other groups in

Paris, in Germany, in England; innovations in acting and stage art were becoming the commonplaces of the foremost public theatres; important revolutionary playwrights were courted by them. The logical course for the manager of the Théâtre Libre was to carry his struggle into a wider field.

The contribution of Antoine to the French stage and to the European dramatic renascence has been discussed hotly in the days of his theatre and since: some dubbed the Théâtre Libre a place of the lost; others, a kind of Mount of Salvation, where the dramatic Sangraal was reverently tended and of which Antoine was the Parsifal.

The least debatable achievement of the Théâtre Libre was its contribution to acting and the art of the stage. Antoine originated modern realistic acting, that which comes from within, as the actor lives fully and directly the life of the character whom he impersonates. Complete absorption in character does away with the elocutionary tricks of the older stage: the long addresses, the unbroken monologues, the tirades. Antoine demolished the conventions that an actor should always speak with his face toward the audience, and that he should insist on rising for his speeches. Paris began by laughing at the back-turning of Monsieur Antoine, which became proverbial. It continued to laugh till it discovered that this back was often more revealing of emotion than many a face.

Antoine found his little group of actors and actresses almost unhampered by traditions of the stage. They were young, busy people of the middle class after long days in office or shop glad to slip into the personalities of their art life. They won their public by enthusiasm, vigor, directness, above all, sympathy in depicting the struggles of modern life. Mademoiselle Barny, one of the greatest, was a dressmaker whom Antoine had known at the Cercle Pigalle and the Cercle Gaulois. She was a persistent worker, during the few years of the Théâtre Libre creating almost seventy rôles with truth and unflagging enthusiasm. When other actors and actresses left the rue Blanche for more lucrative positions on the commercial stages, Mlle. Barny remained loyal; after the close of the Théâtre Libre she acted with Antoine at the Théâtre Antoine and at the Odéon. Louise France, who died in 1903, was a member of Antoine's company during most of its history. Hers was a realistic talent: her favorite plays were *La Fin de Lucie Pellegrin* and *La Prose*. On the stage she lived the part with every motion of her body as well as her voice.

Rehearsed up to the last minute, part in hand. The evening of the première, had forgotten a rôle which she had never known anyway and behold, she found it again word for word, aided *by the memory in her arms, her legs* and by the stage setting.[6]

Mlle. Lucie Colas, gay and charming, appeared in *The Power of Darkness* and many later plays. She left the Théâtre Libre to act with Sarah Bernhardt and with Coquelin.

Of the actors, Mévisto, one of the most powerful, had been Antoine's friend from boyhood and shared his ambitions. As early as the production of *L'Évasion* he was noted for his remarkable facial expressions in the part of the murderous convict. His range of acting appears in his strongly contrasted rôles, Théodore Cottin in *La Sérénade,* Nikita in *The Power of Darkness,* the Christ in the *Amante du Christ.* After his success as Nikita, he was called to the Porte-St.-Martin. Unlike most of Antoine's troupe, Henri Mayer reached the Théâtre Libre by way of the professional stage. A graduate of the Conservatoire in 1882, he joined the Vaudeville, at which he was not given any important part. Antoine persuaded him to appear in *La Sérénade* and *Tout pour l'Honneur* at the Théâtre Libre, in each of which

6 Thalasso, Adolphe, *Le Théâtre Libre,* p. 144.

he scored a great success. His patience was inexhaustible: he would rehearse his speeches thirty times if necessary. Gémier, like Mévisto and Antoine, had been refused admission to the Conservatoire. His first experience with Antoine was a minor part in *La Femme de Tabarin*. Gémier remained with the Théâtre Libre until the end. In 1907, taking a realistic part in a play by Jullien at the Renaissance, he was acclaimed by many Antoine's equal. Other important actors were Janvier and Damoye. A list of even the finer actors and actresses would be long.

Most individual of all was their leader, with his back-turning, his "untheatrical" gestures, his elisions and incoherences as of a careless or halting tongue. His silences, too, were famous,—quivering, devastating, a language more heavily fraught than that of words. He mystified the older critics:

Very intelligent and able as a stage director, this Antoine: [wrote Sarcey] but the devil take me if I know what gives him his reputation as an actor! He recites with an unpleasant monotony; nothing with any effect, not a word which seems forceful or stands out. He finds himself only in the great scene; and there again he is effective only by means of a restrained pathos which is all that his voice allows him. I applaud him all the same because after all he is the soul of this little world and with all his obvious defects, he is yet superior through his intelligence and his will power to many actors who have only their natural gifts and their training.

In his years at the Théâtre Libre, he created eighty-three rôles, many of them of the bourgeois type, represented by the father of Blanchette. Into his rôles he infused a passionate delight in living, a gripping fear of death. In the first months of his little theatre, he became one of the great French actors.

In spite of constant temptation, Antoine never sought to

transform a play into a mere vehicle for his own genius as some actor-managers have done. On the contrary, one of his finest gifts to the stage has been his emphasis upon the need for a perfect ensemble, the coöperation of each actor and manager and the willingness of each to accept any rôle for the good of the play. In this attitude he was strengthened by his observation of the German troupe of the Duke of Saxe-Meiningen (a group which is entitled to fuller study than most historians of the modern theatre have given it). He was also influenced by their acting of mob-scenes, usually far superior to that of the regular theatres, but not always perfect. After seeing the Meiningen performance of *William Tell,* he wrote:

> The only sincere objection to their performance is that in this same *William Tell,* for example, Schiller having written a part for the crowd, all the supernumeraries kept crying the same phrase in the same rhythm. That is clumsy and unreal. But could one not have the replies of this crowd resolve themselves into a skillfully combined clamor?
>
> If we wanted them to cry out, "Vive Gambetta!" for instance, do you know what I would do?
>
> I would divide my two hundred supernumeraries into a dozen groups,—if you wish, women, children, the working class, and so on. I would have the middle class start the *Vi,* the women, accelerating the rhythm, would commence when the others attack *gam,* and I would have the boys drag five seconds after every one else. It is, in short, like directing a choir. I am certain that the audience would hear one great clamor *Vive Gambetta!* and if as in the Meiningen performance the attitudes, the gestures, the groupings were diversified and varied with the same care, there is no doubt but that a general effect would result which would be truthful.

This new interpretation in acting naturally developed new methods of stage decoration: realism in characterizations and dialogue must not be neutralized by flimsy walls, doors, and even stage accessories painted on the flat, by rooms bare of atmosphere, by backgrounds of shabby palaces. Antoine is credited with being the first to use actual door handles and knockers, and many of his scenes were carried out with the most minute detail. Now realism of setting is being superseded, or at least modified; the critic assails the over-conscientious form. But realism is one form of the producer's art, if perhaps a transitional form. Moreover, though Antoine's realistic settings were his most numerous, he was an experimenter in other forms of stage decoration, not limiting his settings to any one kind. For *Un Beau Soir*, for instance, he called in Henri Rivière, the artist of the Chinese shadows of the Chat-Noir. Antoine, though not so engrossed in stage art as Reinhardt was to become, nevertheless by his receptive attitude helped prepare the way for Reinhardt and for others.

Antoine's views on the requirements of the new methods of acting and producing are represented in a letter to Sarcey soon after three realistic plays, one a revival of Becque's *La Parisienne* at the Comédie Française, had proved failures at the larger theatres:

Have you not been struck by this coincidence, namely, that three plays, *La Parisienne, Grand'mère, Le Maître,* all three representing the same general attitude, conceived in the desire for a change, which torments the new school, have all three been unsuccessful, in three different theatres, and, as is generally agreed, have not received satisfactory interpretation though performed by actors who belong, for the most part, to the first rank of Parisian artists?

How explain this triple coincidence; is it not interesting to seek the causes of it? Notice, of course, that I do not allow myself any literary appreciation; that is not my affair: I speak simply from the point of view of my profession. Well, I think that there is here an important technical problem to be explained, a problem which ought to interest all the writers of tomorrow and perhaps also intelligent and wide-awake players concerned for their art and the movement in the theatre as it exists at the present. For *Grand'mère* was a failure, *Le Maître* was a failure, and *La Parisienne* was, you say, a failure.

As far as the three pieces are concerned, the press generally agreed in finding the interpretation mediocre. For *Le Maître* and *La Parisienne*, there had been the original interpretation as a means of comparison. For *Grand'mère*, this method of comparison lacking, it was Ancey who was held to blame and rather more than was reasonable.

Well, the very simple reason for this three-fold happening in which the actors, as a rule excellent, were judged mediocre for one evening (and for this time only) is that no one of the three works was produced and played according to its true meaning.

The fact is that this new (or renewed) drama required interpreters who are new or renewed. Plays founded on observation (or those which claim to be such, if you wish) should not be played in the same way as stock plays are played or as fanciful comedies are produced. To understand these modern people one must leave behind all old conventions; a realistic drama must be played realistically just as a classic drama must have its lines delivered in a certain way since the character is usually an abstraction only, a synthesis, without actual life; the characters in *La Parisienne* or *Grand'mère*, however, are people like us, living not in spacious halls with the dimensions of cathedrals, but in rooms like our own, by their fireplaces, under the lamp, around the table, and not as in the old repertory, close to the prompter's box. They have voices like ours, their language is that of our ordinary life, with its contractions, its familiar tricks of speech, and not the rhetoric and lofty style of our classics.

When Mlle. Reichenberg attacks the opening scene of *La Parisienne* with a voice which proclaims the *actress* and when M. Prud'hon replies with the timbre of Dorante, they immediately falsify the prose of Becque and this they did for three hours the other evening without tiring. Is not the chief characteristic of the new theatre the fact that the characters are never conscious of their actions, just as we do silly and monstrous things without noticing them? The majority of our actors and actresses, as soon as they appear on the boards, seem impelled to substitute their own personality for the good fellow whom they should make live; instead of themselves entering into the person of the drama they let their own personalities enter into the fictitious ones. Thus, the other evening, we had Mlle. Reichenberg and not Clotilde; MM. Prud'hon, Le Bargy, and de Feraudy, but not at all the men of Becque's play.

And that salon! Have you ever encountered one like it in the homes of the Parisian bourgeoisie? Is *that* the home of a head clerk? . . . a dwelling without a spot where one can be comfortable as one can in the home of any one of us, without a place for talking at one's ease, without an armchair where one can relax, when work is done?

I know the objection you may make,—the stage setting is secondary. Yes, perhaps, in the plays of the classic repertory. But why not give the setting the effect of realism when this can be done with some care and without in any way injuring the play, provided—even if I made mistakes (in my own productions)—that this be attempted with moderation? In modern works written in the spirit of truth and naturalism in which the theory of environment and the influence of external things has taken so large a part, is not the setting a necessary complement of the work? Ought it not to assume in the theatre the same importance as description in a novel? Is it not a sort of exposition of the subject? It can never be completely true, certainly, since there is in the theatre, as no one thinks of denying, a (necessary) minimum of conventions, but why not try to reduce this minimum?

The dimensions of the stage or of the auditorium are of slight importance. If the frame is too large why not push forward the space of the acting and reduce it? And as to diction, are not the acoustics of the Comédie Française acknowledged to be excellent? Most of the other theatres, half as large, are less fortunate. Another reason, in any case, for not using enormous settings where the voice is lost in the case of intimate plays. At the Odéon, *Grand'mère* was played with a monumental salon as its setting, the same which, moreover, had completely smothered an act of *Renée Mauperin*.

What do you expect will be the fate of a play drawing its effect from life and intimacy when it is presented in a falsified atmosphere?

The movements of the actors are in my opinion no better understood than the setting. The goings and comings of the actors are not ordered according to the text or the meaning of a scene but according to the convenience or the caprice of the actors who play every one for himself without consideration for the others. And the footlights hypnotize them; each tries to advance as far as possible toward the audience. I have heard of a theatre in which in the days when gas was the means of lighting, all the actors singed the bottom of their trousers.

Mlle. Reichenberg, the other day, spoke her monologues standing and embroidering as good housewives knit at their doorsteps. Not once did Clotilde and Lafont speak directly to each other. But in town, at the end of two sentences, you would say to your interlocutor, "Look at me, can't you! You're the one I'm talking to!" and you would be justified.

The truth is that new actors are necessary for this new type of drama. That is an elementary truth which I am always repeating. . . .

It is impossible to get an actor to speak for any length of time sitting down: as soon as he begins a fairly long speech, invariably he says to the stage director, "I get up, don't I?" The fact is that for actors brought up according to the ancient formula of declamation in the style of Desgenais, the stage is a platform and not an enclosed space in which something is taking place. I remember that at the lecture of Ballande's in 1873 you cited the anecdote of an actor of the Palais-Royal, Arnal or Ravel, I believe, who when he had to hang up his hat walked obstinately along the footlights looking with conviction for a nail upon this fourth wall. That impressed me greatly and you seemed to approve completely. See how one corrupts youth without suspecting it!

I must close. But I beseech you, turn your attention to these things and observe. You will be struck with the complete lack of agreement which is beginning to show itself between the plays with new tendencies and the interpreters whom they find. There is here an important consideration and a curious phase of the present development in the drama. I, indeed, am exceedingly happy, for an evolution is taking shape. I should never have thought of discussing the subject if it had not become a sort of game to down, kindly it is true, but to down the Théâtre Libre each time that a play originally produced there seeks further adventures. Don't deceive yourself—we are going to pile up additional failures, to be hit again, but the start is made. There is more spade-work to be done and you know that the public is already curious. They said at the beginning that our humble little theatre was a fad only and that it would disappear one fine evening just as it had appeared. Now you know that our public grows larger each year and that consequently our domain is widening more and more. The public will come to these new ideas, I firmly expect, but hang it, we must not get excited and naïvely expect all in a minute to win literary success, big box-office receipts, and the favor of the crowd. There will be many plays on the billboards before that time, and we are just beginning to feel our way.

For the moment we must be content with looking back and measuring the ground gained during the last five or six years.[7]

Thus Antoine had created in acting and production the ideal which was to dominate much of the work of the Moscow Art Theatre, the Abbey Theatre, the Court Theatre of London, and many other theatres. His influence in cherishing plays of talent and in encouraging young playwrights was as important. In theory, Antoine was a champion of the new and promising in every vein; his hospitality to many types of dramatic genres was not accidental, but the very essence of the spirit in which he had founded his theatre. He intended to be eclectic, giving encouragement to any new writer of originality and power. Almost from the first, as we have seen, his project had assumed the aspect of a labo-

---

[7] From "Mes Souvenirs" sur le Théâtre-Libre, by Antoine, André, pp. 198-203. Courtesy of the author.

ratory theatre, in which young authors could show their plays to critics, directors, and a small public, and win the judgment which based on a manuscript is difficult. Antoine's announcements in the reviews and in the letters and pamphlets emphasized this desire for freedom from types and coteries. Answering the advice of Bauer in 1889, "If it wishes to continue to prosper, the Théâtre Libre will be naturalistic or it will not be at all," Antoine wrote indignantly:

> I do not at all agree with this opinion. I think that a too strict formula will be death, and that, on the contrary, we must hold ourselves ready to welcome everyone. I feel very strongly that already, here in the rue Blanche, we are turning toward "a little chapel"; the former members of the Théâtre Libre are worried about my eclecticism.

Then he adds a word of the difficulty of preserving his own independence of judgment without injuring the feelings of his friends.

Scanning his programs year by year to see whether they reflected this catholicity of intent, disappointed at the dearth of poetic plays, delighted when a genius of a new form or at least a new mood appeared, Antoine brought to his public a variety of forms, some of them old enough to be nearly forgotten, some of them new—the poetic fantasy, the religious play containing the figure of Christ, the study of amorous intrigue given freshness by exquisite characterization, the sombre psychological study influenced by Ibsen, the chronicle history more human and less pompous than in its early days, as well as the play of the new realism. Numerically the realistic plays were the strongest, for the wave of realism was advancing throughout European literature. The public overemphasized this tendency at the Théâtre Libre, and considered the theatre a house of naturalism. By the third season, Ancey's *L'École des veufs,*

Jullien's *Le Maître,* and Brieux's *Ménages d'artistes* showed the power and variety of the new realistic playwrights: Antoine the critic and producer was a person of admirable impartiality, but Antoine the actor was born to create the characters of the new mood, and to him its playwrights flocked. Later, when, unable to produce Maeterlinck's *La Princesse Maleine* well, he refused to produce it at all, he appeared— against his will—to align himself with the realistic group.

In this attempted liberation of the drama, foreign influences, particularly of Ibsen and of the Russians, had their part. France was drawn, temporarily it is true as far as the larger public is concerned, into the current of European drama. The Théâtre Libre gave little idea of Ibsen's poetry, his love of his nation's past, and his delight in folklore, but of his realism and his absorption in modern problems, it made Paris excitedly aware. Without Ibsen, Curel and Brieux would probably not have written.

A breaking up of conventional technique accompanied this broadening of subject matter. Now Paris sounded the slogan for advanced theatres, "the play that is not a play," and began the revolt against pouring the stuff of life into too rigid a mould. Expositions grew slighter until they frequently left the spectator with as vague a knowledge of relationships and attitudes as does actual life ordinarily. Climaxes were frequently omitted better to reflect the grey monotony of life. Antoine in his pamphlets refers briefly to these theories which are for the most part new to French drama; Jean Jullien, a playwright of the Théâtre Libre, is the fuller interpreter. Several of his ideas spring from Ibsen and Strindberg and others from earlier French realists. He writes:

The serious theatre is the Living Image of Life. The principal purpose of this theatre is to interest the spectator, and especially to rouse him; it must for this reason follow life as closely as possible. The characters will be human beings and no creatures of fancy, the interpreters simple "bonhommes," speaking as they would speak in real life, heightening the style somewhat, and not actors who exaggerate the grotesque or the odious, bombastic speakers who deliver a lecture or develop a thesis for the sake of displaying pretentious qualities of diction. For this theatre, if it is to attain its purpose, everything which smacks of craft or the workshop, everything which might betray the work of the author or the presence of the actor must disappear, (so much the worse for the style of the one and the effects of the other) everything must merge into character. The actor as such may excite our interest, but the actor lost in the character he portrays moves our heart. . . .

The public must lose for a moment the feeling of its presence in a theatre, and for that I believe that it is necessary, as soon as the curtain rises, to have complete darkness in the auditorium. The stage picture will stand out with greater vividness, the spectator will remain attentive, will no longer dare to chat, and will become almost intelligent. . . .

Aside from the necessary concessions as to time, place, and distance, since the infinite cannot be confined within three walls, there is no convention from which one may not be emancipated. . . .

If the actor must always follow carefully the impressions of the audience, he must conceal that fact, must play as if he were at home, taking no heed of the emotions he excites, of approval or disapproval; the front of the stage must be a fourth wall, transparent for the public, opaque for the player. . . .

A play is a slice of life artistically dramatized. They tell us eagerly that the theatre is the *art of preparation* and that the public must before all be taken into one's confidence. I believe the principle false, and the usage absolutely bad. The theatre is action: it is much more than what the spectator sees or hears that makes an impression upon him; the dialogue of action grips him; mere narrative bores him,—and he is right, for narrative is meant for books. Action must make the play throb from beginning to end; it is as if it were its respiration, its heart beat, its life. It is not necessary, of course, to have constantly crowded, intense, violent action (one is not always panting for breath, and one's pulse does not always beat furiously); let there be a minimum of action if you will, but let there be some at each significant moment, and from act to act let it grow in intensity. As for taking the public into one's confidence in advance, never; the public asks to be surprised, for life is nothing but surprise; does it not baffle, as if wantonly, our expectations? I believe that the interest of a play lies especially in this element of the unknown. . . .

What will then, you ask me, become of exposition and dénouement? Two useless things. . . .

It is in the choice of the subject, the character study, the solidity of the framework that the art of the dramatic author lies.[8]

In spite of the extreme to which several playwrights went, like the creation of bourgeois monsters and a dwelling upon some vices, particularly avarice and sensuality, till the inclusion of certain scenes and characters became almost a convention, the realistic play of the Théâtre Libre exerted three powerful influences. In the first place, it taught French playwrights, producers, and audiences something almost undreamed of, that an engrossing drama might deal with some other question than the eternal triangle of husband, wife, and lover, and that the problems of the modern world may appear upon the modern stage. Second, it broke the vogue of the well-made play in which plot rides roughshod over characterization and the people are negligible in comparison with the cleverness of the intrigue. Third, in its closeness of observation of men and women, even though sometimes deficient in fine sanity of interpretation, the realistic play drew the French theatre back to the worship of truth for which classicism had stood.

An objective method for determining the value of the Théâtre Libre to French drama is a comparison of the work of Antoine's playwrights with that of the other playwrights

[8] Jullien, Jean, *Le Théâtre Vivant,* pp. 8-13.

of France during the same period. Professor Frank Wadleigh Chandler, author of *The Contemporary Drama of France,* is not an enthusiast for any one school, and has the impartiality of a foreigner. Statistics are amazing. Of the entire list of two hundred and thirty-four playwrights in his bibliography, fifty-one, almost a fifth, were on the programs of the Théâtre Libre, and thirty-one had their premières there. Of the writers in this book born between 1847 and 1869, that is between eighteen and forty years old at the beginning of Antoine's work, there are seventy-three names. Of these, twenty-eight, more than a third, are Théâtre Libre playwrights. A more revealing comparison is based on the study of eminent playwrights. Professor Chandler considers forty-one of sufficient importance for a treatment of two pages or more. In 1887, three of these, Augier, Dumas fils, and Sardou, were elderly and long established, and seven were not yet old enough to be writing. Out of the remaining thirty-one, fourteen, almost half, belong to the Théâtre Libre.

It is hardly possible, therefore, to over-emphasize the influence of Antoine and his playhouse in modern French drama. He was "the indispensable element about which the crystallization of the modern theatre began"—and much more. During the early months of the theatre Bergerat coined his phrase "Le Petit Odéon" and Zola chronicled the emergence of a new dramatic school and foretold its speedy victory on the other stages of Paris. Later opinions corroborated these: when, fourteen years after the Théâtre Libre had closed, Adolphe Thalasso, its first historian, asked several prominent writers to resume the old discussion, their praise was unqualified. "The only theatre to do real work during ten years," said Emile Fabre. "A decisive influence on a new and brilliant generation of dramatic authors" (Marcel Prévost). "Antoine and his authors aired, purified, and renovated the contemporary theatre" (Gaston Salan-

School

dri). "I believe that the greatest service rendered by the
Théâtre Libre has been to free the modern French theatre
from all schools and literary coteries. A day will come when
greater justice will be done our dramatic epoch and all that
it has gained in originality from its independence will be
felt. It owes this, for the most part, to the Théâtre Libre"
(François de Curel).

Thalasso, himself, is of the opinion: "The Théâtre Libre
was the cradle of dramatic art of our times. The history of
the Théâtre Libre is the history of the contemporary
theatre."

The same general impulse to self-expression which lay
behind the Théâtre Libre in the early nineties later
prompted the founding of several other dramatic organizations. Many of these amateur groups were too trivial or
vague of purpose, or too desirous of social prestige for artistic success. But others experimented freely in many varieties
of dramatic art or chose to investigate the possibilities of
one form. Two of these groups were in process of creation
at the same time as the Théâtre Libre. The Théâtre de
l'Application was organized as a studio theatre for the young
actors of the conservatory of the Comédie-Française by
M. Bodimier at the suggestion of Emile Perrin. Like many
another "little theatre," it was housed in a building originally intended for another purpose, a little tannery in the
rue Saint-Lazare. Though success was slow, the group built
up a loyal audience for its programs of one-act plays, songs
of Yvette Guilbert, not yet famous, and plays by four of
the young writers of the Théâtre Libre,—Georges de Porto-
Riche, Paul Bonnetain, Catulle Mendès, and Oscar Méténier. The director also arranged "conferences" in which
such critics and playwrights as Anatole France, Francis
Sarcey, Ferdinand Brunetière, and Maurice Donnay gave
their opinions upon the drama and the theatre. The Cercle
des Escholiers, which made its bow to the public on the

same evening as the Théâtre Libre, was formed by students
of Faguet, the dramatic critic, and dominated by Georges
Bourdon and Lugné-Poë, lads of seventeen, the one to become a member of the staff of *le Figaro* and the other the
earliest producer of the plays of Maeterlinck and of Ibsen's
symbolic period. Lugné-Poë will be remembered as a close
friend of Antoine and one of his co-workers at the Théâtre
Libre. At first the Escholiers patterned rather closely after
it, favoring Théâtre Libre playwrights of the same literary
tendencies. Somewhat later, Lugné-Poë experimented with
non-realistic drama for the Escholiers and for two other experimental societies: his *Lady from the Sea* at the Cercle
was one of the milestones in the French production of Ibsen,
as Antoine's *Ghosts* and *The Wild Duck* had each been. The
Cercle has always been handicapped by not owning a
theatre. Nevertheless, the group has done distinguished
service.

Meanwhile, innovations became frequent. Albert Carré
conceived the idea of giving Thursday matinées of unusual
plays, a suggestion followed by Sir Beerbohm Tree at his
Afternoon Theatre in London. A delightful experiment was
the marionette theatre of the Galerie Vivienne, in which for
six years Henry Signourtet attempted more ambitious plays
than this ancient art had known. When *The Birds* of Aristophanes and *The Tempest* proved too difficult for the inani-
mate actors, Signourtet encouraged poets, including Maurice
Bouchoir, to write especially for them. The art of pantomime, too, was developing. In 1887, Eugene Larcher was
asked to compose scenarios for some groups in the provinces,
and shortly afterwards collaborated in a book, *Les Panto-
mimes de Paul Legrand*. On May 15, 1888, Legrand opened
the old Cercle Lunambulesque as a house of pantomime,
with *Columbine Abandonnée* by Paul Margueritte and Fern
and Beissier; *L'Amour de l'art* by Raoul de Najac; and
Leandre Ambassadeur by Alfred Copin. The finest plays

which the group discovered were Michael Carré's *L'Enfant Prodigue* and an arrangement of Champfleury's *La Statue du Commandeur*. Another experiment, the Grand Guignol, still very much alive, was founded by a Théâtre Libre dramatist, Oscar Méténier, in 1897. Long one of the sights of Paris, since its extensive tours in Europe and America it is now world-famous, and has inspired both English and American imitators. The Grand Guignol specializes in adroit one-act plays: light farces, ultra-sophisticated comedies, and plays of horror. André de Lorde, "the prince of terror," is a master of the technique of the horrific. His *The Woman Who Was Acquitted* and many other playlets are not for the nervous or the timid.

A theatre opposed to extreme realism was the Théâtre d'Art, important though short-lived. It was organized in 1890 by Paul Fort, the poet, and continued its activities till 1893 when the founder withdrew to give all his time to poetry. For the Théâtre d'Art, Lugné-Poë directed Shelley's *Cenci,* Marlowe's *Faustus,* Paul Verlaine's *Les Uns et les Autres,* and here he continued his championship of Maeterlinck. After the discontinuance of this theatre, Lugné-Poë decided to direct a theatre of his own which should be thoroughly cosmopolitan. The Maison de l'Œuvre accordingly opened October, 1893, with Ibsen's *Rosmersholm.* Since then, Lugné-Poë has brought before his public a remarkable array of foreign drama. Besides championing Ibsen, a difficult task, since the French temperament is remote from the Scandinavian, he has staged plays by Hauptmann, Schnitzler, d'Annunzio, Wilde, Synge, Kaiser. In 1924, an adaptation of Tolstoy's *Kreutzer Sonata* was received enthusiastically. From India came *The Little Clay Cart* and *The Ring of Sakuntala,* and from China, *La Fleur Coupée.* Of French dramas, Claudel's *Annonce faite à Marie* and *Otage* and Francis Jammes' *La Brebis Égarée* are perhaps Lugné-Poë's most valuable discoveries, but the list of his leading authors is almost a roll-call of the present advance-guard: Jean Sarment, *Couronne de Carton* (1920) and *Pêcheur d'Ombres* (1921); Émile Mazaud, *Dardamelle* (1922); Fernand Crommelynck, *Cocu Magnifique* (1920); Jacques Natanson, *L'Age Heureux* (1922) and *L'Enfant Truqué* (1922); Adolphe Orna, *La Dette de Schmil* (1922) and *L'Egoïste* (1924); Marcel Achard, *La Messe est dite* (1923); the Belgian Henry Soumagne, *L'Autre Messie;* Pierre Mille and Jacques Loria, *Le Cadi et le Cocu* (1923). Distinguished actor as well as producer, Lugné-Poë for many years toured widely bringing an acquaintance with French acting to much of the world.

Another of Antoine's group of workers now in charge of an advanced theatre is Rodolphe Darzens, whose *L'Amante du Christ* and translation of Ibsen's *Ghosts* had drawn much attention at the Théâtre Libre. The organization which he directs is the Théâtre des Arts founded in 1906 by Robert d'Humières as a means of freeing the drama from inertia and hidebound conventions. In 1918 this society became affiliated with the newly formed Société Coopérative d'Auteurs Dramatiques, which was founded at the suggestion of Adolphe Aderer, with François de Curel as its president. The members of the Société Coopérative frankly announce themselves as banded together for mutual helpfulness in disposing of their work as a group of factory workers or peasants might be. Though there are occasional programs by foreign writers, most of the plays are those of the members given in an order determined by lot. Dramas by H.-R. Lenormand, Armand Thibaut, Edmond Fleg, Claude Anet have provoked much discussion. The most popular drama so far has been Curel's *L'Ame en Folie;* his *Terre Inhumaine* has also had more than two hundred performances.

This finishes the catalogue of the older advanced theatres, founded and directed largely by men who were Antoine's assistants. The newer Parisian *théâtres à côté* are manned by a younger generation, like their seniors absorbed by a desire for sincere drama artistically presented, but inspired by other direct influences than those of the Théâtre Libre. France of the present can less than ever afford to disregard foreign influences, the development in art and literature of Russia, Germany, and England. During this period the art of stage decoration and the modern idea of the artist-director have been brought to the fore, largely by two men of genius, the Swiss dreamer, Appia, and that volcanic Englishman, Sir Edward Gordon Craig. As subject and technique of the written play were extended marvelously in the earlier period, so now stage decoration, the physical means for giving the drama its objective existence, has grown infinitely more varied and flexible. This book is not a history of stagecraft and cannot give details of the development of Appia's, Craig's, and Poel's theories and of the revolution in the theatre which has partially substituted the architectural, the plastic, or the constructivist stage for the old, enslaving picture-frame setting. But the knowledge of some events is important. In 1899 Adolphe Appia had published *Die Musik und die Inscenirung* at Munich, and Craig the outline of his theory later to be expanded in a pamphlet, *The Art of the Theatre*. These publications, however, were not at all widely known. In 1910, Jacques Rouché, of the Théâtre des Arts of Paris, published a summary of the practise of the Germans, Fuchs and Reinhardt; the Russians, Stanislavsky and Meierhold; and the theories of Appia and Craig in a volume called *L'Art Théâtral Moderne*. This marked the beginning of more general interest.

In 1913 Jacques Copeau, with five friends (Charles Paquement, Gaston Gallimard, Jean Schlumberger, Charles Dullin, and Louis Jouvet), opened the Théâtre du Vieux Colombier. This was almost immediately acclaimed the most important venture in the French theatre since 1887. Copeau is a man of wide general culture and a knowledge of world movements. As a young man—in 1913 he was in his early thirties—he had been a student at the Sorbonne and had traveled to Denmark, Spain, Russia. In 1908, he had been one of the founders of a critical journal, *Nouvelle Revue Française*, to which he contributed his views upon plays and novels. For years he had been writing plays: at the time of the founding of the Vieux Colombier, an adaptation of Dostoyevsky's *The Brothers Karamazov* in which he had collaborated was running at the Théâtre des Arts. Copeau is a dreamer, an idealist, a destroyer of the old, and a builder of the new. He wrote at the time of the founding of his theatre:

A frenzied spirit of commercialization which cynically degrades our French stage from day to day and turns away the cultivated public from it; the monopoly of the majority of the theatres by a handful of entertainers in the pay of shameless business men; everywhere, and especially there where great traditions ought to guard a certain decency, the same spirit of manipulation for profit and speculation, the same baseness; everywhere bluff, over-bidding of every kind, and "exhibitionnisme" of every sort which clings as a parasite to an art which is unquestionably dying and of which no one talks; everywhere weakness, disorder, lack of discipline, ignorance and stupidity, scorn of the creator, hatred of beauty; a production more and more mad and vain, a criticism more and more complacent, a public taste more and more led astray; this is what exasperates us and urges us to revolt. . . .

We think that it is not enough to-day to create powerful works of art; where would they be received? Where would they find either public or interpreters with an atmosphere favorable to their expansion? So we are faced inevitably as by a "perpetual postulation" with this great problem, that of building on absolutely intact foundations a new theatre; and that it shall be the rallying place of all those authors, actors, spectators, who are tormented by the need of restoring beauty to the stage.[9]

[9] From *Paris—Théâtre Contemporain*, by Louise Delpit, p. 21. Smith College, Northampton, Mass. Courtesy of the author.

To be remote geographically and spiritually from the fashionable playhouses Copeau chose for his evenings a hall upon the left bank at the Carrefour de la Croix Rouge, seating less than four hundred. Here he hoped to draw the thoughtful Parisians and foreign visitors by programs which, representing no one school, should contain the best of the past and the best of the present. Opening with Molière's *L'Amour Médecin* and Thomas Heywood's *A Woman Killed with Kindness* in his own translation, Copeau gave in his first season plays by Molière, Shakespeare, Alfred de Musset; *L'Échange*, by Paul Claudel; *L'Eau de Vie*, by Henri Ghéon; *Les Fils Louverné*, by Jean Schlumberger; *Le Testament du Père Leleu*, by Martin du Gard; *La Navette*, by Henri Becque; *Le Pain de Ménage*, by Jules Renard; and *The Brothers Karamazov*. Almost immediately Copeau was invited to tour both Germany and England. Then came the war: Copeau, Jouvet, Dullin were called to the colors, and the Théâtre du Vieux Colombier was closed. But Copeau was not daunted; in 1915 he found a chance to visit Gordon Craig at Florence and under Craig's inspiration and with the help of Suzanne Bing planned a dramatic school for young amateurs and professionals; in 1916 he played for a time in Geneva. The next year he was sent to the United States by the French government,—his mission to familiarize America with French art and to encourage amicable relations between the two countries. He lectured widely and awakened much interest, in particular the sympathy of Otto Kahn, a generous friend of European art, who asked Copeau to bring a group of actors and actresses to the United States and to arrange for a French theatre in New York. Copeau brought to the Garrick Theatre on Thirty-fifth Street almost all his original group, for the French government was glad to release Jouvet and Dullin from military service for this task. Though the audiences were sometimes small and the theatre enjoyed a *succès d'estime* rather than a general popularity, its two seasons were a delight to the thoughtful. Its simplicity of settings and its experiments toward an architectural stage, especially, proved germinal for the American theatre.

With the coming of peace, Copeau and his actors returned to Paris. Then it was that he perfected within certain limitations of space and money the permanent architectural stage of the Vieux Colombier, a stage as famous as the acting of the Vieux Colombier. Sheldon Cheney, distinguished critic of stagecraft and of modern art, calls Copeau's stage "the nearest to a perfectly responsive non-naturalistic platform for acting that the modern Western world has seen," and adds that "in the main this has been at once the pioneer and the most advanced formal permanent stage." Like the Elizabethan, it emphasized freedom of space for the actor. It had a fore-stage as well as a deep stage, and no proscenium arch, no curtain, no painted backdrop. Under gracefully constructed architectural arches the spectator looked toward a permanent wall which might be suffused with light or hidden if necessary. The lower stage, the steps, the inner stage, two entrances at the actor's right, and a gallery at the back were all unchanging architectural elements, though the effects might be infinitely varied by the use of suggestive properties. Here, from 1920 through 1924 Copeau gave over thirty plays of many moods and types, and, with the help of his brilliant assistants, planned each production to the most minute detail. He writes:

This design of a dramatic action is the *ensemble* of movements, of gestures and of attitudes, the harmony of faces, of voices, and of silences. It is the totality of the scenic spectacle, emanating from the one thought which conceives it, rules it and harmonizes it. The director creates this secret and invisible bond and has it control the personages—this bond which is a reciprocal sensibility, a mysterious reciprocal relation, without which the drama, even interpreted by excellent actors, loses the greater part of its effect.

The influence of the theatre and of the school which was affiliated with it in 1920, was attested by its fame, the need for a second company to alternate with the first at the parent theatre and to represent it throughout Europe, and the eagerness with which other theatres looked to the Vieux Colombier for leadership. Jouvet was invited in 1922 to take charge of the Comédie des Champs Elysées at which for a time he used the Vieux Colombier company and repertory. Dullin felt that there was a place for a theatre of his own. Copeau has since moved his school to Burgundy where he can have leisure and quiet to develop the talents of his pupils. Though the Théâtre du Vieux Colombier no longer exists in its original form, the distinguished company of the Vieux Colombier should be named here. The original group who studied with Copeau at Limon, in the Seine-et-Marne, all the summer of 1913, and opened the season with him included Gina Barbieri, Suzanne Bing, Blanche Albane, Jane Lory, Valentine Tessier, Romain Bouquet, André Bacqué, Charles Dullin, Louis Jouvet—the last two acknowledged as co-founders. Additional names in the season of 1923-1924 are those of Renée Garcia, Line Noro, Robert Allard, Auguste Boverio, Jean le Goff, Lucien Nat, Albert Savey, François Vibert, Georges Vitray. Copeau himself sometimes acted.

The greatest contribution of the Théâtre du Vieux Colombier to modern drama has been the fostering of a distinguished group of modern plays: *Le Paquebot Tenacity* by Charles Vildrac; *L'Œuvre des Athlètes* by Georges Duhamel; *Cromedeyre-le-Vieil* by Jules Romains; *La Folle Journée* by Émile Mazaud; *Phocas le Jardinier* by Francis Viélé-Griffin; *La Morte de Sparta* by Jean Schlumberger; *Le Pauvre sous l'Escalier* by Henri Ghéon; *La Dauphine* by

Francois Porché; *La Fraude* by Louis Fallens; *Les Plaisirs du Hasard, La Pie Borgne,* and *Il faut que chacun soit à, sa place* by René Benjamin; *Au Petit Bonheur* by Anatole France; *Saül* by André Gide; *Sophie Arnould* by Gabriel Nigond; *La Belle de Haguenau* by Jean Variot; *Bastos le Hardi* by Léon Régis and François de Veynes; *L'Imbécile* by Pierre Bost; *La Maison Natale* by Copeau. Vildrac's play, especially, has been widely praised. It is often taken as an example of the newer French drama, largely created since the war, which forgets the Parisian types and scenes of the traditional national drama and turns to the life of seaport or village. Copeau's powerful, if sombre play, *La Maison Natale,* was presented in New York with the title, *The World into which We Are Born.*

Even without the advent of the Vieux Colombier the year 1913 would have been a momentous one for the progressive French stage, for it was also the year of the founding of two of Jacques Hébertot's three theatres, the Théâtre des Champs-Elysées and the Comédie des Champs-Elysées, the latter known at first as the Comédie Montaigne from the Avenue Montaigne on which stands the palace which now houses all three groups. The third theatre, organized ten years later, will be described in its turn.

Hébertot, though a less radical spirit than Copeau, is receptive of new ideas and interested in new literary and dramatic movements. He controls several reviews, *Le Théâtre et Comœdia Illustré* among them. He is eager to welcome originality and genius: during one season he had upon his staff of artist-producers Louis Jouvet and the two Russians, Kommisarjevsky and Georges Pitoëff; within a few months he entertained as guest companies the Moscow Art Theatre, the Kamerny Theatre of Moscow, the Jewish Theatre of Vilna, Joseph Kessler's Jewish company, the Italian Troupe of Ermete Zacconi, and Miss Fuller and her School of the Dance. Hébertot's own productions in the

Théâtre, the largest of his three auditoriums, have been intentionally less radical than those of his smaller houses. The stage and auditorium of the Théâtre are well suited to elaborate productions, and several of Wagner's operas and some mammoth spectacles have been given here in addition to modern plays.

The Comédie, on the other hand, is one of the most important theatres in Paris both because of its remarkable plays and because of its ingenious and sometimes inspired producing. In an early season, Hébertot himself produced there several unusual plays including *Le Désir*, which is a French translation of an Icelandic legend by Johann Sigurdjonsonn. The next season Firmin Gémier produced for Hébertot *Le Simoun* by H.-R. Lenormand, *Les Amants Puérils* by Fernand Crommelynck, and plays by Shakespeare, Strindberg, and Shaw. But the most famous period of the Comédie has been the months when Louis Jouvet and Georges Pitoëff were alternating direction.

Jouvet, a distinguished actor, has been mentioned in the account of the Vieux Colombier. Pitoëff is likewise an alert and vital figure. He is a Russian, an admirer of Antoine and Stanislavsky, who before the war had opened his own theatre in St. Petersburg. Exiled in the early days of the struggle, he played at Geneva and at several Parisian theatres, including Copeau's and Hébertot's. Like Jouvet, Pitoëff is a remarkable actor—his endowment the ability to give to an unusual degree a sense of reality and intense emotion. His wife, Madame Ludmilla Pitoëff, who played also at the Comédie, is an actress of understanding and charm. Almost from the beginning of their work, Jouvet and Pitoëff were reaching in many directions for plays which should express the finest spirit of modern French drama or the finest work of other nations. Their list is an amazing one for a single theatre: Jules Romains' *M. Le Trouhadec saisi par la Débauche, Amédée ou les Messieurs en Rang,*

Knock ou le Triomphe de la Médecine, Charles Vildrac's *L'Indigent,* Claude Anet's *Mademoiselle Bourrat,* plays by Chekhov, Gorky, Tolstoy, Andreiev, and Alexander Blok's *The Little Booth,* Sheridan's *The Duenna,* Wilde's *Salome,* and an adaptation of *The Portrait of Dorian Gray.*

Among the novelties which delighted Paris were Jouvet's staging of *Knock* and Pitoëff's of *Salome* and *He Who Gets Slapped.* Jouvet placed his actors against a painted background so simplified and stylized that it gave no impression of reality. Pitoëff for *Salome* hung the walls behind his stage with mysterious curtains of black velvet, and covered the horizontal surfaces of the steps and levels with the same black and the vertical with white satin. The characters symbolizing violent desires were costumed in hot reds and yellows, the thoughtful and sentimental in quiet, retreating colors. Lenormand's *Le Mangeur de Rêves* likewise was played against black curtains with even less scenery for taking a hint from Stanislavsky's production of *The Life of Man* Pitoëff here suggested the necessary locale by ribbon alone; of brilliant soft green placed at the level of the ground for the glory of the Mediterranean, of pink in the form of a shell to designate a boudoir, of red on two sides of a triangle for a limitless desert.

The Atelier, another very original group, owes its existence to Charles Dullin, friend of Copeau and one of the original directors of the Vieux Colombier. For twenty years before the Atelier came into existence Dullin had been longing for a theatre of his own and formulating the principles which should control it. In spite of poverty and lack of influence, in a life packed with adventures, he had slowly moved toward his goal. The youngest of a large family in a little village of Savoie near the Swiss border, he was so frail that his relatives despaired of his ability to do physical work and expected to send him to a college for priests. But the life of the church did not appeal to the boy. While still very young he followed a band of gypsies until he was rescued by his alarmed family. At seventeen he went to Lyons and became a shop-keeper's assistant, measuring cloth during business hours, but in the evenings reciting verses in a café. Here he met another young man, Henri Béraud, also a devotee of poetry. The friends decided to try their luck in Paris, notwithstanding the slenderness of their resources, seventeen francs. Fortunately Dullin was able to pick up a little money by declaiming the ballads of Villon in the streets, but an opening at the small and obscure Theatre of the Gobelins seemed heaven sent though the wage was only the equivalent of fifteen dollars a month. Here Dullin was successful and from this he passed to slightly better positions at the Théâtre Montparnasse and the Théâtre de Montrouge. Then came discouragement, a slipping back into the life of adventure and poverty, illness, a country sojourn for recovery, again the desperate reaching for any kind of work. The first work to offer was with a menagerie,—the recitation of poems from Baudelaire in the lion's den while the lady lion-tamer danced the serpentine. Then followed a round of cabaret entertaining until a fortunate evening lifted Dullin from Bohemia to the world of the art theatres. The discovery of his talent was quite by accident: Robert d'Humières, then in charge of the Théâtre des Arts, was one of the guests at the Lapin Agile, where Dullin was reciting, and noticed both the power of the actor's voice and the beauty of his diction. He at once offered Dullin an opening at the Théâtre des Arts.

This was about 1908. During the next few years under d'Humières and his successor, Rouché, Dullin was an important actor in a radical group. Friendship with Copeau began in 1913 when the adaptation of *The Brothers Karamazov* was running at the Théâtre des Arts and Dullin as Smerdiakov was giving a particularly fine interpretation of the part. The friends have complemented each other in a

remarkable way. Both Copeau and Dullin oppose the selfishness, the conventionality, the reactionary narrowness of
the theatre of commerce; both serve with devoted love what
to them is a true and great art, that of bringing before the
audience plays of originality and power, mounted in as
harmonious and beautiful a way as modern stagecraft can
devise. While Copeau has the finer background of culture, a
more assured place in the world of literature and art, Dullin
seems to possess a larger measure of dramatic genius.

With Copeau in the brief pre-war days of the new theatre
and again in the American years, Dullin, when the group
returned to Paris, began preparations for his own theatre.
He did not wish to depend upon experienced actors versed
in the tricks of the great stages: he would begin at the very
beginning. He recruited his own company of talented young
people and like Stanislavsky and Copeau took them to the
country for a summer of community life and intensive
study. By 1922 these young actors were playing classical
dramas and little farces in the provinces, and looking
toward the conquest of Paris. The metropolitan season
opened in a small motion picture house in the rue des
Ursulines; later the Atelier was established at the Théâtre
Montmartre. Dullin's journal recalls a hand-to-mouth existence which reminds one of the early days of the Théâtre
Libre: while pessimists were prophesying disaster, the
critics of drama and stagecraft wrote in admiration of Dullin's performances and acclaimed the Atelier, "the Vieux
Colombier of the Right Bank."

The Atelier has brought before the public four new stage
decorators, André Foy, Valmier, Touchagues, and Lagier,
and two musicians, Herscher-Clément and Tausmann. It
has given encouragement to young French writers, particularly Jarl Priel (*Les Risques de la Vertu*) and Bernard
Zimmer (*Voulez-vous jouer avec moâ?*) However, the theatre is best known for its large proportion of Italian and

Spanish plays of both earlier and contemporary periods. (Dullin's interest in Spanish drama is said to come from his friendship with the playwright, Alexandre Arnoux, whose wife, a Brazilian, is a student of Spanish literature.) The Atelier has given Goldoni's *Fan* and three of Pirandello's dramas, *Chacun sa vérité, Une Pièce, La Volupté de l'Honneur,* Calderon's *Life is a Dream,* and Jacinto Graü's *Monsieur de Pygmalion* and *Le Comte Alarcos.* Dullin is not interested in sheer realism, but belongs to the group who are bringing back to the stage the play that is frankly a play. He once outlined his theory for the readers of *Comœdia,* and the *Revue de l'Amérique Latine:*

Ask the great dramatists of all epochs and you will see this trait running through all their works. Search out their weaknesses. You will find them in the passages where, their dramatic vein abandoning them, they have resource to rhetoric and literature. The theatre is not a place of contemplation but of faëry. Whether this be by exciting laughter or tears or an exaltation of the soul, it ought to carry us out of our daily lives. But the same thing is true of dramatic acting as of other diversions, the type which pleases one, displeases another.

Another energetic and vital figure in the advanced theatres of Paris is Gaston Baty who organized the Chimère a year after the Atelier opened. Baty had worked for some time with Gémier at the Comédie des Champs Elysées. When Gémier was called from it to the Odéon, Baty brought together a group of his own. His purpose has been to synthesize all the arts of the theatre not, like some producers, by enslaving stagecraft and the skill and genius of the actor in the service of the author, but by creating a beautiful coöperative art. He favors no school of playwrights and dreads all literary cliques: indeed he put the choice of plays completely in the hands of twelve playwrights. The plays of the Chimère were often striking and original.

Among the most-enjoyed were Jean Variot's *La Belle de Haguenau*, Adolphe Orna's *La Farce de Papa Ghéorghé*, Jean Pellerin's *Intimité*, J. J. Bernard's *Martine*, Simon Gantillon's *Le Cyclone*, Marie Diémer's *L'Aube et le Soir de Sainte Geneviève*, Lucien Descaves' *Je veux revoir ma Normandie*, and Denys Amiel's *Voyageur*. For its first year, the Chimère played in borrowed theatres; during the second, it had its own little hall, called Baraque, opposite Saint Germain-des-Prés. But the society could not shoulder this increase in its expenditures. When the little theatre had to close its doors in 1923, Baty accepted an invitation to become scenic director of the Odéon. But his absence from the world of the little theatre was brief, for the next year he was offered the art-directorship of Hébertot's latest venture, the third of the playhouses in the palatial building on the Avenue Montaigne.

This, the Studio, is a natural supplement to the larger theatres above which it nestles. The intimacy of an auditorium seating only two hundred makes this an ideal laboratory for trying out the novel and the daring in both gay and sombre mood. A play with a Chinese atmosphere, *Le Club des Canards Mandarins* by Henri Duvernois and Pascal Forthuny was the opening program; later evenings saw *Les Six Grimaces de Don Juan* and *Facilité* by Jean Sarment, *L'Invitation au Voyage* by Jean-Jacques Bernard, *The Dance of Death* by Strindberg, and *A L'Ombre du Mal* by Lenormand. When I visited it, the Studio was reviving *Maya*, which had opened there in May, 1924, and had played for six hundred nights. This drama by Simon Gantillon, whose *Cyclone* Baty had already produced for the audience of the Chimère, has seen many adventures. In six years, it had been translated into fourteen languages and given in most of the European capitals. Because of its subject, a study of the life of a prostitute, the theatre in which it was being given in New York was closed by the police, and public performance was forbidden in London. (Here, the Gate Theatre, a private society, offered *Maya* refuge.) Willette Kershaw, the American actress, interpreted Bella, the central figure, as thoroughly womanly, a creature of sympathy, love, affection, and imagination, rather than of passion. We see her as she tries to devise means for going to the funeral of her child in the mountain village to which in her poverty she was forced to send her. But poverty is still an unconquerable foe and Bella is not able to see even the dead face of the little girl. Yet the maternal in her lives on, reaching out to bring courage and hope to the seamen whom the Mediterranean sweeps to her door above the quay: a lonely Scandinavian boy, a man half-mad from thwarted love, a stoker whom despair is driving to the breaking point. This kindness is in spite of the hell upon which her life is built, into which we glance now and again, for the soul of the woman is something beyond and above the body's uses. Gantillon has published *Cyclone, Maya,* and *Départs* in a volume entitled *Marines.* This grouping together of three plays of the sea recalls an early volume of O'Neill though the likeness may be accidental.

An organization which like the Chimère entrusts its choice of plays to a committee of authors is Le Canard Sauvage. Its membership includes the distinguished foreigners Schnitzler, Merejskovski, and Bojer. The dramatic authors who have been upon its earlier programs are Yvan Noë, Paul Vialar, André Obey, Denys Amiel, and Philippe Fauré-Frémiet. A slightly younger society, the Griffon, of similar ideas, after one season decided to merge with the more famous society. Other dramatic clubs which have thought of forming a loose confederation with Le Canard Sauvage while preserving their own individuality are the Théâtre d'Art, Athéna, the Grimace, the Pantins. Other less-known theatre societies are La Flamme, La Licorne, Aide et Protection (whose plays are given in aid of wounded soldiers), Les Artisans, Le Cénacle des Œuvriers, the Nouveau Théâtre.

The Théâtre Anglo-Américain, as its name implies, existed for the pleasure of the English-speaking sojourners in Paris. Thomas Van Dycke, who had been the leader of the Dramahouse Players, was behind the venture and its home, the Théâtre Albert Ier. The inaugural season exhibited successful English and American plays of the more thoughtful type, among them *The Skin Game, Outward Bound, A Bill of Divorcement, The Outsider,* and plays of Shaw and O'Neill; the opening program was Milne's *The Dover Road,* chosen, perhaps, because the characters are "Paris-bound."

The season of 1929-1930 saw a new venture in the establishment of an American company to give American plays in the Théâtre Femina. Mr. Carol M. Sax, the founder, had already been a leader in the Vagabond Theatre, Baltimore, and the Romany Theatre of Lexington, Kentucky. For the first season the plays announced were *The Road to Rome, Holiday, The Barker, Let Us Be Gay,* and *The Torch Bearers.*

A special type of play finds a welcome at the Théâtre Ésotérique, whose founders, Paul Castan and his wife, Berthe d'Yd, work under the auspices of two groups, Athéna and Rythme et Beauté, whose hall is the theatre adjoining the Temple Théosophique. Berthe d'Yd is the author of several of the productions, *Au-delà du Seuil, Le Voile du Passé, Sketch Psychique, Germain.* Other writers are Hermann Schilde, Guillot de Saix, Philippe Fauré-Frémiet, René Bruyez, and Maurice Nourry.

Of wider appeal are the plays of the Petite Scène, artists and people of wealth, all connoisseurs of the curious and the beautiful, well suited by taste and background for the field which they have chosen,—the revival of charming comedies and light operas of the seventeenth and eighteenth centuries. It has been suggested that their programs, under the direction of Xavier de Courville, have stirred the Comédie Française to its sudden interest in minor works of earlier periods, as *La Bonne Mère* of Florian played in 1924. The names of these revivals at the Petite Scène are *La Princesse d'Élide* by Molière; *La Foire de Saint-Germain,* by Dancourt, which is said "to make live again the quarter of the old Paris in which Procope opened the first 'caffe'"; *Le Prince Travesti ou l'Illustre Aventurier,* by Marivaux; *L'Ivrogne corrigé ou le Mariage du Diable,* with Gluck's music and Anseaume's text; *Sancho Pança dans son île de Barataria,* with music by Philidor and book by Poinsinet; *La Coquette ou L'Académie des Dames* and *La Sérénade,* by Regnard; *Le Devin de Village,* by J. J. Rousseau; *La Nuit Vénitienne,* by Musset; and *Le Jugement de Midas,* the music by Grétry, the book by d'Hèle and Anseaume.

The Théâtre de Verdure of the Pré-Catelan, an out-of-door theatre in the lovely Bois de Boulogne, delights in poetic drama and delicate and spirited comedy. Some of the most successful plays of its fifteen years—really ten years for there were no performances during the war—might give suggestions to open-air theatres in America. The first performance was *Le Roi Personne,* a four-act verse-play of the story of Ulysses' return, by Bully and Delaquys. *Le Cor Fleuri,* a one-act fairy play, by Ephraïm Mikaël, had been one of the surprises of the Théâtre Libre. Other plays are *Le Chanteur Errant* by Pierre Masson, *L'Heure de Cypris* by André Lamandé, *Les Cerises* by Clénet, a story in three tableaux by Felix Fourdrain, and *La Maison de Banlieue,* an adaptation by Guillot de Saix of part of a novel by René Bazin.

In Paris, as in New York, there has been a growing realization of the love which children have for plays. Humble's Théâtre du Petit Monde, dating from 1919 and playing in various houses, is the oldest of these little theatres for little people. The plays are largely the work of

Alfred Machard (*Minuit, Chrétiens!*, which is a play for Christmas, and *Popaul et Virginie*) and adaptations of the tales of the Countess de Ségur. The ideals and the achievements of this group have been rewarded by a grant from the Minister of Public Instruction. This venture has not been the only one of its kind. In 1924 the Théâtre Albert Ier put on a drama for children played by little girls, *Un Million dans une Main d'Enfant*, by A. Machard. The Théâtre Rose, which borrowed the Théâtre des Mathurins for its performances, opened with the Countess de Ségur's *Jean qui Grogne et Jean qui Rit*. The Comédie Française felt this influence also and in 1924 staged Machard's play for children, *Croquemitaine*.

The most recent of the theatres which declare themselves advanced is the gift to the cause of drama and the newer stagecraft of Baron Henri de Rothschild, the financier. Under the name of André Pascal, he is also the playwright of *La Rampe*, 1909, and *Le Caducée*, 1921. Baron Rothschild has not only erected the theatre, but financed it. His son, Philippe de Rothschild, has supervised the construction, which is in charge of the French architect, Charles Siclis, and the German builders, Siemens Company. The theatre, named the New Pigalle Theatre, standing on what was the site of the Hôtel Scribe, 12, rue Pigalle, represents some of the most recent ideas in both architecture and stage equipment. The foyer is lighted by "a wall of rainbow flame," the interior, including a gallery and exhibition room, is of mahogany and dull rose, and the building is surmounted by a conning tower for viewing Paris. The stage equipment is strongly influenced by the theatres of Germany which the younger Rothschild visited: it comprises four stages on the chain system which can be "alternately mounted, pushed forward, lowered, pushed back." Two hundred and twenty-eight levers control a remarkable lighting system. *L'Histoire de France*, a play in fifteen tableaux especially written by Sacha Guitry to show the possibilities of the new stage, was the first program, October, 1929. This was in charge of Gabriel Astruc, administrative director, and André Antoine, artistic director. Thus a great personality weaves together the stories of the humble pioneer little theatre and the most recent and magnificent of art theatres.

While the French theatre, with few exceptions, is the theatre of Paris, the tourist can find some scenes of great interest far from the metropolis. In Provence, whose people delight in comparing themselves to the cicada which feasts in the summer and starves in the winter but sings the whole year, there is love for the charm, excitement, and beauty of the drama. For several years, there has been a summer festival before the Palace of the Popes in Avignon. Here the spectators are on a terrace close to the lofty walls with their parapet and stairways from which a Gordon Craig might draw his inspiration. Many yards below are the crenellated city walls and the quiet Rhone with the broken arches of the bridge where "tout le monde danse." The setting in itself lends dignity and moving power. Once the play was *Hamlet* and another year the *Alkestis* of Rivollet, based upon Euripides' version, and *On ne Badine pas avec l'Amour* of Alfred de Musset.

Twenty miles of silver road between the mottled gold of plane trees separate Avignon from Orange. Like her sister towns of Nîmes and Arles, Orange holds a glowing memory of Roman culture in her classic architecture. Perhaps there is nowhere in Europe a theatre through which the past surges more irresistibly than the Théâtre Antique d'Orange, in which there is held a summer festival of opera and drama. The "mur d'Orange," as the Provençals call the old Roman architectural background which is one section of the gigantic amphitheatre; the niches for statues, one of which, grotesquely marred, is still in place; the large bank of seats, almost uninjured, carry the imagination back nearly eighteen centuries, while the broken lines of mutilation of part of the amphitheatre recall the fervor of Christian vandals, and the high nasal voices of the girl candy vendors bring one to the present. The present melts into the past during the play itself, for the deep velvet skies of the south are timeless and the dramas, wisely chosen, embody tales of the ancient world as Racine's *Bérénice* or Gluck's *Alceste*. A play by Henri Graivitz, *Cerella*, has for its theme a story of the days when the barbarians were invading this very section, then the Roman province, Gaule Méridionale. In boyhood the author had watched Mounet Sully play *Œdipe Roi* at Orange; the presentation of *Cerella* is the fulfillment of a boyhood dream.

Another development, recalling vividly the fourteenth century, is the religious drama of present-day Brittany, a drama in the Celtic tongue. In this little corner of the world, men and women cling to the old in costume and belief and to the *pardons*, which, like the miracle plays of the Middle Ages, are instinct with drama. One man, with the double purpose of bringing the inspiration of religion more vividly to his people and of keeping what is unique and inspiring in their traditional life and speech, has been largely responsible for native drama. He is L'Abbé Joseph Le Bayon, and his theatre, Le Théâtre Populaire de Sainte-Anne d'Auray.

Le Bayon was born in a peasant home at Pluvigner in the heart of Brittany, April, 1876. He has always been interested in his native literature and drama, since as a boy playing in his grandmother's attic he came across a manuscript of *Le jeu des trois Rois* in the dialect of a Vannetain, and with his young friends, played it from house to house in the manner of the English Christmas mummings. When a student of Professor Loth, the great Celtic scholar, at the University of Rennes, Le Bayon wrote a verse idyll in Breton. Later, at the seminary of Sainte-Anne, he assisted

Buléon, who was soon appointed vicar of Saint-Patern de Vanes, in putting on religious tableaux in the vernacular. Both men had the same enthusiasm. When the older man started publishing a little bulletin for his district, he devoted a section of it, entitled Clocher de Saint-Patern, to the Breton language, and gave the editing of this to Le Bayon. This was not Le Bayon's only contribution to the Breton: by 1902 he had begun a play, a religious mystery in verse on the theme of Keriolet, a native saint. Hearing of this, his superior urged him to finish it for a congress at Auray. The play was received with great delight.

With the appointment of another co-leader, Abbé Louis Cadic, an enthusiastic organizer, the work began to assume the proportions of a folk theatre. Le Bayon continued to write for the group at Pluvigner, and his promotion to the vicarship of Bignan, largely through his devotion to Breton, opened a wider field. By 1909 he had two dramas, *Sant Korneli* and *Nikolazig*, ready for a larger audience, after the festival of Sainte-Anne in late July. The founders lovingly imagined a great throng of worshippers in an open air theatre, under the benediction of a sky of cloudless blue. But Brittany is not Greece. By the next summer the auditorium was covered with a wooden roof. Later successes have replaced the first simple structure with a more attractive one. The stage decoration has also grown more artistic, for a well-known Parisian designer, Boris, a summer visitor in Pluvigner, has given his help.

The Troupe of Sainte-Anne, as these Breton players became known, are unique in one respect—the actors do not go to rehearsals but the rehearsals go to them. That is, since the people represent a wide area—at one time fifteen were from Bignan, three from Pluvigner, one from Camois, and the rest, including the choir and supernumeraries, from Auray—the director must reach them in their own villages. Abbé Le Bayon goes to their homes several times to dis-tribute copies of the already printed play, to comment and explain, and finally to hear the lines. Later there are rehearsals on Sunday after vespers and a long general rehearsal on the day of the play itself. The ages of the actors range from a year and a half to eighty, and the cast may include entire families. The costumes, except for a few borrowed from people who have sojourned in Bible lands, are the loving work during the winter evenings of girls who know the plans of the designers, ideas often taken from paintings and drawings of Tissot and Doré. All service is unpaid, for the tickets, from one-half a franc to five francs, allow of no profit for anyone. During the days of the performances, several a year, peasants leave their farms and tradesmen their shops without grudging the sacrifice. "C'est pour Sainte-Anne et pour la Bretagne."

IV

FROM NATURALISM TO EXPRESSIONISM IN GERMANY

What is needed before everything else in the life of
the German theatre and especially in that of the capital
city is freedom [wrote Maximilian Harden, who has since
championed freedom of thought in other provinces than
that of the theatre, in the pages of *Die Gegenwart* for
July 27, 1889, while plans for the first German free
theatre were under way]. Freedom [he repeats] from
obsolete preconceived opinions, from a notion of morality
vulgarized for the world of the stage alone, from the
exaggerated regard for the taste of the dear public. A
crowd of people,—even if they are merged into an intelligent individuality, which you know is not the case
with a first-night public,—have to be forced continually
into new paths; if we wish to yield the initiative to them,
then perhaps the splendor of our theatre will decay, per-
ishing in the love of shows and exhibitions after the English fashion. And therefore we desire for our stage-direc-
tors and those whom they are called to delight a large
dose of that quality, which would also be an excellent
thing for the critics, giving them a needed balance, that
is, a fine lot of *disregard of the past,* well-shaken and
tossed together. If they enter into the widely rushing
stream of modern life and for a time can forget the thing
named theatre, then the history of the theatre will perhaps
have cause to remember them.

THAT the German drama was in need of some drastic remedy was apparent to all clear-eyed observers and a disappointment to those who dreamed of Germany as a world-
power in literature, as in politics. Her victorious armies had

swept on to Paris in six weeks. Why could not her writers claim some little corner of world-fame for themselves in six years, or thrice six years? To be forced to turn back to Schiller or Goethe for examples of national pride while in other countries science, inventions, the quickening pace of modern life, its revelations, its pity and terror were all finding their reflection in art was an overwhelming humiliation. "Since the seventies," mourned M. G. Conrad, "we have not had a single name in the story, the novel, the epic, or the drama reach the consideration of Europe. It is as if the German triumph of literature stopped at the new German boundary. . . ."

The spirits of national aggrandizement, of commercial speculation, of the triumph of conquerors are hardly the muses to foster great literature: the Franco-Prussian War harmed German letters by dethroning idealism. Germany was not to possess a great modern dramatist till a young man of compassionate heart turned his eyes away from an ideal of material glory toward the sufferings and defeats of Silesian peasants, the problems and anxieties of humble souls, imperfect but aspiring.

Meanwhile, before the advent of Hauptmann, Germany, the conqueror, turned to France, the conquered, for organized amusement. With few exceptions, for twenty years after the Franco-Prussian War, the dramatists of the stages of Germany and Austria were French masters of "the well-made play" or their imitators: Augier, Dumas fils, Sardou, Scribe, Feuillet, Erckmann-Chatrian, Ohnet, Pailleron had their German successes. A week of repertoire at the Burgtheater of Vienna, January, 1886, is representative of the theatrical situation,—a repertoire composed entirely of French pieces by Ohnet, Dumas, Sardou, for two of which the director, Wilbrandt, had bought the right of presentation before he had seen the manuscripts. So eager were the managers to lay their hands on French plays of the light society type that a German playwright is said to have signed a comedy with a French pseudonym to assure its acceptance at the Deutsches Theater of Berlin.

Of the native followers of the French school, Oscar Blumenthal and Paul Lindau were the most prominent. Blumenthal was honored by the production of his *Ein Tropfen Gift* at the Deutsches Theater, which ordinarily received only established playwrights. Paul Lindau's triumphs were his versions of Dumas' *Francillon,* 1888, and Augier's *Lionnes pauvres,* 1889. Like Dumas, he now and then handled contemporary problems, as antisemitism in *Gräfin Lea,* but only superficially. He was the most successful among the adapters and imitators of the French. He had great skill, a feeling for the theatrical, and a nice understanding of what his public wanted. Indeed what the greater number of German theatre-goers between 1870 and 1889 desired was as close as possible an imitation of the lively Parisian farce or comedy with enough weakening and white-washing of the "strong" situations to give the spectators the added delight of a feeling of superiority to those "immoral French." The list of these followers of Scribe and his school might be indefinitely lengthened; they had little with which to endow any new movement.

Aside from the giant Wagner, whose history belongs only partly to the drama and whose innovations at Bayreuth were important for the modern stage in methods of production rather than in dramaturgy, only two figures in the period between the Franco-Prussian War and the emergence of Hauptmann have stood the test of time. The one enjoyed a great vogue in his own day and has suffered a partial diminution; the other, whose life was of hardship and of recognition long delayed, became, in the admiration of the younger men of the nineties, almost a banner-bearer for the dramatic revival.

The first of these is Ernst von Wildenbruch (1845-1909).

The Germans have always been great admirers of historical drama, as their frequent productions of Shakespeare's chronicle-history plays illustrate. Their own playwrights with a bent for history have turned for inspiration sometimes to the stories of other nations, sometimes to those of their own, apparently with little difference in catching the attention of the public, if the theme of the drama is powerful and the handling effective. In the years of the struggle for national unity, when themes from German history were especially welcome, von Wildenbruch became, in a sense, a court poet. His verse tragedy, *Die Karolinger,* 1881, was presented by the company of the Duke of Meiningen at Berlin to great applause, and rival theatres began contending for his work. One of his most moving plays, however, *Das neue Gebot,* 1886, with a "subject of terrible cruelty" frightened the Berlin theatre managers. The period of the action is that of the conflict between Christian and Roman views of life, and the story that of a devout old priest who is forced by the teaching of his church to look upon his wife of many years as a mistress. The greater Berlin theatres took alarm at the theme and the play was given at a suburban house, the Wallnertheater. Here fashionable Berlin flocked for more than a hundred nights. *Die Quitzows* and *Der Generalfeldoberst,* later plays, are from Prussian history. These and other plays have the same merits and the same defects: a feeling both for the theatre and for the vividness and emotional quality of life, but a lack of profundity of thought or richness of expression, and a psychology that is sometimes quite inexplicable. Though *Die Quitzows* contains some realistic scenes and some attempt at dialect, and brought its author the epithet, the "poet of youth," its modern tendencies are slight and fitful; von Wildenbruch is a follower of Schiller rather than a pioneer of the naturalistic movement.

On the contrary, Ludwig Anzengruber (1839-1889), an

Austrian, is generally conceded to be the only dramatist of first rank produced by the German-speaking stage in twenty years. Although he was not a young man at the time of the founding of the first experimental theatre, was but slightly associated with "Youngest Germany," as the disciples of the moderns called themselves, and died within the first year of the Freie Bühne, he anticipated some of the most important tendencies of the radical group. Struggling many years as wandering actor, novelist, playwright, he gained some popularity with *Der Pfarrer von Kirchfeld* (1870), following it by plays which won little honor in his lifetime,—*Der Meineidbauer* (1871), *Die Kreuzelschreiber* (1872), *Der G'wissenswurm* (1874), *Doppelselbstmord* (1876), *Das Jungferngift* (1878), and the only play which is well known outside Austria, *Das Vierte Gebot* (1878). He took the local Viennese play, of the life of the lower classes, particularly the peasants, and freed it of musical and fairy elements, of horseplay, of vulgarities, of untruths. In his hands it became true art showing the surface of life indeed, the customs and language of the peasants, but without exaggeration, and beneath that surface, joy and tragedy more intense for the humble background. The dialect plays of Hauptmann have some resemblances to those of Anzengruber.

In the eighties, then, Germany faced this situation in the theatre: the existence of a host of playwrights willing to imitate endlessly the commercial successes of France; one real dramatist, an Austrian, who had not yet come into his own; theatres which partly through fear of the censor and largely through inertia and complacency closed their doors to any plays not built upon the accepted formulas; and a public which craved the superficial and the cheaply amusing. Yet, in less than ten years, Germany was to have an original and notable dramatic literature. "The drama of modern Germany has broken more completely with the past than any other body of contemporary literature." [1] This change did not come overnight: certain revolutionary influences were already at work.

Four of these influences upon the young men of the eighties can be distinguished,—the influence of the native literature, of the Scandinavians, particularly Ibsen, of Zola, and of the Russians.

The effect of earlier German drama was fitful, slight, often unconscious. Some historians would find the earliest evidence of modern realistic tendencies in Goethe's *Faust;* many in Lessing's *Emilia Galotti* (1772) and Schiller's *Kabale und Liebe* (1784), with their revolutionary ideas, their absorption in social questions, and their attempts to reproduce the language of different groups of people. More direct was the impression made by Hebbel in *Maria Magdalena* (1844) and *Julia* (1851)—the latter with almost an Ibsen theme—and by Otto Ludwig in *Der Erbförster* (1849). Both are fond of the *Familienkatastrophe,* the tragedy of a family, which was to become a favorite theme of naturalism; *Stimmung,* the striving for truth of individual atmosphere; and the belief that character is explained to some degree by environment. They differ in their attitudes towards their material, for Hebbel is only occasionally and unconsciously a realist while Ludwig is a champion of realism both in theory and practice. Georg Büchner, also (1813-1837), was remembered for the vivid dialogue of *Wozzek,* which Goethe admired, and for *Dantons Tod,* 1835, with a theme from the French Revolution, a play which has come into even greater prominence since the World War and the Russian Revolution. These writers are mainly concerned with the middle or lower classes as the naturalistic play was to be. Another type of play which contained seeds of the new movement was the *Volksstück* or *Lokalstück,* the study of a certain locality, a type of

[1] Lewisohn, Ludwig, *The Modern Drama,* p. 103.

drama almost unknown in France. There are plays of this kind in many sections of Germany in the repertoire of the local theatres, but the *Volksstück* of Vienna is the most famous. Ferdinand Raimund (1790-1836) made the form somewhat more delicate, limiting the allegorical elements. In his work there is a feeling of sadness underlying the comedy and pointing toward the peasant tragedy of a later generation. Anzengruber, as we have seen, carried the innovations further. Notwithstanding these suggestive parallels, the impress of either German or Austrian drama upon young Germany of the last of the century was slight in comparison with that of foreign literatures.

The great master of German thought, the germinal poet whose ideas, or rather the selection of them which young Germany chose to emphasize, were permeating the minds of the land of his adoption, was Ibsen. In 1889 he had already been known on the stage or in the library for more than fifteen years. As early as 1872 *Brand, The Pretenders,* and *The League of Youth* found German translators, and on April 10, 1876, under the German title, *Nordische Heerfahrt,* the first Ibsen production in Germany took place in Munich, Ibsen's favorite city. Here, as later in England, early Ibsen performances sometimes confused both producers and audience, and daring young critics attempted to explain the dramatist's work and to conquer a larger public for him. Among these critics were Brahm and Schlenther, fellow journalists on the *Vossische Zeitung,* the former the author of the earliest effective treatment of Ibsen as man and writer; the latter his defender as early as 1878. Both will appear again in this chronicle.

Performances of Ibsen continued throughout Germany, though not with frequency in any one city. *Nordische Heerfahrt* was given at the Vienna Burgtheater in the same year as in Munich, with only moderate success. The first performance of Ibsen in Berlin was *The Pretenders,* by the company of the Duke of Meiningen, June 3, 1876. *Pillars of Society* and *Mistress Inger at Ostraat* were also given there in 1878. With simultaneous performances of different translations of *Pillars of Society* at the Stadttheater and the Volkstheater, in 1879, Ibsen became the gigantic figure in the German theatre world which he has never ceased to be. *Nora,* the German version of *A Doll's House,* was presented in Munich in March, 1880, and at the capital in the following autumn. *Ghosts,* which more than any other play has become a challenge to independent theatres and their communities, was fiven first at Augsburg, April 14, 1886, before an audience of invited guests, and repeated soon after by the Duke of Meiningen's company. It was first seen in Berlin the next January at the Residenztheater, under the direction of Anton Anno and with Frau Anno, a distinguished actress, taking the part of Mrs. Alving. On this same evening Emmanuel Reicher, to become a celebrated actor of Ibsen and Hauptmann rôles, played Pastor Manders. "The most important date in the history of the European theatre in two decades," wrote one critic.

What is most striking in this period and true in only a less degree of the following years is the avidity with which Germany seized upon certain elements in the work of Ibsen and disregarded others. His poetic and symbolic dramas were very nearly overlooked until the tide of naturalism had passed its full. Young critics and writers were looking for socialism, and they found it in Ibsen's plays or read it into them; they wanted naturalism, and it too was there. But subject and technique, form and spirit cannot be easily disentangled; in studying the plays for modern tendencies talented young men were following the mind of a master of technique and a profound observer of human motives. And they profited by their instruction. "You track him everywhere in other men's snow," Dryden's famous criticism of Shakespeare, might be used of Ibsen, for he is constantly present in the work of Hauptmann, his disciple of genius, as in the work of men now half forgotten.

Ibsen was not the only one of the giants of the North to direct the new German movement. Björnson also was known; indeed his *Bankruptcy,* played in 1874, antedated any Ibsen performance. Nevertheless his influence was not in any degree comparable with Ibsen's. On the contrary, Strindberg, both through the originality and cruel power of his best known plays (*The Father* and *Mademoiselle Julie*) and through the brilliant analysis of his dramatic theories, was always a provocative and stimulating figure.

Inspiration was also coming to German drama in the realism of the French Balzac and Flaubert, of the Russian novelists, and the English Charles Dickens, whom the continent persists in considering naturalistic. Russian plays also reached Paris,—before 1889 *The Reviser* of Gogol, *Natalie* of Turgenev, *Raskolnikov* drawn from Dostoyevsky's novel, *Crime and Punishment,* and fathering a long line of plays on the criminal who "comes back," *Der Leibeigene* of Pissemsky, *The Fruits of Knowledge* and *The Power of Darkness* of Tolstoy. The influence of this last play surpassed that of the others together: it was suggested soon after the appearance of *Before Sunrise* that in detail of character description, in careful individualizing of speech, in theme, the moral degradation caused by alcoholism, and in the title, Hauptmann's drama seems patterned on the earlier play. In 1899, in a public address at Vienna, Hauptmann confirmed this belief.

If the average pleasure seekers of the German theatre turned to Paris and the imitators of the Parisian society play for their recreation, the more advanced literary men of Germany turned also to Paris for the realistic novel and the realistic play, the latter, before Antoine instituted the Théâtre Libre, a rare phenomenon. Becque of *The Crows* was known in Germany and admired for his cool, unimaginative observation. Edmond de Goncourt was known also for his novels, for his rather conventional play, and for his thoroughly unconventional preface describing his ideal in dramatic writing:

> The art of the theatre, this sick art, this art which is finished, can have its existence prolonged only by the transfusion into its old organism of new elements, and I have been able to find these only in a literary language with the qualities of actual speech ("une langue littéraire parlée") and in the representing of sentiments according to nature—these make the only extreme realism with which one can endow the theatre.

But the towering figure among the French realists in Germany's estimation was Zola. Now that his fame has suffered a deflation, it is almost impossible to realize Zola's importance between the years 1880 and 1890 in Germany, as well as in France. This influence in Germany was both direct and indirect, for such German novelists as Kretzer, Lindau, Mauthner, followed Zola as closely as their talents allowed. Considered at first a depicter of unusual sex themes (a cheap edition of a German translation of *Nana* was having *un succès de scandale*), Zola was soon exalted by M. G. Conrad and K. Bleibtreu and others as a true artist. Even before *Germinal*, 1885, he was being sought out by young literary men, and his theories began to assume something of the dignity of oracles. Though disagreeing with Zola's belief in the importance of temperament in art, Holz and Schlaf, to become the two extreme theorists of German naturalism, were under his influence.

To these literary influences others only less potent in determining the mood of young Germans should be added, the pessimism of Schopenhauer, Nietzsche's idea of the superman, Marx's criticism of the existing order and his hope of the future betterment of society, and the rising tide of socialistic thought as it seethed in many minds.

Our whole age is an age of unsettled problems and unsettled conflicts [says Professor Kuno Francke writing of this period]. Everywhere, all the world over, there is a violent clash between the old and the new, between the classes and the masses, between capital and labor, between autocracy and freedom, between state and church, between traditional creeds and personal convictions. Nowhere, however, is this conflict being waged with such an intensity as in Germany. Germany is at present the classic land of moral contrasts.[2]

A conflict smouldering between church and state, strife between monarchy and democracy, the struggle between industrialism and the masses all meant a mental and spiritual turmoil. For many, materialism and the new conception of science, as Darwin had revolutionized it, had not yet reconciled themselves with idealism. From the impact of these opposing tendencies were struck the sparks of a new literary art.

The first of these came in the eighties. Young writers felt the pull of a new ambition, the desire to reflect the face and form of human life, modern life, as it appeared to eyes not astigmatized by tradition. *Die Jüngstdeutschen* ("Youngest Germans") or *Jüngstdeutschland* ("Youngest Germany") they called themselves in memory of "Young Germany" of the *Sturm und Drang* period of fifty years before. At first "Youngest Germany" began to find its way into print largely in critical writings. New journals came into existence, some of them short-lived, but all effective in crystallizing the new doctrine. The brothers Julius and Heinrich Hart headed the list with *Waffengänge* (1882-1884), a periodical to which they were the chief contributors, with the motto, "Fort mit der Epigonenwirtschaft." In 1885, Michael Georg Conrad, one of the earliest and most ardent of the Youngest Germans, founded at Munich a

[2] From *Social Forces in German Literature,* by Kuno Francke, p. 557. Courtesy of Henry Holt and Company, Publishers, New York.

review, *Die Gesellschaft, realistische Zeitschrift für Litteratur, Kunst und öffentliches Leben*. This published brilliant articles by Konrad Alberti, Fritz Lienhard, and others, and a satire, "Münchener Parnass," by Kirchbach in which Paul Heyse is made to declare, "Drama is an aristocratic art. To be distinguished, that is the duty of the heroes of the theatre." A much read pamphlet of the same year was Karl Bleibtreu's *Revolution der Litteratur,* which enthralled its readers by the originality and brilliancy of its style. Of realism Bleibtreu writes, "Under this name is meant the tendency in art which denounces entirely Cloud-Cuckoodom and, reflecting life, bases it as much as possible on the earth of reality." Bleibtreu thought that the two basic qualities of a new art should be "objectivity" and "the scent of the soil." Bleibtreu became one of the editors of the *Magazin für Litteratur des In- und Auslandes,* a long-established periodical turned to new uses. There were still other publications in this radical mood.

More influential, probably, were the loosely organized groups of young men who came together to discuss anything in ethics, sociology, art pertaining to modern life. Durch, founded in Berlin in 1886, by Dr. Conrad Custer, included the critic Leo Burg, the poet Holz, his friend, Johannes Schlaf, the novelists Hart, and Gerhart Hauptmann, at the time an undistinguished young man. The revolutionary creed of this group was directed largely toward the reform of literature, and the organization was specially for young writers of modern proclivities. One of the earliest lectures delivered here was upon the future of the drama. Two other radicals, Wilhelm Bölsche and Bruno Wille, friends and ardent socialists, drew a little circle about them at Friedrichshagen, a suburb of Berlin. This "ethical club," formed to discuss modern religious questions and the ideals of social democracy, brought Hauptmann in touch with still other advanced thinkers. Meanwhile, this young man was welcoming in his own home at Erkner several of the most original minds of the day. Here came Holz and Schlaf to read their *Papa Hamlet*, just off the press, with its authorship hidden under the pseudonym, "Bjorne P. Holmsen," which, at the same time, protected the authors from attacks leveled against their inexperience and showed their Scandinavian-mindedness. The short stories in this volume are composed of extremely naturalistic dialogue set within descriptive frames so slight as to be hardly more than stage directions.

Hauptmann, who listened absorbed, was a much travelled and thoughtful young man, who had been in turn farmer, art student, student of sociology, sculptor, and writer, driven on by discontent, which, in itself no proof of genius, is, as Lewisohn points out, often a mark of it. Though his *Promethidenlos* of 1885 had described a hero still hestitating between poetry and sculpture, Hauptmann had at last decided that literature was his destiny, but the form and direction of his writing at that time were not determined. *Papa Hamlet* and its underlying theories of naturalism, which Holz expounded, were the strongest single literary influence in the forming of Hauptmann's genius.

To these groups of young intellectuals the idea of a stage on which modern plays of revolt could be given must have presented itself. Many of the older members had watched the opening, within the same decade, of three large commercial theatres in Berlin, hoping in turn that each would adopt a more liberal policy toward inexperienced playwrights and being again and again disappointed. These theatres and others continued obstinate, even though their managers were concerned over what they called "a theatre-crisis," a period during which the number of spectators dropped alarmingly and many actors were unemployed. The literary radicals were familiar too with the work of that remarkable band of amateurs, the Duke of Meiningen's company, which has been mentioned as having influenced Antoine profoundly. Unfortunately for their influence in Berlin, unusual accuracy of costuming and historical background and finer ensemble acting than the German stage had previously known were lavished upon plays which were rarely considered "modern." The two great impetuses toward a new theatre came from France, the German tours of Réjane and of Antoine and his Théâtre Libre. The first response came from the members of Durch and their friends, who planned a theatre of amateurs to encourage plays of the new spirit. They met with prompt failure. A little later, January, 1889, an article by Bernhard Westenberger in the review *Kunstwart* suggested the founding of a Dichterbühne (theatre for poets) devoted to art aims. This venture, too, received insufficient support.

The suggestion for the theatre which was to revolutionize German drama came from two young Berlin journalists, Theodor Wolff and Maximilian Harden. (Harden was to become one of the leading editors of Germany. In 1892 he founded *Die Zukunft,* noted for its political daring, a constant thorn in the side of Prussian autocracy.) The fullest account of the early days of this first of the German free stages is by Paul Schlenther in his pamphlet, *Wozu der Lärm, Genesis der Freien Bühne:*

It was in March of this year that I was invited one Sunday forenoon to a café in this place to consult about the establishment of a free theatre. I acknowledge that I accepted the invitation more out of curiosity than enthusiasm for I was acquainted with the immense difficulty of such an undertaking. I found eight or nine other gentlemen, besides our proud treasurer and an assistant theatre-agent till then unknown to me. I met with professional men, entirely, journalists who wrote criticisms for dailies and weeklies on literature and dramatic art. When I asked those present what action was being taken and whether someone was able to lay before us a definitely formulated plan, I received no decided answer; the discussion threatened to break into scattering comments. But people were diffident about bringing forward questions of literary principles, because any practical result would have been delayed and hindered.

At that time men were still looking to Paris in all matters of the theatre, and particularly to the example of that Théâtre Libre yonder at which there had been an attempt to present Tolstoy's *Power of Darkness* and similar plays not usually seen on the stage. But a fundamental difference was emphatically pointed out: The Théâtre Libre is the business undertaking of a speculative body, the Freie Bühne shall serve a purely artistic end. What it earns shall be expended for this purpose. On this, I believe, we were at the time agreed, and so we have remained.

As we sat there before the wine table, we came to the conclusion that it was necessary to bind the easy conference into a kind of parliamentary form, and by a unanimous vote of the guests the direction of the debate was entrusted to Dr. Otto Brahm, one of those present. We soon came to a decision to let others know the aim and plan of the Freie Bühne by a challenge to the art-loving public of Berlin.

What were the aim and plan? The outline for the challenge which we the same day determined on and which was sent abroad in many copies was phrased in this way: "We are united in the purpose of forming, independent of the management of the established theatre and without entering into rivalry with it, a theatre free from conventions, theatre-censorship, and commercial aims. During this theatre-year, this group shall give in one of the first theatre houses of Berlin some ten productions of modern plays of decided interest which in their very nature the established stages find difficult to undertake. The aim of a living art shall be opposed to that of patterns and masters alike in the choice of the dramatic works and in their presentations."

Notwithstanding the slighting reference to the Théâtre Libre, the German theatre followed it closely in aims and even in methods. But the internal organization of the Freie Bühne was more elaborate. At the first meeting, a president,

a legal adviser, and a treasurer were elected, and a governing Council of Ten was created. At a later meeting, two
types of membership were decided upon, "regular," or active, and "extraordinary," the second type greatly to out-
number the first. The regular members, numbering ten, were
really a continuation of the first council, a small group
responsible for the whole organization artistically and financially, while the extraordinary members attended plays and
paid the modest sum of the annual subscription.

It became recognized as unfeasible [explains Schlenther] to
grant equal rights to the members collectively and require from
them equal duties when it would not be possible to trouble the
society as a whole about all questions of art and business. We
took our stand on the old experience that a theatre-state must
be as nearly as possible under one rule: the fewer heads, the
sounder thought, the surer results.

At first, the regular members were Dr. Otto Brahm,
elected president because of the general sentiment that a
literary man should be at the head; a successful business
man, Paul Jones, legal adviser; the bookseller Fischer,
treasurer; the two founders, Harden and Wolff; Schlenther;
the brothers Hart; the humorist Stettenheim; and the theatre agent Stockhausen. Any jealousy in the hearts of the
extraordinary members was soon dissipated as they realized
their freedom from responsibility. Nevertheless the society
was not without the friction which seems the lot of stage
societies: before the first performance the two founders,
followed by Stockhausen, had resigned. Perhaps Harden and
Wolff felt a very human irritation at seeing the society of
which they were the "spiritual fathers" pass largely out of
their hands; perhaps they disapproved of the emphasis upon
foreign and naturalistic drama in the program to which
Brahm was preparing to commit the theatre. The Council
of Ten was maintained by the election of the critic Fritz

Mauthner, the poet Ludwig Fulda, and Gerhard Haupt-mann. Later Emmanuel Reicher, the actor, was added.

After this early insurrection the sway of Dr. Brahm was undisputed. He arranged the programs and chose actors and assistants. Under his directorship a publicity campaign was carried on in most of the leading journals, ably supple-mented by many articles in which Harden and Bleibtreu opposed the work of the theatre. A few months after the activities of the Freie Bühne began, the society brought out its own periodical, *Freie Bühne für den Entwickelungs-kampf der Zeit* (Free Stage for the Developmental Struggle of the Time), which besides keeping the plays of the group itself in the mind of the public, included within a short time plays by Max Halbe, Johannes Schlaf, Anne Garborg, and essays on as varied subjects as the French lyric, Walt Whit-man, Darwinism, and Nietzsche. Meanwhile subscriptions for membership were pouring in, three hundred and sixty before any program had been given, nine hundred before the year was over. A little later, at the height of its popu-larity, over a thousand saw each program.

A similar eagerness appeared in the offers of help which reached the new society. Dr. Oscar Blumenthal offered the use of the Lessing Theater, one of the finest German houses; Hans Meery, of the well-known Leipzig Stadttheater, his services as manager; two Berlin theatre-directors put them-selves at Brahm's disposal; and the Vienna Burgtheater, skilled in the production of Ibsen plays, lent a prominent actor. Another actor, even more distinguished, Emmanuel Reicher, left his retirement in the country, and the noted actress, Agnes Sorma, long absent from the stage, returned. Other famous players who volunteered for the cast of the Freie Bühne were Marie Schanzer, Arthur Kraussneck, Theodore Lobe, and Emerich Robert.

Ghosts was selected for the first performance, a matinée, Sunday, September 29, 1889. (Sunday was selected because on that day professional actors were free.) Both art and expediency dictated the choice. Brahm and his friends, long champions of Ibsen, considered the dramatist the "path-finder" or at least the "path-seeker" of the entire new world of thought, and believed that the honor of the first program was his due. *Ghosts,* in particular, was suited to the mood of an experimental theatre by the boldness of its theme and by the fact that in most German cities it was still banned by the censor. It had, however, been given in Berlin, during the preceding January, with enormous success until the authorities caused its removal. One of the members of the Freie Bühne suggested *Brand,* to be countered with Brahm's reply, "If we first gave *Brand* at the theatre, we would sell mighty few seats." The production vindicated the director's choice. Its success can hardly be overestimated. Schlenther wrote, "Four years ago we left the first path-breaking production of *Ghosts* in Berlin with the feeling 'The fight for Ibsen is on.' From this second performance we went with the conviction, 'Ibsen will triumph.' "

To those critics, a substantial number, who objected to the presentation of a foreign drama, even one of Ibsen's, on the ground that the new society should stimulate native production, the second program seemed ideal. *Before Sunrise* (*Vor Sonnenaufgang*) by Gerhart Hauptmann was indeed of the character to test the mettle of an experimental theatre: the first ambitious venture into play-writing of a young author almost unknown outside his own small group. *Gesellschaft,* the advanced journal conducted by Karl Bleibtreu and Konrad Alberti, had indeed published Hauptmann's verse-epic and a novel, *Der Bahnwärter Thiel,* but, through a mistake which the editors later took much care to explain, the manuscript of *Before Sunrise* had been returned to the writer. The author, moreover, was extreme in his theories: the play was dedicated to the fathers of naturalism, under their joint pseudonym,—"To Bjorne P. Holmsen, the most logical of realists, author of 'Papa Hamlet,' I dedicate with joy this play in testimony to my recognition of the decisive influence which his book has exercised upon me."

Now that Hauptmann has long been acknowledged the foremost dramatist of modern Germany and the day of his première the most important date since Goethe and Schiller, early criticisms of his work have a special interest. Men of very different temperaments were enthusiastic: Theodor Fontane, the novelist, wrote the letter of introduction which accompanied the manuscript of *Before Sunrise*. Emmanuel Reicher, allowed to see the text, declared after one reading that this was "the style" for which he had long pleaded. The critic, Schlenther, amused himself in seeking Hauptmann's literary antecedents and in hazarding a guess as to his destinies:

The society believed a strong and original talent of maturity and artistic independence had appeared. Neither the æsthetic and social aim of the unusual piece, nor its unbounded naturalism and its profoundly lucid plan of life ought to be praised, but the writer's intrepid daring in renouncing absolutely all conventions and false tradition, and his gifted attempt to pour a new and complete life into dramatic form. Our German drama stands in danger of being benumbed or withered by two influences: in the serious type, there are descendants of Schiller's poetic dramas, emphasizing history, however, more than poetry, even more bloodless, shadow-imprisoned, narrowly academic; in the lighter type there has nestled a heavy, empty, and foolish phantom, which exhausts itself in external witticisms and conventional humor; an artistic taste would avoid contemptuously that tedious tragedy as this insipid comedy, and the society Freie Bühne has no more to do with one than the other.

Just as little has it to do with that kind of half writing, blessed by a season's success, which, with more or less of a journalistic spirit, in imitation of Parisian society drama, juggles about a pretended German society which does not exist. What "society" signifies to France "the people" (the folk) always signifies to Germany. While for the last fifty years the work of French drama has been the drawing-room play, that of German drama has been the folk-play. What we with high pride place opposite all those others—Scribe, Feuillet, Augier, Dumas, and Sardou—lies in that grasp of the German people, in which Hebbel found his Maria Magdalene, Otto Ludwig his foresters, and Anzengruber his farmer-comedies. There also has young Haupt-mann found his social drama. Like Anzengruber he also employs dialect, like Ludwig he paints the degeneration of a country family, like Hebbel he shows the tragic fate of a girl of the people who is betrayed. And yet Hauptmann binds himself to no one of his masters.

The larger public was soon aroused. The manuscript had been rushed to the publisher Fischer, and the text speedily reached the bookstalls. In cafés and in homes the play was the sensation of the hour even before its presentation. The naturalness of the Silesian farmhouse setting was admired as was also the beauty of Helene's character against the degradation of the newly-rich farmers, on whose land coal had been discovered. Two controversies raged, one concerning art, one ethics: were the scenes which frankly depicted vice necessary for the truth and right emphasis of the theme; should a man renounce the woman he loves rather than let her, innocent victim of heredity, bring to his children a tainted inheritance?

Long before noon of Sunday, October 20, 1889, the time set for the performance, all fashionable literary Berlin was thronging to the Lessing Theater. No one went with an impartial mind: each was vehemently a Youngest German or a member of the old guard, ready to fight to a finish in defence of the good old days.

At first, to their disappointment, as Schlenther relates, the spectators could find little ground for partisanship. The comedy of the home scene in the first act passed lightly, though the audience watched for every trace of naturalism.

"The tiger still lay in his lair," as Schlenther wrote. In the second act, when the conversation between Helene (Elsa Lehmann) and her stepmother began to reveal the moral rottenness of the girl's environment, "the tiger broke out." A noted surgeon and dramatic critic let fly a word "not usual in the vocabulary of a gentleman." Pandemonium was loosed. The theatre went wild as one faction clapped everything upon the stage and the other party hissed till hands were sore and throats hoarse. Some sprang from their seats, stamping, jingling keys, and threatening. Others went about demanding quiet in tones that were themselves an uproar. When during the last act the darkness of Helene's impending tragedy is deepened by the groans from the next room of her sister in childbirth, the same physician sprang up brandishing a pair of forceps. The cast, meanwhile, played the drama painstakingly through.

At the end of the performance there were cries for the author, who was greeted in a characteristic manner by each of the groups.

The young man over whose work the gentlemen in the stalls and the pit were nearly ready to tear out one another's hair, was not at all like the picture which one forms of a wild enthusiast for "storm and stress." As in the confusion he came in sight before the footlights, bowing awkwardly, the eager crowd was nearly disenchanted. A tallish, fair boy, with dark, melancholy, and almost timorous eyes as he faced the people, a very high forehead, which lightly-curling locks combed back left entirely uncovered, a powerful arched nose which taken with the long advancing chin gave the whole physiognomy something of the look of an old woman, great ears, and a mouth moderately broad but with a look of tears and a preacher's earnestness— all this made one think sooner of a modern consecrated spirit of the newest day than of a cruel revolutionary.[3]

[3] Steiger, Edgar, *Das Werden des neuen Dramas*, Vol. 1, p. 3.

In a twinkling, this same surprised young man, identified
by many with Loth, the socialist of the play, had a fine
assortment of epithets bestowed upon him: "the reformer
of art," "political anarchist," "grossest of naturalists," "the
dramatist of the odious," "the most immoral playwright of
the century," "the savior of literary art."

This second production of the Freie Bühne impressed
critics of life and literature for two reasons: first, a Berlin
public had shown interest, no, more, had become violently
factional over an art subject; second, a playwright had
swept aside all veils of theatricality and superficial optimism
and had shown society as he honestly believed it to be. The
note of triumph sounds again and again:

People were fighting over a question of art—who would have
thought that possible in the home of reserve officers? People
were exciting themselves—not over new cannon or gun-model 88,
not over the duty on grain or over trade-treaties, not over anti-
semites or socialists—no, over a new drama that for a few weeks
after it was published people had not simply bought, but wonder of wonders, read! I care not if the narrow circles of young
friends of the dramatist had by open and also secret agitation
prepared anxiously for the great day; the feverish stirring of
souls, the frantic clash of opinions, the blind exaltation, and the
blind hate as they showed themselves at the performance, could
not have been started artificially by foreign whispers, but were
the immediate effect of the drama itself. . . .

For the first time a man [Loth] walked over the German
stage, who openly and frankly gave as his view of the whole
existing society that it with all its furnishings was dedicated to
destruction. And that this creation of the dramatist spoke out
his creator's own view the entire drama proved; in it the filth
and degeneration of society was painted in pictures so grey that
the beholder felt loathing at the sight of human depravity. No
critic of society like Ibsen, who scourged its morals to elevate
them without shaking society to its foundations, was speaking
here to the very pillars of this society, but a citizen of the future

who had lost faith in the existing order and expected no more of it but who perceived in secret strength the upholders of a new structure. The new dramatic style with which this play conquered the stage was, at first, entirely forgotten in questions of the subject-matter, or when one spoke of it, one fused form and contents, art and ethics, so closely that one continually took sides over the truth or falseness of the work. Indeed, it was certainly less the new art garment of the play than its basic observation of society which unchained the embittered contention between the satiated and self-complacent and the conscientious, compassionate, and unacquiescing.[4]

Technique itself to many of the young literary men of Berlin seemed worthy of discussion. The critics combed the play for literary influences. Schlenther and Brahm and others waxed eloquent over the simplicity of the style, the elimination of theatrical conventions, the marvelous exactness of the dialect, which includes the more classic German of Berlin and several grades of Silesian provincialism. Critics did not fail to notice the fullness of character-delineation, approaching that of the novel, the sense of character development, particularly in Loth, who is not labeled for the spectator but gradually reveals his weakness and superficiality of thought as he would in actual existence, the blending of realism with lyric beauty in the love scene between Helene and Loth. (Can a naturalistic play have scenes of pure loveliness?) Already the Freie Bühne was accomplishing what Brahm declares one of the great tasks of the experimental theatre, the fostering of a critical interest in dramatic theory and technique, and a challenging and revaluation of forms.

To the audience of the Freie Bühne, now numbering a thousand, the reasons for the choice of the third program of the new theatre must have been puzzling. No glamor of a great success on a foreign stage illumined the play, no mys-

4 *Ibid.*, Vol. 1, p. 2.

tery of as yet unexplored possibilities. *Henriette Maréchal* was an attempt of the Goncourts, the French brother realists, to conquer the field of the drama, to embody in a play their advanced ideas on dramatic form. In spite of the sincere dramatic ideals of the playwrights and some delicacy of characterization, the drama is mediocre, cumbersome, unconvincing, and filled with conventional stage improbabilities, monologues, and tirades.

The next two evenings, on the contrary, were real successes. Tolstoy's *Power of Darkness* had been one of the triumphs of the Théâtre Libre. *Das Vierte Gebot* (*The Fourth Commandment*) of Anzengruber, though played at Vienna in 1878, was new to the Berlin stage. Fate lent assistance to popularizing the latter play, for the aged dramatist was too ill to accept Brahm's invitation to assist in the production, and died a few days later: the performance became a commemorative festival. Thus the Freie Bühne helped to emphasize Anzengruber's true merits and to establish his play in the repertoire of many stages.

The next evening *Die Familie Selicke* (*The Happy Family*) introduced two writers new to German theatre-goers, who had already exercised an enormous influence upon the German stage. Arno Holz and Johannes Schlaf were the originators of the German brand of naturalism, extreme naturalism, the painting of life which has for its aim an objective reproduction of actuality colored as little as possible by the author's temperament, as illustrated in *Papa Hamlet*. *Die Familie Selicke,* their first play, might have been considered another example of the drama "for the reformation of confirmed drunkards," as *Before Sunrise* had been denominated by the unsympathetic. Without the more revolting elements of *Before Sunrise,* this second play is thoroughly naturalistic in theme and manner. The plot is even simpler than that of Hauptmann's. On Christmas Eve a mother, grown daughter, and two young sons are waiting

by the bedside of the darling of the family, a little girl, who
is very ill, for the return of the husband and father. The
older daughter shows clearly that she is in love with a young
theological student, Toni, their roomer, who adores her and
expects to marry her as soon as he is established in a
parish. It is getting late, and still the father does not come.
Finally the young boys confess that he sometimes drinks a
little. In the second act the drunken father comes home
pathetically and ridiculously laden with Christmas pur-
chases. The mother upbraids him till Toni has to quiet him,
and he falls into a stupor. The child dies. In the third act
the daughter finds herself not only her mother's assistant
but the object of all the affection which had been lavished
upon the little girl. She sees that without cruelty to the
mother it is impossible to tear herself from the family, and
accordingly she and the young theologian renounce their
love or rather postpone it to some distant day which perhaps only a miracle can bring. The play has the heart-break
of monotonous, unspectacular heroism.

In naturalistic workmanship *Die Familie Selicke* is more
nearly perfect than *Vor Sonnenaufgang*. There are no passages which border on rhetoric like Loth's outbursts: Holz
and Schlaf had so great a horror of "paper speech," "paper
style," the words which might stand on the printed page, or
be declaimed from the lips of the actors but which would
never come from the mouths of human beings, that the dialogue is the broken, sometimes incoherent, speech of life
itself. "The authentic speech of men," Lewisohn calls it,
"not speech rewritten and rearranged in its order, nor above
all, heard with the merely literary instinct, but the humble
speech of our daily lives with its elisions, its hesitations and
iterations, its half-articulate sounds and cries, but also its
sting and sob and clutch." The drawing of character is as
exquisitely true as the dialogue: Holz and Schlaf had the
quick perception and the understanding of poets.

Unfortunately *Die Familie Selicke* was more popular with the literary critic than with the average play-goer. Audiences grew impatient at the slightness of the action and the over-abundance of details. Holz and Schlaf were not born dramatists, men of the theatre: they could apply their formula logically, they could create character, but the feeling for great scenes, not necessarily inconsistent with naturalism, was not theirs. In the minds of even the advanced audience of the free theatre this weakness could not be compensated for by even the marvellous atmosphere of the play, "grey and sombre like a day in winter, comfortless like the home of poor people." [5]

The next play, Arthur Fitger's *Von Gottes Gnaden* (*By Divine Right*), given May 4, 1890, succeeded neither with the general public nor with the critics. Conventional dialogue and technique made the play seem much older than its date, 1883. Its only entrée to an advanced theatre was the censor's ban, which its theme and plot had provoked. A young woman ruler of a petty state falls in love with and marries her foster brother, a child of the people who knows their sufferings and aspirations. His belief in their rights clashes with his wife's in the divine right of kings. In the inevitable conflict the people get control of the property of the land owners and the liberal ideas of the prince-consort triumph. Otto Brahm explained the failure of this play as a proof that his audiences were becoming accustomed to naturalism and no longer found the older technique attractive. He compared his hearers with Count Koltwrat, who, going out of an opera-house, remarked:

I detest this Wagner, I cannot understand him.

But, some one objected, it was Italian music which you just heard.

Yes, I know, he replied, it is *Norma*. But that's exactly it—

[5] Arnold, Robert F., *Das moderne Drama,* p. 194.

this music which used to give me so much pleasure I can't listen to today. Wagner has made me lose my taste for it. Wagner I don't yet like and *Norma* I don't like any longer.

The first season of the Freie Bühne closed with a second drama by the greatest of its new playwrights. Hauptmann's *Coming of Peace* (*Das Friedensfest*) was given June 1, 1890. The play has for a sub-title *A Family Catastrophe*. It is a series of scenes of friction and attempts at reconciliation in a family founded on an unsuitable and loveless marriage. The psychology is based on modern theories of heredity, environment, and determinism, showing the author moving in the same new world as Ibsen. Like the Scandinavian, Hauptmann suggests regeneration for one of his characters, a man whom inherited melancholy and unhappiness at home have pushed to the bounds of sanity, through the influence of the woman he loves. In this play, the woman, Ida, seems to have an impossible task. *The Coming of Peace* was successful though it did not awaken the enthusiasm of *Before Sunrise*. The dialogue was even more naturalistic than that of the earlier play.

During the season of 1890-1891 the stage society met for six evenings to see the following seven plays: *The Father* by Strindberg; *Angèle* by Otto Erich Hartleben; *Ohne Liebe* by Marie von Ebner-Eschenbach; *Lonely Lives* by Hauptmann; *The Crows* by Becque; *Der Doppelselbstmord* by Anzengruber; *Thérèse Raquin* by Zola.

The Father was chosen by Brahm as a careful psychological document. Before its production Schlenther wrote in the *Freie Bühne:*

Here [in *The Father*] as there [in *Ghosts*] there develops, up to the final catastrophe, in a style strictly realistic without the customary *pons asinorum* of awkward and hackneyed stage devices, the pathological history of a distraught brain. . . . This work might be called the tragedy of nerves, the man and woman

wear each other out, and in the case of the man, this play of
nerves becomes irritating in the extreme; the woman pushes
the man to madness. [Later, after the performance, he felt that
perhaps he had exaggerated the realistic element of the play.]
The strait-jacket [which the captain is forced to wear in the
final scene of madness] seemed less like the inevitable result of
circumstances than the motiveless and individual ferocity of a
poet who hates woman.

Hartleben's *Angèle* expresses a misogyny, the origin of
which is in Nietzsche. The printed play is headed with the
cynical quotation, ". . . and for how much pure joy, how
much patience, how much kindness are we indebted to our
ability to scorn. Delicate contempt is our liking and our
privilege, our art, our virtue, perhaps." Angèle, the heroine,
plays with and deceives three lovers, a middle-aged man,
his son, and "a good young man," a theological student. Her
contempt is always kept in a vein of serene irony. Written
in 1886, this comedy showed the German liking for the
genre *comédie rosse,* the bitterly conceived play of the clever
and unprincipled. This admiration also determined the
choice of *The Crows.* Zola's name and the brutal melodrama
of the play itself probably determined the choice of *Thérèse
Raquin,* with which the second season and the regular productions of the Freie Bühne closed.

Even after 1891, however, when performances at regular
intervals were discontinued, the Freie Bühne was not entirely disbanded. When need was urgent, it became again the
theatre of the vanguard in the struggle for the new. During
1892 it gave Strindberg's *Miss Julia* its first production in
Berlin; in February of the new year it rose in loyalty to
its best-loved child when Hauptmann's *Weavers* had been
forbidden performance at the Deutsches Theater; later, it
saved *Dämmerung* by Ernst Rosmer from the oblivion to
which commercial producers had consigned it. Even when

there was no need of rescue work Otto Brahm sometimes honored his old friends of the free theatre by giving a promising new drama at the Deutsches Theater under their banner: plays as varied as *The Mother* of George Hirschfeld, *Frau am Fenster* of Hofmannsthal, and *Mutter Maria* of Ernst Rosmer, have appeared in this way.

The Freie Bühne closed, as all historians agree, from a dearth of naturalistic plays, not because such plays were not being written but because an enlightened public and awakened managers were making possible their performance at the larger theatres. The warfare which had begun with the Freie Bühne's production of *Ghosts* and *Before Sunrise* had been marked by victory in 1891, when L'Arronge accepted *Lonely Lives* at the Deutsches Theater soon after its performance by the society. At the same time Sudermann, with *Die Ehre,* and Max Halbe, with *Freie Liebe,* both plays of realism, were able to reach the large stages at once, and dramatists of the old school like Wildenbruch and Ludwig Fulda were undergoing at least a temporary conversion to naturalism. New dramatists of naturalism seemed to emerge each day. When, in 1894, Otto Brahm passed to the directorship of the Deutsches Theater, naturalism triumphed. The experimental theatre did not have the means or the desire to compete with these larger theatres. "It lies in the nature of the experiment," Brahm has written of the Freie Bühne, "that its greatest victory is its end."

Though short-lived compared with its French prototype, the Freie Bühne had a definite influence upon the course of modern drama. In the first place, like the Théâtre Libre, the Berlin stage society was a much-needed means of introducing its audiences to foreign drama, particularly the plays of Ibsen and Strindberg which elsewhere in Berlin could be seen only during some momentary lapse of the censor. Second, to a limited degree, the Freie Bühne was an encourager of young writers: while Antoine's theatre in its first season introduced ten new authors, Brahm's theatre discovered only three. But one of these was Hauptmann. Third, the Freie Bühne was a force for raising the standards of commercial drama though its influence came as much through its proclamation of aims as through its somewhat inconsistent practice. Although frequently a leader in the use of new subjects and new technique in play-writing, the first German free theatre was not revolutionary in acting and stage production. Its standards in these arts were those of the better public theatres, which the actors and managers usually represented. Finally, in the work of several of its playwrights and in Holz's remarkable analysis of the principles of art, the theatre pushed the theory of naturalism to its uttermost bounds. This theory merits some explanation.

Arno Holz, disciple of Zola, brooding upon the nature of art, found that he was unable to accept a statement of the master's, "Art is life seen through a temperament." Rather, to be accurate, he accepted this statement, but found it a truism, of slight general application, like many another fact, that rats have tails, for instance. One day he picked up a paper upon which a small child had been drawing. "What is this?" he asked as he held up the quite indecipherable sketch,—to be answered, "A soldier." The idea of the child's approach to art became the starting-point of the theory which Holz evolved. The child, he reasoned, was not successful, both because he had defective instruments and because he did not know how to use them. Revolving the whole matter in his mind, he passed to the contemplation of a theory of "logical" naturalism, which has never been equalled in its rigor,—a naturalism which should reflect life with absolute photographic accuracy. Instead of admitting and approving the presence of temperament in art as the French had done, in the belief that the so-called "raw slice of life" must be subjected to some slight culinary process, Holz deplored any departure from absolute objectivity.

He expresses his views in a series of equations. The ideal of the artist should be, he thinks, faithful imitation of nature. If man, he says, were only able to imitate nature completely, the relation of art to life could be stated thus: *Art = Nature*. But, unfortunately, man's talent and knowledge are limited: therefore, Holz alters the equation to *Art = Nature* — x, with x representing the lack of complete power and knowledge. X will diminish with experience but can never be reduced to zero. And yet observation shows Holz that even this formula is imperfect. It must be modified by the objectionable element of temperament, y. In reality, *Art = Nature* — x + y; in ideal, *Art = Nature*.

Such a discussion would almost justify the definition of the naturalistic writer which an art critic has given:

A naturalist is a man with a native gift for science who has taken to art. His purpose is not to extract the material and spiritual significance of objects, thus communicating them to us more rapidly and intensely than we should perceive them ourselves and thereby giving us a sense of heightened vitality; his purpose is research, and his communication consists of nothing but facts.[6]

For we do not have to be poets to realize that Holz's view disregards not only imagination and fancy, but all reflection, invention, all reactions to the recurring problems of existence. To correct the formula we must add z, *Art = Nature* — x + y + z. Z is indefinable, boundless, the power of selection, of vision, of creation. In z are the Gothic cathedral, the Greek temple, the seacoast of Bohemia, tragedy, farce, fairyland.[7] Nevertheless, by its very exaggera-

[6] Berenson, quoted by Meyer, E. Stockton, "The Modern German Drama," the *Critic*, July, 1905, p. 66.

[7] Benoist-Hanappier, L., *Le Drame Naturaliste en Allemagne*, p. 42.

tions, logical naturalism was the curative which its age needed: close observation of men and women, their environments and their longings, and an emphasis upon the hidden drama of humble and monotonous lives. This is perhaps the greatest contribution of the German experimental theatre in its early days.

The Freie Bühne had many imitators, which may be grouped in three general divisions: stage societies, people's theatres, and art theatres.

The first of these stage societies, organized in Berlin the year after the Freie Bühne, was the Deutsche Bühne, whose sponsors were Karl Bleibtreu and Konrad Alberti,—leaders of the new movement in literature and art who had not been invited to share in the management of the older society,— Max Stempel, and George Zimmerman, the Saxon dialect writer. The Deutsche Bühne did not approve of the *Ausländerei,* the emphasis upon foreign drama of the older group, and sought to present exclusively the work of young Germans, particularly those of socialistic tendencies. At the opening performance at the Central Theater, Bleibtreu's own play of Napoleon, *Schicksal,* was presented. Later came Adam Guttenbrunn's *Irma,* Alberti's *Brot,* Hermann Bahr's *Neue Menschen,* and Stempel's *Morphium.* This theatre was not epoch-making. Another Berlin society, the Fresko-Bühne, also failed of great success.

Munich, center of art and of music as well as of drama, watched the experiment within the Berlin theatre from its early days. An unsuccessful attempt at a free theatre two years after the founding of the Freie Bühne was followed in 1895 by Max Halbe's Intimes Theater (Intimate Theater). Here on a bare stage, even for naturalistic plays, a group of young writers acted before a small audience, also of writers. The theatre was unique in drawing its players, except the Hungarian actress, Juliane Déry, from its own circle of amateurs. Prominent among these were Julius

Schaumberger, Ernst von Wolzogen, Franz Held, and Halbe himself.

Meanwhile, many student societies, Akademische Vereine, were springing up, particularly in Berlin, Munich, and Vienna. By giving striking plays, both classical and modern, these groups often influenced the commercial stage. Berlin students gave *Œdipus the King* and *Orestes* in a German translation; Munich students, Hebbel's *Julia*, von Hofmannsthal's *Der Tor und der Tod*, Wilde's *Salome*, Ibsen's *Ghosts* and *Rosmersholm*, Sudermann's *Sodoms Ende* and Hirschfeld's *Zu Hause*, while the Munich Hoftheater and Gärtnerplatz Theater were still closed to plays of their type. The founder and moving spirit of the Munich society was the Ernst von Wolzogen of the Intimes Theater. In 1896 he also founded in Munich the short-lived Deutsches Theater, after the model of the Berlin house of the same name, and, two years later, he was one of the organizers of the Litterarische Gesellschaft. The Vienna dramatic association staged the first German production of *Peer Gynt* and gave many dramas by Euripides, Goethe, Maeterlinck, and Hauptmann.

Immensely important for the size of their audiences and the extent of their influence were and still are the folk-theatres or people's stages. Until the Great War nothing like them had existed outside Germany, though there had been attempts to introduce the idea in both England and America. This offshoot of the general experimental theatre movement was inspired only in part by a desire for the reform of the existing theatre and owes much of its driving power to German socialism. Long before the establishment of the Freie Bühne a number of advanced thinkers in Berlin had proposed a great theatre for working men with dramas at popular prices selected for their appeal to the worker and for their bearing upon socialism and other modern subjects. The Verein zur Gründung deutscher Volksbühnen under the leadership of Baron von Malzahn, the painter Karl Emil

Doepler, and other art lovers held several meetings without accomplishing their purpose. Another suggestion was that a royal theatre should be established with free performances for the poor, in the fashion of the Roman emperors' gifts of *panem et circenses* (bread and festivals).

The first plan to come to fulfilment was modeled on Brahm's stage society and founded by a young man who had watched its career, Dr. Bruno Wille. His interests were not exclusively dramatic: he had been a theological student and was now a philosopher of materialistic and atheistic tendencies, much concerned with problems of modern life. Associated with him were the ex-actor, Julius Türk, and Wilhelm Bölsche, a student of philosophy and æsthetics who had lived much in Paris and had carried on investigations into the scientific basis of literature. All three were active members of the social-democratic party. Their union in a folk-stage movement was a particularly happy one, for Wille and Bölsche were known as fellow-socialists to thousands of working men, and Türk was familiar with their dramatic tastes and demands. Wille's name drew together two thousand workmen for a public discussion on July 29, 1890. The presence on the platform of the socialists, Wildberger and Baake, and of the literary man, Otto Brahm, was significant of the double aim of this people's theatre: to advance a political party and to serve the dictates of true dramatic art. Its ideal, as Wille outlined it, was a social-democratic organization bringing before its audiences plays which offer a social criticism of life; it was to turn its back on the out-dated drawing of the beautiful and concern itself with an honest facing of actual existence. "And this was the word," Brahm wrote, "which like a *leitmotiv* rang through the assembly: Give us truth! We will not have classical and romantic works; we want realistic, in which the pressure toward truth and actuality of the time expresses itself; we will see life as it is, not as it is not."

This Freie Volksbühne (the Berlin Free People's Stage), with a membership of six hundred, opened at the Ostend Theater, Sunday afternoon, October 19, 1890, with *Pillars of Society*. The second performance, imitative of the Freie Bühne, was *Before Sunrise*. Then followed several brilliant seasons, with plays, foreign and native, largely in the realistic mood: Schiller's *Die Raüber* and *Kabale und Liebe;* Hebbel's *Maria Magdalena;* Otto Ludwig's *Der Erbförster;* Ibsen's *Ghosts;* Anzengruber's *Der Doppelselbstmord;* Zola's *Thérèse Raquin;* Gogol's *The Reviser;* Pissemsky's *Der Leibeigene;* Fulda's *Das Verlorene Paradies, Dis Sklavin;* Sudermann's *Die Ehre;* Hauptmann's *Die Weber;* Halbe's *Eisgang*. Season tickets, drawn by lot, were at first fifty pfennigs, later ninety. By 1908 the society numbered twelve thousand. The custom of Sunday performances here, as at the Freie Bühne, became so popular that several of the commercial theatres adopted it and the society had occasional difficulty in providing itself with adequate casts.

The other great free folk stage of Berlin, the Neue Freie Volksbühne, also founded by Wille, resulted from a rather amusing incident. The police of Berlin, long accustomed to hearing the Folk Stage referred to as a social-democratic theatre, decided to treat it as a political organization and attempted to bar women, who were then without the right of political assemblage, from its audiences. Wille drew a fine distinction between socialistic propaganda and the artistic expression of socialistic ideals, and won his case in the courts. On his return to the society which he had saved from dissolution, he was startled by an accusation that he was no socialist; indeed, the members, who had much power, voted him out of the directorate. His next theatre was organized on the same plan as the first except that the members were not given majority representation on the executive committee. Wille's helpers in this second plan included Maximilian Harden, Hartleben, the brothers Kampfmeyer—now successful playwrights—Emil Lessing, who later became a prominent theatre director, and the composer, Victor Hollander.

This New Free People's Theater opened November, 1892, with Goethe's *Faust,* at the Belle-Alliance Theater. The greatest success of its early years was Hauptmann's *The Weavers,* which tripled the membership of the society and aroused the helpless wrath of the police who had forbidden its production before a general audience. Later the authorities retaliated, at the time of the presentation of *Alone,* by demanding to censor all pieces. Wille kept the society inactive for some time and by secret diplomacy managed to win his own way. Later directors have been Ludwig Jacobowske and Joseph Ettlinger. Except for a brief period of financial stress in 1903, the society has been prosperous. At the time when Reinhardt was staging *Salome* and *A Night's Lodging* at the Kleines Theater, the New Free Folk Stage was able by special arrangement to include certain performances at the Kleines and then at other theatres in its season, at an additional cost of about fourteen marks to a subscriber. In 1914 the fifty thousand members could make their choice of a varied repertoire at their own playhouse and special Sunday afternoon performances at a dozen theatres. The theatrical fare in one year included works by Schnitzler, Strindberg, Wedekind, Wilde, Ibsen, Shaw, and Tolstoy.

A year or two before the Great War both of these powerful organizations, affiliated at last though not completely merged, had dreamed of theatre homes of their own and had made significant beginnings. The New Society in particular had been most ingenious in encouraging small contributions from a great number of people by adding a tax of ten pfennigs to each ticket and selling building fund stamps. A comparatively small sum allowed the giver to vote upon questions connected with the new project. Though a great deal of money had been collected in small amounts there was not enough to finance an undertaking involving the equivalent of several hundred thousand dollars. Finally the city of Berlin decided to take a mortgage on the building. In the fall of 1913 ground was broken on Kaiser-Wilhelm-strasse for the first real People's Theater of modern times, the possession of the New Free People's Stage Society. The next difficult years saw only slow progress; however, the building was completed before the coming of peace.

The work is a triumph for Oskar Kaufmann, the architect, Franz Metzner, the sculptor, and many other artists. An impressive building of grey stone, austere and dignified, modernistic rather through the formalism of the simplified human figures in its ornamentation than through any startling quality of its architecture, is this crystallization of the vision of a multitude. The statues of men and women whose bodies, distorted by life and toil, are yet curiously decorative in an almost symbolic treatment give way to figures with a suggestion of more classic beauty between the superbly plain columns grouped about the entrance, above which are the carved words, "Die Kunst dem Volke" (Art for the People).

Within, the spacious auditorium faced with red mahogany, comfortable corridors, and refreshment rooms care for the well-being of many thousands who come to this, their club, their home. The stage possesses every device which a German producer considers desirable for the interpretation of a play according to old or new methods. With a group of other Americans, little theatre producers and teachers of the drama, I was shown these wonders,—the inner adjustable proscenium arch for narrowing the playing space for intimate drama, the cyclorama, the projectors for throwing a pictured background of unmoving lines or all the moving lights and shadows of clouds or changing waves, the revolving platform. I visited also, under the guidance of Herr

Fuhr, scenic designer, the studios where the settings and costumes originate in enthusiastic and untiring hands. As I paused at the rehearsal platform for a last view of the auditorium, looking toward the stage where soon a rehearsal of *Danton's Death* would begin, and again toward the seats in which, assigned by lot and paying only a mark and three-quarters for a play and two marks and a half for an opera, one hundred and fifty thousand people in the course of a few evenings would behold the same drama, I caught, as I believe I never had before, a realization of what the will, the unfailing devotion, and the careful organization of an enormous number of people of humble means can accomplish. My wonder grew as I was told of the activities of a minority—but a minority of thirty thousand—which finances a special communistic program.

No question can be more interesting to a student of the experimental theatre than what one hundred and fifty thousand people, many of them just escaping actual privation, demand of their playhouse. The answer is heartening, for there has never been any catering to an inferior taste: indeed many of the plays chosen are those which so-called "high-brow" theatres in other countries offer to limited audiences. Anzengruber, Shaw, Fulda, Shakespeare, Grillparzer, Ibsen, Sudermann, Halbe, Hauptmann, Strindberg, Maeterlinck, Dreyer, and Schnitzler have been favorites. In the official list of plays of the five years between 1914 and 1919 Shakespeare leads with twelve plays; Ibsen is second with ten; Hauptmann, third with eight; Goethe and Schiller follow, with five each; Anzengruber, Schnitzler, Sudermann, with four. There are evidences of the emergence of the new post-war drama in the work of Kaiser and Werfel.

Other theatres with the folk-ideal, less successful than Wille's, were established during the next few years: the Schiller-Theater in Berlin under the direction of Raphael Löwenfeld, which had for its première *The Robbers*, August

30, 1894; the Freie Volksbühne of Hamburg, under Gustav Falk and Otto Ernst, opening with *Before Sunrise* in 1893; a Charlottenburg group which presented Hartleben's *Die Befreiten* in March, 1906; since 1907 a Charlottenburg branch of the Berlin Schiller-Theater; a Vienna Free Folk Stage, led by Grossman, showing the influence of Russia in producing Andreiev's *To the Stars*. The Hofburgtheater at Vienna has also joined the movement with classic matinées at popular prices. The Vienna stage has always followed the ideals of the German stage.

This idea of the people's stage society has traveled through much of Germany until now almost three hundred groups in other cities and towns are affiliated with the great organizations of Berlin. These other societies, many of them weak and struggling, make what arrangements they can for the good of their members, sometimes a large part of the inhabitants of the town. Several stage societies work through the local theatres, others support town-owned playhouses, still others encourage traveling companies, particularly three sent out by the general federation.

Combining the aims of stage societies and people's theatres are the Freie Litterarische Gesellschaften (The Associations of Free Literary Societies) branches of which have sprung up in several German cities,—Leipzig, Hamburg, Breslau, Attendorn, Stettin, Nuremberg among them,—with the ambition of becoming people's colleges, including in their work not only producing plays, but arranging lectures and recitals. At these associations men of letters have been glad to appear. One of the most successful of these people's clubs is that of Leipzig, organized by Dr. Walter Harlan and helped by Carl Heine, well-known director and scenic artist, which gives an amazing number of important plays in a single year. For mutual assistance many of these societies and other free theatres have banded together as a Verband deutscher litterarischer Gesellschaften, with the dramatist, Ludwig Fulda, as president and their organ of expression the *Magazin für Litteratur.*

This list, of course, is not a complete catalogue of German stage societies, people's theatres, and other organizations experimenting with the new in theme or technique. Besides names of theatre societies whose work was too intermittent to leave any significant record, as the Probebühne, the Versuchsbühne, and the Dramatische Gesellschaft, there are undoubtedly others. In 1894 a touring company, the Theater der Modernen, headed by Emil Messthaler, traveled across Germany awakening much enthusiasm. In its repertory of twenty-eight plays were *Musotte, Jugend, Ghosts, Thérèse Raquin, Sodoms Ende,* and *Lonely Lives.* In Austria by 1890 the Deutsches Volkstheater began to give "modern" plays, *Der Fleck auf der Ehr'* of Anzengruber; *Eva* and *Schuldig* of R. Voss; *Sodoms Ende; Die Haubenlerche* of Wildenbruch; *Ghosts* and *The Wild Duck.* Meanwhile the Burgtheater under Dr. Max Burckhardt became fitfully naturalistic, including in its repertory plays by Fulda and Hauptmann. In 1898 Paul Schlenther, biographer of Hauptmann, became Burckhardt's successor.

Of the German art theatres with their new types of stages and new methods of stage setting much has been written in the last few years; nevertheless, since the art theatre is an experimental, even revolutionary form, any historian of the new, at the risk of the charge of superficiality, must include at least a brief summary of it and an account of its leader, his conquest of the German stage, his part in elevating Berlin to the capital city of the European theatre, and his latest vision of creating out of a little mountain city in the Austrian Alps the festival center of the world.

Reinhardt's activity within the theatre, spanning more than half a lifetime, began in 1894 when, at nineteen, leaving his home in Vienna, he started acting in the Municipal Theatre at Salzburg, in the Austrian Alps. He was enjoying the elderly character parts in which he was appearing and was entranced by the charm and beauty of the mountains, the castle on the hill, the river, when Otto Brahm of the Deutsches Theater, still the leading figure among German producers, happened to spend an evening at Salzburg and was taken to the Municipal Theatre to see the performance of a favorite leading man. The Berlin director surprised himself and Reinhardt by offering him and not the star a two-year contract at the Deutsches. Reinhardt signed this, later repenting as he contemplated the loveliness of Salzburg. Only Doctor Brahm's firmness brought the boy into the stir and excitement of Berlin at a period which was already giving indications of artistic expansion.

The Deutsches Theater, built a decade before in the intent to provide a German rival to the Comédie Française and the Burgtheater of Vienna, was still engrossed in realistic productions in the mood which the Freie Bühne had fostered. Here Reinhardt had the opportunity to study the conscientious following of a theory of acting and stage setting which evolved consistent, if somewhat drab, and now and then uninspired, productions, for, on the whole, the Deutsches Theater was superior to the other German stages. Here he became one of Brahm's ensemble, acting very successfully parts of old men, Foldal (*John Gabriel Borkman*), Baumert (*The Weavers*), and Luka (*The Lower Depths*). Meanwhile he amused himself and his friends in a very original cabaret, Schall und Rauch, "Sound and Smoke," which gave him the longing for a tiny, intimate stage.

This desire was fulfilled in the Kleines Theater, the first real stage of his own. Here and at the Neues Theater, from 1902 to 1905, he produced nearly fifty plays representative of many countries and of many artistic tendencies: *The Pretenders* and *Rosmersholm*, rather than Ibsen's plays of realism; *Pelléas et Mélisande, Sister Beatrice; Candida,* before it had been produced in England; Lessing's *Minna von Barnhelm* and Schiller's *Kabale und Liebe* (Love and Intrigue); and plays by young writers now famous largely through Reinhardt's early understanding and sympathy,— von Hofmannsthal's *Elektra*, Richard Beer-Hofmann's *Der Graf von Charolais* (The Count of Charolais), Wedekind's *So ist das Leben* (Such is Life), Schnitzler's *Der Grüne Kakadu* (The Green Cockatoo) and *Der tapfere Cassian* (The Gallant Cassian). Though the list is most eclectic, including comparatively little of naturalism and of the classics, the play in which Reinhardt conquered the Berlin public was *The Lower Depths,* and the play in which he became known throughout Germany was *Midsummer Night's Dream,* produced in 1905. In his fantastic and lovely presentation of this comedy, which, like other Shakespearean plays, had lost much of its light and humanity through over-zealous academic enthusiasm, Reinhardt encouraged the neo-romantic movement. This had been silently budding even during the period of naturalism, that naturalism which reached its height with *The Weavers* and showed a waning in the transitional *Hannele*.

In 1905 Reinhardt followed Lindau, Brahm's immediate successor, at the Deutsches: ten years had seen the young actor and producer climb from the obscurity of a provincial stage to the managership of the most famous and influential house in Berlin. Here no production could escape comment; Reinhardt was forced by dramatic critics to compete with Doctor Brahm now at the Lessing Theater, and to hear its adherents label with wearisome monotony the Deutsches productions "mere stage decorations." But Reinhardt continued to hold his Berlin public whether he revived Greek tragedy or Shakespearean comedy or gave the first performance of a drama of super-subtle psychological analysis or of elaborate spectacle.

No lover of plays has believed more fervently than

Reinhardt in the composite nature of the acted play, the coöperation and interdependence of playwright, actors, producer, scenic artists, and the audience. To this list might be added the auditorium itself, which Reinhardt treats as though it possessed a soul. Remembering the days of Schall und Rauch and the Kleines Theater, he dreamed of a tiny playhouse, a jewel casket which should contain the more fragile or the more intimate of his creations. As chamber music is to a giant orchestra, so this little theatre should be to the greater. Brown, quietly paneled in oak, the Kammerspiele recalls to its admirers the violin, that poignant, intimate, single voice. The Kammerspiele, opening with *Ghosts* in 1906, has housed Wedekind's *Frühlingserwachen* (*The Awakening of Spring*), tragedy of childhood; *Man and Superman; The Coming of Peace; Love's Comedy; The Doctor's Dilemma; Lysistrata* of Aristophanes in Greiner's version; Halbe's *Freiheit;* and a myriad more. Reinhardt's policy has been to produce here only what really benefits by the smallness of the auditorium; the plays which do not require this individual atmosphere go directly to the larger house. Occasionally a play opening in one theatre proves better adapted to the other, and a change is made.

This management of two theatres has given Reinhardt an unusual opportunity to experiment in many moods and to build up a superb organization of players, artists, and designers. Among his players have been Alexander Moissi of Italian and Albanian blood, in whose genius Reinhardt believed before the German audiences were convinced even of his talent; Max Pallenberg, rescued from the musical comedy stage; Rudolf and Joseph Schildkraut, and Emil Jannings, now as famous in America as in Central Europe; Else Heims; Gertrud Eysoldt; Agnes Sorma; Helene Thimig; Asta Fleming; and many others. The madonnas of his three productions of *The Miracle,* Lady Diana Manners, Maria Carmi, Rosamond Pinchot, have come from England,

Italy, America. Richard Ordynski, now producing in the United States, was trained under Reinhardt; Edvard Munch, Max Rée, Alfred Roller, Mahler, Fritz Erler, Wilhelm Dietz, Emil Orlik are artists of several nations who have designed for the Reinhardt playhouses. Richard Strauss, the composer, and Hugo von Hofmannsthal, the dramatist, have worked for these same theatres and other theatres which Reinhardt has discovered and made his own, —the square before an Austrian cathedral, a church interior. He has taken suggestions from revolutionaries like Craig and from stages of Oriental nations: in *Sumurûn*, a runway from the wings was used most effectively; in *Julius Cæsar*, a long flight of steps down which the dictator fell under the knives of the conspirators; in *The Miracle*, elaborate ecclesiastical architecture. Reinhardt's catholicity of taste in both choice of plays and methods of production appears in his world-famous successes,—*The Lower Depths, Midsummer Night's Dream, The Yellow Jacket, The God of Vengeance, Œdipus Rex.*

The repertory system at the Deutsches and the Kammerspiele during Reinhardt's Berlin years was a model for Europe. It combined the opportunity for careful production, simple or elaborate as the individual play demanded, with that economy, born of true appreciation of dramatic art, which does not let a play perish after its first long run. Granville Barker has described a representative week at the Reinhardt houses in the autumn of 1910: the Deutsches Theater presented *Sumurûn*, a pantomime based on the Arabian Nights, twice; *Midsummer Night's Dream, Faust,* Hebbel's *Judith*, and Fulda's *Herr und Diener* each once; the Kammerspielhaus, *The Comedy of Errors* and *Le Mariage Forcé* three times; *The Doctor's Dilemma*, Edward Stucken's *Gavân*, and William Schmidtbonn's *Der Graf von Gleichen* one performance each. Of these Reinhardt productions *Midsummer Night's Dream* dated from the days of the

Neues Theater and had passed its five hundredth performance; *Faust,* from the preceding season, was playing for the one hundred and fourteenth time; *Sumurûn,* only a few months old, for the fiftieth; *The Doctor's Dilemma,* for the one hundred and thirteenth time. The others were much more recent, *Herr und Diener* having just appeared in the repertory. The theatres together were showing some twenty new productions a season, and, Granville Barker stated, "in one week a greater variety of good drama than any two London theatres will give in a year."

The work of these theatres and of the Düsseldorfer Schauspielhaus in a German manufacturing city under the direction of Gustav Lindemann and his wife, Louise Dumont, prompted Granville Barker to reaffirm his creed of the repertory theatre:

A repertory theatre is not an institution for producing plays successfully and removing them from the bill as soon as the public manifests a wish to see them. Nor is it a theatre for producing plays foredoomed to failure, though some do maintain that there is evidence in support of this definition. Repertory is not the production of one new play a week or a fortnight or a month. It is not the putting on of the "new" drama; or the "uncommercial," or "intellectual" or even the "serious" play. Nor has it anything particular to do with Socialism. It is not necessarily a philanthropic enterprise nor is it the idea of a lunatic.

It is the putting plays in a theatre as books are put in a well-used library. A book must be upon the shelves that one man may take it down. Plays are hardly as portable as that. But a theatre so organized that, having produced a play and justified its production, it can keep the play reasonably ready for use while it is likely that five or six hundred people at a time will want to see it, is a repertory theatre.[8]

[8] From "Two German Theaters," by Granville Barker, *Fortnightly Review.* Courtesy of the Publishers, New York.

The Kammerspiele was only the beginning of Reinhardt's innovations. In 1908 he was called to Munich by a group of artists to experiment at the Künstler Theater with an adaptable proscenium arch over a narrow stage on which the actors and actresses were to be thrown into relief in a moving silhouette design. This "relief stage" proved too limited for Reinhardt to carry its method into many plays, but the experience helped him in his Molière revivals at the Kammerspiele. At the same time he was amusing himself with the possibilities of the revolving stage, the invention of Lautenschlager, first used for Mozart's operas at the Munich Residenztheater. These elaborate revolving and sliding stages of a few years ago marked a great increase of interest in the problems of the stage and are still being modified and improved in the German theatres.

In contrast to the Kammerspiele, the house for the few, Reinhardt long ago began to toy with the thought of a gigantic playhouse, "the theatre of the five thousand." This should hold as many spectators as the sky-vaulted amphitheatre of the Athenian tragedy, the market-place of a medieval mystery, or a great cathedral on a festival day. He meditated upon the need of self-expression in the impoverished lives of the masses, on the stupidity and coarseness of many of the films devised for their benefit, and also on a likeness,—capable perhaps of being pushed too far,—between the "release" of the individual sharing the emotion of a throng at a great dramatic spectacle and the consolation and atonement of religion.

A vast hall in Munich became the scene of Reinhardt's first festival drama, Sophocles' *Œdipus Rex*, 1906. This was later given in Vienna, Budapest, Berlin (Zirkus Schumann), London, many Polish and Russian cities, and Stockholm. Here, as in later festival dramas, every device possible narrowed the physical and spiritual distance between spectators and actors: the proximity of audience to the actors, the use of lights and shadows to throw into relief only what the director chose to emphasize, the magnificent training of the chorus till, whether words were spoken or sung, the group became a tremendous instrument for awakening emotion, and the drenching of everything with music.

Here [writes one of the critics discussing Reinhardt and his training of the chorus] he does change into the dictator. *His* will penetrates all these players, *his* feeling pulses through them all, with *his* voice they all shout. When we see these masses of humanity changed into one being, as it were, torn between passionate hate or love, fear or joy, as in "Julius Caesar," "Oedipus Rex," "Danton," or "The Miracle," a terrible thought suddenly strikes us: Was not the whole world recently such a mass of humanity, such a "theatre chorus," when the dreadful tragedy of the late war was staged? Was it not merely such a shouting, gesticulating mass driven by instinct, it knew not why nor whither? Truly, indeed, the stage is the symbol of life.[9]

At the beginning of the Great War, Reinhardt had already produced besides *Œdipus Rex, Æschylus' Oresteia, The Miracle* by the playwright Karl Vollmoeller and the composer Humperdinck. The last, by which Reinhardt is best known in America through Morris Gest's production, is an elaboration of the medieval story of the nun who escapes from the convent into the world while the Madonna steps from her shrine to perform her duties. It was first given in Olympia Hall, London, a building erected for exhibitions that require much space. In the necessary reconstruction a rose window, three times the size of that of Notre Dame, was opened to illuminate dimly the forms of thousands of performers and more than twenty thousand spectators. In Berlin, Reinhardt used two great interiors, the Zirkus Schumann and the Zirkus Busch. The War and the Revolution

[9] From "The Evolution of Reinhardt," by Frank E. Washburn-Freund in *Max Reinhardt and His Theatre,* edited by Oliver M. Sayler, p. 56. Courtesy of Brentano's, Publishers, New York.

were over before he was to possess his own gigantic play-house.

No one can appraise the recent accomplishment of Max Reinhardt and his countrymen without understanding something of the spirit of the German theatre during that great conflict, the ensuing days of confusion, and the organization of the republic. Equally amazing are the vigorous life of the German theatre throughout these troubled years—a history paralleled only by the Russian—and its profound search for reality during the last decade. Since warfare ceased, this search by young writers whose lives at a critical period had been touched by a devastating force has been magnificently scornful of all convention in theme and technique. Many critics find this body of dramatic literature the most original produced in Europe since pre-war days.

For in London and Paris the theatre as anything more than a house of entertainment nearly ceased in the early days of the War. The little theatres of the advance guard could rarely maintain their personnel before the inroads of the recruiting officer; the commercial theatres were absorbed in securing unforeseen profits out of the multitude of soldiers on leave, and discovered, or thought they discovered, that the lower the appeal the greater the receipts. They pushed on to the stage every kind of farce, revue, and dubious hybrid performance.

But it was not so in Germany. The German theatre was doubly protected, first, by the historic attitude of the nation toward drama, the belief that it should handle deep and fundamental situations and problems, retelling man's eternal warfare with himself and with the external world; and secondly, by the almost perfect organization of the German theatre system. This system includes the state or municipally-owned theatres which present the classics, ancient or modern, the subscription theatres which are alert for the new and experimental, and the large commercial theatres which introduce recent playwrights who have survived the test of the little theatre. Nearly all the important theatres are stabilized by their dependence upon the repertory system, which is accepted as a matter of course. The work of these theatres all over Germany was little affected by the war. Two typical state playhouses of Cologne, a city within the zone of air raids, in 1916-1917, were giving between them over two hundred performances of opera and even more of drama. They gave much Shakespeare (the Teutonic claim to Shakespeare, often asserted during this period, rests upon the German enthusiasm for him), Goethe, Schiller, Grillparzer, Hebbel, and present day writers, Hauptmann, Sudermann, Schnitzler, Fulda, Wedekind. In Berlin Wedekind's *The Box of Pandora* was very popular. Indeed Wedekind's disillusionment and cynicism, the mood of the "danse macabre," one of the dominant themes of recent German drama, made him anticipate the spirit of the next period; he is often claimed by the expressionists.

Gradually a new emphasis began to appear in the choice of plays for revival, the importations from foreign drama, and the mood of the younger German playwrights,—this last expressed furtively during the struggle but openly after the Revolution had ended censorship. The main currents just before the War, which was, of course, several years after naturalism had declined, were the historical drama of Wildenbruch under the influence of Schiller; modern treatments of classical subjects, as *Der Zorn des Achilles* of William Schmidtbonn and *Achill* of "Ernst Rosmer" (Elsa Bernstein); a fitful neo-romanticism; and a mystical and at the same time decorative use of the Arthurian legends in the plays of Edward Stucken, *Gavân, Lanvâl, Lanzelot*, in which Avelun, the Avalon of the English poets, becomes a symbol of the longing for death. The German playwrights had reacted from the ethical and social subjects which have stimulated other nationalities to their best work. With the war came a new worship of national heroes in revivals of Schiller's *Wallenstein* and Goethe's *Götz,* and a deepened understanding of the tragedies of the Greeks and of Shakespeare. Meanwhile a spirit conceived under the militaristic régime but in revolt against it, gloried in the downfall of tyrants as Kleist's Hermann, Hebbel's Holofernes, Grabbe's Kaiser Heinrich VI, Grillparzer's Ottokar; conversely, it exalted revolutionaries almost to deification.

It was in the midst of this surging of awakened democracy, of hatred of oppression, and of abhorrence of war that Reinhardt attained his dream of a festival theatre, the Grosses Schauspielhaus, "Theatre of the Five Thousand." It was designed by Hanz Poelzig, leader among German architects. The lighting, which comes from hundreds of stalactites encrusting the dome, is gay enough to be in itself an incentive to a festival mood. When the auditorium vibrates with music and comes to life in thousands of faces each part of the enormous space seems to join in the drama. Here the stage makes no pretense to being a room with a transparent fourth wall: the stage is frankly the *podium,* the platform, from which the actor addresses his audience. And such a stage! Three planes—an orchestra extended into the audience, a forestage rising above that, and somewhat higher the largest of the three—give an abundance of space for the surging movements of the crowds which almost engulf the spectators, for the individual actors who must by some means gain the emphasis which their parts need, and for the scenic backgrounds. The theatre owns an enormous revolving stage, an almost perfect lighting equipment, a sky dome, and several stereopticon lanterns for reproducing moving clouds.

Here at prices lower by half than those of other Berlin theatres and supported in some degree by the people's theatres, Reinhardt began a remarkable series of performances, stretching over three years. Opening the giant playhouse in November, 1919, with Æschylus' *Oresteia*, he presented Romain Rolland's *Danton* which like Büchner's version of the same story appealed to the spirit of revolution and the newly awakening democratic consciousness; *Helios*, by Gerhart Hauptmann; *Antigone*, rearranged by Walter Hasenclever, a young revolutionary in the drama, to express a more explicit hatred of tyranny than the original; and *Julius Cæsar*. The second season brought *Europa*, by Georg Kaiser, another young writer of genius; *Florian Geyer* and *Florindo* by Gerhart Hauptmann; *La Passion* (The Hobby) by Raoul and Simon Greban; *The Merchant of Venice; Midsummer Night's Dream*. In 1921 *The Robbers* by Schiller, *Dantons Tod* (Danton's Death) by Georg Büchner, and *Orphée aux Enfer* (Orpheus in the Underworld) by Jacques Offenbach closed the season and the work of the theatre.

The Theatre of the Five Thousand has been the battleground for almost as many critics. "The Arena is the medium which opens the soul of the people once more to the drama and makes this very soul visible," and "The Grosses Schauspielhaus is a belated product of pre-revolutionary German megalomania," show strongly contrasted attitudes. Reinhardt's reasons for closing this theatre and withdrawing from Berlin are not certain. Probably there is much justice in the explanation offered by an admirer of Reinhardt's:

No wonder he was loth to see his life-work imperilled by the irresistibly progressing commercialization of the artistic theatre, a process which is visible in the displacement of the ever-changing repertory system by long runs of single plays, in the relaxation of the artistic standard of the ensemble, through "stars." Economic exigencies; diminished appreciation of cultural values, one of the consequences of the war; competition by the financially stronger film industry; resulting corruption and indifference among the actors; growth of labor and other industrial organizations, as detrimental to real art as the trusts of the moneyed interests in the theatrical business—all these factors are digging the grave of the artistic theatre.[10]

But there is a special source of weakness in an arena stage, namely the difficulty in discovering dramas which are suited to magnificent spaces and which are yet of universal enough appeal to reach each individual among the thousands of spectators. As a corollary, of course, there is the constant temptation to bowdlerize a more subtle, delicate form. Reinhardt, even his enemies agree, was superb in the management of crowds and scenes of revolution, but not every play includes such scenes. In an auditorium in which lines are almost shouted, Kaiser's *Europa,* idyllic in mood, became a hybrid of musical comedy and circus, and the more fanciful scenes in *Midsummer Night's Dream* suffered grotesquely.

Before closing the Grosses Schauspielhaus, Reinhardt was already interesting himself in Salzburg, for which he had always longed. Far from the rush and ugliness of industrial Berlin, it is now Reinhardt's haunt and the inspiration for most of his recent experiments. This little city in the Austrian Tyrol, only a few miles from Bavaria, has a loveliness both of natural beauty and of storied past. Hohensalzburg, the fortress-crowned height above the River Salzach, is compared to Edinburgh in boldness and contour, while the gentler slope of Nonnberg saw the building of the camp of Marcus Aurelius and his death. In the square a few yards from the river is the Dom, the marble cathedral, and near at hand the Kollegienkirche, the Jesuit church of Fischer von Erlach, a fine example of the baroque. A few blocks across the stream is the birthplace of Mozart. Beyond the Hohensalzburg, reached by a beautiful walk through moun-

[10] From "Reinhardt as Stage-Director," by Arthur Kahane in *Max Reinhardt and His Theatre,* edited by Oliver M. Sayler, p. 77. Courtesy of Brentano's, Publishers, New York.

tain paths and a mountain tunnel, is Schloss Leopoldskron, a baroque castle erected by a prince of the church in the eighteenth century, now the palace of Reinhardt.

Salzburg is not only a joy to the spirit: it has contributed to Reinhardt's art something which the metropolis could not teach. To his life in Berlin he owes valuable gifts, a realization of the pleasure of work (not always an Austrian trait), an emphasis upon restraint and economy in the acting of plays of the more northern nations, and an acquaintance with their dramatic literature. What he desires now is more of the spirit of play, of the spontaneous mingling of gaiety and seriousness, of the impromptu, of the varied emotional appeal of music. All these moods are part of the folk drama of the Austrian and South German: across the border lies Oberammergau with its miracle play centuries old; the Austrian Tyrol has its own little folk festivals, particularly in the Salzburg regions, in the local dialect. In the town itself there exists a little puppet theatre, the delight of American tourists and small Austrian boys, whose ragged jackets are forgotten as they absorb the adventures of a charming puppet hero in a world of Austrian fairy lore and peasant speech. A more sophisticated though no truer love of beauty contrived the Marionette Theatre at Schloss Hellbrunn, a delicate and complicated little stage operated by water power. Civic pride built the Mozarteum for the music and music dramas of Salzburg's most famous musician.

In his plans for Salzbzurg, Reinhardt selected for his assistants two friends of many years, fellow-workers in the Berlin theatres, the Austrian poet, Hugo von Hofmannsthal, and the composer, Richard Strauss. To these he added a group of idealistic and public-spirited citizens. The whole endeavor has been actuated by the love of art and the love of the little city, and much of the service has been unpaid. (The high-mindedness of the community can be seen in its indignation at a recent proposal of an outside corporation to make the section into another Monte Carlo, a gambling resort for Central Europe.) Within a few seasons the Salzburg Festival has become known to those who were already familiar with the summer charm of this mountain country and to devotees of the drama all over the world.

Most famous of the Salzburg productions has been *Everyman—Jedermann* in the German version—which is von Hofmannsthal's expansion and adaptation of the medieval English play. The story in general outline is unaltered,—the summoning of Everyman by Death and his frantic endeavors to persuade someone to undertake the fearful journey with him. The adapter has added some vivid characterizations and much illustrative action: Everyman's frivolity and callousness are stressed by his mother's anxiety for his soul, by his lack of sympathy with the debtor who is being led toward prison, by the lavishness of the banquet in honor of his mistress. This scene heightens the effect of the play by comic relief in the gaiety of the women guests and the humors of the Thin Cousin and the Fat Cousin. The performance is skilfully manipulated, for rows of parallel platforms with concealed spaces below give opportunity for the sudden appearances of visitants from heaven or hell. The delight in technique, however, comes after the play is over: during the performance the moving story upon a universal theme grips the audience too deeply for analysis.

For *Jedermann* in the Domplatz with the portals of the cathedral as background and its towers drawing the eyes toward a sky against which gleam mountain and castle is worth a long journey. Some things about the performance are unforgettable,—the voice of God speaking from within the cathedral and the sound of the organ, the devout old mother like a figure from a Flemish painting, Moissi as Jedermann with his look of mischievous good-humor turning to horror at the premonitions of evil, the naturalness of the debtor's wife,—a peasant woman with her children clinging to her skirts,—the exquisite figure of Glaube (Helene Thimig) with her grave and lovely face above nun-like robes. Most powerful of all in its effect upon the imagination is Death's summons not in one voice but in many, from the domes of the cathedral, from the fortress above the city, from each turret and cloister, freezing and terrifying as though Death had a myriad heralds. No wonder that the peasants have taken the drama to their hearts and that it is being repeated by their own actors in several mountain valleys.

Only less impressive, to judge by the report of critics, is *The Great World Theatre,* von Hofmannsthal's version of a theme from Calderon, which has found its setting in the Kollegienkirche of Salzburg and has been repeated with other actors and other producers in a Congregational church in far-away London. In this morality the king, the beggar, the rich man, the peasant-farmer, beauty, and the nun typify all varieties of humanity. Von Hofmannsthal's most radical change in using the old material has been his drawing of the beggar, not the meek recipient of charity but a disturbing figure deeply touched by communistic ideals.

Von Hofmannsthal felt that the material for festival plays is inexhaustible. He once catalogued as some of the more important sources,—parts of *Faust, A Midsummer Night's Dream, Le Misanthrope, Hero and Leander, Prometheus Bound,* the Hindu drama, *Life is a Dream,* and certain plays of Euripides.

These are only the beginning of Reinhardt's plans and ambitions for Salzburg. In the old Outdoor Riding School, a tilting yard from the later days of tournaments, a curious inclosure, with galleries and spectators' boxes carved from the solid rock, he has presented *Twelfth Night.* Another Riding School, the Indoor, has been elaborately adorned with paintings in modernistic vein as a suitable meeting place for artistic temperaments. The auditorium above this has been renovated by Alfred Roller for indoor productions of Mozart's compositions. Sometime there will stand a little garden theatre near Schloss Leopoldskron and sometime, not very soon, perhaps, because of its costliness, a gigantic festival house or possibly a group of auditoriums on a spacious meadow near the site of the first out-door theatre in Europe, Hellbrunn; the architect of the Grosses Schauspielhaus, Hanz Poelzig, has already submitted drawings. Let us hope that in more sumptuous quarters the Salzburg festivals will be able to draw the past of the race and to preserve the vigor and integrity of folk origins as surely as they have done in church interior and cathedral square.

Reinhardt undertook an experiment of a very different type in 1922 when the Theater in dem Redoutensaal, Vienna, was entrusted to him. Maria Theresa's exquisite ballroom in the ancient Hofburg had been transformed a few months before from an assembly room of royalty to a state theatre under the direction of the republic. Without injuring the individual loveliness of the room, President Vetter of the bureau in charge of state theatres, Sebastien Heinrich and Alfred Roller, the latter one of Reinhardt's foremost designers, had created a permanent stage and architectural background. Baroque in inspiration like the room itself, harmonizing in cream and gold with the exquisite molding, the brilliant chandeliers, and rare Gobelins, a curving background with two or three openings forms an unsurpassable setting for the few types of plays which do not fall outside its artificial mood. The range of plays which can be given here is smaller than that for Copeau's permanent setting at the Vieux Colombier, as the Redoutensaal suggests a definite period and a sophisticated society. The Viennese stage is not fitted for plays of realism, even less of naturalism. As Kenneth Macgowan, distinguished critic of the modern stage has remarked, "Plays for the Redoutensaal must have some quality of distinction about them, a great, clear, emotion free from the bonds of physical detail, a fantasy or a poetry as shining as crystal, some artificiality of mood, or else an agreement in period with the baroque." Here Reinhardt presented Goethe's *Clavigo* and *Stella,* Calderon's *Dame Kobold,* and Rey's *Beautiful Women.*

Far in mood from the cream and gold delicacy of this eighteenth century ballroom have been some productions of Reinhardt which are more important historically than any evocation of a charming rococo past. These were the evenings between 1917 and 1920 in which Reinhardt lent his aid to the new drama which had been fermenting for years, but which came to the surface more frequently after the Armistice. Stupendous in conception, anarchistic in literary form, this group of plays is the most original and outstanding contribution to the drama made by any European nation since the beginning of the war. This drama represents the confluence of two streams of thought, the one largely literary and artistic; the other the mood of disillusionment of a war-torn people. The literary movement needs explanation.

The elucidation of *expressionism,* the German *expressionismus,* is not easy. Its enthusiasts tell us in one breath that it is both a world tendency and inexpressible,—inexpressible because it goes more deeply into life than do thought and reason, and "is rooted in the instinctive, the intuitional, the esoteric." Like Italian futurism and dadaism with which its origin is connected, expressionism has no desire to reflect actuality of outward form as realism does, individual temperament as romanticism, or moods of nature as impressionism:

The summary of the Expressionistic creed or formula may be stated as follows: The immediate expression which the artist receives and transfers to canvas or to paper is not art. Nor is the presence of feeling or temperament in the work to be considered as art. Nor is art to be attained by the reproduction of an object, a feeling or an impression, *but only by the trans-mutation of this impression into art,* into an artistic relationship of means of rhythm.

The reproduction of an impression [says Blümner] is not art; it remains impression. It is only through transformation to the purely artistic, that is, the pure, abstract vision of this impres-sion—that we attain to expression—*Expressionism.* The forma-tion of the individual experience (impression) by virtue of art, results in the work of art.[11]

The true expressionist indeed regrets that, whatever his medium, he must use words or forms which have existed before in this world, even though there may be no more apparent arrangement in them than in the kaleidoscopic colors which dance before closed eyes. He does his best to break with all traditional art forms. Among his admirations in art are primitive things, friezes of the Egyptians, un-tutored Negro art, Polynesian simplicity. The child spon-taneously creating not what he sees but what he chooses to fancy is the expressionist's archetype. Yet now and then the disciple of the new movement deigns, according to Herman Scheffauer, to accept as expressionistic widely scattered works of earlier genius, a painting by Giotto, Dürer's *Mel-ancholia,* the engravings of William Blake. The expression-ist hunts for the abstractions behind human life—the geo-metric, the mathematic; he lets down all bars between con-scious and unconscious life, the day of activity and the night of sleep. He is often Freudian in his psychology. The earlier American expressionistic plays, Elmer Rice's *Adding Machine* and Kaufman and Connelly's *Beggar on Horse-back,* illustrate the expressionist's opposition to realism, as do also Kaiser's *Morn to Midnight,* Toller's *Masse-Mensch* and many other continental plays.

Other definitions of expressionism might be gathered.

[11] From *The New Vision in the German Arts,* by Herman George Schef-fauer, p. 35. Courtesy of The Viking Press, Inc., Publishers, New York.

Herwarth Walden, a German expressionist even before the war and leader of the Sturm group, declares "Kunst ist Gabe, nicht Wiedergabe" ("Art is production, not reproduction"). Huntly Carter, thinking particularly of the drama, writes, "Expressionism is simply expression taking the form of a new technique for the purpose of giving the most intense effect—say a one hundred percent effect—to the species of drama that expressed pre-war and war-time insurrectionary tendencies. Dramatists found it necessary to put a punch into their plays, to make them violently aggressive, in order to arouse the play-goers into active sympathy with their insurrectionary ideas." Scheffauer considers the central idea of expressionism "direct action in art—the forthright naked impulse, delivered without intermediaries, straight from the imagination to the outer world—like a child from the womb." To him expressionism is also "a new search for God"—"It is not only the flight from reality, nature, space and time which is the motive force behind this new dispensation in art. It is also the triumph of the cosmic over the personal, the destiny of all humanity in opposition to the destiny of the individual man."

The first German expressionistic group, whose organ was *Der Sturm*, appeared in 1910 with the purpose of giving "expressionistic drama in expressionistic style." Under the encouragement of Herwarth Walden the Sturmbühne presented insurrectionary plays by August Stramm, Lothar Schreyer, Herman Essig, Oskar Kokoschka, Kurt Schwitters, and Walden himself; several of these have since reached much wider audiences: Lothar Schreyer's *Mann* was produced at the Deutsches Theater, Berlin, in 1920 and caused much comment by the use of such characters as Movement and Color; Walden's *Sünde* was performed several times in Hamburg, and in 1920 his *Trieb* and a pantomime, *Die vier Taten der Fiametta*, became a nine days' wonder. In 1910 *Offiziere* (*Officers*), in which a Prussian officer regarded militarism with a very un-Prussian criti-calness, was part of Reinhardt's season at the Deutsches Theater. Three years later he produced at Breslau *The Centenary Festival 1813* by Gerhart Hauptmann, in which the leading dramatist of Germany handled the ideals of militar-ism with such unconventional frankness that he ruffled the emperor, and was accordingly mentioned, nearly ten years later, as a possible candidate for the leadership of the first German republic. During the next few years Reinhardt put on several of the plays of Wedekind, whom the expression-ists consider one of themselves, and plays by Carl Stern-heim, whom they also acknowledge,—*Der Riese* (*The Giant*), *Die Kassette* (*The Small Box*), *Don Juan, Burger Schippel* (*Citizen Schippel*).

The end of the war found Germany as a nation in a mood which had many analogies with the new spirit in art and drama. Here in life as in art was a furious distrust of con-ventions, of previously accepted truths, a vehement desire to get at the foundations of everything, even though the in-vestigation might throw human thought into chaos. War, which had been shortly before a religion, became for many thinkers the most immoral thing in existence. The ever-changing Germany became an absorption; the ideals of social democracy, a new inspiration. Now came the burst of creative energy in the dramatic form which to many seems equal to that of any great creative period in the nation's history. These expressionistic plays, several of which were written by members of a group called "The Dramatic Will," were given on many stages and under the aid of several dis-tinguished producers, especially Leopold Jessner, Jürgen Fehling, and Emil Pirchan. But no man of the theatre helped the movement more than did Reinhardt. Between Decem-ber, 1917, and 1920, Reinhardt produced for Das Junge Deutschland, the most prominent group of the advance guard in Berlin, plays of the new mood: *Der Bettler* (The

Beggar) by Reinhard Sorge; *Seeschlacht* (A Sea Battle) by Reinhard Goering; *Der Sohn* (The Son) by Walter Hasenclever; *Der Besuch aus dem Elysium* (The Visitor from Elysium) by Franz Werfel; *Kain* (Cain) by Friedrich Koffka; *Ein Geschlecht* (One Family) by Fritz von Unruh; *Der Sturz des Apostels Paulus* (The Fall of the Apostle Paul) by Rolf Lauckner; *Die Wuppur* (The Wuppers) by Elsa Lasker-Schüler; *Der Brennende Dornbusch* (The Burning Briar Bush) by Oscar Kokoschka; *Die Sendung Semaels* (Semael's Mission) by Arnold Zweig. In addition Reinhardt gave plays by several of these playwrights and other dramatic revolutionaries upon his public stages. In the list are Georg Kaiser's *Die Koralle* (The Coral), *Der Brand im Opernhaus* (The Fire in the Opera House), *Von Morgens bis Mitternachts* (From Morn to Midnight) and *Europa* (Europe); Reinhard Goering's *Der Erste* (The First One); Paul Kornfeld's *Himmel und Hölle;* Walter Hasenclever's *Jenseits* (Beyond); and August Stramm's *Kräfte* (Powers).

Benefiting indirectly by Reinhardt's interest are several other playwrights of the new movement. The work of many of Das Junge Deutschland and these others is hard to classify except as all represent some phase of expressionism. Several are expressionistic only in mood, pouring the new wine into old wine skins; others only in form; still others in spirit and form. There are playwrights of what one critic has called "the drama of definite political purpose" as opposed to "the drama of social indignation" as Shaw and Galsworthy write it: Fritz von Unruh in *Offiziere* attacked militarism before the war, and his *Ein Geschlecht*, finished in 1916, again attacked it, this time as a mother and her son see its results; Goering in *Seeschlacht* was a prophet of the German naval revolt; Hasenclever in his adaptation of *Antigone* wrote scathingly against a tyrannic monarchy under the thin disguise of the Greek story. The most advanced psychology has touched the drama: Arnolt Bronnen has looked for beauty in what is usually considered depravity; Werfel, whose historical drama, *Juarez and Maximilian,* has been given by the Theatre Guild in New York, has often shown himself deeply moved by Freudian concepts in a portrayal of the difficulty of adjustment of old and new generations. These two men typify the finest and best of the new movement.

Georg Kaiser, whose work is becoming well known in America and in England—indeed *From Morn to Midnight* was the first German play to be given across the Channel after the Armistice—is an "apostle of energy" as he told Barrett Clark.

Energy is the driving force of the world. Without energy there is nothing. Sentiment, pity, romance are only the refuge of the weak, who must inevitably go down. The unfortunate are hindrances. Go out into the world and see what men really are. They are brutal, self-seeking, egotistical, heartless, energetic. It is only through will power that injustice and stupidity can be done away with.[12]

Of nearly twenty plays, *The Burghers of Calais, Europa, From Morn to Midnight, The Fire in the Opera House, Hell, Way, Earth,* and the amazing trilogy, *The Coral Charm, Gas I,* and *Gas II,* are the most widely known. Everywhere Kaiser is attacking the powers which threaten man—his own stupidity, capitalism, the machines which he has created and which now threaten to become his master. His nobler characters are actuated not only by strength of will but by a deep love of humanity. This spirit and also his tremendous energy in theme and dialogue appear in a scene of *Gas I.* An engineer and a billionaire's son are watching the delicate apparatus which is giving warning of an explosion which takes place almost instantly:

[12] From "New Trends in the Theatre in Germany," by Barrett Clark, *The Forum.* Courtesy of the Publishers, New York.

Engineer: It works out—and does not work out. We have reached the limit—works out and does not work out. Figures fail us—works out—yet does not work out. The thing sums itself up, and then turns against us—works out and does not work out!

Billionaire's Son: The Gas—?

Engineer: It is bleeding in the sight-tube! Flooding past the formula—going red in the sight-glass. Floating out of the formula —taking the bit in its own teeth. I have done my duty. My head is quite clear. The impossible is going to take place—it cannot come—yet it is coming! . . .

Workman: Report from Shed Eight—Central—White cat bursts—red eyes torn open—yellow mouth gaping—humps up crackling back—grows round—snaps away girders—lifts up roof —bursts—sparks! sparks! (sitting down in the middle of floor and striking about him). Chase away the cat—Shoo! Shoo!— Smash her jaws—Shoo! Shoo!—Bury her eyes—they flame— Hammer down her back—hammer it down—thousands of fists! It's swelling, swelling—growing fat—fatter—gas out of every crack—every tube! (once more half erecting himself). Report from Central—the white cat has exploded! (he collapses and lies prone).

Billionaire's Son: (Goes to him.)

Workman: (Gropes with his hand.)

Billionaire's Son: (Takes his hand.)

Workman: (With a cry.) Mother! . . . (dies).

Billionaire's Son: (Bending low above him.) O man! O mankind! [13]

Here the compressed, direct dialogue has been compared to "the discharge of mechanisms each discharge preparing the mechanism for a new charge." [14]

More daring even than Kaiser is Ernst Toller, in whose work is reflected the struggle of the proletariat and the

[13] Kaiser, George, quoted by Scheffauer, H. G., *The New Vision in the German Arts*, pp. 204, 205.

[14] Scheffauer, *Ibid.*, p. 29.

bourgeoisie, the great struggle of present-day Europe. If agony, physical and spiritual, gives a man a right to speak, his is a voice which cannot be disregarded. At the outbreak of the war, a youth of twenty, he was on his way to France to study. He started instantly for Munich, where he volunteered in what he was led to believe the one type of righteous war, the defense of a fatherland. Thirteen months later he was invalided home. Next he studied in Munich, and in a short time became a rebel, a conscientious objector to any war. He found kindred spirits, particularly at the "Kultur" congress at Burg Lauenstein and later at Heidelburg, and joined an idealistic and social group who dreamed of uniting the youth of all warring peoples in an effort to end war and to build a League of Nations. Plans for the systematic circulation of propaganda were ended by the action of the General Staff, which at once conscripted several of the leaders without determining their physical fitness. Toller, however, escaped. Going to Berlin, he came under the influence of Kurt Eisner, a radical thinker and playwright, and read articles which astonished him by proving Germany the offender. His next action, logically, was a part in the strike of munition workers in Munich, a strike to end the war and bring about a peace without annexations and with self-determination for every country. After the arrest of his friend Eisner, Toller became a member of the strike committee, and was shortly conscripted and sent to military prison. Here he began his play, *Wandlung*. In the November Revolution he returned to Munich and helped the revolutionary forces in several capacities: as chairman of the Central Committee of the Workers' Peasants' Soldiers' Soviet, the first German soviet in Bavaria, chairman of the Independent Social Party, and chairman of the Central Committee of the Soviet Republic. Gradually he came to feel that Bavaria was not ready for soviet government and, the situation in Munich proving hopeless, tried to dissolve the soviet. Indeed the crime for which a price was set upon his head and for which in July, 1919, he was arrested and court martialed, was an attempt to restrain the mob from excesses. Yet in spite of the intercessions of Hauptmann and other men of prominence, Toller was forced to serve a sentence of five years in the fortress of Niederschönenfeld.

The plays which soon issued from this Bavarian military prison depict the passions of man as an individual and as a unit in a mass swept by a mob's peculiar psychology, and are a poignant cry against war, against violence. The first, *Wandlung* (*Transformation*), begun in the earlier imprisonment, falls into scenes which are called by Scheffauer "six stations of the via crucis of war." In the first scene, War Death in helmet and uniform and Civilian Death in high hat and gaiters meet in a cemetery. At War Death's command ghosts of the slain rise in a ghastly parade. A little later comes the breaking of a statue entitled "Our Victorious Nation," and by implication the hurling down of a narrow patriotism. Another drama, *Die Maschinenstürmer* (*The Machine Wreckers*), given by Reinhardt in his Grosses Schauspielhaus, was suggested by the Luddite riots of English workers at Nottingham in 1816, and shows the panic of the handworkman at the coming of the machine-laborer. The prologue of this presents the House of Lords voting upon the resolution, "Whoever destroys a machine shall pay for it with his life," with Lord Byron speaking against the measure and Lord Castlereagh in favor of it. Curiously, in a later scene, the face of Lord Byron is repeated as a weaver's and the face of Lord Castlereagh as a manufacturer's, for Toller believes that different as are class interests under the conditions of modern industry, human emotions and attitudes are not confined by artificial barriers. The one bit of hope in the play is the strange figure of Old Man Reaper with his philosophy of love, a philosophy which leaves its imprint upon much of Toller's work—"We must help one another and be kind."

The most powerful of Toller's plays is his second, conceived in two and a half days in prison, while he refused all food and all companionship, and reworked painstakingly for nearly a year. *Man and the Masses (Masse-Mensch)* was given first at the Berlin Volksbühne, September, 1921, with Jürgen Fehling as producer and Hans Strohbach as stage designer. Three years later the New York Theatre Guild repeated it at the Garrick Theatre. Both productions were expressionistic, divining the inner meaning of scenes which alternate between reality and dream. Both caught the sinister implications of strife between the masses and the bourgeoisie and the decisions which face man as an individual and as a member of a group.

There can be no question about it: [writes Toller] that which in the social world and its artistic representation seems to the bourgeois a fight in barren phrases is to the proletariat a tragic problem, a disintegrating strife. And what to the bourgeois seems "deep" and "important" as an expression of most agitating mental conflict leaves the proletariat unmoved.

I need not emphasize [he adds] that proletariat art no less than all other must spring from a human source, must in its depths be all-encompassing, all-enfolding like life, like death. There is a proletariat art only in so far as its creator shapes the manifold forms of proletariat life and feeling into the eternal humanities.[15]

In the drawing of Sonia Irene L., The Woman, the only character in the drama with a name, Toller triumphs in a new mood. Sonia, a pacifist, is inflamed with love of humanity and faith in the masses. Leaving The Man, her husband, an official and upholder of the existing government, she throws in her lot with the proletariat only to discover them

[15] From *Man and the Masses,* by Ernst Toller, translated by Louis Untermeyer, pp. X, XI. Courtesy of Doubleday, Doran and Company, Publishers, Garden City, New York.

to be as ruthless and indifferent to human life as the representatives of any capitalistic government. She refuses her
husband's help and that of The Nameless One, the embodiment of revolution, when she learns that she can be saved
only by the death of a guard. "A leader has the right to sacrifice no one but himself." Enclosing these scenes of her life
are the dream-pictures, satiric, horrible—a council of bank-
ers, brokers, and clerks making cold, bitter plans for the
pushing on of a war, a dance of prostitutes and condemned
men, a vision of a prison cell. A strain of beauty runs
through the darkness of the play: two passages of molten
poetry are in Sonia's cry of love for The Man and her
brooding upon the loneliness of death, "the last road"—

The last road runs across a snowfield.
The last road never knows companions.
The last road winds without a mother.
The last road we walk alone.

V

THE INDEPENDENT THEATRES OF ENGLAND

George Bernard Shaw in 1921 wrote to Mr. J. T. Grein of *The London Illustrated News,* his friend and colleague since the nineties, those momentous days in dramatic history:

It is now very close on thirty years since you madly began an apparently hopeless attempt to bring the English theatre into some sort of relation with contemporary culture. Matthew Arnold had suggested that step; but nobody in the theatre took the slightest notice of him, because nobody in the theatre knew of the existence of such a person as Matthew Arnold. That was what was the matter with the theatre then. . . .

When you first desperately stuck an advertisement into the papers to say that an unheard-of enterprise called the Independent Theatre would on a certain Sunday night and Monday afternoon perform an unheard-of play, totally unlike any play then current in the theatrical market; when the papers thereupon declared that the manager of the theatre ought to be prosecuted for keeping a disorderly house, and that you and the foreign blackguard named Ibsen who was your accomplice, should be deported as obvious undesirables, you made a hole in the dyke; and the weight of the flood outside did the rest. When you declared that you would bring to light treasures of unacted English drama grossly suppressed by the managers of that day, you found that there was not any unacted English drama except two acts of an unfinished play (begun and laid aside eight years before) by me; but it was the existence of the Independent Theatre that made me finish that play, and by giving me the experience of its rehearsal and performance, revealed the fact

164

(to myself among others) that I possessed the gift of "fingering" the stage. That old play now seems as remote and old-fashioned as Still Waters Run Deep or London Assurance; but the newspapers of 1892 raged over it for a whole fortnight. Everything followed from that: the production of Arms and the Man by Miss Horniman and Florence Farr at the Avenue Theatre, Miss Horniman's establishment of Repertory Theatres in Dublin and Manchester, the Stage Society, Granville H. Barker's tentative matinées of Candida at the Court Theatre, the full-blown management of Vedrenne and Barker, Edie Craig's Pioneers, and the final relegation of the Nineteenth Century London theatre to the dust-bin by Barrie. At present the cry in the papers is that the theatre is hopelessly out of date, that it needs fresh air, new ideas, scrapping of traditions and conventions. The most famous apostle of the new theatre has declared publicly that what has been holding the theatre back for twenty years past and making all reform impossible is not Sardou but Shaw. If only we could give the young lions a ride on Wells' Time Machine and take them back to 1892!

Well, more power to their elbows! I am always delighted to hear a clamor for new ideas, or indeed for ideas of any sort, in the theatre. So, I have no doubt, are you. But the clamorers will hardly see a revolution like the one you began by making the hole in the dyke. It is the second revolution that England owes to a Dutchman.

After this, [adds Grein, the founder of the first true experimental theatre in England] the less I say about myself, the better. I am very well content to be the man who made the hole in the dyke. In letting Ibsen in I let the ocean in; and I certainly look round sometimes in bewilderment at the extent to which the old landmarks have been obliterated.[1]

Indeed the ocean obliterated many landmarks and floated vessels of many cargoes, for in no other country has the dramatic revival been more diverse in its manifestations or

[1] From *The World of the Theatre; Impressions and Memoirs,* by J. T. Grein, pp. V, VII, VIII. Courtesy of William Heinemann, Ltd., Publishers, London.

appealed to a greater variety of playgoers. The stage societies of London modeled on those of the continent and the
repertory theatres of London and of several of the provincial cities were established in antebellum days; since the
Great War the expansion of every kind has been remarkable.

For more than a decade after the beginning of the final
quarter of the nineteenth century, English drama, like that
of the continent, was in dire need of reform. However, there
were a few hopeful signs. Many magazines,—*The Review,
The Athenæum, The Saturday Review,* and *The Fortnightly
Review,*—gave space to dramatic criticism. *The Theatre* and
The Journal of Dramatic Reform were both founded in
1880. Percy Fitzgerald, Clement Scott, William Archer, and
George Bernard Shaw were leaders among a group of critics
who regarded the drama as an art which like other arts must
be taken seriously. The universities, too, were becoming
conscious that English drama did not end with Shakespeare
or even with Goldsmith and Sheridan, and called noted
actors to lecture. At Oxford University, a dramatic society
was founded in 1884. Within the theatre itself, the Kendals,
Sir Beerbohm Tree, producers, and Sir Arthur Wing Pinero,
Henry Arthur Jones, and Sidney Grundy, playwrights, were
eager for surer workmanship and finer art. How much of
this quickening of interest was due to Ibsen is hard to
determine: Shaw, perhaps, does not exaggerate in declaring
him "the hero of the new departure." Soon after Edmund
Gosse had introduced Ibsen to English readers through the
pages of *The Fortnightly Review* in 1873, he had been
championed by William Archer, who translated many of his
plays and kept his genius before the minds of the public.
The stage history of the plays began with *Pillars of Society,*
in Archer's translation, performed at the Gaiety Theatre one
morning in December, 1880. In 1889, Miss Janet Achurch

and Charles Charrington gave *A Doll's House,* the first of their many Ibsen productions.

But if Ibsen and Scandinavia quickened the spirit of English lovers of the drama, Antoine and France suggested the form of the revolution. William Archer and other admirers of continental drama, as well as George Moore, knew of Antoine and his courageous little group. Even before the establishment of the Théâtre Libre, however, they had tried to diagnose the malady of the London theatres. In 1884, George Moore had pointed out one cause in the long-run system, contrasting the three hundred nights of a modern successful stage play with the twelve performances of an Elizabethan, and deducing the fact that the public could expect only triteness and mediocrity from a play written to attract many thousands. Later, he had reiterated this unpalatable truth by rating the leading English playwrights as literary men of the third and fourth class. When a Mr. Crawford had referred to the idea of a free theatre to stimulate great work in London, Moore called on any wealthy gentleman to give ten thousand pounds—or five—a year and reminded potential donors that "it would be equally meritorious to endow a theatre or a hospital" for "the man who gives pleasure is as charitable as he who relieves suffering." In 1891, when William Archer was also urging the foundation of a free theatre, George Moore included in the volume with his essay on the French experimental theatre another on *The Necessity of an English Théâtre Libre.*

A free theatre, in Moore's opinion, should appeal not to the general public but to the small minority—three or four thousand persons among the London multitudes—who are interested in artistic work and experimentation. It should not present plays which could succeed on the commercial stage, for the regular theatre can give more elaborate production and people will not come to see the usual type of play given in an inferior manner, but it should above all attempt something that is different, great plays if attainable, but if they are unattainable, plays which at least have something original and distinctive in them, "even though that something is not always deeper than the charm which we find in a piece of *bric-à-brac,* or a piece of old china." Neither realism nor any other form of art should prevail: the taste which should guide the theatre should be above all eclectic, seeking only for the rare. Such a playhouse could scorn the accepted rules of the stage, among them that every play should contain a love-interest, and that any theme touching problems of religion and morality should be so weakened as to be innocuous.

The question arose whether such plays existed in England or were confined to France. Moore began to canvass the opinions of men who had access to manuscript plays, Sir Beerbohm Tree, who confessed his disappointment at the quality of plays submitted for his Afternoon Theatre, William Archer, who had never met an English example of "those curious literary experiments in dramatic writings which Antoine produces in the Théâtre Libre," and a professional reader, who was even more emphatic in his expression of discouragement,—"I never met a play that was literary either in conception or in language."

Moore's optimism did not flag. A free theatre, he consoled himself, need provide for only one season at a time and need not depend entirely upon English playwrights: Tolstoy's *The Power of Darkness* and Ibsen's *Ghosts* might be supplemented by several of Antoine's French successes such as Hennique's *La Mort du Duc d'Enghien* and *Jacques Damour* and Méténier's *En Famille.* If English plays did not exist, they might be written. Two possible sources were in existence, the work of eminent novelists and the work of the more alert and sincere of the playwrights of the commercial stage. Stevenson and Henley could be urged to collaborate on unusual themes, Meredith to dramatize a story, or Hardy to put in dramatic form "unconventional scenes of the sordid avarice and crime that lurks among sheepfolds and hayfields as well as a city's slums and by-ways." Perhaps to Grundy, Pinero, Jones, came sometimes ideas which they knew to be without value to the established theatres.

In the midst of this theorizing, the first English independent theatre was organized, like the French, not by a beneficent millionaire but a poor young man of far vision. J. T. Grein, a native of Holland, who had come to London in his early twenties, was occupied with many other activities, among them the Consulship General of the Congo. His great delight, however, was modern drama; in 1891, at the time of the founding of the Independent Theatre, he had been the dramatic critic of *Life* for several years. He has left his own account of the event:

Strange as it may seem the basis of the Independent Theatre was laid through the production of two English plays in Holland. There stands in my house a grandfather's clock, upon which is inscribed the following dedication: "From Arthur W. Pinero and Henry Arthur Jones to J. T. Grein, in recognition of his efforts for the British drama abroad, and especially of the production of 'The Profligate' and 'The Middleman' at Amsterdam." This was in 1890, and the first time that English authors were duly remunerated in Holland, although that country does not belong to the Berne convention. It was one of my hobbies in those days to obtain for the British drama, which was in very bad odour abroad, some recognition, and among the most successful plays which I transplanted were the aforesaid works of our leading playwrights. So great was the success of these English plays at Amsterdam that the managers of the Royal Subsidised Theatre sent me a cheque for £50 to be used in the interest of art in England. At the same time I had received another cheque for £30 for the translation of an English play. With these gigantic sums, in the wake of Antoine in Paris, I founded the Independent Theatre.

Thus with funds which, as Shaw declared, "fell far short of those with which an ambitious young professional man ventures upon giving a dance," Grein announced Ibsen's *Ghosts* for his first program and began his preparations. He expected to give the performance in an inexpensive hall in Tottenham Court Road, and was agreeably surprised to receive enough support to make possible the use of the Royalty Theatre. The performance was given early in March, under the direction of the actor, Cecil Raleigh, and with the help of George Moore. Among the charter members of the society, who presumably witnessed this historic production, were George Meredith, Thomas Hardy, A. W. Pinero, H. A. Jones, Mrs. J. R. Green, and G. B. S., the last less famous than he was soon to become.

The little theatre needed all the help it could get, for a storm of popular indignation burst upon the heads of Ibsen's admirers, as ancient conservatism became aware of the new freedom. The epithets collected by Shaw in *The Quintessence of Ibsenism* illustrate the coarse violence of the abuse heaped upon the new theatre and its leaders, particularly Grein.

[Shaw adds] throughout the following week he [Grein] shared with Ibsen the distinction of being abusively discussed to an extent that must have amply convinced him that his efforts had not passed unheeded. [Grein himself refers to this first performance as eliciting] no less than five hundred articles mostly vituperating Ibsen, whose "Ghosts" inaugurated the movement and obtained for me the honorary, if somewhat unflattering, title of "the most abused man in London." In parenthesis, I should add here that this distinction clung to me for many years, that some families closed their doors against me because I had produced an immoral play, and that a well-known journalist, since dead, refused to be present at a banquet if I were invited. It cost me practically ten years of my life to overcome the prejudice created by an undertaking which even the enemy must admit has left its mark upon the history of our stage.

Grein's course was now difficult. While several prominent critics were his defenders, he had a considerable part of the English press against him and apparently an overwhelming majority of the English public. For a time there was a possibility that the opposition would succeed in closing the house even though it did not come under the rules applying to ordinary theatres. There were other complications: timidity kept many from expressing their interest, and thus crippled Grein's resources; theatre-owners, afraid of hampering alliances, were reluctant to offer their stages. For a time the Independent Theatre seemed marked for early death.

But Grein's few friends were loyal. Several of them, including Frank Harris and Frank Danby, contributed generous sums. Unfortunately for a swift recovery, the next program, *Thérèse Raquin,* was assailed almost as bitterly as the first; however, the third, both wider in appeal and less provocative in theme, did much to establish the theatre. On this triple bill was an adaptation of a story by Frank Harris, *The Kiss* by Théodore de Banville (translated by John Gray), and *A Visit* by Georg Brandes.

Thus far the theatre had approached one ideal, offering the English public stimulating continental drama, but not the other, presenting daring original English plays, though Grein was reading eight or ten manuscripts a week. Fantastically enough, the earliest English play of length and serious theme was the result of a wager. As Moore records the incident in *Ave,* Mr. George R. Sims, a well-known playwright, who had received what he considered rough treatment at Moore's hands (Moore had said of him in *Our Dramatists and their Literature,* "his appeal to the intellectual habits of the middle classes is so frank and undisguised that no part of his work can be said to come within range of literary criticism"), remarked to a reporter that he "would give a hundred pounds if Mr. George Moore would

write an unconventional play for the Independent Theatre."
Moore caviled at the word "unconventional" on the ground
that Mr. Sims would not recognize the unconventional if he
saw it, but offered to write the play if "the objectionable
word" were withdrawn. When his enemy rephrased the
challenge, Moore betook himself seriously to dramatic composition. The result, *The Strike at Arlingford,* found an interested audience and for its day represented extreme realism. A comparison with Galsworthy's *Strife,* on a similar
theme, shows the change in technique which the next few
years brought.

Moore's play, not comparable with his novels, could not
maintain a radical theatre for long, yet no other English
playwright appeared. Again the enthusiasts of the Independent Theatre grew discouraged: the Théâtre Libre had
cradled a new French drama, but where was an "artistic
Messiah" of the Independent Theatre? "Never was Messiah
more eagerly awaited," wrote William Archer. "We are all
on tiptoe, with our trumpets at our lips, ready to hail his
advent. And yet he comes not. We do not even cry, 'Lo,
here!' and 'Lo, there!'—no one appears who can for a moment be mistaken for the master that is to be."

When there seemed no proof of even the tiniest flowering
of a "New Drama," George Bernard Shaw, as he says,
"manufactured the evidence." The discovery of this man of
destiny Grein records briefly,—"It was my good fortune to
obtain from George Bernard Shaw the MSS. of his first
play, 'Widowers' Houses.' " Eden Greville, one of Grein's
helpers, gives a delectable account in his article, *Bernard
Shaw and His Plays:*

> Next we cast about for some home-made play, as we did not
> wish the critics and the public to say that we produced nothing
> but foreign works. Gazing round the literary landscape of the
> day we discovered George Bernard Shaw, sitting in picturesque

solitude, wild, red-haired, shaggy, aggressive, looking like an untamed wolf. . . .

Shaw had shown himself to be the possessor of an original viewpoint, a brilliant and somewhat irreverent style, and a strong tendency to hit at every head in sight, whether that of a friend or that of a foe.

He was not an easy man to approach, but taking our courage in both hands, we ventured to suggest that he should write a play for the Independent Theater. At first he treated the proposal with scorn, as he usually treated anything suggested by anybody else; but finally he mentioned that he had at home the fragments of something more or less like a drama, which he had commenced, in collaboration with William Archer some six or seven years before. Of course the co-authors had disagreed over their work, which had been abandoned, and had lain on the shelf in a London lodging ever since.

We urged Shaw to complete the fugitive fragments, and eventually he began to think that the idea of doing so was his own and not ours. When we had carefully led him up to this point, the rest, of course, was easy. The way to deal with an advanced and original thinker of Shaw's caliber is to flatter him judiciously—to tell him that as a man he is greater than any king or sage, and that as a writer he far transcends Shakespeare or Milton. You can then get out of him anything you want. Of course he does not like flattery, but then he does not know that you are flattering him. He only thinks that you are an unusually intelligent and appreciative person.

An appointment was therefore made to dig up Shaw's dramatic fragments. Many of the readers of *Munsey's Magazine* may know London, where soft coal is burned, and may realize how much soot would accumulate on a shelf in seven years. My recollection is that the papers were buried about a foot deep. It really was an excavation which might compare, for difficulty and for danger of choking, with some of the searches for ancient manuscripts in Egypt.

However, we eventually dug out the fragments, which turned out to be the beginning of a play afterwards known as "Widowers' Houses." By this time Shaw had firmly persuaded himself

that he had discovered us, not we him. He no doubt thinks so
still.[2]

This is Shaw's own account:

. . . but its [the Independent Theatre's] search for native dramatic masterpieces, pursued by Mr. Grein with the ardor and in-
nocence of a foreigner, was so complete a failure that at the end of
1892 he had not produced a single original piece of any magnitude
by an English author. In this humiliating national emergency, I
proposed to Mr. Grein that he should boldly announce a play
by me. Being an extraordinarily sanguine and enterprising man,
he took this step without hesitation. I then raked out, from my
dirtiest pile of discarded and rejected manuscripts, two acts of
a play I had begun in 1885, shortly after the close of my novel
writing period, in collaboration with my friend Mr. William
Archer. . . .

Exhuming this as aforesaid seven years later, I saw that the
very qualities which had made it impossible for ordinary commercial purposes in 1885, might be exactly those needed by the
Independent Theatre in 1892. So I completed it by a third act;
gave it the far-fetched mock-Scriptural title of "Widowers'
Houses," and handed it over to Mr. Grein, who launched it at
the public in the Royalty Theatre with all its original tomfool-
eries on its head.[3]

The play was received with furious applause by socialists
and independents and with hoots by conservatives. Shaw,
who was in excellent practice as a mob-orator, finally suc-
cumbed to repeated calls for a speech. He expressed his
approval at the serious way in which the play had been
taken, repeated the unpleasant facts of slum-landlordism
which it depicted, and expressed his hope that the day would

[2] From "Bernard Shaw and his Plays," by Eden Greville, *Munsey's
Magazine*, Vol. 34, March, 1906, pp. 765, 766. Courtesy of the Publishers,
New York.

[3] From *Plays Pleasant and Unpleasant*, by George Bernard Shaw, Vol.
I, pp. XI, XII. Courtesy of Brentano's, Publishers, New York.

come when this evil would be so completely obliterated that the play would be unintelligible. Later, *Widowers' Houses* was published with prefaces by Grein, Archer, and Shaw himself, as well as "several elaborate controversial appendices in the author's most energetically egotistical fighting style,"—an Independent Theatre play was again a topic of the hour. Thus the most voluminous and perhaps the greatest genius among modern English dramatists was discovered, the Independent Theatre's most valuable gift to the public. Grein wrote years after,—"If the Independent Theatre had done nothing else for the British drama than to give a hearing to George Bernard Shaw, I contend that it justified its existence and fulfilled its mission."

Widowers' Houses was the only one of Shaw's plays staged by this group, for *The Philanderers,* written especially for them, proved too difficult to cast. Several more English plays found their premières at the Opéra Comique (the house used after the Royalty), plays by Michael Field, Mrs. Oscar Beringer, Dr. Todhunter (*The Black Cat*), Dorothy Leighton (*Thyrza Fleming*), and others. Foreign plays,—Dutch, French, German,—however, were in the majority. In March, 1895, the theatre was host to Lugné Poë of the Théâtre de l'Œuvre of Paris, who played *Rosmersholm, The Master Builder, L'Intruse,* and *Pelléas and Mélisande* and introduced the new symbolism to London.

Notwithstanding the power of several of its twenty-six plays, the Independent Theatre was rarely out of the shadow of financial anxiety. Its audiences were small, the membership never exceeding one hundred and seventy-five. In 1894 there was a temporary prosperity when Miss Dorothy Leighton, the novelist (later Mrs. Ashton Johnson) joined Grein as co-director and helped him incorporate the Independent Theatre, Ltd., in which many friends took shares. But by 1897 the Independent Theatre could struggle no longer and performances ceased.

Perhaps the quality of the plays of the Independent Theatre has in the eyes of historians rather dwarfed its other achievements, but contemporaries tell us that it was renowned for a spirit of *ensemble* which even enemies acknowledged to be unique on the London stages in the nineties, and that like its Parisian prototype it developed a new standard of realistic acting. Under the banners of the Independent Theatre many actors and actresses first won success. The distinguished actor, James Welch, first became known as Lickcheese in *Widowers' Houses*.

Grein's interest in the contemporary theatre did not terminate with the Independent group. He had already established the review, *Tomorrow*, and the Anglo-Dutch paper, *Hollandia;* subsequently, he became dramatic reviewer for several papers, and still holds that position on the *Sunday Times* and the *London Illustrated News*. He helped to found both a German and a French theatre in London, later receiving distinguished honors from France and Germany for his services. Twice he served as president of the Playgoer's Club, and seven times of the Dramatic Debaters, societies which have supported the new movement. In 1914, he closed his long fight for Ibsen with a signal victory, the license to produce *Ghosts* publicly in England,—a gala event under the patronage of King Haakon of Norway. Later, through the kindness of a London business man, Mr. Grein was able to announce his intention of giving occasional performances in the spirit of his early theatre. During these years, he has been a loyal supporter of the Stage Society, a direct descendant of the earlier theatre. With Mrs. Grein he translated Sudermann's *Midsummer Fires* for a program in May, 1906.

The second experimental theatre was suggested by Frederick Whelen, a banker, later literary secretary to Sir Herbert Beerbohm Tree. He sent a circular letter to a hundred and fifty people known to be interested in the drama, discussing the feasibility of organizing a small society to give modern plays, continental and English, high comedy as well as serious dramas. The last suggestion was probably to appease those who, with some reason, had accused the Théâtre Libre, the Freie Bühne, and the Independent Theatre of reveling in depictions of gloom. The idea was to give plays very simply, in costume but without scenery, in large studios. The performances were to be arranged for Sunday afternoons when professional actors and actresses were free. On July 19, 1899, fifty people attended a meeting in the old rooms of William Morris, 17, Red Lion Square, and the Stage Society began. Its objects then, as now, for incorporation in 1904 did not alter its ideals, have been officially stated:

To promote and encourage Dramatic Art; to serve as an Experimental Theatre; to provide such an organization as shall be capable of dealing with any opportunities that may present themselves, or be created, for the permanent establishment in London of a Repertory Theatre; and to establish and undertake the management and control of such a Theatre.

That is, the society was to foster dramatic art by continuing the search of the Independent Theatre for new playwrights, by familiarizing its members with classical and contemporary foreign plays, and by producing thoughtful plays refused license by the censor. The society was to do all that it could to advance the type of theatre which ideally, at least, is free from the two chief evils of the commercial stage, the star system and the long run.

The strength of the Incorporated Stage Society has lain in enlisting the interest of a great number of people in the many activities of any production. The Council of Management, numbering about twenty, at different times has included Sidney Colvin, J. M. Barrie, Gilbert Murray, Mr. and Mrs. Bernard Shaw, Granville Barker, Edith Craig, St.

John Hankin, Ashley Dukes, W. L. George. During the first few years more than six hundred people had acted and more than fifty had been in charge of productions. The membership, too, has been large.

Before the idea of studio production was abandoned, the group was limited to three hundred regular members. When this restriction was removed the membership sprang quickly to five hundred and, before the World War, to over fifteen hundred; in June, 1919, after many tragic losses, the number had climbed to a thousand.

The annual dues, later slightly increased, were for many years a pound each, entitling the subscriber to one orchestra or two gallery seats. The entrance fee is an additional pound. Like many other experimental theatres, the Stage Society is not technically a theatre, and can choose what plays it wishes. With careful management of its funds, it can produce from four to eight programs a season, averaging three hundred pounds each.

"The work of the Stage Society during the past ten years has been 'a labor of love' practically to every one who has been connected with its activities," said the report of 1909, and the statement holds true of later years. Many professional managers have lent their theatres; many distinguished actors and actresses have been as willing as untried beginners to give their time and efforts to these Sunday performances, and later to the Monday matinées, added when one performance was no longer sufficient. The generosity of these professionals has kept the Stage Society free from the stigma of amateurishness.

Appropriately the society began its career, November, 1899, with Shaw's *You Never Can Tell*, in which James Welch appeared as the waiter, William, thus linking the new venture with the earlier. Other programs of the first year were *Mrs. Maxwell's Marriage* by Sidney Olivier, *The League of Youth* by Ibsen, *The House of Usna* by Fiona

Macleod, *Interior* and *The Death of Tintagiles* by Maeterlinck, and late in the season, *Candida* by Shaw. Miss Janet
Achurch or her husband, Charles Charrington, both distinguished professionals, produced most of these plays;
while in *The House of Usna* and the plays of Maeterlinck,
Granville Barker found part of his training.

Sir Owen Seaman has testified to the variety of fare at
the Stage Society and the richness of the continental influence:

WHEN WE SLEEPING BEAUTIES AWAKEN

(Lines written for a dinner of the Stage Society. With acknowledgments,
for the title, to the Master.)

There was a time, as I am told,
   Back in the dim Victorian Age,
When antic Custom, dull and cold,
   Wrapped like a pall the British Stage;
And some among the best "reporters" said:—
"Dramatic Art is practically dead!"

But ere they fixed the funeral site
   A race of Thinking Men arose,
Clapped on the corpse a searching light
   And found her simply comatose;
(Four years ago they took this fearless line,
That is to say, in 1899).

Before the lapse of many days,
   The Sleeping Beauty stirred in bed
And used the Tennysonian phrase:
   "O love, thy kiss would wake the dead!"
From Mr. Whelen came that Clarion sound;
His was the smack that brought the lady round.

They fed her up (for she was weak
   And swelled with swallowing windy puffs)
On German, Belgian, French and Greek,
   On Norse and even native stuffs;

With urgent appetite the patient drank in
Essence of Hauptmann, Heijermans and Hankin.

Exotic fish and local fowl,
    With these they plied her generous maw—
Curel and Barker, cheek by jowl,
    And Ibsen jostling Bernard Shaw;
Thus, if *The Lady from the Sea* looked foreign,
For British Matrons there was *Mrs. Warren.*

Her moral frame expanded too
    On transcendental meat and drink;
Of thoughts that ranged quite near the blue
    She caught the missing Maeterlinck;
And after meals of more than earthly manna
Inhaled the stiffish fumes of *Monna Vanna.*

Taught, in *The Good Hope's* crib, to know
    The salient signs of healthy growth,
With every second word or so
    She rapped you out a ribald oath;
Showing that, should her other powers go wrong,
Her language still could "suffer and be strong."

Such is her progress, large and free,
    Whose nerve, of late reduced to pulp,
I now and here propose that we
    Should drink in one exhaustive gulp;
Long may her history, freed from hoary fossils,
Live in the Acts of You, her Young Apostles! [4]

At the end of the first ten years the society could pride
itself on having introduced the work of Granville Barker
(*The Marrying of Ann Leete,* January, 1902, *Waste,* November, 1907), St. John Hankin (*The Two Mr. Wetherbys,*
March, 1903, *The Cassilis Engagement,* February, 1907,

[4] By Courtesy of Sir Owen Seaman.

The Last of the De Mullens, December, 1908), W. Somerset Maugham (*A Man of Honour,* February, 1903), Charles McEvoy (*David Ballard,* June, 1917), W. Kingsley Tarpey (*Windmills,* June, 1901), Arnold Bennett (*Cupid and Commonsense,* January, 1908, *What the Public Wants,* May, 1909). In the days when Shaw was still caviar to the general he and the Stage Society found mutual benefit in *You Never Can Tell, Candida, Captain Brassbound's Conversion,* December, 1900, *Mrs. Warren's Profession,* January, 1902, *The Admirable Bashville,* June, 1903, *Man and Superman,* May, 1905.

Among continental plays of distinction were those of the Russians, Leo Tolstoy, Gorky, Gogol, Turgenev; of the French, Brieux, Curel; of the Germans, Hauptmann, Sudermann, Wedekind; of the Belgian, Maeterlinck; of the Italian, Giacosa; of the Scandinavian, Ibsen. Many of these are the work of playwrights who had been encouraged by the continental free theatres. More than once the Stage Society carried out its early intention of thwarting the censorship: *Monna Vanna, Waste,* and *Mrs. Warren's Profession,* while still under the ban, were all given before London audiences. Curiously, though Archer and Grein had praised heartily *Mrs. Warren's Profession* in the reading, they were shocked by the actual performance. Grein's account is an interesting social document in the history of the last three decades:

It was an exceedingly uncomfortable afternoon. For there was a majority of women to listen to that which could only be understood by a minority of men. . . . And, sure as I feel that most of the women, and a good many of the men, who were present at the production of "Mrs. Warren's Profession" by the Stage Society, did not at first know, and finally merely guessed, what was the woman's trade, I cannot withhold the opinion that the representation was unnecessary and painful. It is mainly for these reasons that, in spite of my great admiration for Bernard Shaw, the play was not brought out by the late Independent

Theatre. As a "straight talk to men only" it is not sufficiently true to life to be productive of an educational effect. As a drama it is unsatisfactory, because the characters have no inner life, but merely echo certain views of the author.

. . . Now he [Shaw] has merely philandered around a dangerous subject; he has treated it half in earnest, half in that peculiar jesting manner which is all his own. He has given free reins to his brain and silenced his heart. He has therefore produced a play of a needlessly "unpleasant" understructure to no useful end.[5]

If the second decade of the society appears less momentous, there are reasons for the slight decline. First, several of the playwrights of the early years had already reached the commercial stages and were no longer available; second, these later years are still too close to possess quite the glamor of the preceding ones; third and most important, for almost half the period England was at war.

In spite of many difficulties and tragic withdrawals these years saw more than one memorable evening. George Moore returned to play-writing in a dramatization of his own *Esther Waters* in 1911 and *Elizabeth Cooper,* a three-act comedy, in 1913. With *The Outcry,* 1917, Henry James experimented in the dramatic form. Echoes from the Moscow Art Theatre reached London in Chekhov's *Cherry Orchard,* 1911, and *Uncle Vanya,* 1914. *Eyvind of the Mountains* of Johann Sigurjonsson, in the translation of Sidney Olivier, represented a far distant drama, the Icelandic. During these years discoveries of the younger experimental societies founded in imitation of the earlier continental and English organizations, began to appear on the Stage Society programs: Masefield in *Pompey the Great,* 1910, *Good Friday,* 1917, and *The Faithful,* 1919; Stanley Houghton in *Hindle Wakes,* 1912; Harold Chapin, *The Philosopher of Butterbiggens,* 1917; Yeats, *The Player Queen,* 1919. A comedy

[5] Grein, J. T., *Dramatic Criticism, 1900-1901,* p. 293.

which passed to success on the regular stage is a translation of *The Man Who Married a Dumb Wife,* by Anatole France.

An innovation resulting from war conditions and the scarcity of new plays was the revival between 1914 and 1918 of several Restoration comedies, *The Recruiting Officer* by George Farquhar, *The Double Dealer, Love for Love,* and *The Way of the World* by Congreve, and *The Provoked Wife* by John Vanbrugh. In justification of these revivals, a historian of the society writes in the *Twentieth Annual Report:*

If the Council feels one regret it is that the Society remains, in this regard, a light shining in the darkness. Now that our living British dramatists have almost ceased to write, and London is fast becoming, in the theatre, little better than a suburb of New York, the Council hold that there can be no better refreshment and encouragement than the contemplation, on the stage, of these glories of our past dramatic literature. The Comedies of the Restoration were an obvious starting point, but the dramatists of the Elizabethan, Jacobean, and Caroline periods offer a province vast and rich upon which the Society is inclined to levy tribute in the future. Of the audiences' approval there can be no doubt; while the attitude of those few critics who, though doubtless well versed in English literature from Chaucer to Fielding, persist in regarding and indicating one aspect only of these merry comedies, is both instructive and illuminating.

These revivals were so well liked that, when the society returned to its search for contemporary plays, a separate society, under its auspices, was established to carry on the new work. The Phoenix is organized on much the same plan as the parent society, except that an executive committee of four takes the place of a large council of management. The committee in 1918 consisted of W. S. Kennedy, Montague Summers, Alan Wade, Norman Wilkinson. The programs of the first season were Webster's *Duchess of Malfi,* Dryden's

Marriage à la Mode, Heywood's *Fair Maid of the West* (*Part I*), Otway's *Don Carlos,* and Jonson's *Volpone.* "The Phoenix," read the announcement of its first season, "takes its name from one of the most celebrated of the old theatres, the Cockpit or Phoenix, constructed in the Cockpit in Drury Lane *circa* 1617. It was dismantled by the Puritans in 1649, but again opened at the Restoration. Pepys frequently visited the house. It was here he saw *Othello* and several of Fletcher's comedies. This theatre was last used in 1664. And in the words of Ovid:

> Inde ferunt, totidem qui vivere debeat annos,
> Corpore de patris parvum phoenica renasci."
> *Met.* XV, 401-2.

Though there may well be a Phoenix to complement the work of the older society, one cannot but feel that the true task of the Incorporated Stage Society should remain what it has been for thirty years, that of the laboratory theatre,—the agency for introducing new playwrights and the work of unusual foreigners. In its first twenty years the Stage Society had produced one hundred and twenty-three plays, of which eighty-one are English and forty-two continental; of these one hundred and six had not been previously given in England. In the season of 1918-1919 the Council read and considered seventy-eight plays, seventy-one English plays and seven English translations. "A real force in the dramatic world," A. W. Ward called the Society, while Henderson compares its achievement with that of the Théâtre Libre, or L'Œuvre, or the Freie Bühne.

Grein, looking back at the history of the Incorporated Stage Society in June, 1920, on the occasion of its hundredth performance, ascribed its success to its "three great helpmates," the serious students of the drama, the actors, and the authors. He wrote:

If many actors have risen to greater fame by the aid of the Stage Society, it cannot at the same time be gainsaid that the Stage Society owes a great deal to the actors. To study a part as long as Hamlet—as was not infrequently the case—for the sake of two performances only, is evidence of loving one's art beyond all dreams of avarice! At length—third in the triumvirate —came the authors. Practically from the beginning "G. B. S." lent his storehouse to the Society, and whenever Shaw was on the programme up went membership, interest, and prestige. No fewer than eight plays by Shaw appear in the list of a hundred, and six of them—mostly world-famed by this time—were ceded by him for first production.

It has made its mistakes—what human being or institution has not?—it has sometimes created the impression that it was running into grooves and ruled by cliques, but that is of small account when the work done is thrown into the scale. In our Theatre the Stage Society, in spite of its not having a fixed abode, has cemented its own place; and it is, perhaps, not presumptuous to express the hope that henceforth it will be looked upon by the regular managers not merely as a kind of freakish museum, an intellectual refuge of the destitute, but as a splendid auxiliary channel to increase the répertoire of the Commercial Theatre.[6]

Four years later Desmond McCarthy, writing in *The New Statesman,* gave his idea of the accomplishment of the society:

During the intervals betwen the acts of *The Bright Island,* by Mr. Arnold Bennett, I studied the back of the Stage Society's programme. I had often glanced at it before, but it occurred to me now to read it carefully. . . . How many modern dramatists the Stage Society had helped to launch, Shaw, Granville Barker, Hankin, McEvoy, Munro. True, Shaw would have made his mark anyhow; but after *Widowers' Houses* had had its brief scandalous success at Mr. Grein's Independent Theatre, his second play, *The Philanderer,* failed to find a theatre, and his third, *Mrs.*

[6] Grein, J. T., *The World of the Theatre; Impressions and Memoirs,* pp. 52, 53. Courtesy of William Heinemann, Ltd., Publishers, London.

Warren's Profession, was prohibited. Though *Arms and the Man* amused and had a run at the Avenue Theatre, it was the Stage Society's famous performance of *Mrs. Warren's Profession* which opened people's eyes to the importance of his talent. To how many literary men of eminence the Society had given a chance to show what they could do as dramatists: Hardy, Conrad, Henley, and Stevenson, Bennett, Henry James, George Moore, Sturge Moore, Masefield! How very ignorant we should be of continental drama during the last twenty-five years if it had not been for 36, Southampton Street! Who first introduced Tchekhov to us? How many of us would have seen a play by Tolstoy, D'Annunzio, Hauptmann, Gorki, Hermann Heijermanns, Strindberg, Turgenev, Wedekind, Brieux, Benavente, Gogol, Schnitzler or Maeterlinck, if it had not been for the Stage Society? Some of these dramatists' plays have been produced elsewhere, but in almost every case the Stage Society led the way.

It has been our only reliable channel of communication with continental drama. And what a cheap one, 42s. or 21s. or 10s. 6d. a year! They have been accused of not keeping pace with the times and showing an undue preference for the problem or slice-of-life play; but I noticed as I studied the back of my programme that before the Phoenix started they had produced three of Congreve's plays, *The Double Dealer, Love for Love, The Way of the World.* I had not forgotten that admiration for Pirandello in this country dated from their admirable performance of *Six Characters in Search of an Author* two years ago, or that we owed to them our peep at the new German drama; Georg Kaiser's *From Morn to Midnight,* Scholz's *The Race with a Shadow;* Toller's *Machine Wreckers,* were plays we ought to have seen. . . .

The program of the Phoenix recalls the work of a much older and more influential organization. Indeed the Elizabethan Stage Society with its origin in the Elizabethan Reading Society, which antedated the Stage Society by more than a dozen years, could claim the honor of being the first English experimental theatre if what is now its main activity had been developed sooner. The Elizabethan Stage Society, or rather William Poel, for the founder has been the heart and soul of this organization, has had an almost inestimable influence upon one form of production and upon Shakespearean criticism. Mr. Poel's lifelong contentions have been two, and most of his revivals have been attempts to prove them:

No play of Shakespeare's is a play unless it is being acted.

The greatest honour we can do Shakespeare is to show the world what are the dramatic limitations under which Shakespeare himself was content to work, and that these so-called "limitations" had exceptional advantages both for the author and for his actors in his own day.

In 1881 the members of the reading group under their leader's direction gave a remarkable performance of the First Quarto *Hamlet* on a stage of the Elizabethan type,—the first attempt to reproduce the conditions under which Shakespeare's plays were first acted. Success led to other productions and to the forming of the Elizabethan Stage Society. By 1919 the group had given performances of forty plays or parts of plays, including twelve of Shakespeare's, among them *Measure for Measure*, 1893, and *Troilus and Cressida*, 1912, till then almost unknown on the modern stage.

The surroundings being left, as they were in Shakespeare's day, [writes Mr. Poel] almost wholly to imagination, scene can follow scene without pause. It is therefore possible to show the whole action, to deliver nearly all the words, and to convey those effects of contrast between scene and scene which are obliterated by intervals. All this is necessary if one wants to get the theatrical result at which Shakespeare himself aimed, and if one shares the appetite of the Elizabethan audience for his poetry.

This revival of the Elizabethan method is one of the steps toward the liberation of Shakespeare's plays from the academic attitude which would magnify the achievement of the poet and overlook the very means by which the poetry and delineation of character find their expression, the achievement of a genius who was at once actor, man of the theatre, poet, and dramatist.

The productions have not been confined to Shakespeare. Of Elizabethan and Jacobean dramatists Marlowe, Middleton and Rowley, Jonson, Ford, Beaumont and Fletcher have been presented. The morality play, *Everyman*, first revived in London in 1901 and later brought to America, was one of the most impressive of the productions of the society and a revelation to the average playgoer, ignorant of the existence of any drama before Shakespeare. Occasionally, the society has turned to plays of other nations and sometimes to a dramatic poem which can be adapted to the stage,—Calderon's *Life's a Dream*, Kalidasa's *Sakuntala* from the Sanskrit, *The Bacchae* and the *Alcestis* of Euripides, *Samson Agonistes*, Coleridge's translation of Schiller's *Wallenstein*, and Scott's *Marmion*. Mr. Poel has also been devoted to the ideal of a national theatre, in form preferably the Elizabethan. That theatre which is as yet England's nearest approach to a national theatre, the Old Vic, is baptised in his spirit.

Another group called The Pioneers, organized much after the fashion of the Independent Theatre and the Stage Society, gave its inaugural program on December 17, 1905. The most famous program of this society was May 24, 1908, John Masefield's *Tragedy of Nan*. Of this Granville Barker was the director; his wife, Lillah McCarthy, Nan; A. E. Anson, Dick Gurvil; H. R. Hignett, Gaffer Pearce. As Professor Dickinson says, "This is one play of the new theatre that is not a little play." In it indeed, as Masefield wished, "the truth and rapture of man are holy things not lightly to be scorned," and "the beauty and the high things of the soul may pass from the stage to the mind." [7]

[7] From *The Tragedy of Nan*, by John Masefield, Introduction, p. 1. Courtesy of The Macmillan Company, Publishers.

The Pioneer Players, a reorganization of the earlier group, was formed in March, 1911, with two main objects, first, "to produce plays dealing with all kinds of movements of contemporary interest," and second, "to assist societies which have been formed all over the country in support of such movements, by helping them to organize dramatic performances, it having been asserted that one play is worth a hundred speeches where propaganda is concerned." From the list of plays one judges that the propaganda is often for feminism. In 1911 Miss Ellen Terry was president; in 1919 her daughter, Miss Edith Craig. Unusual productions have been Laurence Housman's *Pains and Penalties,* a defense of Queen Caroline, and Evreinov's monodrama, *The Theatre of the Soul,* translated by Marie Potapenko and Christopher St. John. This second play has for its scene the chest of the human body; for its characters a professor, and the three "entities" the rational, emotional, and the subliminal which make up his soul, two "concepts" of his wife, and two of a dancer, besides a porter, Death. The setting was unusual and the play created a sensation.

The New Century Theatre was also founded in imitation of the Stage Society. William Archer was one of the managers. The theatre opened with *John Gabriel Borkman;* later Barker staged for it Sir Gilbert Murray's translation of *Hippolytus, Trojan Women, Electra,* and *Medea.*

"The Play Actors Society," as its leaflet announces, "was founded in May, 1907, by members of the Actors' Association for the production of original works by English Authors, Shakespearean plays and other classic works, translations of well known foreign works, and to benefit the position of the working actor and actress." This is the second oldest of "the Sunday societies" now in existence. It follows very closely the Stage Society in organization, in the plan of Sunday evening and Monday afternoon performances, and in the scale of prices. Sir James M. Barrie has been its president, and its vice-presidents Oscar Asche, Arnold Bennett, Fay Compton, Gladys Cooper, Norman McKinnel, Marie Tempest, Irene Vanburgh, and Hugh Walpole. The chief purpose of the society is to give the young playwright the opportunity which otherwise he might never have. For a long time the society has given only "first productions," largely of original plays, though sometimes of an English translation or an adaptation of a foreign play. "We prefer to do modern plays," the secretary writes, "as it gives us wider scope for helping new playwrights. We like to be as progressive as possible."

For choice of plays, as well as for acting, this society has been commended by William Archer, J. T. Grein, and others. The society has now presented nearly one hundred plays and has brought some twenty-five successfully to the attention of theatre managers. The society has been particularly fond of the work of Elizabeth Baker, Harold Chapin, and Harold Brighouse. The list of "successes" also includes Ibsen's *Brand*, three of Bjørnson's plays, and Israel Zangwill's *The Melting Pot*. Miss Baker's *Chains*, later bought by Mr. Frohman, is perhaps the most important discovery of the theatre. A young author who through the help of The Play Actors has lately come to the front is Benn W. Levy; *This Woman Business*, given by the society in October, 1925, gained a great success at the Haymarket Theatre.

Another group wishing to assist the beginning playwright and the young actor are The Repertory Players with a first production in April, 1921. Their president is Matheson Levy and their vice-presidents are Lillah McCarthy, Normal McKinnel, Sir Johnston Forbes-Robertson. Prominent actors and actresses are among their patrons,—Lena Ashwell, Gladys Cooper, Sybil Thorndike, Irene Vanburgh, Sir John Martin-Harvey, and Nigel Playfair. Like the Incorporated Stage Society, they have given one play by Eugene O'Neill.

The Fellowship of Players, another of the younger Sunday night organizations, restricts its programs to Shakespeare, who in 1922 and 1923 was rarely seen in London except at the Old Vic, and gives an opportunity in Shakespearean rôles to many artists who are usually in modern plays. The society is proud of having presented Lilian Braithwaite as Hermione, Sybil Thorndike as Rosalind, Godfrey Tearle as Hamlet and Othello, Leslie Taber as Richard II, and Jean Cadell as Mistress Ford. The committee feels that it is partly through their efforts that there have lately been several West End revivals of Shakespeare.

"Sunday Societies" in London are multiplying. A critic from one of the groups finds a decided danger in this:

The rapidly increasing number of Sunday play producing Societies raises, however, a serious problem. . . . Theatre Managers justly complain that they are overwhelmed with applications for the loan of their theatres; dramatic critics justly complain of the number of performances they are invited to attend; and what endless difficulties have to be faced in the actual production of plays on Sundays can only be realized by those who have undertaken the task.

These obstacles arise entirely out of the rapid multiplication of play societies that have no definite aim. Any individual has the right to form a play society, but the point is that the position may become so untenable that all play producing societies, whether they be good, bad, or indifferent, will cease to exist.[8]

A somewhat different purpose animates The International Theatre Society of which Miss Kitty Willoughby is founder and director, as the sentence at the head of her leaflets suggests:

[8] Program of The Play Actors, May 30, 1926.

Every Nation has its Art—but Art has no Nation.

The idea was born [writes Miss Willoughby] through my being asked to read some Roumanian Folk Tales at a public dinner at the Lyceum Club, of which I am a member. This peep into Roumanian literature proved so very interesting that I resolved then and there to form an International Theatre Society in order to present the plays of all the nations who had a dramatic literature, preferably the lesser known, to the London Public. The society was formed and as you will see by the page heading practically every Embassy and Legation in London is represented in our membership. . . .

The ultimate aim of the Society is to establish a permanent International Theatre in London, where Dramatic Authors of every nationality will be represented. The idea is to put each play on for a week only at the International Theatre and to invite all the Managers of other theatres, so that it would act as a clearing house for foreign as well as English talent. We also believe that the friendship between the various countries will be fostered by these means.

There can be no true friendship without understanding and the easiest means of understanding a nation is through its dramatic art.

Other less important societies founded in imitation of the Incorporated Stage Society or the Elizabethan Stage Society are the English Drama Society, which in the winter of 1906-1907 revived three of the Chester Mystery Plays, the New Stage Club, which in the same year with *The Stronger Woman* and *Simoom* first introduced Strindberg to English play-goers, the Drama Society, founded in 1911, the Morality Play Society, The New Plays, The Ibsen Club. The Oncomers Society between 1911 and 1913 produced some twelve or fourteen plays at the Little Theatre, London, to introduce new playwrights and to aid actors from the provinces in becoming known to London managers. Another organization, the Adelphi Play Society, in April, 1912, produced Tolstoy's *The Cause of It All.*

A novel society for assisting young playwrights, The English Play Society, was carried on four years by Mr. Lyddell Sawyer, "mostly as a personal hobby," and ended with the withdrawal of his interest. The society, which had among its patrons many of the leading actors and producers of London,—Sir Charles Wyndham, Lena Ashwell, Charles Frohman, the Kendals, Cyril Maude, Marie Tempest,—offered to read and grade new plays according to a standard examination form, and to give a diploma to each play deserving production. The society also staged a few plays.

A little apart from these others in purposes and ideals is the Play and Pageant Union of Hampstead Garden Suburb. The interest of this group, formed in 1910 as the Pageant Committee, has been stimulating the residents of Hampstead Garden to authorship. There is an annual competition for a play or masque suitable for out-door performance. The out-door theatre in the Little Wood seats nearly six hundred people and has a stage of turf outlined with trees, which will hold a cast of two hundred. In winter there are four programs of contrasted types. The annual Christmas entertainment, like the pageant, is always the work of one of the group.

Two unusual organizations of recent years are The Gate Theatre Studio and the Three Hundred Club. The second was founded by Mrs. Geoffrey Whitworth to produce plays by young Englishmen and thus to bring their names before a larger public. The first evening *The Discovery,* by the mother of the dramatist Sheridan, in an adaptation by Aldous Huxley, was directed by Sir Nigel Playfair; ordinarily the society does not foster revivals. It has encouraged Welsh drama by presenting Richard Hughes' *Comedy of Good and Evil.*

Not to be confused with these play-producing groups are

several organizations which have for their purpose the advancement of the drama by play-going and discussion. Chief among these are the Playgoers' Club founded in 1884, and numbering among its presidents J. T. Grein, Max Beerbohm, and A. B. Walker; the Gallery First Nighters' Club, the O. P. Club, and the Dramatic Debaters. Their influence on the drama, though indirect, must be important.

Three national organizations, though not in themselves play-producing, have an important influence upon many thousands of men and women who are directly concerned with English little theatres in town and country. In 1919, Mr. Geoffrey Whitworth, who had long been a devoted member of the London Incorporated Stage Society, founded the British Drama League, with Lord Howard de Walden as president and Granville Barker as chairman of the council. The League seeks to affiliate acting groups of non-professionals and thus form channels of intercommunication for advancing the drama as an art and a social force; there are over seven hundred societies on its books. It organizes conferences, sends out costumes and stage properties, and plans an annual Festival of Community Drama in London to which six companies, the winners in district competitions, are sent. The League has also collected the material for some famous loan exhibits, the International Theatre Exhibit at the Victoria and Albert Museum, South Kensington, the Historical Exhibit of Theatre Art at the British Empire Exhibition, 1924, and the Exhibition of Community Theatre Art at the Summer Meeting at Oxford, 1925. The Village Drama Society, the creation of Miss M. E. Kelly and Miss D. Kelly, with headquarters first in North Devonshire and now in London, in its special field parallels the work of the League. The English villages, according to the leaders of the Village Drama Society, are passing through a difficult transitional period in which they are attempting to reconcile the ideals of their somewhat isolated past with those of the outside world. The Society puts the acting groups in touch with the finest plays for which they are ready and encourages play-writing by criticising manucripts for young writers and publishing a few dramas of country life. The organization has a Welsh branch which is very successful. The National Federation of Women's Institutes—the Women's Institute corresponds to the Women's Club of the United States—also holds competitions both in production and in original writing.

The second phase in the advance of the experimental theatre movement was the repertory theatre. What is the "repertory" idea of which there has been so much discussion in the last twenty years? To turn to William Archer:

When we speak of a repertory, we mean a number of plays always ready for performance, with nothing more than a "run through" rehearsal, which, therefore, can be, and are, acted in such alternation that three, four or five different plays may be given in the course of a week. New plays are from time to time added to the repertory, and those of them which succeed may be performed fifty, seventy, a hundred times, or even more, in the course of one season; but no play is ever performed more than two or three times in uninterrupted succession.[9]

From this definition the reader can see that repertory is not a new development in the history of the theatre but an established method favored by the actor-manager eager to show his versatility in several parts during one week, by the old stock companies, and by that great home of French classical drama, the Comédie Française.

What is new in the repertory movement of the last few years is its spirit,—its attempt to appeal to intelligent theatre-goers who have grown weary of the abuses of the commercial stage. These people have tired of the long run system which keeps on the stage the play of hackneyed plot

[9] Quoted by Howe, P. P., *The Repertory Theatre*, p. 37.

and conventional ideas, which the manager believes have stood the test of time, and of the star who spends many months in one rôle while he should be gaining power in several rôles. For the actor repertory means variety of opportunity and training, freedom from long periods of unemployment, and continuity in the organization of his company; for the manager it means the opportunity to experiment without overwhelming initial expense and with the assurance that under the repertory plan of frequent revivals a play can make a gradual appeal to its own particular audience.

The first London repertory theatre of modern ideals was the Lyceum during the season of 1899-1900, under the management of F. R. Benson. Mr. Benson for more than a dozen years had been touring the provinces of England, Scotland, and Ireland in Shakespeare, and since 1886 had produced a play annually in the Shakespeare Memorial Theatre, Stratford. In this particular London season, he gave *The Rivals* and seven of Shakespeare's plays, including the complete texts of *Henry VI* and of *Hamlet*. The company reached a high order of achievement.

Granville Barker, the next experimenter in repertory, had thought much about the problems and destinies of the modern theatre, and as actor, playwright, or producer, had been connected with the New Century Theatre, the Elizabethan Stage Society, and the Stage Society, and with several professional companies. In 1901 his conversion to socialism resulted in deeper interest, for the theatre came to seem to him "a great instrumentality in the life of our time," and the repertory system, or rather a modified form of it, the most effective method of reaching the public.[10] In 1904 his opportunity came: J. H. Leigh of the Court Theatre, Sloane Square, invited him to assist the manager of that theatre, Vedrenne, in a production of *Two Gentle-*

[10] See Henderson, Archibald, *George Bernard Shaw*, pp. 368, 369.

men of Verona. Mr. Barker accepted on condition that he might give six matinées of *Candida,* a decidedly daring experiment in the days when Shaw was still considered the darling of the ultra-intellectuals. These matinées proved so successful that Mr. Barker and Mr. Vedrenne formed a partnership which lasted during the next three years.

These years were a veritable triumph. There were nine hundred and forty-six performances; seven hundred and one performances of Shaw gave the house its nickname, "the Shaw Repertory Theatre." Among the eleven plays of his which the Court produced, the three great favorites were *Man and Superman* and *You Never Can Tell,* beloved of the intellectuals, and *John Bull's Other Island,* which promptly appealed to "the man in the street." Other successful plays were Barker and Housman's *Prunella* and Galsworthy's *Silver Box.* St. John Hankin's *The Return of the Prodigal* and Masefield's *Campden Wonder* had several performances. In fact, hardly a contemporary English dramatist was absent from the boards, except Pinero, Jones, and Barrie, who had long been established. Foreign drama, also, was well represented, especially the Greek tragedy in Sir Gilbert Murray's translations. Before producing these dramas Barker considered the three methods of revival,— giving the play as nearly as possible under the original conditions, supplementing the Greek method by the modern, and acting the plays as though written for the present day. He chose the last.

The acting of the Court Theatre, as well as its choice of plays amazed thoughtful Londoners, many of whom had never before realized the delight of a careful ensemble. There was unusual acting of the central rôles, Gertrude Kingston's Helen, Edith Wynne Matthison's Electra; but there was no less unusual interpretation in minor ones, Granville Barker's messenger, Lewis Casson's Castor, Michael Sherbrooke's Marzo (in *Captain Brassbound's*

Conversion). The delight of the audience indeed came partly through the relief of not having to watch one personality constantly,—against a background of mediocrity,—and partly through the truth with which sincere acting in even small parts illuminates a play. The attempt was always to get away from the insincere, the artificial. Because of the same desire the scenery of the Court was inexpensive and suggestive, rather than realistic and elaborate. Harmony of colors, agreeable lights and shades were put before exactness of detail. As MacCarthy says, Barker and Vedrenne had grasped an important principle overlooked by London managers, "that good acting can make poor scenery seem real but that real scenery cannot do the same for poor acting."

There underlay the Court Theatre in a degree perhaps never surpassed a happy mingling of artistic endeavor and strong business sense. The managers presented the most advanced drama of their decade, but they did not continue to run plays (one by Harcourt and Fenn, for instance) which received almost no support. On the other hand, they resisted the temptation to offer for many months popular plays like *You Never Can Tell* and *John Bull's Other Island*. Though possessing in a high degree the repertory spirit, the Court, it should be noted, in arrangement of programs was not strictly a repertory theatre: instead of offering three or four different plays a week like the municipal theatres of the continent, Barker and Vedrenne's theatre presented one play during the evenings of several weeks and new programs at matinées.

By showing that a theatre of high ideals and a taste for advanced drama need not be a financial failure, the Court achieved several important results. (1) It broke ground for other repertory theatres, as the pioneer experimental theatres, the "Sunday societies," had broken ground for it. (2) It drew back to the theatre many hitherto disgusted playgoers and welded them into a regular audience. (3) It established the reputations of half a dozen important playwrights who had not before emerged from the smaller audiences of the stage societies. (4) It convinced a hitherto sceptical public of the greatness of Shaw. "The most notable achievement in modern dramatic production," says Desmond MacCarthy of this theatre, "the most interesting chapter in the history of the development of the contemporary English drama . . . very like a revolution in the art of dramatic production in England," while Howe gives the Court Theatre even greater emphasis,—"The Stage Society was formed to carry on the movement, (begun by Grein) but it is with the little body of dramatists who came into prominence at the Court Theatre during its three years' season that the new dramatic movement may most usefully be regarded as beginning."

In September, 1907, Barker and Vedrenne moved to the larger Savoy Theatre and conducted another repertory theatre with the same aims and similar programs, adding to the repertory of the Court, *The Devil's Disciple, Cæsar and Cleopatra, Arms and the Man,* Murray's translation of *Medea,* and Galsworthy's *Joy.* Though the audiences of the smaller Court Theatre were not always able to fill the Savoy, the season was reasonably successful, but disappointment on the refusal of the censor to license Barker's *Waste* brought the attempt to a close the following March. During the same winter Barker and Vedrenne managed *The Devil's Disciple* at the Queen's Theatre and a series of special matinées of *Getting Married* and *The Tragedy of Nan* at the Haymarket. Galsworthy's *Strife* was also given afternoon performances at the Duke of York's Theatre, and later taken to the Haymarket Theatre.

These experiments drew to the repertory supporters one of the most prominent and respected of the managers of the commercial theatre, Charles Frohman. He opened the Duke of York's Theatre as a theatre of the new type and gave Barker a power of direction theoretically unlimited. Mr. Frohman was so avowed an enthusiast of the new as to advise young playwrights to learn the conventions of the stage chiefly for the sake of disregarding them. "I have no preference for any particular kind of play," he said. "I want what is good of any kind. One sometimes hears it said, 'A good thing, but not a play.' This is one of the kinds I want."

Beginning February 21, 1910, the Duke of York's gave a season of seventeen weeks with one hundred and twenty-eight performances of seventeen plays. Galsworthy's *Justice* was the opening program. Arranged in order of popularity the plays are as follows: *Trelawney of the 'Wells'* (forty-two performances); *Justice* (twenty-six); Barrie's *The Twelve Pound Look* (twenty-six); *Prunella* (seventeen); Miss Baker's *Chains* (fifteen); Shaw's *Misalliance* (eleven); Barker's *Madras House* (ten); Meredith's *Sentimentalists* (six); Barrie's *Old Friends* (six); Anthony Hope and Cosmo Gordon Lennox's *Helena's Path* (two).

The Duke of York's illustrated again the versatility of several of the Court Theatre actors and actresses,—Lewis Casson, Hubert Harben, Frederick Lloyd, Mary Barton, Sybil Thorndike, and Donald Calthrop,—and introduced two others of distinction in widely contrasted rôles,—Dennis Eadie, who was Falder in *Justice* and Philip in *The Madras House;* and Mary Jerrold, Lyra in the *Sentimentalists,* Miss Yates in the *Madras House,* and Doll in *Prunella.*

To the surprise of every one the Duke of York's, unlike the Court Theatre, proved a heavy loss. Various reasons have been suggested for this: a lack of unity in direction as Granville Barker was gradually given less freedom, the illogical attitude of the public in persisting in considering the repertory gloomy even though it included comedy and fantasy, and, perhaps most important, the greater expenditure needed for advertising and managing a larger house.

Apparently the London audience for serious drama, except that of the Old Vic, is not numerous enough to support a great repertory theatre. The many theatres in the metropolis taken together are a kind of repertory house.

"A theatre of character," the biographer of the Old Vic calls this playhouse, the more formal but rarely heard appelation of which is the Royal Victoria Hall. This theatre, more than a century old, has seen unusual vicissitudes. Over a generation ago it could scarcely have been described in the terms of its present admirers: it was rather *without character*, prostituting art to gain, in an outrageous fashion. Indeed this playhouse in its sensational career is like a would-be lady of fashion, striving for social leadership, then, when unsuccessful, sinking rapidly to the gutter, and finally, to her surprise, rescued and brought back to a life of usefulness and idealism.

The building of the Royal Coburg Theatre, as it was first called after Prince Leopold of Saxe-Coburg, husband of the young Princess Charlotte of Wales, later King of the Belgians, was inspired by a laudable belief in progress and the patronage of royalty. It owed its existence to the building of the Waterloo Bridge in 1817, an event which was expected to bring expansion to Lambeth and its surroundings upon the Surrey side of the Thames. In encouraging theatrical enterprise in this district the Royal Coburg followed a tradition, for this bank of the river had been the home of the Globe and other Elizabethan playhouses. But the early days of the theatre and the life of the royal patrons seemed alike ill-fated: between the time of the laying of the corner-stone of the Royal Coburg "by Their Serene and Royal Highnesses' proxy, Alderman Goodbehere" and the completion of the building, Princess Charlotte had died, and the theatre which had hoped for fashion and distinction never quite succeeded in rivaling the playhouses of the West End.

Not that it did not make a gallant struggle. The Royal
Victoria Hall, as it was rechristened in honor of the next
little princess, followed the theatrical vogues of the day.
With its adaptations of Shakespeare (Ophelia married her
Dane), its long bills compounded of amazing elements, its
system of *half-prices*, (admissions at eight-thirty when the
evening was half over), this playhouse illumines much of
the stage history of the nineteenth century. Great actors
were sometimes billed here: Edmund Kean, Macready,
Junius Brutus Booth, Brooke ("the Hibernian Roscius"),
Phelps, the Keeleys. But denizens of Hyde Park and the
West End did not relish an awkward trip by coach or river-
boat in quest of the sort of entertainment which they could
find close at hand. More and more the clientele of the Old
Vic came from Lambeth and expressed the taste of Lambeth,—as the managers conceived it,—for coarse and obvious comedy, and above all, for melodrama.

> Look always on the Surrey side
>   For true dramatic art;
> The road is long—the river wide—
>   But frequent buses start
> From Charing Cross or Gracechurch Street
>   (An inexpensive ride);
> So, if you want an evening's treat,
>   O seek the Surrey side!
>
> I have been there, and still would go,
>   As Dr. Watts observes;
> Although it's not a place, I know,
>   For folks with feeble nerves.
> Ah me! how many roars I've had,
>   How many tears I've dried
> At melodramas, good and bad,
>   Upon the Surrey side.
>
> Can I forget those wicked lords,
>   Their voices and their calves,

The things they did upon those boards
　　And never did by halves?
The peasant, brave though lowly born,
　　Who constantly defied
Those wicked lords with utter scorn
　　Upon the Surrey side?

　　　．　　　．　　　．　　　．　　　．

I gape in Covent Garden's walls,
　　I doze in Drury Lane;
I strive in the Lyceum stalls
　　To keep awake in vain.
There's naught in the dramatic way
　　That I can quite abide,
Except the pieces that they play
　　Upon the Surrey side.[11]

By the seventies of the last century the Old Vic was at its lowest ebb, "on the bottom," to use a phrase of Chekhov's,—both artistically and morally, "the most degraded" theatre in London, haunt of "the vulgar and ignorant," house of "atrocious melodramas fit only for an audience of felons." Charles Kingsley fulminated against it in *Alton Locke,* describing "the beggary and rascality of London" pouring in at half-price time, "from the neighboring gin palaces and thieves' cellar," and made the need for the withdrawal of its license the text for one of his appeals for the Charter and the representation of the working classes in Parliament. In this period the theatre was living on its "wet money," the intakings of the bar, which encouraged drunkenness and other forms of vice.

But its reformation was approaching. Miss Emma Cons, who brought this about, was an energetic and courageous woman, always a pioneer. Friend and admirer of Ruskin, for whom she illuminated several manuscripts, she was

[11] Leigh, H. S., *Carols of Cockayne,* quoted in *The Old Vic,* by Cicely Mary Hamilton and Lilian Bayles, pp. 88, 89.

swayed both by his conception of art and by his sympathy for the poor. After being one of the first women in England to enter the delicate craft of watch-engraving and the first woman to design stained glass windows (she restored several of the windows in Merton College, Oxford), she turned to public affairs, particularly those connected with the life of the London slums. She was an active suffragette and a member of the first London County Council. She founded one of the first hostels for girls, many clinics and crèches, and the earliest "coffee tavern" in the city. "The Safe Shop," as it was nicknamed, furnished good, inexpensive food, without selling alcohol or allowing gambling, and provided the men and women of the laboring classes a quiet, respectable place, where they might read their papers, talk, or listen to an occasional concert. Later came her improvements in housing the poor, in which she assisted Mis Octavia Hill, Ruskin's agent. Miss Cons' connection with the Old Vic was a logical sequel to her study of housing conditions: she saw first that her people had light and air about their houses and then made her gallant and successful fight for more light and air about their souls.

Her life at Surrey Lodge [Miss Bayles writes] only strengthened Emmie's conviction of the necessity of separating drink from entertainment. Again and again there were violent scenes in the building, when men came home drunk from the neighboring music-halls—and she made up her mind that the only remedy for the evil was a counter-attraction, the provision of clean entertainment. When she came to Lambeth the Coffee Tavern Company was in a fairly prosperous condition; she conceived the idea, therefore, of extending its sphere of operations and opening a music-hall where the only drinks sold were coffee, tea and lemonade. The Old Vic, at the time, was standing empty, so the venture was possible if others would follow Emmie's lead.

This idea of using the Old Vic originated with John Hollingshead of the Gaiety, but the plan for a reformed music-hall was Miss Cons' own, and hers was the enthusiasm which drew together the first Council of the Coffee Music-Halls Company in control of the project. Arthur Sullivan, Carl Rosa, and Julius Benedict were important members. The aims, according to the leaflet which heralded the new enterprise, were as follows:

The present company has been formed to provide several large music-halls in various parts of London, at which a purified entertainment shall be given and no intoxicant drinks be sold. The popularity of music-halls is shown by the fact that in London alone, to say nothing of the large provincial towns, they exist, as compared with theatres, in the proportion of eight to one.

The visitors at these places are essentially family visitors; that is to say, men go there and take their wives and children, whereas if they go to a public-house or a coffee tavern they generally go alone.

It has long been felt that the influence of the existing music-hall is for the most part far from elevating. General complaints have recently been made as to the impropriety of many songs now sung at these places, and the present Home Secretary, Mr. Cross, has just addressed a circular letter on this subject to the licensing magistrates. . . .

It is not proposed to provide for a higher class of audience than that which at present frequents music-halls, but only to offer that class an entertainment which shall amuse without degrading them, and to which men may take their wives and children without shaming and harming them.

Thus on Boxing Day, Monday, December 27, 1880, the Old Vic began its modest program with an evening of variety acts revolutionary only in their freedom from indecency. The building, altered and redecorated at the cost of three thousand pounds, no longer housed a bar; it became a center for amiable and appreciative audiences, "including whole families taking their tea and coffee." But the building up of a large audience proved a difficulty, for the

respectable playgoer had not yet dissociated the name of
the Old Vic from its recent epithets, and the disreputable
longed for the old days and his "licensed pit of darkness."
A deficit of three thousand pounds within less than a year
was to the majority of the trustees reason enough for closing the theatre. But Miss Cons, heading the minority, urged
its continuation on the ground that the founders had never
anticipated any profits and that in its moral influence the
theatre was already a success. New gifts came in, notably a
thousand pounds from Miss Martineau, and from Lord
Mount Temple a promise to pay any debts for the next nine
months.

The work went with new enthusiasm under a reorganized
committee. Within three years the performances had
steadily improved, and other activities had been undertaken. Weekly lectures, with admission a penny, sometimes
must have proved disconcerting to the distinguished men
who gave them, for "play-goers accustomed to exchanging
back-chat with red-nosed comedians saw no reason why they
should not also exchange back-chat with professors. When
one eminent scientist paused in his speech to arrange his
mechanical apparatus, the pause was mistaken for a failure
of memory,—a dry-up—and a shout from the upper regions
bade him 'Go home and learn his lessons.' " [12] Strangely
enough these lectures and the rough-and-ready discussions
developed into a college, Morley Memorial College for
Working Men and Women, which has the distinction of
being the only institution of its kind ever founded by a theatre. Its premises continued in the theatre building, *under,
above,* and *behind* the stage for the next twenty-five years.
In 1921 a London County Council more alert to structural
requirements than the Council of a quarter century before,
served notice on the Old Vic that Morley College and the
theatre must be housed under separate roofs and that cer-

[12] *Ibid.,* p. 185.

tain alterations must be made in the playhouse. Now followed one of the most serious campaigns for money in the history of the theatre. At last, in August, 1922, through the benefaction of Sir George Dance, a large-visioned theatrical manager, Morley College was enabled to move to new quarters in Westminster Bridge Road nearby, and the Old Vic to transform itself into a modern playhouse.

To return to the story of the Old Vic itself. Under the authority of Miss Cons and her co-workers, including William Poel of the Elizabethan Stage Society, by 1898 the Vic had become a theatre devoted to decent variety programs, lectures, concerts, and operas, the last presented mainly in tableau form. In that year Miss Lilian Bayles, Miss Cons' favorite niece, joined her as manager, later, after her aunt's death, to shoulder the main responsibility for the theatre. No lengthy analysis of her character is necessary, for the Old Vic is her self-expression. Her broadcasted message on "The Art of Living and the Need for the Theatre," is her expression of faith:

I so believe the theatre is our greatest power for good or evil, that I pray my earnestness may give me words in which to express this faith and to hold your attention. . . . I am cast to-night to speak on the Art of Living and the place of the Theatre in that life. The Theatre isn't an excuse for wonderful evening gowns and jewels; it isn't a fad of people with long hair and sandals or the perquisite of 'varsity men and women; good drama isn't only for the students of training colleges and boys and girls swotting for the Oxford and Cambridge Locals; it is a crying need of working men and women who need to see beyond the four walls of their offices, workshops and homes into a world of awe and wonder.

Furthermore, all art is a bond between rich and poor; it allows of no class distinctions; more than that, it is a bond between nation and nation, and may do much to help widely differing peoples to understand the peculiar problems of life in each country; I think it was Dr. Dearmer who said: "Art is a spiritual necessity. Civilization cannot exist in its absence for without it civilization is but organized savagery." The theatre is perhaps the most important and accessible and the most easily understood branch of art for the man and woman in the street.[13]

Of the two activities for which the Old Vic is famous, one was brought to its present success by Miss Bayles and the other was inaugurated by her. These are the presentation of opera in English and the frequent presentation of Shakespeare.

Miss Bayles realized the love of music in the hearts of her Lambeth audience when even the simplest production, hardly more than the singing of a few of the best-known airs, could draw an audience of two thousand to Waterloo Road, and began to give complete operas as often as she could afford them. In the early years she was never able to pay understudies; even in 1925 she could not afford a full-time chorus. But amateurs and professionals have been generous in their assistance and in some way the work continued in the face of obstacles. Non-copyright operas of necessity came first, those of Verdi, Mozart, Balfe, and the young Wagner; later the range was extended. In 1924-1925 the season included *Carmen* (Bizet), *Cavalleria Rusticana* and *Pagliacci* (Mascagni and Leoncavallo), *Faust* (Gounod), *Tannhäuser* (Wagner), *Il Trovatore* (Verdi), *Lucia di Lammermoor* (Donizetti), *La Traviata* (Verdi), *The Bohemian Girl* (Balfe), *The Magic Flute* (Mozart), *Lohengrin* (Wagner), *Maritana* (Wallace), *The Marriage of Figaro* (Mozart), *Rigoletto* (Verdi), *Mignon* (Thomas), *Elijah* (Mendelssohn), *The Lily of Killarney* (Benedict), *Don Giovanni* (Mozart), *Aïda* (Verdi). The next year the company added Puccini's *Madame Butterfly*. Modern music has been represented by Ethel Smyth's *Bosun's Mate* and *Tête Galante*, Nicholas Gatty's *Ferelon* and *The Tempest*,

[13] From *The Old Vic*, by Cicely Mary Hamilton and Lilian Bayles, pp. 188, 189. Courtesy of Jonathan Cape Limited, Publishers, London.

and Rutland Boughton's *Immortal Hour*. The last is called
the first really popular English opera since Balfe and Wallace.

To the outside world the Old Vic is the "Home of Shakespeare and Opera in English," but perhaps few know that
in this surprising theatre Shakespeare owes his place indirectly to the cinema. The Vic was a pioneer in the giving of
motion pictures, simple clean films principally of out-door
scenes once a week before large audiences of children. Even
at a penny a seat these entertainments netted the organization two thousand pounds in two years. When more sensational were released, Miss Bayles came to feel that the
movies were not an elevating force for her audiences of
children. Shakespeare occurred to her as a substitute.

To propose Shakespeare at all in the autumn of 1914 took
daring. Three years before Bridges Adams had suggested
a season of Shakespeare and had been refused; in the early
part of 1914 Rosina Filippi had brought her People's Theatre with its Shakespearean repertoire to the Old Vic, and
played to slender houses,—her failure partly accounted for
by the fact that some of the performances were scheduled
on nights which the Lambeth audience had considered
sacred to opera. In 1914, too, money was needed for another
cause than the drama, and young actors were beginning to
play their parts upon a different stage. But Miss Bayles
persevered: to her the experiment, if successful, would
mean three things, the establishment of a permanent company, more valuable than a haphazard group, the opportunity of developing unknown or provincial talent, and,
above all, the privilege of bringing beauty and delight to
her thousands of little patrons as well as to the grown-ups.

From the beginning, the venture had the assistance of distinguished men and women, both professionals and amateurs. Estelle Stead, Matheson Lang, Mrs. Lang (Hutin

Britton) were active in the first plays, *The Taming of the Shrew, Hamlet, The Merchant of Venice;* Lang lent costumes and produced the plays, while Mrs. Lang acted Katherine and Portia. Ben Greet between 1914 and 1917 produced thirty-eight plays, twenty-seven of them by Shakespeare. Other actors and actresses spoke at the Vic to advertise its new purpose. Here Sir Herbert Tree made his last speech on an English stage. Such assistance and Miss Bayles' own courage and artistic conscience held the playhouse to a standard almost unique among English war-time theatres: while its wealthier compeers on the other side of the Thames were pandering to the lower elements in their audiences the Old Vic gave of its best, Shakespeare or opera. As each difficulty appeared the Vic met it; when the company had sent too many members to France to make possible the mob scenes in *Julius Cæsar,* Miss Bayles asked for volunteers among the audience. The theatre, too, recognized no national boundaries in art: the Wagnerian operas were never banished; indeed *Lohengrin* was sung during the war to help Belgian refugees.

These war days demanded courage of players as well as soldiers. "We'll play to-morrow," replied Miss Bayles when, during the period of the worst air-raids, she was advised to close her house temporarily. "That is, unless they blow off the roof to-night." On the night of the performance of *King John* the Germans were taking Waterloo Station, nearby, for their target. Miss Bayles encouraged the little girl who was playing Prince Arthur, by reminding her that the day was sacred to Saint Michael and All Angels. The little child said afterwards that she was no longer afraid for she knew that these saints would protect her. At the height of the raid came the lines, seemingly devised for the moment,—

> Some airy devil hovers in the sky
> And pours down mischief.

At Falconbridge's lines,—

> This England never did and never shall
> Lie at the proud foot of a conqueror,

the audience rose in an ecstasy of enthusiasm. These words were placed over the proscenium arch "for the duration." For another purpose, the honoring of the sacred dead of the Old Vic, the inscription also came from Shakespeare:

> The benediction of the covering heaven
> Be on their head, for they are worthy.

To Miss Bayles and her helpers the belief that the theatre is an incomparable influence for joy and solace is more than a theory: it was proved true many times during these anxious years. Here in her own words is an example:

A nurse in charge of our blind boys found how they delighted in opera. One of her patients was so depressed that nothing could be done to rouse him. The doctor thought there was little chance of his recovery if he did not regain an interest in life. An entertainment was given at the hospital and the nurse noticed how he lifted his head for a few moments while a beautiful song was being sung; and she felt, if she could make him come to an opera, it might be the first step towards recovery. So she urged him, and eventually he gave in with a bad grace saying, "I'll do it for you, Nurse, as you believe it's good for me, but I don't think anything will do me any good." Saturday afternoon came; and Nurse came with three blind boys. The poor fellow seemed as bad as ever; so Nurse talked to the other two of opera and plays. They entered our doors and climbed the stone staircase and sat on the rather hard balcony seats. The opera was *Mignon* and, as the charming overture started, the boy clutched Nurse's arm and said, "What is this place? Where am I?" She replied, "I told you I was bringing you to an opera." "Oh, I thought you said 'operation'— I wasn't half listening." "But we talked of the theatre," she persisted. "I thought you meant an operating theatre," he said. "I've

never heard an opera before—oh, it is lovely!" . . . And from
that time he began to enjoy life again.[14]

The Old Vic is continuing its programs of Shakespeare
and opera. *Measure for Measure, King John,* and *Antony
and Cleopatra* can attract the Surrey Side if West End
managers hesitate over them. On November 7, 1923, the eve
of the Tercentenary of the First Shakespeare Folio, Miss
Bayles gave *Troilus and Cressida,* thus completing the production of all the plays which it contains, a stupendous
achievement for any theatre and an indication of a most
unusual audience. Since seats at the Vic range from reserved orchestra and balcony stalls at five shillings, to seats
not reserved at five pence, it is apparent that a delight in
Shakespeare is not the prerogative of the wealthy or the
cultivated.

Any account of the Old Vic must mention the fellow-
workers who by their directing have helped bring Miss
Bayles' vision to an actuality, Matheson Lang, Hutin Britton, Estelle Stead, Andrew Leigh, Fisher White, and Ben
Greet during the war years; more recently George R. Taso,
Russell Thorndike, Charles Warburton, Robert Atkins, and
in 1924, Andrew Leigh again. Of the actors and actresses
discovered by the Old Vic, Russell Thorndike and his sis-
ter, Sybil Thorndike, now known everywhere for her St.
Joan in Shaw's play, are perhaps the most famous. Long
before she played to the West End Miss Thorndike was
Prince Hal for her Lambeth audiences. Ion Swinley, George
Hayes, John Lawrie, and Hilton Edwards have been among
Miss Bayles' prominent actors.

To many Englishmen the Old Vic has come to stand
as a partial realization of their dream of a national theatre.
As such it was invited by the Belgian minister of art to
Brussels a few years ago for a three-day Shakespearean

14 *Ibid.,* pp. 202, 203.

festival. Miss Bayles is the only woman, except Queen Mary, to whom Oxford University, long the traditional foe of players, has presented an honorary degree of Master of Arts. Recently the faith of the public in the Old Vic and its director has been again evidenced in the success of the campaign undertaken to restore a famous old theatre at the other end of London, Sadler's Wells, and to add its management to Miss Bayles' activities. These two theatres under the same direction, alternating Shakespeare and opera, can be run much more economically and effectively than as separate units, and can bring beauty into the lives of the poor of two large and congested districts.

Another playhouse in an outlying district is making theatre history under a director of genius. This is Sir Nigel Playfair's Lyric Theatre in Hammersmith.

Mr. Playfair is often accused of knowing, in some occult way, the tunes which the public really likes. He has much more valuable knowledge than this: he knows the tunes which he himself really likes—and is not afraid of them. His *flair*, of which people talk, is the *flair* which a few women have, of exploiting, not their toilets, but their personalities by means of their toilets; a flair, however, beyond most women, whose horizon is bounded by the minatory words, "stock size." [15]

It was in 1918 that Mr. Nigel Playfair, now Sir Nigel, discovered this old theatre in a remote and dreary section of London, and as Arnold Bennett says, "before a baby could learn to talk," made it one of the most vivid spots of delight in the English theatre world. A notable actor in modern plays on the regular stages, Sir Nigel had long been on the side of the angels in matters pertaining to modern drama. He believes thoroughly that the theatre should be "a stimulant, not an anodyne," that its influence should be toward a

[15] Milne, A. A., Epilogue to Playfair, Nigel, *The Story of the Lyric Theatre, Hammersmith*, p. 222.

strengthening of sympathy for other people's problems, "problems, I mean, which may not present themselves in the comparatively narrow sphere in which each one of us of necessity has to move during his ordinary working days. That is the duty of the theatre as I conceive it, translated as it may be in terms of music and tragedy, of laughter and of song. With its exposition of problems it must bring, too, its own comfort and mercy." [16] Arnold Bennett, Alistair Taylor, and a group of share-holders whom Mr. Bennett persuaded to contribute a thousand pounds apiece with the warning that they might never see their investment again, have been Sir Nigel's supporters. The Lyric stands half way between "the Sunday Society" and the ordinary theatre, for it presents whatever play it believes in and will endure a reasonable amount of loss, but after all, as its founder says, it must be "subsidized by its successes." It cannot use a borrowed theatre and actors and actresses who are donating their services for one or two performances, but must employ men and women who earn their living on the stage.

The Lyric chooses modern dramas, Shakespeare, and early plays not often seen elsewhere. It made the London reputations of St. John Ervine's *John Ferguson* and Drinkwater's *Abraham Lincoln*. It is probably best known for its revivals of "period" plays and operas, *The Way of the World, The Beggar's Opera, Polly, The Duenna, The Rivals, When Crummles Played* (which is Lillo's *George Barnwell* seen through the eyes of the theatre troupe of *Nicholas Nickleby*) and *Dandy Dick*, in which Pinero begins to "date." The plays are given with a touch of gay burlesque made more piquant by the originality and beauty of costume and background. This theatre has done more for modern stage design and the art of the theatre, one is inclined to think, than the other English experimental thea-

[16] *Ibid.,* p. XXV.

tres taken together. Claud Lovat Fraser, who was severely wounded in the Great War, and whose death a few years later was a great loss to English art, did the charming designs for *Beggar's Opera* and others only less delightful for *As You Like It* and *La Serva Padrona*. William Nicholson, George Sheringham, and Doris Zinkeisen are now brilliant designers.

London, however, has not been the only English city to feel the stirrings of the new enthusiasm. The North, the region of modern industrial development, was the first section of the provinces to resent the limitations of the commercial theatre and to awaken to the importance of modern plays. In the south of Lancashire and the north of Cheshire, especially, there have been activities rivaling in many ways those of the London experimental societies.

The oldest stage society in the provinces, the Stockport Garrick Society, in 1901 "broke away from a Unitarian Sunday School for the purpose of studying, and giving performances in dramatic literature." It is still in existence, stronger for the passing years. Like the Incorporated Stage Society, it has introduced to its community many of the finest works of continental and English writers during its early years, specializing in the work of Ibsen and Shaw. The society has always enjoyed Shakespeare's plays and has given many performances of them for children in the elementary schools, as well as for its usual audiences. It has been conscious also of the work of other "little theatres" and has given plays by members of the Irish theatre, of some of the English groups, and in the last few years, of similiar organizations in America: the program announced for 1926-1927, for instance, included *Edward About to Marry* by F. Sladen-Smith of the Unnamed Society, Manchester, *Autumn Fire* by T. C. Murray, now one of the leading playwrights of the Abbey Theatre, *Woman's Honour* and *Trifles* by Susan Glaspell, *The Locked Chest*

by Masefield, and *Gold* by Eugene O'Neill. First performances of plays by J. R. Gregson, Ross Hill (president of
the organization), O. Channon Collinge, H. M. Richardson,
"X. Y. Z.," and many others of its own members are an indication of a truly creative spirit.

The achievement of the Stockport Garrick has been determined partly by the excellence of its organization. Managed by the few in its early days, it was "decentralized"
some time ago and has a large group of workers busy with
the plays, and also with the arrangement of lectures and of
exchange performances, the publication of its little magazine, and the building up of a dramatic library. The size of
the membership, often five hundred, frees the producers
from many cares and in 1925 made possible extensive alterations in Garrick Hall, in which the society plays, which is
now a well-equipped little theatre owned by the Stockport
Garrick, Ltd. The society has always maintained a high
standard of plays. The suggestion of "R. H.," writing in the
Garrick Magazine, April, 1926, is not a reproach but a challenge:

The Plays Committee must remember that in one sense it is
the most important of all, for if its work is faulty or ineffectual,
the work of the Society, to a large extent, falls to the ground. It
has roughly a total audience of some 15,000 people to consider,
in addition to the Society's members, so that even one poor or
ineffectual play ought to weigh heavily on its conscience. Unfortunately, in practical life all kinds of pettifogging considerations
impose themselves, and most of us have a habit of some kind of
compromise and the usual comforting excuses.

If, however, I were asked to formulate any principles for the
Plays Committee, I should be inclined to say "No compromise"
for the first, and for the second, "Be bloody, bold, and resolute."
A committee which wobbles between the Finance Committee and
the spectre of "popularity" is going to come an artistic cropper.
The Finance Committee I shall deal with in a following para-
graph, and popularity is for the commercial theatre to worry

about; let the Garrick stick to its last. The utter and absolute financial failure of a play would not result in bankruptcy.

Imbued with the best of the repertory spirit, the Stockport Garrick Society prepared the way for the first true modern repertory theatre in the English-speaking world, Miss Horniman's Manchester Repertory Theatre Company, which opened in the autumn of 1907. Because of her modesty and her withdrawal into her work, Miss Horniman is a shadowy figure compared with that other beneficent woman of the pioneer days, Lady Gregory of the Abbey Theatre. Yet Miss Horniman's influence upon modern drama is as profound. In the nineties she had already financed a season of *Arms and the Man* with Miss Florence Farr at the Avenue Theatre and helped prove the genuineness of Shaw's appeal; in 1903 she played lady bountiful to the Abbey Theatre; four years later, encouraged by both the Irish movement in Dublin and the Court Theatre venture, Miss Horniman launched her work in the English province. Since then she has had the joy of seeing "the growth of Lancashire drama which has made Lancashire live for thousands where before it was no more than an empty name." [17]

Miss Horniman's management was notable for the union of idealism and common sense. Her aims she announced as follows:

(a) A repertory theatre with a regular change of program not wedded to any one school of dramatists but thoroughly catholic, embracing the finest writing of the best authors of all ages and with an especially wide-open door to present-day British writers, who will not now need to sigh in vain for a hearing provided only that they are worth listening to, and say it in an interesting and original manner.

[17] Payne, Iden, in Introduction to Brighouse, Harold, *Hobson's Choice,* p. VI.

(b) A permanent Manchester stock company of picked front-rank actors.

(c) Efficient production.

(d) Popular prices.

In all her arrangements she was fair and business-like, as, for instance, when in rebuilding the Gaiety Theatre for her second year she made certain that every seat from the seven shilling stalls to the eight pence rear of the gallery should have an unobstructed view of the stage.

> I give these business details [she wrote the author] to make it clear that this is nothing like the semi-amateur Little Theatre elsewhere. I was in management before the word "repertory" was common in the language and I avoid it as it has come to carry an impression of dullness, amateurishness, and impropriety to the public mind.

And again:

> I look on the Drama as an Art and to use it for personal vanity, as in the case of the semi-amateur schemes, or for financial gain without any conscience as to the means, is to prostitute the Art.

The same insight which made Miss Horniman believe the time ripe for a more ambitious theatre than Manchester had known led her to choose as her first manager Mr. Edwin T. Heys, honorary secretary of The Stockport Garrick Society, and her director, Mr. B. Iden Payne, who knew conditions in this part of England. Her first play was Charles McEvoy's *David Ballard,* given its première that spring by the Incorporated Stage Society, a delineation of lower-middle-class life familiar to many in the audience. Eight other programs followed during the first season, including seventeen plays, many of them one-acts. What was striking was not the presence of an occasional continental drama but the fact that of the English plays half were given for the first time. This discovery of new playwrights has been Miss Horniman's delight. Like Yeats and Lady Gregory, she is possessed of the magic which calls playwrights into being. To the "Midland School" or "Lancashire realists" besides Charles McEvoy, belong Basil Dean (*Marriages Are Made in Heaven, Mother to Be, Effie, Love Cheats*); Allan Monkhouse of the *Manchester Guardian* (*Reaping the Whirlwind, The Choice, Mary Broome, Nothing Like Leather*); and Stanley Houghton (*The Master of the House, The Dear Departed, The Younger Generation, Hindle Wakes*). Though the Gaiety cannot lay exclusive claim to Harold Brighouse and Harold Chapin, who worked also for the Scottish Repertory Theatre, Manchester gave several of their plays, including Brighouse's *Lonesome Like*, early recognition.

Hindle Wakes is an outstanding example of the fact that not only may the individual playwright acquire his training in the provincial theatres and later emerge in London, but that a play may assert its power in the smaller city and pass to the metropolis. This play, written late in 1911, was accepted by Miss Horniman after it had been declined by London and by Liverpool. In June, 1912, when asked by the Stage Society to put on a play of Lancashire atmosphere, preferably new, Miss Horniman decided upon Houghton's. It was given two performances at the Aldwych Theatre, under the direction of Lewis Casson, with acting so remarkable that several of the cast received immediate calls to other companies. The play was later given in Manchester, London (by Cyril Maude at the Playhouse), New York, and Chicago. At one time, five companies were traveling with it through the provinces. Before Houghton's death there had been over eighteen hundred performances.

Unfortunately the Gaiety Theatre was not able to weather the adverse conditions which followed the war. Perhaps another reason for its closing is that the hour of realism seems to have passed in Manchester as on the continent, and the play of romantic imagination, of fantasy, or of expressionism is now in the ascendency—till dramatic fashions change again. At least,—the most interesting of the present-day Manchester experimental theatres was founded in direct opposition to the older ideal.

The Unnamed Society [writes Mr. L. Stanley Jast] is another attempt at creative drama, but its compass needle swings right away from that grey North which provided the magnetic satisfaction of its predecessors. It emphasizes everything the earlier school of dramatists ignored, and ignores most of what the earlier school stressed. Its aim is not to reveal Manchester, but to forget it. The Manchester of the earlier school of dramatists is disappearing. The 'Manchester Man' is already half a relic, and the unlovely city he built (but long ago ceased to live in) is slowly but none the less surely changing its outward presentment. A semi-metropolitan air is beginning to pervade it, and though it still struggles to preserve its sturdy provincialism, the fresh bloom of it is gone forever.

From its beginning when a few people meeting in the Midland Hotel in 1915 watched a little play given very simply and stayed to talk of the art needs of Manchester, the Unnamed Society has been not merely a producing organization but a banding together of many professions and crafts to think and work for "a more beautiful Manchester." The drama has gradually received the strongest emphasis, its composite art offering the fullest opportunity for the abilities of many individuals. For fusing the art of the playwright, the actor, the scenic artist, the electrician, the costume-designer, and many individuals of humbler but necessary tasks the society has felt that plays by its own members are the best. Among the few plays by outsiders have been Geoffrey Whitworth's *Father Noah*, Maurice Baring's *Catherine Parr*, Lawrence Housman's *The Queen*,

God Bless Her, Brighouse's *The Happy Hangman,* and Lascelles Abercrombie's *Phoenix.*

So far the Unnamed Society has two playwrights well-known in Manchester and becoming known in London through the agency of the British Drama League. One, Mr. F. Sladen-Smith, was introduced to America with *St. Simeon Stylites,* a play of fanciful plot and brilliant dialogue, chosen by the Huddersfield Thespians for their entry in the Little Theatre Tournament in New York, May, 1926; the other, Mr. L. Stanley Jast, needs recognition here. Their plays may interest American little theatres which are looking for the non-realistic. F. Sladen-Smith has written. *Bazhouka meets the Gods, Paradise Perplexed, St. Simeon Stylites, The Tower of Babel, Henbury, The Nod of Osiris, The Invisible Duke, Chimp, The Saint's Comedy;* L. Stanley Jast, *The Lover and the Dead Woman, Aladdin, The Geisha's Wedding, The Lovers of the Elements* (a lyrical ballet with music by Georgia Pearce), *The Call of the Ninth Wave, The Eugenic Cupid, Estelle Discovers Herself, Venus and the Shepherdess, Harbour,* and *A Florentine Irony.*

Mr. Sladen-Smith is interested in many other activities centering about the society and its tiny theatre in a room on Lomax Street. He directs the study of methods of production, staging, and lighting, and encourages and trains younger writers. As his helpers, he has artists and designers of originality, Eric Newton, Lilian Reburn, William Grimmond, H. R. Barbor, Paxton Chadwick, and Margaret Nicholls. Few theatres have attained such unity of method as these producers. One of the leaders ascribes much of this success to "a stage hung with blue curtains":

To say that the curtain-hung stage (which, far from being an invention of the Society's own, is of course a well-established convention among experimenters in non-realistic stage craft), has conditioned everything the Society has done, from the character of the plays it produces to the nature of the smallest stage property, is no exaggeration. Such a stage resembles nothing, and for precisely that reason it can be made to resemble anything. Say, for instance, you want to represent an interior with a door. Put in a real door or an imitation of one and the result is ludicrous. Nothing could be more absurd than a real door let into a room whose walls are manifestly made of thin cloth. The first step towards realism has defeated its own object, and your stage is less like a room than ever. But part your curtains at the place where your door is needed, just sufficiently to reveal a vertical strip of the unearthly gloom behind the stage, and you have a door indeed—one more fraught with mystery than any door that ever swung on hinges and flaunted its knob and keyhole. You have in a flash transformed your stage into a room, and a room with a meaning (not to mention the incidental saving in time, timber, canvas, paint and curses).

"But," it will be objected, "why all this striving after mystery and significance in connection with so simple and homely a piece of furniture as a door?" For the reason that if you do not want it to be significant you may as well leave it out altogether. If the door is an essential part of the meaning of the play, and not merely a convenient way of entering or leaving the room, then put it in in all its stark and mysterious "door-ness": if not—why then, it's easy enough to slip in and out through the curtains.[18]

Liverpool was the first provincial city to follow Manchester in providing excellent drama for a large community. The Liverpool Repertory Theatre was organized in 1911 and put under the direction of Basil Dean, who had been one of Miss Horniman's assistants at the Gaiety. Though for financial reasons this theatre has not been able to take the same risks as some of its rivals, and has accordingly failed to develop a school of local playwrights, it has given well many of the finest plays of the commercial stage. The innovations of this theatre have been largely in methods of creating an audience and paying expenses. The first method

[18] Newton, Eric, *The Unnamed Book,* pp. 14, 15.

tried was the so-called "limited liability plan," with an association of eight hundred stockholders. When this failed, the "commonwealth plan," new to England but similar to that of the Moscow Art Theatre, was introduced: every one connected with the theatre except the audience shares all obligations and profits.

The Birmingham Repertory Theatre is of greater significance artistically. "I will not consent," says Sir Barry Jackson, "to put on bad plays in order that I may have money to provide good plays." It is owing to Sir Barry's generosity that the Birmingham Theatre has comparative freedom from anxiety, for the little theatre, seating four hundred and fifty, is his property. Before the opening in February, 1913, Birmingham was already interested in the modern movement for a group called the Pilgrim Players for seven years had been playing in local halls once a week. To his little theatre Sir Barry Jackson has brought the gifts of a versatile and stimulating personality and talent in acting, stage-designing, and play-writing. In his desire "to produce plays of a definite literary value, beautifully, but without undue elaboration," [19] he has lured distinguished literary men to a more immediate concern for the theatre: Gilbert Cannan's *Everybody's Husband,* Eden Phillpotts' *St. George and the Dragons* and *The Farmer's Wife* were first played in Birmingham. John Drinkwater is an enthusiastic supporter of this theatre and was for some time its general manager; with *Puss in Boots, Rebellion, The God of Quiet, The Storm, X=O, A Night of the Trojan War,* he was a favorite of this audience before *Abraham Lincoln,* first played here, made him known throughout the English-speaking world.

"The first Repertory Theatre in the country which has started with direct civic encouragement," a writer in the

[19] Letter of Mr. Bache Matthews, business manager of the Birmingham Repertory Theatre.

Times calls the Bristol Little Theatre. Another interesting fact in the history of this theatre is the assistance which it has received from a local Rotary Club. It opened December 17, 1923, in Lesser Colston Hall, remodeled by a committee of the city corporation, with the blessing of St. John Ervine and of Sir Arthur Wing Pinero, who gave the first address. Mr. Rupert Harvey, an outstanding figure at the Old Vic, was called to head a permanent stock company. There has been some attempt at original writing, but on the whole, the management has preferred to give a large number of modern plays, many of them comedies, already successful on the stage, and has become a factor in improving the standards of the Bristol commercial theatres. After five hundred performances, an anonymous historian of the Little Theatre wrote:

When the Little Theatre movement was initiated by the Rotary Club of Bristol, in association with other clubs and societies, the promoters made plain their intention of catering, not for the special tastes of any limited audience, but for all intelligent theatre-goers who are capable of enjoying a well written and competently acted modern play. No enterprise of this kind, well advanced in its third season, could hope to have disarmed all criticism; but regular patrons who to-night look back and review as a whole the fare hitherto provided, will agree that the Little Theatre in practice has steadily maintained the original idea which marked its inception.

It has been admitted by not a few Bristolians that they have acquired, in the past two years, the habit of genuine play-going, as distinct from a casual inclination for miscellaneous entertainment. Many people have discovered what before, from lack of opportunity, was unknown to them; the fact that actual life, contemporary manners, and current speech are material for drama not less stimulating, certainly not less amusing, and distinctly more instructive, than the old romantic conventions and stock sentimentalisms which they regarded, once upon a time, as inseparable from theatrical art.

The aim of the Little Theatre has not been, and probably never will be, purely experimental. It does not set out to be a pioneer of wholly novel dramatic forms, nor to present to the public those more poetic, symbolic, exotic, or cryptic types of play which, though often of intellectual value and fruitful in suggestion, are mainly caviar to the general. That plays of this type should be performed at times, somewhere, is very desirable: but no provincial British city has yet been discovered in which considerable audiences, for six successive nights, will pay for the privilege of exposing themselves to mental strain, even when accompanied by the gratifying sense of mental superiority.

An unusual theatre which stands half way between the professional repertory theatre and the little theatre of amateurs is the Maddermarket Theatre, Norwich, with a salaried producer, a building of its own, and unpaid actors. This theatre represents a theory opposite from decentralization, for Mr. Nugent Monck, the director, formerly of the Abbey Theatre, Dublin, is, as he says, "in sole charge of every detail of every production," expects "nothing less than implicit obedience from all," and invites his own actors, people from every class and profession, who find it "easier to act than to refuse his invitation." These at first are called "associates" of his theatre; later, after their success is established, "players."

The Maddermarket Theatre takes its name from an old market in which madder, a substance used in dyeing, was sold when weaving was an important Yorkshire industry. The building has witnessed a drama of its own, as it has been, during the last two hundred years, successively a Catholic church, a baking-powder factory, and a center for the Salvation Army. A drama society, the Norwich Playgoers, saw the possibilities of the structure, and rebuilt it in 1921 at a cost of more than three thousand pounds. The little theatre—it seats only two hundred and twenty—is unique among English playhouses because of its permanent architectural stage, similar to that of Copeau's Vieux Colombier, except that the Norwich stage is almost purely Elizabethan. Mr. Monck finds this a thoroughly practical type of construction, ideal for Shakespeare and almost ideal for modern comedy.

Mr. Monck has strong opinions on the choosing of plays. He believes that a play should have both "an intellectual and a spiritual content" and admits a fondness for high comedy: to his mind *Hamlet* and *The School for Scandal* are the two most popular plays in the language, with *Twelfth Night* and *The Critic* not far behind. With some exceptions, as Shaw's, which delight the Labor element, modern plays, Mr. Monck finds, are a risk and frequently a loss. On the contrary, Sir Gilbert Murray's translations of *Hippolytus, Electra,* and *Alcestis* are much enjoyed by English audiences, who are deeply moved by the verse and the beauty of the words. The Maddermarket must be self-supporting as a proof that it is not "becoming too high-brow." Mr. Monck believes that many people who have left the churches find in the theatre some of the elements of religion, "colour, ritual, and discipline."

An account of the work in the English cities should mention an unusual dramatic club at Oxford and the Festival Theatre, Cambridge. At the second, Mr. Terrence Gray has experimented remarkably with settings made of adjustable blocks.

Another little theatre of high standards is that belonging to Citizen House, Bath. In 1913 Miss Helen Hope founded this settlement in a beautiful eighteenth century mansion, built for the Duke of Chandos by the architect Wood, who is responsible for much of the stately loveliness of the city. "It has panelled walls everywhere, and a vast oak staircase from ground to attics, powder-closets, several ghosts, windows on which diamond rings have scratched records of old loves and hates, and, in the noble room which is sometimes a drawing-room and sometimes a lecture-room, a 'sun-ray' fireplace which is an antique as famous as Katisha's left shoulder blade." [20] In the midst of this beauty those who have charge of the destinies of the settlement are trying to satisfy the urge to self-expression which is often thwarted by factories and machine-made things.

Creative hunger [says Miss de Reyes, one of the leaders of Citizen House] is the basis of all the difficulties of to-day. It is a difficult thing to satisfy. People *want to do and to make things,* not merely to learn theoretically. Drama is possibly the highest form of art and of education, because it combines the service of all other arts. A boy discovers his own genius for architecture in the line and design of a scene, a girl her genius for colour and painting in the colour-motif of a scene. Dancing, music, needle-work, drawing, painting, principles of lighting, the value of the spoken word are all combined. Many of the Players have had their life work determined by their Citizen House training. One boy has become a stage electrician, one a poster designer to a Fleet Street firm, two professional dancers, four professional actors, and this has arisen from an avowedly non-professional organisation. They have merely discovered themselves.[21]

The theatre, in a new wing of Citizen House, and the roof-garden theatre, in a disused factory, were constructed in the early days of the war for the Soldiers Club. Until after the war soldiers packed both. The first play, a mystery for the Christmas season, was followed by plays for other festivals and by those reflecting the life and ideals of other countries, including when possible something of their music and folk lore, usually accompanied by exhibitions of arts of the people. Since the end of the war the scope of the project has been much extended: the majority of the plays are by members of the organizations, but modern plays by Clifford Bax, Lady Margaret Sackville, and G. K. Chesterton have

[20] *The Drama in Adult Education,* p. 73.
[21] *Ibid.,* pp. 71, 72.

been given, and interesting revivals. Both players and audiences have a special interest in plays of the eighteenth century which reflect the life of Bath in its most brilliant period. The Players have received several honors,—an invitation for their Child Players to give four plays at the Conference on New Ideals in Education at Stratford-on-Avon, and frequent requests from the City Council to revive miracle and mystery plays. Bath is fortunate in the variety and hospitality of its auditoriums; when plays overflow the Citizen House Theatre they are housed in local playhouses, in the historic Pump Room, or in parks under the open sky.

Largely since the war, another section of England has become conscious of the present-day movement in the theatre,—York, Leeds, Huddersfield, Bradford, and the industrial centres which adjoin them in the southern and central part of Yorkshire. The enthusiasm here is very real.

The Huddersfield Thespians, who began their career in 1920, are an unusually talented group. Their nucleus was the amateurs who had been giving a private performance of a drama by Mr. James R. Gregson, the most prominent of the Yorkshire playwrights. Though the Thespians will consider any unusual modern play, their special purpose is to encourage the creation of a local drama in the Yorkshire dialect. Among these Yorkshire playwrights besides Gregson are George Beaumont, F. A. Carter, and Captain O. Lord; Gordon Bottomley, though an accomplished poet and playwright long before the Thespians were organized, is interested in them because of his Yorkshire birth. Mr. Gregson's plays are *Youth Disposes, Young Imeson, Liddy, T'Maisdens, The Shining Steps, Lai' Alice,* and *The Way of an Angel.* The organization is now increasing the building fund for a Huddersfield Little Theatre. In the spring of 1926 the players were greatly encouraged by winning first place in the British Drama League competition with Sladen-Smith's *St. Simeon Stylites.* Special performances at home and the generosity of their mayor and other townsmen enabled them to send the cast to America, where the play was adjudged one of the four most successful productions, though it did not receive the Belasco Cup. (The next spring a group from Welwyn Garden City, a new factory community, not far from London, which is radical and interesting in many ways, secured the cup, winning over the American contestants.)

"The Settlement is a place where any man or woman, however poor, can share in Leonardo and Beethoven, Shakespeare and Goethe, and become himself or herself something of a thinker and a poet and an artist," is the statement of the Sheffield Educational Settlement to which a Little Theatre is attached. Almost all of its actors and workers are poor, many of them unemployed (membership in the settlement is only a penny a week for those out of work). One might suppose that the dramatic fare would be of the gayest and the lightest. On the contrary this little theatre has one of the most ambitious programs in England: Goethe's *Faust (Part I)*, Marlowe's *Dr. Faustus*, Pushkin's *Boris Godunov*, *Androcles and the Lion*, *Peer Gynt*, *The King's Threshold*, and *Iphigenia in Tauris*. The programs bear the warning that "young children, including infants-in-arms, will not be admitted" and offset this by the offer, "the management undertakes to mind children of all ages." The Little Theatre is the parent of the Sheffield Repertory Company, which in 1923 began its rather more conventional programs. Even this theatre group once gave *Heartbreak House*.

Difficult and unusual dramas are also the order of the day at the Leeds Art Theatre and the York Everyman. The York society has chosen *Everyman*, *The Adding Machine*, *The Duchess of Malfi* (given under the direction of Mr. Nugent Monck in a thirteenth century guildhall), *The Machine Wreckers*. Miss Edith Craig, the daughter of Miss Ellen Terry and the sister of Gordon Craig, is producer for the Art Theatre. Since 1925 she has had at her disposal a theatre in the Alexandra Hall. Her plans include only the best in modern plays. *Philip the King, John Gabriel Borkman,* and *The Great World Theatre* were early choices. This last, from Reinhardt's Salzburg festivals, was also given for three weeks at St. Edward's Church, Holbeck.

Leeds must be especially favored by the experimental spirit. A year or two after the war a clergyman of Leeds, the Reverend Mr. Percival Gough, finding that many of the working people in his parish enjoyed drama, helped them in methods of study and in putting on scenes from Shakespeare. Meanwhile Mr. W. B. Dow, a director of the firm of Simpson, Fawcett and Company, manufacturers, had discovered a similar interest in his employees. He arranged lectures for them and made possible their attendance at various plays. When Mr. Gough and his actors came to the factory, enthusiasm for plays and play-producing spread like wildfire. Mr. Dow helped most generously, building a permanent stage at his own expense, installing a lighting system, organizing his own people, and enlisting the enthusiasm of the workers at other factories. In November, 1921, he called Mr. Gregson of the Huddersfield Thespians as Welfare Coach.

During the next three years, this Leeds Industrial Theatre presented an amazing spectacle, in actual plays and in methods of organization. The members, actors and audience, contributed a penny a week (later increased to twopence) toward the rent of the hall. They were divided into units of fifty, with one member to collect the fees and represent the unit on a general council. In the most successful season, the second, there were some thirty plays given, including eight by the factory group itself and the rest by visiting little theatres. Shakespeare, Ibsen (*Peer Gynt*), Maeterlinck, Strindberg, Shaw, Barrie, Galsworthy, George Calderon, Cicely Hamilton in America might be considered above the heads of factory workers, but they succeeded in Leeds. Two operas, *Il Trovatore* and *The Bosun's Mate,* were also given. Though the standard of acting could not be professional, there was much accomplished, and the theatre was an important bit of pioneer work. "Mr. Gregson was instructed to regard the whole matter primarily as an educational experiment, and anyone who evinced a desire to take part in a production, whether suitable or not, had to be encouraged. This policy was modified later for certain productions but never abandoned." [22]

The closing of the theatre after three years was caused by business depression, the impossibility of procuring a hall, and Mr. Gregson's summons to other work. Moreover, the ideal of the Industrial Theatre has been merged in a greater dream, that of combining the Leeds Art Theatre and the Industrial Theatre and keeping "the artistic attainment" of the first and "the larger popular appeal" of the second. The fortunes of the Leeds Civic Theatre are assured by three townsmen, one of them Mr. Charles F. Smith, a founder of the Leeds Art Theatre and director of the York Everyman Theatre. He is director of the new enterprise, and Mr. Gregson is producer. The hope of the management is to attract the best amateur actors throughout Yorkshire and later to form a semi-professional stock company. *Œdipus Rex, The Little Plays of St. Francis,* and *The Adding Machine* were to open the season.

Directly influenced by the Leeds Industrial Theatre is the Bradford Industrial Theatre launched at a public meeting held at the call of the City Council after the city officials had invited the Leeds group to play in Bradford. This Bradford society is a confederacy of various groups belonging to different factories trained by one producer.

This account of the little theatres and the repertory theatres in Yorkshire, naturally, cannot be inclusive, for

[22] *Ibid.,* p. 58.

new organizations are doubtless being formed rather frequently. The importance of the whole movement here and in
many industrial sections can scarcely be over-estimated.
There must be others besides Mr. Gregson for whom the
little theatre has been a liberal education. This is his own
account of his life:

You must know in the first place that I am a working-man. At
the age of twelve (twenty-four years ago) I commenced work
in a cotton-factory. Since then I have been office-boy, foundry
clerk, railway clerk, business manager of a professional theatre,
business manager of a kinema theatre, producer and coach for
The Leeds Industrial Theatre and am now a cost clerk in a
perambulator factory. I have lived all my life in a small working-
class house in an industrial district of Yorkshire.

From the age of five to twelve I attended a board school and
received the usual working-class education. But, ill-health driving
me from the factory to the office at the age of seventeen, I had
the additional schooling to be derived from three winters' attendance at an evening technical school.

About this time a dawning interest in Sunday School work led
me to take up other studies and to take part in the performance
of short sketches and dramatic dialogues. I thus found my hobby
and the pursuit of it has brought me into close and responsible
touch with all kinds of dramatic ventures, both amateur and
professional.

. . . My subsequent development came as a matter of course.
Only in the drama did I find the fullest scope for this vital
activity and in the service of the drama I have acquired, as a bye-
product, what real knowledge I possess and what real mental
ability I exercise.

In the course of my career as an actor and a dramatist I have
met men of every class and kind, and I have noticed invariably
that those who are the most alive, those to whom life means the
most, are neither the men who are walking encyclopedias of
knowledge, nor those whose wits are the sharpest or whose brains
the most supple. The best men, the happiest men, are those who,
knowing much or little, quick in mind or pedestrian, labourers

or professional, are men of understanding, sympathy and insight, who see life as a means of expression and service and therefore as a thing of infinite beauty and wonderful opportunity. I have met these men in every class. . . . And a study of them has always resulted in the discovery that the difference is due to this spiritual rather than intellectual development.

I believe that this education of the spirit is the real need of my own class to-day. Let other classes speak for themselves. I know what modern industry means in terms of monotonous routine tasks. I know what a working-class home-life means, with few outlets for emotional "release" save the "pub" and the "chapel." I know the mental apathy and the crippled spirit they engender. I have spent my life fighting against this state of mind and temper, both in myself and in my fellows. The working-man's first instinct is to distrust beauty when he is made to see it. Talk to him of what life means to you, and he will confide to his neighbour—behind your back—that you are a bit funny sometimes!

I therefore conclude that what the working-man needs to-day is not more cramming, but digestive medicine. Not more education but the vision to use what little education he already possesses. This is the essential. By all means let him have his clear path from the day-school to the university, but don't let it become, in the savage description of one working-man, a clear path from the cradle to the grave, for you may unfit him for the humdrum industrial life without finding for him that compensation which makes any life a matter for joy and gratitude. We are sour dough awaiting leaven. Give us the real education of an informed, sympathetic and vital spirit—the yeast of life which will transform the sour dough into living bread. And, incidentally, in the happiest easiest fashion, we shall, pursuing the one thing needful find all these other things, mere knowledge and intellectual equipment, added unto us.

If education is release, the function of the drama is readily perceived. I cannot help noting the origin of Greek drama. It sprung out of religious and ceremonial rites the effect of which, speaking broadly, was the "release" of emotion, an exercise of the spirit. The plays which sprung from these rites carried on this essential service but gradually widened the scope, multiplied the occasions, and refined the qualities of this spiritual exercise. The development of our own drama from the monkish mysteries to the Elizabethan plays is, I think, a fair, if rough, analogy. This quality of "release" is the mark of true drama, either comedy or tragedy, for laughter is "release" as well as tears.

This is not theory or hearsay, this dramatic "release." I have proved it myself and seen and helped others to prove it. I believe that the most valuable result of the work at the Industrial Theatre was that it allowed, nay demanded, that the workpeople-players should break their shells and "come out of themselves." This, to me, is the first and all-sufficient justification of the drama. Before a player can be anything but a stick he must try, at the cost of violence to his timid reserve, to become someone else. He must conquer his inbred repression, rouse his dormant spirit, practise insight and a sympathetic understanding of the "other fellow," and the pleasure of this, the freedom and relief it brings in its train, will result in the practice of the imaginative faculty off the stage as well as on. As one workman put it, "It's no use trying to be somebody else unless you try to feel what he feels." Another description of this sensation of release is most pithy. Said one of my actors in *The Merchant of Venice*, "Eh, I've been miles away from myself to-night, and I feel pounds lighter for it." [23]

Some of the most fascinating experiments of the kind in England are not in London or the great provincial cities but in the countrysides, under the leadership of men and women who have enough knowledge of the outside world to appreciate the flavor of the local dialect, for dialect-speakers themselves are not usually conscious of any peculiarities.

"A dialec' play!" exclaimed Neddy Kier, who was sharing a two-handled cup with Farmer Boggis in the tap-room of the "Mildmay Arms" at Queen Camel. "Broad talk upon a stage avoor the parish! Do I hear aright!"

"Thee dost," said Farmer Boggis.

[23] *Ibid.*, pp. 164, 165, 167-169.

"Well then," said Neddy, "I'll tell thee. Vust thing: 'twoulden be understanded. There idden no dialec' nowadays. Tidden a-spokt, I tell 'ee. Not here to Camel tidden. Tidden a-spokt nowhere. 'Thouse midbe in liddle outstep plazen like West Camel. And 'twoulden be understanded there, mind, not by the uppermost volk." [24]

An interesting group producing dialect plays are the Grasmere Players of Westmorland in the heart of the Wordsworth country. Their history began over thirty years ago. Their first play, *The Dalesman,* was written by Miss Charlotte Fletcher; the later plays are largely adaptations of novels or stories arranged by Mrs. Rawnsley, who has long been the leader of the group. She attributes her success partly to the traditional love of acting in this section of England, where village children still give fragments of an old mumming play at Easter.

In a region of literary shrines to the south is another company of players eager to preserve the beauty of the past, the Hardy Players of Dorchester in Dorset, the Wessex of the novels. Mr. Frederick E. Hansford, their representative, after conferring with Mr. Thomas Hardy, once wrote:

The Players are bent on faithfully representing what is usually described as the "atmosphere" of the Wessex novels. All that the works of Mr. Hardy owe to the ancient dialect, customs, and folk-lore, the quaint rustic wit and wisdom, the home-crafts and field-crafts—is dear, too, to the hearts of the Hardy Players. Not only are these things dear to the impersonators, but they are able to present them upon the stage by the instinct of relationship. For they are local men and women who, pursuing their daily rounds amid Dorset dialect and scenery, have been long familiarised with the speech, the dwellings, and the habits of the characters portrayed in the novels.

[24] From "Somerset Dialect Plays and Players," by John Read in *Somerset and the Drama,* p. 89, by S. R. Littlewood and Others. Courtesy of Somerset Folk Press, London.

Plays drawn from Hardy's novels have been given since 1908 when the dramatic section of the Dorchester Debating Society turned from short plays and Shakespearean comedies. A few of the adaptations were the work of Mr. Hardy himself; others of Mr. A. H. Evans and Mr. T. H. Tilley. Before the war there had been performances of *The Trumpet Major, Far from the Madding Crowd, The Mellstock Quire* (from *Under the Greenwood Tree*), *The Three Wayfarers, The Distracted Preacher,* and *The Woodlanders.* More recently the Players have given Wessex scenes from *The Dynasts, The Return of the Native, A Desperate Remedy, The Famous Tragedy of the Queen of Cornwall,* and *Tess of the D'Urbervilles.* Parts of *The Dynasts* and *The Distracted Preacher* were given at Weymouth (Budmouth), the scene of the actions. Outdoor performances often have backgrounds of unusual beauty and traditional interest, the manor-house of Bingham's Melcomb, the castle grounds of Sturminster Newton, a smooth sheet of green at Cerne Abbas. On the evening when *The Mellstock Quire* was given, the members of the present Mellstock (Stinsford) choir were invited guests. As in almost all the English rural groups the actors represent all classes, for the basis of choice is histrionic ability. The players have been particularly ingenious in building up their own methods, as there is no opportunity to see any similar production on the commercial stage,—this absence of theatric tradition is probably a real advantage. For many years Mr. Hardy encouraged and helped the players.

Not many miles from Dorset as the crow flies, in the heart of the Westcountry, are men and women eager for expression in a kindred dialect, Somerset people who have always loved playing, and did not allow the Christmas mumming plays to die out till the nineteenth century. Students of earlier drama have discovered that the Somerset dialect was the accepted one for countrymen upon the Elizabethan stage (see Edgar's feigning in *King Lear*) and that, for a time, an actor was expected to have the ability to "speak Somerset." There is a possibility also that *Gammer Gurton's Needle* may be in the dialect of this county. Perhaps these connections with the stage were known to the peasants; certainly the glories of the Theatre Royal in the days of Mrs. Siddons must have been, for pastures and farms are just over the rim of the green cup in which lies Bath.

The most important figure in the dialect drama of Somerset is Mr. John Read, who does not come among the native folk as a "furriner" but knows every cadence of their language, each bit of folk-lore and folk-song. To him the dialect play is both an abiding record of the past and a means for making attractive the country life of the present.

It is sad [he writes] to read of so many well-meant but ill-conceived efforts to "restrain the drift from the land" and to "brighten up village life" by the introduction of alleged amusements which make no appeal to the folk-spirit; it is passing sad to witness the inroads of modern education upon the same folk-spirit, and to realise that the tendency of the age is towards the repression of individuality and the establishment of a standardised human unit: such reflections are sad beyond expression, when one feels that so much could have been done, by a judicious cultivation of the folk-spirit, to develop the interest of the countryman in his environment and his rich heritage of lore and song; to preserve the wonderful tradition of English agriculture; and to retain the subtly charming atmosphere of old English country life.[25]

Mr. Read adopted the dramatic form when he found that the dialect play appeals more widely to the Somerset farmer than the dialect novel or short story. In 1910 the Camel Play-actors began to appear at Queen Camel and West Camel,—later journeying far afield. Mr. Read's plays usually reproduce the language of the present or of a period only slightly earlier; one, *Latter-Lammas* is written in "the

[25] *Ibid.*, pp. 95, 96.

archaic dialect of old Somerset, harking back to the days of the ballad." In subject matter they fall into two groups, those which emphasize old beliefs and customs and those which mirror the life of the present. The list includes *Conjuror Lintern, Dumbledore's Droa, The Wheel-Heaver, Wold Ways a-Gwain,* and *Latter-Lammas.* Other Somerset groups, particularly at Burton and Cheddar, have repeated several of these plays.

The English dialect-play movement, slight in its beginnings, has great potentialities. Why, as its spokesmen ask, should not the English villager be bilingual, retaining the best of the old life while reaching for the new? Certainly much of the beauty of the Irish plays comes from the flavor of the speech. Championship of the dialect is open to all kinds of misunderstandings, most of them removable by sympathy and knowledge:

"But is the dialect-speaker capable of appreciating a play?" "Even if he is, will he want to listen to his own dialect?" "Then, surely, he will not be interested in the things he does every day? Why not give him something novel, something to lift him out of his environment?"

In answer to the first question one might point out that the whole trend of folk-lore and song is towards the dramatic, and that the commonest dialect superlative of excellence is expressed in the words, "Why, 'tis so good as a play!" The second and third objections could be met by counter-queries "Do you prefer to attend plays written in English or in Dutch?" "Would you not be interested in a play dealing with your own vocation?" [26]

Another experiment recreating the beauty of the past for more than ten years had its home in Somerset,—at Glastonbury, close to the Vale of Avalon, as legend-haunted as Tintagel on the cliffs of Cornwall. Here the Arthurian tales and others of the Celtic past have been wedded to music in a

[26] *Ibid.,* pp. 85, 86.

new form of opera. Two impulses led to the founding of the Glastonbury Festival Movement, the desire of Rutland Boughton, a young composer, to establish a colony where young artists could combine creative work and the life of the farmer, and the eagerness of a young poet, Reginald Buckley, to develop a festival theatre, somewhat like the Wagner Theatre at Bayreuth, as a center for plays and operas founded on British Legends. Their little book, *The Music Drama of the Future,* was published in 1910 before a location had been decided upon; the appropriateness of Glastonbury was suggested in 1912 by Mr. Philip Oyler, who undertook to interest important local people. He carried on negotiations for Chalice Wells, a large building suitable for a festival school, but, although several prominent musicians backed the project, there was not enough financial support, and Chalice Wells was shortly afterwards purchased by Miss Alice Buckton, author of *Eagerheart,* who established there her own Guild of Glastonbury and Street Festival Players. Conquering their disappointment, the organizers, with the help of Mr. Dan Godfrey, gave at Bournemouth *The Birth of Arthur,* the first scene of a proposed series of Arthurian operas by Mr. Buckley and Mr. Boughton.

Though the members of the audience were the rather haphazard group of a summer resort, the evening was successful enough to warrant further experiment. During the next summer, 1914, a holiday school opened in Glastonbury giving Fiona Macleod's drama, *The Immortal Hour,* with Mr. Boughton's musical setting. This is the most successful drama of the Glastonbury circle: it has been performed in Bournemouth, Bath, Bristol, and London by the Festival Players, in Birmingham by the Repertory Company, and has now been published with the funds of a Carnegie First Award. At the outbreak of the Great War local interest in the Festival School had grown so strong that the Glaston-

bury people continued rehearsals, preparing a musical Nativity Play and Purcell's *Dido and Æneas,* which had at
that time been revived only once (by Gordon Craig at the
beginning of the century).

By 1915 the musical world of London was aware of Glastonbury, and many visitors saw a richer program: *Dido and
Æneas, The Immortal Hour, Oithona,* an opera based on a
Celtic story by Edgar Bainton, a young Englishman, pris-
oner in the German camp at Ruhleben, and *Bethlehem,* by
Boughton. This is a version of the Coventry Nativity Play,
including early English carols, folk tunes, interludes from
the Arthurian cycles, and lullabies for the Virgin. The next
season, with performances at Easter and Whitsuntide, saw
the following: Gluck's opera, *Iphigenia in Tauris;* a children's ballet, *Snow White,* with scenario by Margaret Morris and music by Boughton; *Everyman;* and two new British operas, *The Sumida River,* by Clarence Raybould, and
a continuation of the Arthurian operas, *The Round Table.*
When Mr. Boughton was called into military service the village, not willing to give up the delight of the plays, put on
for themselves *The Land of Heart's Desire* (Yeats), *Columbine* (Arkell), *The Dark Lady of the Sonnets* (Shaw), *The
Robin, the Mouse, and the Sausage* (Bostock), *Sacrifice*
(Tagore), and *Paddly Pools* (Malleson).

After the war the festival school sustained a great loss in
the death of Mr. Buckley. Since that time there has been
little hope of a permanent theatre building. Experiments,
however, continued with a musical drama founded on
Euripides' *Alcestis* in 1922 and Boughton's *The Queen of
Cornwall* somewhat later. Lawrence Housman, who had
joined the group, allowed them to produce his Franciscan
plays.

Though the work of the Festival Players is now at a
standstill, its record is inspiring: by 1925 there had been
three hundred and eighty-eight stage performances, with

tours to London and to many towns and country districts. The managers estimate that other companies have given nearly seven hundred performances of the Festival operas and plays. Many of the Festival singers have joined professional companies.

Whatever the future of this festival movement, it has three accomplishments: (1) the stimulating of interest in legendary British and Celtic themes as material for operas, (2) the proof that operas may be admirably given with simple stage settings and comparatively little expenditure, and (3) the working out of certain new theories in musical composition. Mr. Boughton's own description of these is perhaps the best:

Dramatic art arose in the choral dance, and only gradually became prosy instead of poetic and musical—only gradually tended to outline the disagreements of individuals rather than the play of vital forces. As a musician it was forms of choral song and dance which had chiefly interested me, while opera with its crude and realistic settings made but little appeal. Now it happened that when Buckley wrote his librettos he had made no arrangements with any musician to collaborate, and with the literary man's usual, and not unwarranted disdain for the intelligence of musicians, he had inserted in his dramas whole passages of poetry—not with the idea that they should be set to music, but to keep the composer's mind in the right emotional path during the purely instrumental portions of the works. But these particular lines, with their interesting use of verbal phrases, corresponding in music to Wagner's use of the Leading-motive, seemed to me often to give the best of the author's thought, so I decided, with his approval, to set them as choral passages on the plan of the Greek Tragedy; and inasmuch as these sections generally proclaimed the scene of the action, just as Shakespeare's first lines of a scene generally picture the forest or chamber where he would have the audience's imagination to be, so it seemed that this form of Choral Drama might enable us to dispense with that conventional part of stagecraft which has been so seriously in the way of the appreciation of opera-forms by lovers of the arts.

At Bournemouth we staged the scene where Queen Igraine waits in the castle of Tintagel for the coming of Uther the King. Men in hard and squarish costumes of grey and earth-red sang the music of the castle with stiff poses and movements, while women in blues and greens and purples delivered the rushing and wild music and dance of the sea.

. . . .

The Sumida River was a lovely setting by a then unknown composer, who has since made his way in the Beecham Opera Company. His opera gave us a chance still further to develop our methods of stage-craft. There is in the course of the play a journey by boat quite impossible of effective staging in the ordinary way of theatrical realism; and there are passages of description and comment sung by a kind of Greek chorus. By causing the choral singers to carry out a sort of flowing water-dance during the Ferryman's narrative of the journey the necessary stimulus was given to the imagination of the audience with the minimum of upholstery and no risk of the kind of disaster which so often attends the use of mechanical appliances on such occasions.[27]

The preceding account by no means does justice to the activities of Somerset, which a few years ago, exclusive of Bath, numbered almost thirty organizations. One society gave a dramatization of *Tom Jones,* with special attention to the dialect of this, Squire Western's native county. Two or three other interesting experiments might be mentioned. In a tiny village of three hundred, Buckland Dinham, Mrs. Cynthia Rowena Starey once organized and managed a passion play, the *Bethlehem Tableaux,* given by performers "who have no name, no personality, beyond the person they represent," before a reverent audience. In another community, near Frome, Mrs. E. D. Lear of Mells Rectory has

[27] From "The Glastonbury Festival Movement," by Rutland Boughton, in *Somerset and the Drama,* pp. 58, 59, 70, by S. R. Littlewood and Others. Courtesy of Somerset Folk Press, London.

trained her players in Shakespeare, Sheridan, and Goldsmith. Miss Elizabeth Blake of Crewkerne, born and reared
in the countryside and knowing the limitations in amusement of the average village, has drawn together a small
group of actors and toured with them several times. The
circular letter which she sends out when planning her visits
says:

> I travel with a small professional company of educated people,
> and we aim at giving a performance of good standard in the
> simplest way. People everywhere are waking to the fact that
> there is a great need to improve our standards of recreation,
> which have a direct effect on the manners and morals of the
> nation, and we need to overcome the desire for coarse and degen-
> erate amusements by developing the enjoyment of the wholesome.
> My village tours are an effort in this direction.

She believes that the right kind of recreation should be
on a stable basis, tax-supported, and that every community
of five thousand should have "its own small community
theatre, self-supporting, with regular seasons, sharing
trained producers with other small towns."

Several other village groups, like the Hardy Players
formed under the direct influence of men and women of letters, may be grouped together: the Hill Players, the Cotswold Players, and the Shoreham Village Players. Mr. John
Masefield organized the Hill Players, devoted to poetic
drama and fortunate in the possession of a small theatre
which he has built for them. He has also helped the Cotswold Players of Gloucestershire. This society was founded
in 1912 by Constance Smedley and Maxwell Armfield, then
of Minchinhampton, Gloucestershire, with the object of
taking educational drama to the villages of Gloucestershire
and the Cotswold hills and dales. This purpose continues,
though more recently several large towns of Gloucestershire

have been visited with the purpose of stimulating interest in a small repertory theatre when the time is ripe.

The Cotswold Players are not bound exclusively to either the long or the short play. When their program consists of one-acts, there is usually a combination of two plays of the more popular type, a fantasy, and a play of ideas. The standards of acting are high: the productions of *The Tragedy of Nan* and of *Will Shakespeare* were praised enthusiastically by their authors. Recently the group has discovered two playwrights of its own, F. Morton Howard and Henry Atkinson. Among the Cotswold successes are *The Burcombe Scandal* (F. Morton Howard), *If Four Walls Told* (Edgar Percy), *The Storm* (Drinkwater), *Hall-Marked* (Galsworthy), *The Little White Thought* (Malleson), *Money Makes a Difference* (F. Morton Howard), *The Victory* (F. Morton Howard), *The Curious Herbal* (Constance Smedley), *The Gilded Wreath* (Constance Smedley), *Breaking Point* (Henry Atkinson), *Columbine* (Reginald Arkell), *Everybody's Husband* (Gilbert Cannan).

Lord Dunsany is president of the Shoreham Village Players near Sevenoaks, Kent, founded by Mr. Harold Copping and Mr. H. R. Barbor. In 1924 when Shoreham had a public hall suitable for dramatic performances these gentlemen announced an open meeting, addressed by Lord Dunsany, and interested eighty people in a village drama society. The society is as yet too young to have developed any school of playwrights; its claims to distinction are its fine enthusiasm, its spirit of coöperation, and the marked success with which the society has put to work all classes and ages within the little community. For the first play, *A Midsummer Night's Dream*, the boys of the village school erected an apron stage. So many volunteered for the cast that the comedy was finally performed twice by entirely different groups. In the summer it was twice repeated by invitation of Lord Dunsany at Dunstall Priory, his home in Shoreham. The next year the choice was Dekker's *The Shoemaker's Holiday,* not performed on the London public stage for two hundred years. The following season saw *Hops,* a rustic review, which included *The Deluge* from the Chester cycle of miracle plays, sailor songs, country dances, Dunsany's *A Night at an Inn,* and a Kentish adaptation of one of Chekhov's farces. In this type of program Mr. Barbor and his fellow-workers hope to keep alive Kentish folk-lore and to foster such old merrymakings as "hop-picking" and "harvest-home." Partly under the influence of the Shoreham Players, the Rural Community Council of Kent is attempting to encourage local drama. Mr. Barbor, as technical adviser, is organizing drama conferences with well-known lecturers and demonstrations of methods of production.

If the work of the Glastonbury Festival Players recalls Bayreuth, that of another group, the Stoneland Players, recalls Oberammergau. Since 1910, Mrs. Godwin King, a few of her friends, and the villagers of West Hoathly, Sussex, have given annually a Greek play, in Gilbert Murray's translation. The original suggestion came from Mrs. King's mother when her daughter was interested in a university extension course in Greek literature. The aged woman helped cast the play, plan the costumes, and train the voices. In spite of her blindness and frailty she attended all rehearsals until her final illness and lived by sheer force of will to within a few days of the date set for the performance. When the play was given this spirit of unselfishness and devotion seemed to hallow it, for the villagers thought of this as a memorial for the woman they had loved: "one old man asked if he might stand in the crowd in order to show his respect." This devotion lingers still, intensifying the players' sense of loyalty to the group, eliminating rivalries,—the program is printed without the names of players and the press is asked to respect this anonymity,—and creating an atmosphere which approaches the religious awe in which the Greeks enacted the struggles of their gods and heroes.

The exquisite simplicity of the performance—I was privileged to see the *Hippolytus* in 1927—conceals, as all art should, the infinite pains which have made it possible. About seventy people have a share either in the chorus or in interpreting the Greek gods and heroes. These actors range from childhood to old age: on this particular afternoon from a little baby carried by one of the women, perhaps because it could not be left at home, to a man of seventy-four. The village choral society furnishes the women's chorus, the music of which, like that composed by Mrs. King for all the dramas, is sung in unison without accompaniment. In the early days some members of the group studied Greek statues and vases in the British Museum for details of costuming; now the players own an extensive wardrobe. The men and boys consent to leave even gardening and cricketing to attend rehearsals on summer nights, and gradually more are essaying important parts, though there is still a preference among them for the chorus. The physical endurance which allows them to stand many hours after long days in the field is remarkable. The players have given more than forty performances, largely of Greek plays, though in winter Shakespeare, Shaw, and Dunsany have been acted. *Hippolytus* has been played most often; *Trojan Women* and *Œdipus Rex* are also favorites.

By insight and long experience Mrs. King knows the taste of her audience. Any excellent play well acted, she thinks, appeals to them, but during many rehearsals the actors weary far less quickly of a Greek play than of a modern. This she accounts for by the mood of Greek tragedy, the rhythm and fullness of sound of the verse. One of the crying needs of the village is for modern plays of the right kind, not "the mistress-and-servant" type and not those which confound silliness with simplicity. People want the drama to give them emotion expressed in universal experience. In this opinion the postmistress of West Hoathly, one of the players, concurs. She feels that since village life includes as much tragedy as comedy people are glad to find in the plays "ideas which they had felt but had never been able to express." She recalled an old man's sobbing during the last scene of *Œdipus*, although he had attended every rehearsal.

I wish that I could mirror the beauty of the *Hippolytus* as I saw it at Stonelands in the covered yard of an ancient cattle shed, an amphitheatre both for chorus and spectators, with the afternoon light slipping through the open sides of the stalls, now box-seats, across the warm colors of the robes of actors and chorus and the enigmatic, archaic faces of the shrined deities. Many of the voices were beautiful and all were nearly flawless in articulation, speaking the rounded and golden syllables of a classic English. When the peace of resignation had succeeded passion and the figures of the tragedy had passed quietly out along the flagged walk by the sculptured box garden, toward the Elizabethan manor, the audience was silent with the sense of a restrained and assured beauty akin to religious ritual.

These village drama societies, the work of which has just been discussed, and scores of others are organizations of amateurs; there remains the amazing history of one professional group which has played in nearly six hundred towns and villages of England, Scotland, and Ireland: the Arts League of Service Travelling Theatre. Its influence is almost immeasurable, not only upon its own audiences, but upon local dramatic groups which have been formed under its inspiration.

The Arts League of Service was founded in 1919 by a group of prominent people, many of them experienced in other dramatic associations; Lord Henry Cavendish-

Bentinck was their president. It was born of disquietude after the Great War when thoughtful men were wondering what importance Art was to have in a chaotic world. The aims of the society are "to establish a closer bond between the community and the Artist, to create in the public a greater interest in his work, and to rouse in the Artist an understanding of the community and its needs, and thus to stimulate both the demand for, and the supply of Art." The activities of the League are many,—organizing lectures, exhibiting modern paintings, sculpture, pottery, and textiles, sending out portfolios of drawings and prints, and planning dramatic programs. These are composed of folk-songs, tableaux suggested by poem or song, and various other types of gay and artistic amusements called "absurdities," often with a prominent folk-element; for instance, the command performance before the royal family at Balmoral Castle included five folk-songs, a poem arranged for músic, two nursery rhymes—one of them *The King's Breakfast* by A. A. Milne,—two dances, two "absurdities," and Allan Monkhouse's play, *The Grand Cham's Diamond*.

Early in 1919 the League sent out a small professional company in a borrowed wagonette for a fortnight's tour of Sussex villages. In the next eight years the tours extended to fifteen weeks twice a year into every English county but one and across the border. Now, thanks to a Carnegie grant, a second company can travel at the same time. In each village or town the local organizers engage the hall, manage the advertising, provide for the entertainment of the players,—usually in homes,—and promise the sum of £20 for each evening. Profits in excess of that amount up to £15 belong to the organizers; above this amount they are shared. The League carries all expenses of actual production. However, since the directors have discovered that many remote villages are too poor to look after the entertainment of guests or to provide even a small guarantee, they have decided to gather an additional smaller company, to procure a motor caravan for housing the cast, and not to require any guarantee. For these tours all stage settings must be easy to handle, as the actors have no assistance. The background is always of reversible curtains with one side blue, the other buff. Little painted canvases on light frames are sometimes added to give atmosphere. These, like the costumes, are designed by artists.

The programs are naturally influenced by the small stage and cast, which bar plays of Shakespeare and many moderns. At the beginning of the season the League sends to its patrons a list of about thirty numbers, from which twelve or fourteen, including a one-act play, are to be chosen.

Since the League company appears before every type of audience, including that of large city, university town, agricultural village, and drab mining-center (the last in its reaction from the ugliness of its daily surroundings is the most appreciative of all) a list of its successes is valuable. These, like those of the Old Vic, contradict the belief that a manager must "play down" to the audience: *Wurzel Flummery* (A. A. Milne), *Sister Clare* (Laurence Housman), *The Fool's Errand* (Housman), *The Curious Herbal* (Constance Smedley), *The Conquest of Humility* (Susan Richmond), *The Shepherd* (Charles Forrest), *The Grand Cham's Diamond* (Allan Monkhouse), *Pages from our Magazines* (Margaret Drew), *Catherine Parr* (Maurice Baring), *The Old Firm's Awakening* (A. J. Talbot), *The Statue* (Leslie R. French), *Cloudbreak* (A. O. Roberts), *Crabbèd Youth and Age* (Lennox Robinson), *Monday* (Alfred Kreymborg), *The Unknown Hand* (Clifford Bax). Two great favorites are *Riders to the Sea* (Synge) and *Campbell of Kilmhor* (J. A. Ferguson), both tragedies.

What the Arts League of Service has been doing for town and country another organization, the Lena Ashwell Play-

ers, has been attempting for the poor of London. Miss Ashwell writes:

> The English do much for the drainage of their cities: they
> light, sweep and police the streets: they arrange trains and trams
> to carry the people to and fro: they tend the hurt, vaccinate the
> young, pension the old and bury the dead, all rather well or very
> well; better than most people.
> What do they do for the people's joy?
> What joy is offered to the millions who live in mean streets
> and come home tired every evening?
> No doubt many make joy for themselves in little gardens or
> window boxes: many have wireless sets, or subscribe to libraries.
> What else is there, except the cinema? [28]

In the war days Miss Ashwell had organized the "Concerts at the Front," in soldiers' camps, and experience had
again and again shown her the strengthening and consoling
power of the drama,—when the troops burned the huts at
Honfleur "the authorities sent for the 'Concerts at the
Front' party; they played *Candida* and all was quiet again."
"Because we are haunted with the memory of those years
with the armies, because we recall the great use we were in
healing the sick and encouraging those who fought, because
we broke the deadly monotony of life out there, we know
we can be of use to the masses of the people in this country." With a small sum of money turned over to her after the
war, Miss Ashwell collected a group, many of whom had
been with her on the continent, and held entertainments
first at veterans' hospitals and then at Bethnal Green. She
then formulated a program of coöperation with the London
boroughs, and persuaded the mayors of Stepney and other
boroughs to allow her to rent halls at low prices and also
to assume a certain amount of advertising.

Beginning with Shoreditch, Limehouse, and Stepney in

[28] Leaflet, *Recreation and the Drama,* published by the Lena Ashwell
Players.

their first year, by the season of 1924-1925 the players were visiting Ilford, Battersea, Edmonton, Winchmore Hill, Greenwich, Deptford, Watford, Sutton, Camberwell, Staines, Hounslow, and, in summer, Bath and York. In 1924, these strolling players had their longings for a permanent home gratified by the purchase of an old theatre, the Century, once the Bijou, at Westbourne Grove. (Before they had rehearsed in a garage, "though it was a lovely garage," as one of them loyally wrote.) Here they have an opportunity for polishing their plays before starting around the circuit. By running three companies, Miss Ashwell can allow three weeks for the study of each new play.

Prices of admission are purely nominal. Miss Ashwell believes in a small charge for all entertainments as a means of creating genuine interest. An association, named Friends of the Players, was founded to bring theatre and public into closer acquaintance. This numbers eighteen hundred, and several branches have more than two hundred each.

As to repertoire—though Shakespeare and Shaw have continued to be the backbone of the program (they were also the favorites of the English armies), the list includes representative work of distinguished modern English playwrights with a sprinkling of Restoration and of foreign plays and plays by the talented younger group. Occasionally, Miss Ashwell has been able to give a play its first London production. Her catalogue of successes and comparative failures is illuminating; with the exception of *Everyman*, which she declares depends largely on an atmosphere which at the time her company was not able to create, each play in the third list would probably be admitted to have some decided weakness or at least slightness.

I. *Successes: Twelfth Night, The Taming of the Shrew, As You Like It, The Merry Wives of Windsor, The Merchant of Venice, Othello, Much Ado About Nothing, Macbeth, You Never*

Can Tell, Man and Superman, Candida, Fanny's First Play, Pygmalion, The Devil's Disciple, The School for Scandal, She Stoops to Conquer, The Country Wife, The Tragedy of Nan, A Doll's House, The Skin Game, His House in Order, Lady Windermere's Fan, Mrs. Dane's Defence, Caroline, Mr. Pim Passes By, Belinda, The Younger Generation, The Witness for The Defence, The Lion and the Mouse, The Romantic Young Lady, The Bill of Divorcement, Caste, The Bathroom Door, Ann, Passers By, A Pair of Spectacles, The Child in Flanders, The Likes of Her, Merely Mary Ann, Leah Kleschna, Diana of Dobsons, Trilby, Hobson's Choice, His Excellency the Governor, The Message from Mars, The Purse Strings, The Beggar Prince, The Brave and the Fair.

II. *"So So": The Morals of Marcus, Getting Married, The Importance of Being Ernest, The Gay Lord Quex, The Liars, The Thief, Diplomacy, The Walls of Jericho, The Duke of Killiecrankie, Mrs. Gorringe's Necklace, The Celluloid Cat, The Mock Doctor, Sweet Lavender, The Young Person in Pink, Rutherford and Son, Woman to Woman, Doormats, The Elder Miss Blossom.*

III. *"No": Widowers' Houses, Everyman, A Christmas Carol, Prunella, Paola and Francesca, Liberty Hall, The Mollusc, Cousin Kate, The Easiest Way, Niobe, Our Boys, The Rivals, Smith, The Case of Lady Camber, The Naked Truth, Shortage, John Glayd's Honour.*

For lack of resources and for other reasons, the Lena Ashwell Players do not favor elaborate production. John Masefield, a great admirer, has written of the players in *Recreation and the Drama:*

Perhaps all that these players do is done with what most theatrical managers would call "insufficient means." These "means" are taken by many as excuses for the neglect of essentials. Want of them has always stirred these people to give the essentials their fullest value. The play is the thing with them. The problem always before them is not what effects can be produced by an avalanche in Act I., an eruption in Act II., an inundation in Act III., a tidal wave in Act IV. and the Day of Judgment at the end, but what is the very soul and purpose of the author, to get at that by spiritual effort and to let all deficiencies help them, as they can be made to, if there be the will.

Generally, the inspiration of all little communities that are worth their salt and are doing memorable work, comes from one person. Probably that is so in this company. Inspiration is a vague word for several qualities: such as faith, that the work is worth doing; hope, that the world may some day know this; and courage, to keep the thing going, in the midst of adversity. It is always by such qualities of soul that the individual inspires the little band to go down into the trouble to alter the thought of the world.

In their acting Masefield commends "a spirit and a grace which I had not seen before in any English company," a beauty of speech both in prose and verse, and "freshness, clearness and gaiety." Mr. Lennox Robinson writes of *The Winter's Tale,* which was played first and foremost for its poetry:

In a dismal suburb on a cramped stage, the Lena Ashwell Players presented this lovely thing. It shone like a jewel in its poor setting, catching its chief fire from Miss Esme Church's Hermione. Miss Church has not got the qualities that go to the making a star; she is not magnificent, her voice is not startlingly fine, but in herself she is radiant, and her Hermione was beautifully noble. Beautiful, too, were Mamillius and Florizel, Camillo and the Old Shepherd, and Miss Wilson's passionate Paulina. The play swept through like a lovely poem, like a piece of music heard in the distance on a summer's night.[29]

Conceived in love, born in a time of intense national emotion, this remnant of the Concerts at the Front has for its audience the consecration of a sacrificial past. Though several members have joined much more recently, playgoers know that their chief and some of her helpers have appeared

[29] *The Fifth Lap,* April, 1925.

four times a day before the men of the trenches; they know that "our Esme" is the Esme of the Tommies. ("Cheer oh, Esme, God bless you." "Where's the little 'un with the red hair?" "Where's the red haired girl wot makes us laugh?") On Armistice Night the company gives a "Concert at the Front" exactly as it did in France, and one of their favorites, *The Child in Flanders,* Miss Cicely Hamilton's modern miracle play, first played by them at Abbeville, stands to Miss Ashwell for the very spirit of her endeavor.

On the clock which the poet laureate has given these players, standing in an honored position in their theatre, is this inscription:

The Clock to the Lena Ashwell Players

On Their Comedy	On Their Tragedy
I tell the time; but you within this place Show to the passing Time its fleeting face.	Without, the passing city roars her tides; I tell the Time, you show what it abides.

I tell the Time; and bring a Poet's prayer
That Time may bless such players everywhere.

VI

THE NATIONAL THEATRE OF IRELAND

As the long line of the mountain coast unfolded before me [writes Chesterton, of Ireland], I had an optical illusion; it may be that many had had it before. As new lengths of coast and lines of heights were unfolded, I had the fancy that the whole land was not receding but advancing, like something spreading out its arms to the world. A chance shred of sunshine rested, like a riven banner, on the hill which I believe is called in Irish the Mountain of the Golden Spears; and I could have imagined that the spears and the banner were coming on. And in that flash I remembered that the men of this island had gone forth, not the torches of conquerors or destroyers, but as missionaries in the very midnight of the Dark Ages, like a multitude of moving candles, that were the light of the world.[1]

FOR Ireland has no reason for shame in the household of nations. Alone among the nations north of the Alps did she not keep her national life inviolate till the eighth century and almost untouched by the later classical renaissance? Was it a disgrace, this insularity, this working out of her own beauty, her truth, in her own terms? Wilde bewailed "the dreary Classical Renaissance," which superimposed itself upon "Christ's own Renaissance, which has produced the Cathedral at Chartres and the Arthurian cycle of legends," and many other deeply loved and national things. The whole course of the Irish literary awakening in this

[1] From *Irish Impressions,* by G. K. Chesterton, p. 43. Copyright, 1919, by Dodd, Mead and Company, Inc.

present generation has been the germination and stirring of national impulse, bringing into the hearts of her own race a fuller consciousness of a "hidden Ireland," [2] of whom the Gaelic poets of the eighteenth century were only a part, that whole body of Irish thought and tradition and dreaming which is not a musing upon a dying language or a people, but a fusing of past and present, with a challenge for the future. Nationalism has been immeasurably strengthened by the revival in Irish literature of this brooding love of country. Past and present interpenetrate each other reaching toward some vision of perfection, some *Tir n-an-Og*, the Land of Youth, some country of the Ever-Living.

> We would no Irish sign efface,
> But yet our lips would gladlier hail
> The firstborn of the Coming Race
> Than the last splendour of the Gael.
> No blazoned banner we unfold—
> One charge alone we give to youth,
> Against the sceptred myth to hold
> The golden heresy of truth.[3]

The Irish national drama is one of the voices of a fervent, consecrated spirit. Though known throughout the world its intent is not to influence Europe, as in the centuries when Irish Catholicism and Irish culture spread their way almost across a continent; the Irish dramatic movement has a nearer and more abiding purpose: to save its own race by holding up to it not only a portrait of the old heroic days, but a mirror of the present marked with perplexities and anguish but in its very lineaments a prophecy of a fuller, more exultant life.

Four great influences have merged in the development of

[2] See the brilliant introduction to *The Hidden Ireland*, by Daniel Corkery.

[3] From *Collected Poems*, by George William Russell, p. 230. Courtesy of The Macmillan Company, Publishers, New York.

Ireland's national drama: the love of a deeply wronged land; the instinct to cherish whatever is racial and individual in her history and her people; the desire for what is intense and passionate in literature (of which drama is the acme); and the knowledge of the European theatre in the days of its rekindled genius. If the continental, last-named of these four influences, seems minor, picture what might have happened to a young Irish theatre under the direction of men who loved Ireland, the legendary Ireland of gods and heroes and the Ireland of today, and knew nothing of the drama of other nations. A play is a highly concentrated art form resentful of propaganda. An untrained patriotism, sincere but unskillfully and bombastically expressed, such as had marred many Irish lyrics of the early nineteenth century, might have worked havoc with the art of the drama.

The beginning of the Irish literary revival, of which the national theatre is a part, is hard to date exactly. Interest in Gaelic, a language identical in sections of Ireland and Scotland for centuries, had never died down since the eighteenth century controversy over Macpherson's *Ossian*. In 1842 in the first issue of *The Nation*, the organ of his movement, Davis pleaded for a nationality which should find its expression in literature, "of the spirit as well as the letter—a nationality which may come to be stamped upon our manners, and literature, and our deeds." An occasional poem of the group which included Charles Gavan Duffy, Mangan, Walsh, Callanan, John Mitchel, Sir Samuel Ferguson is either a free translation of the Gaelic or upon a Gaelic theme, as Sir Samuel Ferguson's poems upon the Cooly Cattle Raid and his translations of modern folksongs. Dr. Sigerson translated some Irish poets metrically in *Bards of the Gael and Gaul*. In 1878 Standish O'Grady published the first volume of his *History of Ireland*, a reshaping of ancient Irish tales, and gained the right to be considered at least an inspirer, and by many the father of the modern movement. Eleven years later William B. Yeats published *The Wanderings of Oisin,* which the Irish patriot, John O'Leary, then an old man, helped bring to the attention of the political and intellectual leaders of Ireland. Within the next few years Yeats, who had written *The Death of Cuchulain,* several poems of peasant life, and *The Land of Heart's Desire,* was accepted as an authentic Anglo-Irish poet and a power in the literary revival.

The Gaelic revival, in the stricter sense of a language revival, made a great bound forward in 1893 when Dr. Douglas Hyde, who had already written a book in modern Irish and in the next year was to publish his *Love Songs of Connacht,* most beloved of the translations of Irish lyrics, founded the Gaelic League, "for the preservation of the Irish language and for the encouragement of spoken Irish." The time was ripe for this. Again, as in the Davis era, Ireland was disheartened in politics, for the struggles of Fenians, nationalists, and land reformers against English oppression and English rule received a setback in the Parnell split in 1890 and in that leader's early death a year later. No longer with an "uncrowned king of Ireland" around whom to rally, Irishmen sought liberation in the language which was theirs long before the invasions of Danes, Normans, or English, a language which has a longer continuous history than that of any other people north of the Alps. For hundreds of years English influence had been against the native language. It received a great setback in the terrible famine years of 1846 and 1847 when nearly a million Irish people, many of them native Irish speakers, died. After this, English gained rapidly over the Celtic tongue. When Hyde was beginning his translations of Irish, the Board of National Education had almost decided to blot out a language which the University of Dublin found at the best merely trivial. Now, after many years of teaching and writing and a long term as president of the Gaelic League, Dr. Hyde sees early Irish acknowledged a treasury of one of the most beautiful folk-literatures of Europe and modern Irish taught by government sanction in over nine out of ten elementary schools.

It cannot be too strongly emphasized that the Gaelic revival is more than a language movement, an attempt to stay what was a waning speech. Unfortunately the difficulty of the language has thrust into undue prominence grammar and lexicon, all the paraphernalia of the schoolmaster. The movement is an attempt to revive and develop Irish culture, everything that is traditional, beautiful, national, in literature, folk-song, dance, or sports, with a "bold educational ideal of building up a national character, which makes it not so much a language movement as a thought movement." [4] The influence of this Gaelic revival on modern Irish thought is almost limitless; there is something mysterious in its shaping power: under this magic, Standish O'Grady has brought again to Ireland a vision of heroic days; Douglas Hyde has encouraged and himself helped create a modern Gaelic literature; Lady Gregory, from a teller of little anecdotes, has become a writer of delightful comedies and of moving historical plays; and Synge has caught a reflection of his own soul with its Celtic beauty, melancholy, grotesqueness, in a series of plays which contain in their Anglo-Irish idiom much of the really poetic in contemporary English drama. Even those who have not learned the language have felt its influence: "A. E." (George William Russell) in his descriptions of the life of ancient Ireland for his audiences has helped the Coöperative movement for agricultural reform as no mere economist or professional organizer could have done; George Moore in his ardor for "the little languages" has rediscovered Ireland much to his own and Ireland's benefit and recorded his adventures in *Hail*

[4] Bourgeois, Maurice, *John Synge and the Irish Theatre*, p. 115.

and Farewell; and Yeats, in his versatility perhaps the most influential figure of all, has metamorphosed the lyric poet into the dramatic, organized a national theatre, and by the force of his personality (the Irish have always been great admirers of personality) turned many a man of talent and at least one of genius into the road of their best endeavors.

This account can be only a chapter in the history of Irish drama, not of Irish politics, except in so far as the two are interwoven. Ireland has certainly moved toward Yeats' ideal: to bring into importance again the kindred arts of an earlier world, the association of literature, music, speech, the dance; and he has done much to bind by a common love of beauty the humble day-laborer, the artist, and the poet. The Irish Free State has had other founders besides its statesmen:

The Literature of the past quickened the imagination of the present; because it is not far wrong to say that Mr. W. B. Yeats and the poets associated with him in the early years of the last decade of the nineteenth century sowed the seed that has blossomed into the Irish Free State; an examination of the ideals of the Irish literary revival, and a study of its development, give the spiritual background for an understanding of political events.[5]

Curiously, Ireland,—like Celtic Scotland and Wales,— has had a retarded development in an art the love of which is considered instinctive. The delight in strong and varied characters which the Irish possess, their joy in conversation, their impulsive bravery, their life of national struggle would all seem to predestine them to dramatic achievement. Yet the nineteenth century was almost over before a distinctly Irish play appeared. The reason ordinarily given, the presence of unrest and struggle in Ireland during the years when western Europe was developing the miracle play and redis-

[5] From *Changing Ireland,* by Norreys Jephson O'Conor, p. 94. Courtesy of Harvard University Press.

covering classical drama seems scarcely adequate when one realizes the amount of fighting in England and on the continent. A truer reason is almost certainly the unbounded enthusiasm of the Irish for story-telling,—by the bards in the great houses and the *shanachies* in the cottages of the poor. This delight was so absorbing and the tales themselves so filled with emotion and action, two characteristics of drama, that the listeners felt no need for the play. Another reason is the fact that the guilds, which in England assisted the new art, never fitted the Irish temperament, which preferred a looser method of organization, and, accordingly, whatever guild performances were given in the larger Irish cities were the entertainment of the Ascendency, the English in Ireland. Again, the Irish Catholic clergy never favored the religious drama, and after the Church of England had separated itself from the Church of Rome, religious differences further alienated their sympathies. This attitude continued; the theatres of the eighteenth and nineteenth century belonged to the English in Ireland, never to the native Irish. Not until Boucicault, a favorite of the Irish in America, turned to audiences at home was there Irish drama of any kind, and not till Yeats' *The Land of Heart's Desire,* produced in London in 1894, was there any distinctly Irish play of artistic beauty. (For two centuries, of course, Irishmen had been writing in England for English audiences. The list is overwhelming: one hesitates to think what English drama would be without the names of Congreve, educated though not born across the Irish Sea, and the Irish-born Farquhar, Goldsmith, Sheridan, Oscar Wilde, George Bernard Shaw. Fertility and brilliancy of dialogue, humor, wit, and ingenuity, particularly in satire, have marked all these "English" dramatists.)

The dream of an Irish theatre had been in existence for several years before the first program of the first Irish Theatre. Lady Gregory would have the beginning of modern

Irish drama a winter day in 1898 when Douglas Hyde as an
actor in a Punch and Judy show at a school party at Coole
amazed the children by "the grand curses"—in Irish—
"which An Craoibhim had put on the baby and the police-
man," [6] but neither Lady Gregory nor Douglas Hyde was
the real founder. Edward Martyn, George Moore, and William Butler Yeats were the ones from whom the initial impulse came. According to George Moore, the spirit was
already groping in 1894 when his cousin, Edward Martyn, in
his room in the Inner Temple, London, startled him one evening by a wish to know enough Irish to write plays, and set
him wondering over the place of "the little languages" in culture, whether English might not be waning, whether a man
of letters might be reborn through the influence of a new or a
newly revived language, and whether Irishmen needed exile
or the inspiration of long native tradition. But the actual inception of the organization belonged to Yeats. For over
thirty years he has been a great figure in Dublin as well as
one of the most distinguished of English poets, and his is the
outstanding individuality of the Irish theatre.

Genius can be defined as the power within a man which
draws everything within the circle of his destiny—his inheritance from his forebears, each apparently trivial activity, each friendship, each contact. For the man of genius
each bye-path is a march forward upon a direct road. So life
has been for Yeats. As the leader of a dramatic movement
he needed both unusual emotional power to envisage the
conflicts of life and critical ability to disentangle prejudices
and escape from an insular attitude, and his inheritance
supplied both. His mother, of the Pollexfen family, partly of
Cornish blood, was, as Yeats tells us, by nature a woman of
unusual intensity, a trait which first attracted her artist husband. The affairs of the outside world meant little to her; in
the often-straitened home of an artist not yet famous, she

[6] "The pleasant little branch" is Dr. Hyde's Irish name.

sewed for her children and told them tales of the Irish country and its people. "She read no books," her son writes, "but
she and the fisherman's wife would tell each other stories
that Homer might have told, pleased with any moment of
sudden intensity and laughing together over any point of
satire." [7] Many of Yeats' tales were first of his mother's tell-
ing. His father, far more analytical, discussed theories of art
and of literature, and read aloud at the breakfast table
poetry chosen for its deep emotion. The bit of praise which
the poet values most is that spoken by one of the Yeats
family, "We have ideas and no passions but by marriage
with a Pollexfen we have given a tongue to the sea cliffs." [8]
Yeats' childhood and youth were passed in Sligo in the
northwest of Ireland, in art circles of Dublin, and among
artists and writers in London. As a boy he delighted in the
poetry of Wordsworth for its nearness to nature, and like
the English poet was given to nocturnal investigations. Once
he harried various members of his family until he was
allowed to take out a boat in the early morning to find what
seabirds are the first to cry at dawn. He was an admirer of
William Morris and of certain doctrines of the pre-
Raphaelites. Like some of them, he hovered between painting and poetry until three years in art schools made him
realize his preference for literature. This early training
proved a background for scenic experimentation later. He
was a friend of many of the younger writers, notably Lionel
Johnson and Oscar Wilde, of the artist Aubrey Beardsley
and others of "the tragic generation"; of the Irishmen in
London, Edward Martyn and George Moore, and others;
of a group interested in psychical research.

Yeats, in these years before 1899, can be made to seem
dilettante and poseur, as he appears in some of George

---

[7] From *Reveries Over Childhood and Youth*, by William Butler Yeats,
p. 75. Courtesy of The Macmillan Company, Publishers.
[8] *Ibid.*, p. 27.

Moore's pages. But under his amazing versatility he was thinking deeply and arranging life's values according to his own scale. For a time he was much troubled over the relationship of art to life: if "poetry and sculpture exist to keep our passions alive," how can we justify them in the eyes of the puritanical who believe that passions are wrong? Again if it makes people more sensitive, more susceptible to sorrow, has the individual any right to follow art? He brooded much upon the connections between what he named the solar and the lunar influences in literature, the influence of the individual art and the influence of the folk mind. From the early days of collecting of Irish legends in *Irish Fairy and Folk Tales,* (which opened to him sources for his own *Countess Cathleen* and *The Land of Heart's Desire*) he has praised the folk-mood and the folk-imagination for their beauty and for their constructive influence in Irish literature. Some of his most exquisite prose comes in passages like these:

These folk-tales are full of simplicity and musical occurrences, for they are the literature of a class for whom every incident in the old rut of birth, love, pain, and death has cropped up unchanged for centuries; who have steeped everything in the heart; to whom everything is a symbol. They have the spade over which man has leaned from the beginning. The people of the cities have the machine, which is prose and a *parvenu*.[9]

I thought that all art should be a Centaur finding in the popular lore its back and its strong legs.[10]

If we would create a great community—and what other game is so worth the labour?—we must recreate the old foundations of life, not as they existed in the splendid misunderstanding of the eighteenth century, but as they must always exist when the finest minds and Ned the beggar and Seaghan the fool think about the

[9] Yeats, W. B., *Irish Fairy and Folk Tales,* p. XII.
[10] Yeats, W. B., *Plays and Controversies,* p. 214.

same thing, although they may not think the same thought about it.[11]

Intent on bringing a unity in Irish thought through the life of the spirit, Yeats joined or organized Irish literary societies wherever he could. From membership in the Southwark Irish Literary Society in London he passed to the founding, with the help of T. W. Rolleston, of the Irish Literary Society, at the house of his father in Bedford, a society which soon included all the Irish authors and journalists in London. Later in Dublin he was responsible for The National Literary Society affiliated with the Young Ireland Societies in country towns; the group included John O'Leary, John F. Taylor, Douglas Hyde, Standish O'Grady, Dr. Sigerson, Count Plunkett, and others prominent in literature or politics. Yeats proposed to organize lending libraries throughout Ireland, to establish an Irish publishing house, and to create an Irish theatre to begin with a travelling company. Though no one of these objects was realized by this group, the interest which the plans awakened and the publicity given the society helped create the enthusiasm for later phases of the movement.

Yeats had long been of the opinion that the drama from its very nature, its intensity of emotion and the direct appeal of actor to audience, is the most powerful art for awakening interest in a national literature. He had also been concerned over the difficulty of producing verse-plays before any audience which could support them. He had once suggested to the Irishman, John Todhunter, that if a poet would be content to stage a poetic play once or twice in a small suburban theatre, and then follow it the next year in the same house and at the same season, he could, if his plays had real merit, gradually build up a following and be sure of a modest success. This suggestion Dr. Todhunter

[11] Yeats, W. B., *Cutting of an Agate,* Edition of 1912, p. 33.

accepted for his first venture, a pastoral drama in verse, but carried away by a response which surpassed his hopes, in 1894 he gave his next, *The Tyranny of Tears,* in the Avenue Theatre, a much larger and more expensive playhouse—unsuccessfully. Both Dr. Todhunter's undertakings benefited Yeats. In the first play Miss Florence Farr acted. Then an amateur, but already one of the few beautiful speakers of verse on the English stage, she became Yeats' close friend, experimenting with him in arranging musical notation for speaking verse. The second program, at Miss Farr's suggestion, offered a chance for Yeats' lovely *Land of Heart's Desire* as a curtain-raiser.

At the same Avenue Theatre Yeats could also see *Arms and the Man,* one of Shaw's early successes. In other ways, at about the same time, Yeats came in contact with English and continental movements: indeed with Miss Farr he became a champion of Ibsen, though with reservations, for much as he admired the technical skill and the courage of the Norwegian, he found the speeches trite and flavorless, lacking joy, as he did the novels of George Eliot. The pioneer little theatre of London, the Independent Society, one of the bravest of Ibsen's defenders, at first seemed to Yeats a model for an Irish theatre, but he gradually became hopeless of poetic drama in London. His dream theatre should not be realistic but romantic,—a home for his own plays, for Martyn's, for Bridges,' and for whatever the Celtic enthusiasts, Standish O'Grady and Fiona Macleod, could be persuaded to write.

It was neither in London nor in Dublin, however, that the actual plans for an Irish theatre leaped into being, but appropriately enough in an old estate on the Galway coast in a very Gaelic section of Ireland. The plans came about as epochal things sometimes do, almost by accident. In the summer of '98 Lady Gregory came from her home at Coole, near Gort, and Edward Martyn from his neighboring estate of Tillyra to spend an afternoon at the home of the old French nobleman, Count de Basterot, at Duras. Martyn had brought Yeats with him. In the course of the afternoon Yeats and Lady Gregory found themselves discussing plays. They were, at this time, only slight acquaintances, though Yeats had already interested Lady Gregory in collecting Irish folk-lore. Before that she had been absorbed in historical studies, after her husband's death spending her leisure in writing his biography and in editing letters belonging to his family, a distinguished one which had always championed Ireland. When Yeats spoke of Martyn's plays, which had been refused by London managers, and of his own dreams of a theatre, dreams hopeless because of Ireland's poverty, Lady Gregory, who up to then, as she admits, had had little interest in any theatre, heard herself suggesting the founding of an Irish one. Before evening, the initial program, Martyn's *Heather Field* and Yeats' *Countess Cathleen*, had been decided upon, and a guarantee fund started with Lady Gregory's contribution. Not long afterwards, Yeats and Martyn sought George Moore and persuaded him that Dublin might be more hospitable to literary plays than London. Ireland, which had been "a little speck down on the horizon" of his life, suddenly grew to "tremendous bulk," calling him to herself and to a realization of an unsuspected continent of his mind, that of *The Lake,* of *Evelyn Innes,* and of *Hail and Farewell.* Least Irish in temperament of the four perhaps, by his knowledge of play-producing learned at the Independent Theatre, he saved the Irish Literary Theatre from being still-born.

Mr. Andrew Malone, the most recent historian of the Irish drama, has pointed out the significance of Connaught in the lives of all four organizers of the Irish Literary Theatre: George Moore was born and reared in County Mayo, Lady Gregory and Edward Martyn in County Galway, and Yeats spent much of his childhood in Sligo. These leaders, devoted as they have been to Ireland, are not of pure Irish descent: loving the Gaelic west, they have had the background of general European culture and the sympathy with world literature to appreciate the richness of this native source. In the wildly beautiful surroundings of this remote section, the peasants have kept an originality of language and a grace of phrasing from their earlier tongue, and a direct belief in the rich folk-lore of a Celtic past, which "still lives and is still vivid in speech, in stone, and in misery . . . in an environment that has changed but little in five hundred years."

The manifesto of the theatre drafted by Lady Gregory and Yeats breathed an eagerness not limited by any partisanship, political or sectarian:

We propose to have performed in Dublin, in the spring of every year certain Celtic and Irish plays, which whatever be their degree of excellence will be written with a high ambition, and so to build up a Celtic and Irish school of dramatic literature. We hope to find in Ireland an uncorrupted and imaginative audience trained to listen by its passion for oratory, and believe that our desire to bring upon the stage the deeper thoughts and emotions of Ireland will insure for us a tolerant welcome, and that freedom to experiment which is not found in theatres of England, and without which no new movement in art or literature can succeed. We will show that Ireland is not the home of buffoonery and of easy sentiment, as it has been represented, but the home of an ancient idealism. We are confident of the support of all Irish people, who are weary of misrepresentation, in carrying out a work that is outside all the political questions that divide us.

The founders hoped to secure £300, a sum which would finance the Irish Literary Theatre for three experimental seasons. Their appeal brought a wide response from members of the Irish National Literary Society, members of the Gaelic League, writers, political leaders, and others: Aubrey de Vere, W. H. Lecky, John O'Leary, Douglas Hyde, Sir Horace Plunkett, John Dillon, John Redmond, Professor Mahaffy of Trinity, and a New York lawyer, John Quinn. One or two who were approached, scenting the taint of continental and English movements, the "London Independent Theatre" and "Ibsen & Company," refused.

Meanwhile life was becoming complicated for the two playwrights and their adviser in London, who were to rehearse the plays, and for Lady Gregory in Dublin. Anyone ever responsible for a dramatic performance knows the multitude of difficulties which can develop. Martyn's play was a delicate and subtle tragedy written under the influence of Ibsen and perhaps of Strindberg, to be given when Ibsen actors and actresses were not easily obtainable; Yeats' mystic verse could be crushed even more surely by poor production. Both plays, in spite of their Irish characters and settings, had to be entrusted to English impersonators because no Irish actors were obtainable. The entertaining quality of the account in *Hail and Farewell* does not conceal the fact that hard work was required and that in this department of the enterprise Moore's services were invaluable. In Dublin Lady Gregory was beating against an old law which forbade any performance for money in an unlicensed building. For a time the only feasible plan appeared the organization of a closed society like the London Stage Society; to those looking toward a national theatre this type of society would have represented a defeat at the very beginning. Fortunately Lady Gregory had powerful friends in Mr. Lecky and others, who were able to append a clause to a bill then going through the House of Commons, making possible the granting of an occasional license for a stage play if the proceeds were for charity or to aid a society of scientific, artistic, or literary purpose. Still another anxiety came from distorted rumors of the nature of Yeats' play in which some well-meaning people suspected heresy and others not so well-meaning hoped to find an excuse for a theatre fracas.

The first performance of the Irish Literary Theatre was May 8, 1899, at the Ancient Concert Rooms, Dublin. The atmosphere was cleared and mellowed by the reciting of Lionel Johnson's beautiful poem, the cadences of which have echoed on the first nights of other little theatres on both sides of the Atlantic, in prologues never quite so graceful as their original:

> The May fire once on every dreaming hill
> All the fair land with burning bloom would fill;
> All the fair land, at visionary night,
> Gave loving glory to the Lord of Light.
> Have we no leaping flames of Beltaine praise
> To kindle in the joyous ancient ways;
> No fire of song, of vision, of white dream,
> Fit for the Master of the Heavenly Gleam;
> For him who first made Ireland move in chime,
> Musical from the misty dawn of time?

> Ah, yes; for sacrifice this night we bring
> The passion of a lost soul's triumphing;
> All rich with faery airs that, wandering long,
> Uncaught, here gather into Irish song;
> Sweet as the old remembering winds that wail,
> From hill to hill of gracious Inisfail;
> Sad as the unforgetting winds that pass
> Over her children in her holy grass
> At home, and sleeping well upon her breast,
> Where snowy Deirdre and her sorrows rest.

> Come, then, and keep with us an Irish feast,
> Wherein the Lord of Light and Song is Priest;
> Now, at this opening of the gentle May,
> Watch warring passions at their storm and play;

Wrought with the flaming ecstasy of art,
Sprung from the dreaming of an Irish heart.[12]

The Countess Cathleen was received with interest by both
stalls and gallery, except for a few trouble-makers whose
hisses and boos were not loud enough to require any action
by the force of special police. The next morning the Dublin
newspapers were so enthusiastic that several London dramatic critics, among them Max Beerbohm, attended the second program, *The Heather Field*. Of the success of this
there was no doubt. While the Ibsen influence delighted,—
or troubled,—only a minority, the theme of the play, idealism at war with materialism, appealed to the Irish heart.
That the general trend of the plays, however, was not distinctly national did not escape the critics. Stephen Gwynn,
somewhat later, gave his opinion that to a considerable extent the first programs of the Irish Literary Theatre, instead of being "representatively Irish" were "in reality
exotic":

No normal Irishman would have expected an Irish audience to
regard with equanimity an Irish peasant kicking about, no matter
in what extremity, an image of the Virgin. The mind of Mr. Yeats
and his artistic sympathies had been moulded away from Ireland;
the public which he conceived or assumed was the public that
applauds Maeterlinck. And the same alien element was apparent
in the work of Mr. Martyn, who, although a land-owner and a
Deputy-Lieutenant of County Galway, had lived and made his
friendships in Paris. It was a coincidence that he should have hit
upon a dramatic idea previously treated by Strindberg—the
dilemma of a wife who feels herself impelled in self-protection to
swear her husband into a lunatic asylum—but the coincidence
proved that Mr. Martyn was working under the influence of
Ibsen and his imitators, and every line of the play bore out that
suggestion. Nevertheless, *The Heather Field* had in Dublin a

[12] From *Our Irish Theatre*, by Lady Gregory, pp. 23, 24. Courtesy of
G. P. Putnam's Sons, Publishers, New York and London.

genuine success. I read it in London, and I saw it played in London, and it did not attract or interest me; but then I read it and saw it under the impression left by Mr. Moore's preface. The Dublin audience saw, and welcomed, a sincere attempt to present one of those amiable and talented individuals through whose hands money slips like water, who are careful neither how they pay or how they shall be paid, who see a possible Eldorado in the reclaiming of a Connemara hillside, and the situation of the wife, with beggary full in front of her and her children, and no one to blame for it but a well-intentioned man, had a strong appeal for them. The dramatic interest was Irish, though the exposition of it affected me as if it had been a translation from the German.[13]

Yet, the plot of Yeats' play, the story of a devoted and saintly woman sacrificing her soul for others, with analogues as remote as the Greek story of Alcestis, is recorded in a collection of Irish folk-lore with a variant in a well-known Donegal tale, and the character of Cathleen seemed to the playwright, as he worked upon it, a symbol of Ireland's soul. At moments the dialogue of both Yeats' and Martyn's plays had the distinction of style, the beauty of words which, next to plot itself, Yeats, in another connection, had declared the touchstone of great drama. Tyrrell cries joyfully as insanity liberates him from sorrow,—

See, the rain across a saffron sun trembles like gold harp strings, through the purple Irish Spring! . . . The voices—I hear them now triumphant in a silver glory of song.

Cathleen bids farewell to her dear ones,—

Bend down your faces, Oona and Aleel:
I gaze upon them as the swallow gazes
Upon the nest under the eave, before
He wanders the loud waters. . . .[14]

[13] From "The Irish Literary Theatre and its Affinities," by Stephen Gwynn, *Fortnightly Review*, Vol. 76, pp. 1052, 1053. Courtesy of the Publishers, London and New York.
[14] From William Butler Yeats, *Plays and Controversies*, Vol. II, p. 121.

Though the acting of the plays had been somewhat disappointing (Yeats' verse in particular had fared badly) the directors felt sufficiently pleased to continue their experiment the next February at the large Gaiety Theatre. The programs were *The Bending of the Bough,* which was George Moore's revision of Martyn's *The Tale of a Town,* and Martyn's *Maeve,* preceded by Alice Milligan's *The Last Feast of the Fianna,* more of a masque than a play. *Maeve* is dreamlike and legendary, the story of a young Irish girl who, influenced by an old nurse at night a fairy, chooses death and a dream lover rather than marriage with a prosperous English suitor. *The Bending of the Bough,* which Martyn turned over to Moore rather than bring any note of discord into the national theatre, is a satire upon Irish municipal politics. The central figure is a young Irishman who first champions his town against the unfairness of a neighboring English seaport, then through love of an Englishwoman betrays it. It was the first play dealing with a vital Irish question that had appeared in Ireland.

Before the plays, Yeats made a little speech pointing out their significance for Irishmen. To him Peg Inery of *Maeve,* by day the poor old woman, by night "a queen in an ideal world," represented Ireland. In the other play, one aspect the financial, of Ireland's relation to England was made the theme of the story because upon it all parties could agree.

The materialism of England and its vulgarity are surging up about us [Lady Gregory quotes Yeats as saying]. It is not Shakespeare England sends us, but musical farces, not Keats and Shelley, but *Tidbits.* A mystic friend of his had a dream in which he saw a candle whose flame was in danger of being extinguished by a rolling sea. The waves sometimes seemed to go over it and quench it, and he knew it to be his own soul and that if it was quenched, he would have lost his soul. And now our ideal life is in danger from the sea of commonness about us.

Both plays were successful in spite of the unfamiliarity of the English actors with the allusions to Irish legends and politics. There were many of the Gaelic League in the audience who sang Irish songs between the acts and cheered for the authors and for their own president, Dr. Hyde. As Lady Gregory points out, the Irish Literary Theatre was not carrying on any campaign for Home Rule but preparing a people for it.

The third and last season of the theatre was at hand. The directors realized that notwithstanding the merits of the programs of these early seasons there had as yet been no play in Irish and no play which was strictly folk-drama. The final program was conceived in the hope of making up both these deficiencies.

Perhaps no play has a more curious history than *Diarmuid and Grania,* the *pièce de résistance* of the program of October, 1902. As one of the two most famous love stories of ancient Ireland—the other is that of Deirdre and the three sons of Usnech—the theme came naturally to Yeats' mind. The material is perhaps more difficult to handle than the Deirdre story for even in some of the old versions Grania's motives are not always above question, but the devotion of the lovers "whose beds were the cromlechs," as many country people still tell the tourist, and the names of Tara and Ben Bulben are in themselves evocations of magic. Yeats had profited by George Moore's ability in untangling some difficult technical knots as they talked over *The Shadowy Waters* and asked him to collaborate in the Grania legend. The task was impossible: two strongly individual men of letters, one a realist, the other a poet and romanticist, were engaged upon material which might conceivably be treated by either but not by both; even Lady Gregory's gracious hospitality and the woods of Coole could hardly prevent a rupture. The debate over the language of the play did not settle the question whether the heroine should be a

peasant Grania or a heroic Grania speaking with the simple
dignity of Biblical idiom. A scornful suggestion of Moore's
that the play might be written first in French was taken by
Yeats, who planned its various transmigrations:

Lady Gregory will translate your text into English. Taidgh
O'Donoghue will translate the English text into Irish, and Lady
Gregory will translate the Irish text back into English.[15]

How many of these changes actually took place only the
collaborators know. The play as a whole has never been published. A few pages inserted in *Ave* which Moore declares
were "if not in French, in a language comprehensible to a
Frenchman," testify to partial following of the curious
method. The result, as might be expected, was not a masterpiece. The audience was cool in spite of the excellent acting
of Mr. F. R. Benson and his company, brought from England for the performance. One critic, Stephen Gwynn, remarked that in treating a theme among the most beautiful of
Celtic story, "Mr. Moore and Mr. Yeats had gone to Irish
legend to find in epic tradition the plot of an average
French novel."

On the contrary, Douglas Hyde's little play, *Casadh an
t-Sugáin* (The Twisting of the Rope), the first Gaelic play
given in Dublin, though less ambitious, was welcomed with
demonstrations of pleasure. People shouted in Irish, caught
up phrases, cheered the dancers, broke into Irish song.
Much of the applause was for the acting. Here were no Englishmen attempting alien ways: every actor was an Irishman, a member of the Gaelic League, and the president of
the League himself took the part of the wandering poet,
catching the Celtic exaggeration of his love-making, his
passion, his gaiety, and his pride in his art. Never afterward

[15] From *Hail and Farewell*, by George Moore, p. 366. Courtesy of D.
Appleton and Company, New York.

did those with the success of the Irish theatre at heart doubt that its real future lay in the hands of native actors.

The play itself was delightful. Dr. Hyde had adapted one of Yeats' Hanrahan stories from *The Secret Rose,* a tale which was based on an old song, the creation and possession of "the folk." To a cottage in Munster more than a hundred years ago comes the wandering poet, an uninvited guest, to join in the dancing at a neighborhood gathering. He is now gay, now melancholy, reckless, boasting, hated by all men and loved by many women. During his few minutes in this household he has almost bewitched the daughter, Oona, in spite of her betrothal to Sheamus O'Heran and the disapproval of her mother, Maurya, and a neighbor, Sheela. The poet sings to her with all the Gaelic freedom of imagination,—she is "the swan of the brink of the waves, the royal phoenix, the pearl of the white breast, the Venus among women. . . . O star of women, show me how Juno goes among the gods, or Helen for whom Troy was destroyed. By my word, since Deirdre died, for whom Naoise, son of Usnech, was put to death, her heir is not in Ireland today but yourself." [16] Clearly something must be done. Hanrahan could easily be forced out, but no one would have the temerity to assist in the expulsion for nothing is more dangerous than a poet's indignant "rann," and the curse of such a mighty poet could "split the trees" and "burst the stones." Finally Sheela suggests that Hanrahan be set to twist a hay rope of the kind that Connachtmen understand and which Munstermen do not, a rope needed to repair a mail bag in the coach said to be overturned at the foot of the hill. Twisting the rope and singing of the ingenuity and skill of Connacht and of the poor-spiritedness of Munster, Hanrahan steps beyond the threshold—to find the door bolted against his return.

[16] From *Poets and Dreamers,* by Lady Gregory, pp. 208, 211. Courtesy of Hodges, Figgis and Company, Dublin.

The three years of experiment were now ended, and the theatre had taught its organizers and its public many things. Native Irish drama certainly could be depended upon since a society of amateurs had been able to obtain seven plays, all of them with Irish scenes and Irish people, including a poetic play of rare beauty, the earliest drama in English written in the spirit of Ibsen, a timely dramatic satire on Irish municipal government, and a comedy in Gaelic. With the coöperation of Miss Florence Farr, Yeats had been able to carry on some experiments in the speaking of verse, an interest in which was destined to make Ireland the greatest home of poetic drama in the countries touched by the dramatic revival. By theories outlined in *Beltaine*, the little periodical representing the theatre, as well as by means of several of the plays themselves, the group was seeking to withdraw Ireland from her insularity and give her a part in the general European movement. Except for the discovery, late in the experiment, of the power of Irish actors the theatre had contributed little to acting for Miss Florence Farr and Mr. Benson were already well-known in England and the other members, English or trained in England, hampered by the strangeness of their material, gave only mediocre performances. In spite of all difficulties the Literary Theatre had proved that Dublin had an intelligent audience for sincere and original work.

The movement was now at a standstill. Yeats and Lady Gregory believed more strongly in the future of a national drama as their ideals evolved under the criticism of Edward Martyn and George Moore, who did not sympathize with the ideal of a theatre of poetic drama and folk plays. They, accordingly, separated themselves from the group (Martyn more than a dozen years later was to return to his old dream of a playhouse to give literary drama,—continental masterpieces and Irish dramas inspired by them—in the founding of the Irish Independent Theatre). Two possibilities suggested themselves to Lady Gregory and Yeats. One was the establishment of a stock company under the management of Mr. Benson composed of experienced actors who should at first take the difficult parts while gradually training an Irish company, eventually to give Irish and continental plays in many parts of Ireland and in English towns with a large Irish population. This expensive project could be financed only by asking the Corporation of Dublin for a subsidy and such cities as Cork, Limerick, and Waterford for halls, attendants, and lighting during the semi-annual visits of the players, a plan which would entail the exclusion of politics from all programs and the directorship, probably unsatisfactory, of many interrelated committees,— a constant struggle between artistic ideals and commercial success. The other plan, simpler and less ambitious, was to encourage play-writing and to turn over all promising manuscripts to some group of actors, Mr. Benson's or Mr. Fay's for example. While the founders of the Irish Literary Theatre hesitated, the initiative was taken by others and for a time the leadership of the dramatic movement passed out of Lady Gregory's and Yeats' hands.

The second phase of the Irish dramatic renaissance was inaugurated not by men of letters but by two actors, the brothers W. G. Fay and Frank Fay, and their associates in an amateur dramatic society. In this truly remarkable group were Dudley Digges, Miss Maire Quinn (later Mrs. Dudley Digges), P. J. Kelly, Fred Ryan, Miss Marie Walker, Padraic Colum. Like Antoine's company, of whom they had probably read, they were hard-working people who could devote only their evenings to acting. They belonged to the Ormond Dramatic Company which W. G. Fay had organized a few months after the beginning of the Irish Literary Theatre. Among this group, art and nationalism were inseparable. Indeed the nucleus of the company was the members of the women's nationalist associations and the Celtic

Literary Society; and the group for some time was connected with a political organization, the forerunner of Sinn Fein. Many members belonged to the Gaelic League, speaking Gaelic from childhood or toiling to acquire it after the work of the day. All were enthusiasts to whom love of country was a religion: they longed to put their power at the service of Ireland, the Ireland of their dreams, not torn by strife, broken, impoverished, but glorified, exalted, the newest home of the muses. While the society could procure little but trivial farces and ephemeral plays, now and then it had better fortune, as in 1900 the opportunity to give *The Daughters of Erin* and a few months later *The Deliverance of Red Hugh* by Alice Milligan. From this group came many of the Gaelic cast of *The Twisting of the Rope,* a performance which stirred the Fay brothers deeply. Soon afterward the Fays came to George Moore asking for his intercession with the Gaelic League to make possible a small touring company to act Gaelic plays, or Gaelic and Anglo-Irish. While Moore was attempting to overcome some trivial but persistent objections of the officers of the League, the brothers happened to read the first act of *Deirdre,* by "A. E." (George W. Russell), poet, artist, publicist, mystic, in the new *All Ireland Review.* This act so delighted them that they gave up the idea of touring and while the rest of the play was still unwritten, gained the author's permission to give it in Dublin. "A. E." introduced the Fays to Yeats, whose *Cathleen ni Houlihan* was also put in rehearsal.

The plays were given by W. G. Fay's company, rechristened the Irish National Dramatic Company, on April 2, 1902, at St. Teresa's Hall, Clarendon Street, Dublin, with a greater enthusiasm than had ever marked the acting of the Irish Literary Theatre. Both patriotism and delight in true art made the audience a demonstrative one. Though *Deirdre* did not prove strongly dramatic, the poetic quality of the dialogue, the beauty of the scenery and of the costumes designed by the artist-playwright, and above all the nobility of a theme drawn from the heroic days of Ireland touched the audience. *Cathleen ni Houlihan* at the first performance stirred the depths of each Irish heart as it has never ceased to do. On this opening night, Maude Gonne, one of the leaders of the Irish national societies, idolized alike for her beauty and her patriotism, played the part of the old woman.

Almot immediately Yeats' connection with the Fays company was made official. The presidency of the Irish National Dramatic Company was offered Russell, who, retaining only a vice-presidency for himself, sent the founders to Yeats. Other vice-presidents were John O'Leary, long in prison and later in exile for his political beliefs, and Maude Gonne.

Here, because the tendency of some historians has been to associate this company intimately with the Irish Literary Theatre, it must be clearly stated that the Fays organization had a separate origin and a separate existence. Yeats was invited into its membership and for some time, although this was not later true, his power was simply that of one officer in a directorate. Yeats himself stresses this. Mr. Padraic Colum, now well-known playwright and poet, a member of the original group, speaks of the Irish National Dramatic Company as being at first "indistinguishable from the political society which had helped to form it by specialization." *Samhain,* organ of the new theatre, announced that the Irish Literary Theatre had "given place to a company of Irish actors," which it saw "take up the work all the more gladly because it had not formed them or influenced them." Nevertheless, the brilliancy of Yeats and George Moore, masters of English prose, and the individual charm of Lady Gregory, a born narrator, have made the story of the early Literary Theatre and of the later Abbey Theatre one of the most absorbing chapters in modern literary history and have led, against their intention, to popular underestimation of the Fays, who are men of the theatre and not of the pen.

The debt of the Irish National Theatre to these two can hardly be exaggerated. From the early days of the society they were great actors, W. G. Fay, a born comedian, and Frank Fay, as remarkable in tragedy and in the fine rendering of verse. In addition W. G. Fay developed unusual power as stage manager and trainer of actors, and Frank Fay as a teacher of poetic dialogue, both contributing practical knowledge of the stage before Yeats and Lady Gregory had been able to acquire it. No other actors could have been a more suitable instrument for the ideal of the theatre, at first dimly imaged but gradually maturing: the expression of the folk element in Irish dramatic material; the play of peasant life as it is lived today with much of humor and much of sadness; and the poetic play, in prose or verse,— likewise with something of a peasant flavor,—of the heroic days celebrated in folk tale and legend.

The work of the Irish National Dramatic Society, later called the Irish National Theatre and still later, at the Abbey Theatre, the National Theatre Society, has passed through three clearly defined periods and now seems to be in the midst of a fourth: (1) a period of beginnings through the year 1903; (2) of the great achievement for which the theatre is internationally known, 1904 through 1908; (3) of marked decline, 1908 to 1918; and (4) since the Great War and especially the Easter Uprising, another outburst of genius as yet too recent for a prophecy of its attainment or duration.

The chief mood of the autumn programs of 1902 was that of folk art. Though Fred Ryan's *Laying of the Foundations*, like *The Bending of the Bough*, draws its theme from municipal politics, Yeats' *Sleep of the King* is based on heroic legend, a vein which he was to work again and again, Seumas O'Cuisin's *Racing Lug* is a tragedy of the sea and

its people, and Yeats' *Pot of Broth,* in the humor of which
Lady Gregory had a part, is a traditional story of a joke
played in a peasant cottage. In the next year with the first
modest attempt of her own, *Twenty-five,* Lady Gregory began the series of high-spirited farces of Irish village life
which have brought much joy to the theatre, a relief as she
intended for the predominating mood of tragedy. At about
the same time appeared Padraic Colum's *Broken Soil,* later
rewritten as *The Fiddler's House,* one of the most thoughtful and beautiful plays of the theatre, a play which strengthened the interest of the National Theatre in drama of
peasant life and became a powerful influence upon many
playwrights to follow. In the autumn the theatre introduced
the dramatist who in the view of many is up to the present
its authentic genius, John Millington Synge. His first play
was *In the Shadow of the Glen.*

But even before the emergence of Synge, the fame of the
Irish theatre was spreading. In May, 1903, at the invitation of the Irish Literary Society of London, the Dublin
group gave two performances of *The Hour-Glass, The Pot of
Broth, Cathleen ni Houlihan,* Ryan's *Laying of the Foundations,* and *Twenty-five.* Before one of the programs Yeats
explained the ideal of the Irish National Theatre in a statement which he later amplified in *Samhain.* The Irish theatre, he said, wishes for plays written in the mood of literature, that is, absorption and delight in a noble subject, by
men who think more of their vision than of their audience,
for the drama, as he has recorded elsewhere, is "the praise
of life" and cannot be confined to realism, which is often
dreary and counsels despair. Against a too conscious
modern art of cities and social problems native drama rooted
in a people's soul must rediscover "an art of the theatre
that shall be joyful, fantastic, extravagant, whimsical,
beautiful, resonant." For this there is needed not the speech
of office and drawing room, a speech wearied and sapless,

but beautiful, vivid language like that of the Gaelic speakers of Ireland or of those whose Anglo-Irish is moulded in the terms of Celtic imagination and the remembered cadences of the older tongue. For its plays this theatre should devise its own means of stage production, its own methods of declaiming verse, its own scenery: to imitate even the greatest masters of other forms would be to misunderstand the very nature of art.

The force of Yeats' theories and the originality of these London programs brought to the Irish theatre the generous help of an Englishwoman who was later to become for a decade perhaps the strongest single force in the English repertory movement, Miss A. E. F. Horniman. The Fays, Lady Gregory, Yeats, and others were giving the theatre all their time and thought; Miss Horniman fortunately was able to supply the financial aid without which their work would have been infinitely more difficult. She gave the Irish National players for several years a small subsidy and rebuilt for them the old Mechanics' Institute on Abbey Street, assuring them its use free until 1910. Thus Ireland had "the first endowed theatre in any English-speaking country." This little theatre (it holds less than six hundred), beautified by the work of Irish craftsmen, has housed the National Theatre through many successes and some defeats. After the six years of Miss Horniman's subsidy it was purchased by popular subscription and became to some degree a people's theatre. During the more recent years since the Great War it has received an annual appropriation from the Irish Free State, an ideal arrangement apparently, since the theatre retains its own directorship—unless it is menaced by the dangers of bureaucracy in the person of one director appointed by the government.

Here under its own roof the Irish National Theatre was able to play more often and under more favorable conditions than in a temporary home. Instead of three performances a month in Molesworth Hall, the managers began to present a different play every week for ten months of the Dublin season and have continued to do this through most of the intervening years. Though the opposition of the Gaiety Theatre and the Theatre Royal prevented the grant of an unrestricted patent to the Abbey, the limitation of its range to plays written by Irishmen or on Irish subjects or to foreign masterpieces other than English has interfered little with the ideals of the theatre; [17] indeed, basing its case on the Irish birth of George Bernard Shaw, the Abbey Theatre was once able to defy British authority by presenting *The Shewing-up of Blanco Posnet* while it was still under the ban of the censor. For a long time both playwrights and actors at the Abbey made their work a labor of love, for the theatre could afford neither salaries nor royalties. By 1908, however, the actors were paid, and now for many years the theatre has paid royalties to its authors.

In 1904 the National Theatre Society entered on the period of its greatest plays—if we except Sean O'Casey's dramas—and its greatest interpretation of them. Première after première was of some play now widely known outside Ireland: Yeats' *Shadowy Waters, On Baile's Strand, Deirdre,* and, in collaboration with Lady Gregory, *The Unicorn from the Stars;* Lady Gregory's own *Spreading the News, Kincora, The White Cockade, Hyacinth Halvey, The Jackdaw,* and an early version of *The Workhouse Ward;* and Synge's *Riders to the Sea, The Well of the Saints, The Playboy of the Western World.* Other unusual plays, less familiar in America, are William Boyle's *The Building Fund,* Padraic Colum's *The Land,* and George Fitzmaurice's *The Country Dressmaker.* As though in reward for the courage of the directors, the theatre had discovered a seemingly inexhaustible reservoir of folk inspiration, in the com-

---

[17] These restrictions have since been removed.

edy of the peasant cottage, in poetic legend, in the tragedy of humble lives.

Nothing else in the first five years of the National Theatre provoked so much excitement or covered so much space in the newspapers of the English-speaking world as the controversy over the work of Synge. This began with the production of *In the Shadow of the Glen* October 8, 1903, and culminated in Ireland with *The Playboy of the Western World* played through nightly turmoils for a week in January, 1907, followed by milder riots in America when the Irish group were on tour. Indeed Yeats declares that no first performance of this play before an audience of Irishmen has ever taken place "without something or other being flung at the players." On Synge's native soil raw potatoes were preferred as missiles; in New York a currant cake and a watch, the owner of which later called for it at the stage door. Before the Dublin week of *The Playboy* had ended, seventy policemen were in attendance and five hundred are reported to have been stationed in front of the theatre and on streets nearby. The advertising value of these riots and near-riots was immeasurable: the fame of Synge and of the theatre leaped around the world. But there was a tragic aspect to this unintentional and triumphant heralding of the work of the Abbey: Synge, who was of extraordinarily sensitive nature and often ill, was much shattered by the experience. The cause of this seven-day battle was the last play which he lived to finish; *Deirdre of the Sorrows*, without the revision which he intended, was given after his death.

To a non-Irish reader the furor over these two plays was out of proportion to anything questionable in their texts. But one must remember that the Irish had long been thwarted and goaded in politics and caricatured in literature. They are constantly on the lookout for any shadow of "the stage Irishman," which many of them felt in the draw-

ing of Christy Mahon. They also believe themselves the
guardians of morality in their attitude toward women. To
many of them there seemed an insult in the thought that a
woman of their race would consider leaving her husband
for a lover under any circumstances, or that an avowed mur-
derer could win the hero-worship of a countryside. It was
certainly unfortunate for Synge's early reputation—he has
long come into his own—that *Riders to the Sea,* a drama as
powerful and not so controversial, which was already in the
hands of the directors, should not have had earlier production. Again it was unfortunate that *The Playboy* at first
was too realistically produced with Christy's father a horrible, wounded creature, and Christy himself almost devoid
of lightness. Perhaps if the play had been originally given
in a vein of fantasy as it is now, even the lines "a drift of
the finest women in the County Mayo standing in their
shifts around me" might have escaped jeers.

Nevertheless, about 1908 the Abbey Theatre entered upon
a period of decadence or at least of comparative decline.
This decline followed natural causes. In the first place, the
very success of the theatre in its championship of Synge
had created in the audience an appetite for the startling and
the unusual,—the playgoers expected the Abbey to live up
to its reputation for notoriety. Spectators who were less
sensitive to the beautiful in Synge's imagination than clam-
orous for his grotesqueness encouraged playwrights who
could imitate something of the attributes of genius without
catching its spirit. They rapidly developed the so-called
"gun-shot school of drama," substituting for the naïve
humor of countrymen and villagers undistinguished farce
and melodrama. The breaking down or at least weakening
of the great tradition of acting was a second principal cause
of this decline. In 1908 the Fays, discouraged by the constant strain of inadequate audiences in the days of the controversy over Synge and probably feeling themselves not

in accord with Yeats and Lady Gregory in their selection of
plays, left the Abbey. For a short time powerful actors and
actresses who had been associated with the brothers took
their places and maintained much of their tradition. Gradually these followed the example of the Fays. After the loss
of Sara Allgood, Moira O'Neill, Maire nic Shiubhlaigh, and
Eithne Magee, there was little to hold the newer members
to the ideals of the founders. A late comer, Arthur Sinclair, a great actor, chose more often to appear in broad
comedy than in the serious rôles of which he was also master. In 1910 the situation was further darkened by financial
anxiety for the Abbey, no longer subsidized, had become a
rival of the commercial theatres with a watchful eye on box
office receipts and lucrative tours. Serious problems in organization also arose, for W. G. Fay's resignation came
when there seemed no other Irishman suited to the managership of the Abbey. For a time Lady Gregory and Yeats
turned reluctantly to an Englishman and later to St. John
Ervine, who, though Irish, had spent many of his years in
England and had become interested in the Irish movement
only after it had become well known in London. Later Lennox Robinson, literary child of the Abbey, took over the
responsibility. Whether English or Irish, these men, sincere
in their interest in the Dublin theatre, have too often committed the Abbey to the ideals of an English repertory
theatre rather than those for which the theatre was once
unique. An Irishman, Boyd, was typical of many disappointed critics when he wrote, at this period, "The Abbey
Theatre is now at the disposal of rising and accepted London playwrights, whenever their usual market is not available, and it will tend to be so increasingly unless some halt is
called for."

But even these days of the Abbey Theatre must not be
painted in too dark colors. Irish melodrama, at its worst,
is less conventional than English: the figures of the insane,

of the weakling, of the brutal peasant are somewhat fresher than those of the white-souled innocent and of the blustering villain. While the Abbey often brought ephemeral plays to the public and too frequently revived the little farces of Lady Gregory, modestly intended as comedy relief to Yeats' and Synge's more ambitious dramas, it never entirely ceased to recognize true art. This is proved by the production of Synge's unfinished *Deirdre of the Sorrows*, January, 1910, of Yeats' occasional new plays, and of Lady Gregory's translations of several comedies of Molière, done into the "Kiltartan" dialect, the Anglo-Irish speech of the village which she knows best.

Nor did the theatre decline in an entirely logical way. Even those who fifteen years after its founding were prophesying death began to notice symptoms of recovery; perhaps the theatre which had for years absorbed the hours and the devotion of some of the finest souls of Ireland bears a charmed life. However that may be, there were hopeful developments in the theatre soon after the war. One was the growing firmness in technique and wider interest of the later plays of Lennox Robinson. Robinson, son of a country clergyman, had been drawn to the service of the theatre by his enthusiasm for the Abbey Players when they visited Cork, first depicting the life of country and small Irish town in plays which to frequenters of the Abbey suggested the dramatic irony of Synge. Later he chose political subjects in *Patriots* (1912), *The Dreamers* (1915). In *The Whiteheaded Boy* (1916), quite unpolitical and not very original in subject, he displayed a fineness of character-drawing, humor, and skill of dramaturgy, which make this one of the greatest and most deservedly popular of the Abbey comedies. *The Lost Leader* (1918) followed,—a brilliant satire upon the Irish parties, Unionist, Nationalist, Sinn Fein, combined with a haunting fancy of a Parnell who has never died. More recently a comedy, *Crabbed*

Youth and Age (1922), has won Yeats' whole-hearted endorsement,—"The new Ireland overwhelmed by responsibility begins to long for psychological truth." Later plays are *The Round Table, Never the Time and the Place, The Big House, The Far-off Hills,* and *Give a Dog*—.

Another playwright of the middle years who has lately surpassed the critics' expectations is T. C. Murray of the early *Birthright* and the later *Autumn Fire,* and other plays. Brinsley MacNamara who salts his comedies (*Look at the Heffernans* is the best known) with a generous amount of satire of Irish life, is also well liked. George Shiels, an invalid who writes for a theatre which he can never enter, is a popular figure, sometimes mingling humor of characterization with vigorous corrective of national shortcomings. His finest plays are *Paul Twyning, Professor Tim,* and *Mountain Dew.* In the summer of 1929, when I visited Dublin, the plays chosen for revival—the summer is largely a period of revival—were *Mountain Dew, Look at the Heffernans, Full Measure, Blanco Posnet, Autumn Fire, John Ferguson, The Whiteheaded Boy, The Countess Cathleen, Professor Tim,* and *The Far-off Hills,* the last two of which alternated during the famous Horse Show Week.

To these writers the Abbey Theatre must look for its immediate future; and to one other, the most picturesque figure and the most richly endowed with genius among the Abbey playwrights since Synge, Sean O'Casey. Child of the tenements of Dublin, a city in which forty thousand families live in single rooms, by turn newsboy, builder's assistant, laborer on the docks, stone-breaker in a city in which the untrained workman is legion, O'Casey has won through bitter knowledge the right to interpret the life of the Dublin poor as his predecessors at the Abbey have interpreted the life of the peasant. Moreover, he knows the pulse of the time, a rapidly changing time, for he was in the great dock strike of 1913 and a member of the citizen army of 1916, though convalescence from an operation kept him from actual participation in the fighting of Easter Week—but not from the inconvenience of arrest and the horror of anticipating execution. Under the humor of his plays is understanding of Ireland, satire of Irish weaknesses, as well as admiration for Irish strength and sympathy for the humble worker everywhere. He has been compared with the German Toller and with Eugene O'Neill: all three write of the dwellers of the slums and are exponents of expressionism, "that genius that is much too insistent and far too pregnant with meaning to be bound by the four dismal walls of orthodox realism." [18]

O'Casey is popular in Ireland as no other Irish dramatist has been. The little playhouse, in which on many an evening a few visitors from the provinces and the Abbey management tried to create the illusion of an audience, now for an O'Casey program sells in advance every seat that can be booked and watches a long line stand for hours in the street. Patriotism, the sad delight of remembering the events of "the trouble" which surged within a stone's throw of the theatre, and the amusement at recognizing Dublin types and "oul' back-parlour" neighbors attract many who are quite oblivious to the poetry of Yeats' plays or the tragedy of cottage drama. There are gleams of the universal alike in the grimness and mirth of O'Casey's Dubliners.

The Plough and the Stars was characteristically honored by the audience in a riot which, if it did not reach the proportions of that over *The Playboy*, was of the same kind. In the midst of the hubbub caused by a dozen women climbing on the stage and attempting to involve the actors in a debate over the importance of "morality, patriotism, and the virtues of home life," and the scuffling of others who knocked down the young man who attempted to lower the

[18] Johnston, Denis, "Sean O'Casey: an appreciation," *Living Age,* Vol. 329, April 17, 1926, p. 163.

curtain, there arose the voice of Yeats: "You have disgraced yourselves again. Is this to be the ever-recurring celebration of the arrival of Irish genius? The news of this will go from country to country. The fame of O'Casey is born tonight. This is apotheosis." Did many catch the poignancy of that moment when the elder dramatist, the inspiration of whose life has been the dream of Ireland's freedom and who must have often felt that he was weaving only "in little sedentary stitches as of making lace," welcomed to the fellowship of genius the representative of the generation which has brought the dream to reality? Through political and social satire the Abbey has entered upon another great creative era.

The Abbey Theatre had a coming-of-age party on December 27, 1925, and chose for revival *The Hour Glass, In the Shadow of the Glen*, and *Hyacinth Halvey,*—the first, perhaps the most dramatic of all of Yeats' plays, a fine handling in morality form of the universal theme of Man confronted by Death; the second, in its early performances, a famous battleground and a famous victory; and the third, a comedy which has brought delight to thousands, by that gracious and devoted woman whose personality has been one of the great forces of the theatre. Frank Fay returned to take the part of the Wise Man in Yeats' play, and Gordon Craig designed its setting. The Minister of Finance of the Free State proposed a vote of thanks to the players and was seconded by an officer of the Gaelic Drama League; Lady Gregory answered in behalf of the theatre. The program summarized the work of the Abbey:

Since that evening twenty-one years ago, when the Theatre was opened, the Society has produced two hundred and sixteen plays, the work of eighty-six authors. It changes its programme each week and it performs in Dublin for about ten months of each year. Many of its plays have become part of the dramatic literature of Europe, and have been translated and played all over the world; its players have won fame not only in Ireland, but in England, in America, in Australia. The national importance of the Society's work has lately been recognized by the government of Saorstat Eireann, and the Theatre has received a subsidy from the State.

The Abbey Theatre is now under the directorship of W. B. Yeats, Lady Gregory, Lennox Robinson, and a fourth member appointed by the Minister of Finance of the Irish Free State, which has granted this theatre the annual subsidy of £1000. The first representative of the government was Dr. George O'Brien of the National University; the present member is Dr. Walter Starkie, a fellow of Trinity College, vice-president of the Dublin Drama League, and student of Benavente and Pirandello. Robinson is producer, with Arthur Shields his assistant. Yeats hopes that the Abbey will become a state theatre; younger men think that they already detect a conservative influence and are alarmed by a statement of Robinson's, in 1927, that new and unknown dramatists cannot hope for presentation at the Abbey but can produce what they please at the little Peacock Theatre in the Abbey building—at their own expense. While there is a disturbing element in such an attitude, great liberalism may develop—the theatre in the past has weathered many difficulties and solved many problems. It now has a company which in the work of Barry Fitzgerald, F. J. MacCormick, Eileen Crowe, Maureen Delany, and May Craig, is said to approach the best of its earlier days.

In summary of the Irish dramatic movement one might say that The National Dramatic Society was born under happy stars. Except for the earlier Literary Theatre, it was the first attempt to offer dramatic expression to a people hungry for it. That the Irish nature is distinctly, even preeminently, dramatic, no one can doubt who has travelled in Ireland and found every railroad compartment "as good as

a play" and one's fellow-travelers the best conversational-
ists in the world or who remembers the delight in dialogue
of the biographers of St. Patrick, the excitement in action
of the unknown narrators' tales of the heroic cycles, the
moving words and deeds of many leaders in Irish history.
Only the peculiar conditions of Irish history had prevented
an earlier manifestation of this instinct in Ireland, and it
had often been shown on other English-speaking stages,
where many great Irish men and women have acted. It is
said that every new development in the English drama in
the last two hundred years has had an Irishman as its
leader. Another reason for the triumph of the Irish drama is
the patriotism, the nationalism, which has touched with
flame its theatre, taking it out of the scorn which some people attach to the merely literary and giving its workers the
sense of a great and sacred cause. And third has been the
remarkable balance of the local and the cosmopolitan in the
attitude of the directors, an attitude maintained consciously
and sometimes against serious opposition. In the early days
of the theatre, for instance, a majority of the officers, including William Fay and Yeats, on the question of an
artistic ending for a little political play of Colum's, out-
voted the nationalists, Arthur Griffith and Maude Gonne,
who resigned their vice-presidencies. If the Fays, Lady
Gregory, Synge, and particularly Yeats had not been people
of broad literary interests and knowledge of the continental
movements, the Abbey might easily have become merely
the home of propaganda. It cannot be too strongly emphasized that the Abbey Theatre is the child both of the
Irish renaissance and of the general Ibsenite free theatre
movement.

Memories of the early history of the Abbey Theatre will
always weave themselves about three names. Yeats, in his
response to the speech in which he was awarded a Nobel
prize in 1924, has referred to his comrades:

I am speaking without notes and the image of old fellow-workers comes upon me as if they were present, above all of the embittered life and death of one, and of another's laborious, solitary age, and I say, "When your King gave me medal and diploma, two forms should have stood, one at either side of me, a woman in vigorous old age and a young man's ghost. I think that when Lady Gregory's name and John Synge's name are spoken by future generations, my name if remembered, will come up in the talk, and that if my name is spoken first their names will come in their turn because of the years we worked together.[19]

It is no disparagement of Synge, whose dramas for many epitomize the work of the Abbey, of Lady Gregory, who has mothered the younger generation of Irish writers and whose home at Coole is the most important shrine of modern letters in Ireland, to say that William Butler Yeats has been throughout the years the strongest personality in contact with the fortunes of the Abbey. The force of his individuality, rather than any unusual knowledge of the stage, has been the most powerful element in holding together the Abbey Theatre and in drawing to it playwrights of distinction. Yeats, like Goethe and Ibsen, had long possessed an ideal of drama and the desire to experiment in his own theatre; opportunity came soon after Miss Horniman's benefactions to the Abbey, when a special committee for reading and choosing plays was created. The members were W. G. Fay, Lady Gregory, Synge, and Yeats, who after the resignation of the Fay Brothers received greater power.

Yeats' original idea of a theatre [wrote George Moore for a Boston newspaper when the Irish players were on tour in America in 1911] was a little mist, some fairies and a psaltery, and his achievements are realistic plays and an admirable company of actors and actresses. . . . Yeats knew how to stoop to conquer,

[19] From *The Bounty of Sweden*, by William Butler Yeats, pp. 27, 28. Courtesy of The Cuala Press, Dublin.

and he conquered, because he was possessed of an idea, and an idea is always sufficient to secure success.

Yeats had no knowledge of the technique of the stage and no aptitude for learning it. I doubt if to-day he would be able to produce a play efficiently; instead of acting he preferred and perhaps, still prefers a sort of chant which he calls "the speaking of verse." He certainly seemed the last man in the world who would succeed in running a theatre, and I thought this because I overlooked the fact that he was possessed of an idea. . . . If an epigram be permitted in an article, I will say that though there be nó high road to Parnassus the boreen will take us there. Boreen is Irish for a little road, a by-way, and Yeats and his company have reached Olympus by following the boreen; that is to say, the dialect.[20]

After the early days of the National Theatre group there was no doubt concerning the path which the dramatic renaissance was to take: the peasant play, the peasant speech, the folk legend still lingering on peasant lips. Yeats' famous dictum, in *Samhain* 1902, that for the countryman and the artisan plays must represent their own life or that of the ideal world of poetry as a theory may be questioned, but one should remember that he was writing for a country in which the stage importations, largely society comedies, were as a rule artificial and vicious, and a country in which for lack of joy in rural life communities were being nearly destroyed by emigration. A theory may be partly justified if it stimulates more than a decade of original and moving art.

Yeats explained his ideals to an audience of the Boston Drama League in September, 1911:

We are putting upon the stage a real life where men talk picturesque and musical words, and where men have often strange and picturesque characters; that is to say, the life of far-away villages where an old leisurely habit of mind still prevails.

[20] From an article by George Moore. Courtesy of the *Boston Evening Transcript,* Boston.

From the first start of our intellectual movement in Ireland, our faith in success has come from our knowledge of the life of the country places, and the imaginative beauty of their speech. One discovers thoughts there not very unlike those of Homer, not very unlike those of the Greek dramatists. . . .

In Ireland the country life has for us the further fascination that it is the only thoroughly Irish life that is left. Everywhere else English influence has made a conquest more thorough than any that the sword could make. All our patriotic movements go back to the peasant, just as similar movements have done in Norway. We try to re-create Ireland in our Irish way by mastering what he knows, and by using it to understand what the old manuscripts contain. To understand the peasant by the Saga, the Saga by the peasant—that was the Norwegian formula. If you keep this in mind, it will show you that our theatre of folk art is no artificial creation of a literary clique, but an expression of the Irish mind of today.[21]

Thus the Abbey Theatre returned to the foundation of true art: " 'Fool,' said my Muse to me, 'look in your heart and write.' " The intimacy of the revelation has been a deep experience for Ireland, while the very remoteness and strangeness of the life described has contributed much of its charm for the outside world.

By the sincerity of its approach, the Irish Theatre has assailed the old artificiality of the stage and broadened its themes. "We do not make love at the Abbey," Miss Allgood once said, meaning that the theatre has not considered any of the themes of the older stage a necessity. For years Lady Gregory and Yeats conducted what was almost a correspondence school as they read the first attempts of young authors, sent to them from many counties, and gave suggestions, directing them for technique, not theme, to Galsworthy and Ibsen. The form which accompanied the individual criticism was as follows:

[21] Courtesy of the *Boston Evening Transcript*, Boston.

The Abbey Theatre is a subsidised theatre with an educational object. It will, therefore, be useless as a rule to send it plays intended as popular entertainments and that alone, or originally written for performance by some popular actor at the popular theatres. A play to be suitable for performance at the Abbey should contain some criticism of life, founded on the experience or personal observation of the writer, or some vision of life, of Irish life by preference, important from its beauty or from some excellence of style; and this intellectual quality is not more necessary to tragedy than to the gayest comedy.

We do not desire propagandist plays, nor plays written mainly to serve some obvious moral purpose; for art seldom concerns itself with those interests or opinions that can be defended by argument, but with realities of emotion and character that become self-evident when made vivid to the imagination.

The dramatist should also banish from his mind the thought that there are some ingredients, the love-making of the popular stage for instance, especially fitted to give dramatic pleasure; for any knot of events, where there is passionate emotion and clash of will, can be made the subject matter of a play, and the less like a play it is at the first sight the better play may come of it in the end. Young writers should remember that they must get all their effects from the logical expression of their subject, and not by the addition of extraneous incidents; and that a work of art can have but one subject. A work of art, though it must have the effect of nature, is art because it is not nature, as Goethe said: and it must possess a unity unlike the accidental profusion of nature.

The story of Yeats' finding Synge in Paris, of the poet's intuitive recognition of genius in the almost unknown young man, and the winning of that genius for Ireland has been recounted many times. Synge's art, which has been the subject of several books, can scarcely be discussed in detail here. Yeats compared *Riders to the Sea* to a Greek tragedy; George Moore once called *The Playboy of the Western World* "the most original piece of stage literature that has

been written since Elizabethan times." Not long after the
first production of Synge's plays, a critic writing in *The
Irish Review* spoke of elemental emotions and most ancient
energies, the high grave note of true tragedy, wonderful
women who take the lead in love-making and liberate the
spirits of the men as this dramatist's gifts to literature.[22]
For many people whose longing for beauty and reality
craves something different from realism or the drama of discussion there is nothing which quite stands beside the work
of Synge. Yeats has a remote beauty, lovely in itself but
often far from human life; Masefield in *The Tragedy of
Nan* has sordidness and the exaltation of beauty and sadness; but Synge mingles joy, exaltation, grotesqueness,
ugliness, humor, beauty, in a way which gives both the
sweet of life and its tang of bitterness and frustration. He
is, besides, a master of beautiul language, prose poetry, in
this Irish school which values dialogue highly, and he is
said with fairness to be the only modern dramatist whose
dialogue creates for us the landscape, thus reflecting the
natural magic of the Celt.

This highly original genius drew his inspiration from
many sources if one can analyze genius whose ways are
those of an eagle upon the rock. From his highly eclectic
reading, including Villon, Baudelaire, and early French
farces, from knowledge of Gaelic and of the Gaelic speaking peasant of the Aran Isles and the west of Ireland, and
the vagabonds of many roads, came hints and suggestions.
For Synge, even more than for Yeats and for Lady Gregory, Douglas Hyde's translations of Irish songs, *The Love
Songs of Connaught,* was an inspiration. Like Yeats, looking
for "the springing foot" in literature, Synge ever hungered
for the gaiety and the joy that are a racial yearning of the
Celt. "Leave off," said Yeats, "writing articles on Anatole
France, Francois Coppée, and Baudelaire, and come back

[22] Maguire, Mary C., "John Synge," Vol. i, No. i, pp. 39-43.

to Ireland and write plays for me." A shy man of an ailing body, Synge must have felt that like his own Deirdre "of the sorrows," he was under the doom of early death: his plays are in reality subjective, as he creates in the men and women of the roads, of the tiny village, of the remote glen, the passions, the desires, the exaltations, the glooms of his own spirit. He is closest of modern dramatists to the mood of the Middle Ages with which Ireland has never broken.

The Abbey Theatre acting has been as famous as its playwrights,—in Synge's full-flavored language, as well as in Lady Gregory's Kiltartan dialect and the exquisite verse of Yeats' poetic dramas. Here, too, continental influences were at work, for one of the Fays was a collector of books upon the French stage and Yeats an experimenter in many subjects, some of them suggested by the continental stage. He attempted to work out a system for reciting verse in which violence was to be done to neither sense not meter, no word prolonged unnaturally, or changed into a mere musical note, but in which the rendering should be diversified according to the poet's intention, "regulated declamation, the song almost indistinguishable from the dialogue, the country song, the rapid incantation, or the song to be given with minute passionate understanding." But stronger than any foreign influence was the whole-hearted enthusiasm of the actors and actresses. These young men and women, clerks and artisans, were sustained by one vision, the ideal of acting truly and beautifully the plays of a national literature; they formed their own tradition of acting, reproducing lovingly phrase or gesture from the life of the Irish country which lay behind them in childhood or in the tales of mother or grandmother. This acting, which reminded Yeats of that of Sara Bernhardt and De Max in *Phèdre,* was that of the actual peasant with "quiet movement and careful speech . . . arising partly out of deliberate opinions and partly out of ignorance of the players" with the "awkwardness and stillness of bodies that have followed the plow." Besides being masters of moods of sadness or of grave beauty, the Irish players are always delightful in the scenes of gaiety and frolic in which they give the sense of the impromptu merry-making of a fair or a country dance.

Some great rôles of the Abbey theatre have been those of Frank Fay as Cuchulain (*On Baile's Strand*), Forgael (*The Shadowy Waters*), Sheanchan (*The King's Threshold*), Naisi (*Deirdre of the Sorrows*); of W. G. Fay in the tramp (*The Shadow of the Glen*), Martin Doul (*The Well of the Saints*), and Christy Mahon (*The Playboy of the Western World*); of Maire O'Neill as Deirdre. Other remarkable actors and actresses, scarcely less famous, are T. Dudley Digges, Sara Allgood, Mr. O'Donovan, Mr. Kerrigan, Arthur Sinclair. A fact often noted is that with few exceptions these Abbey players leaving Dublin have not been equally successful in English plays.

This raises the question whether something of the appeal of the Abbey Theatre has not been due to its audience. This audience is unique: in unity of impression—shown occasionally in violent disapprobation—it has approached that of the Greek theatre. One reason for this is the smallness of the Abbey; another is the recurrence of themes from Irish heroic legend and folk-lore in the material used by its playwrights, for the majority of the playgoers have been enthusiasts in regard to anything which touches the Celtic Renaissance, which for most of them, hard-working people whose opportunities for education have been restricted, has been the key to the world of poetry and thought. This audience which Padraic Colum compares to a community with "a community's history, a community's memory" has been the envy of other little theatres. What Stephen Gwynn writes of the audience of the earlier Irish Literary Theatre is even more true of the Abbey:

But the Stage Society, which makes an ideal audience for wit, is perhaps too sophisticated for poetry; too much under the domination of modern comedy. Over in Dublin Mr. Yeats and the rest had a hall full of people not less intelligent but less over-educated, less subservient to the critical faculty, in a word, more natural. This audience had all the local knowledge necessary to give dramatic satire its point (and that is scarcely possible in a place so big as London) and had also a community of certain emotions arising out of distinctive ideas. And, above all, the people composing it came to the theatre much as they might have gone to church or to a political meeting, ready to be moved by grave sensations or by serious ideas.

Contrary to its record in play-writing and acting, the Abbey Theatre has accomplished little in the art of production. Twenty years ago it was among the theatres preaching a rather new doctrine, that of simplicity and sincerity in stage decoration: the beauty of its settings lay in the artistic arrangement of common materials as backgrounds for costumes such as the characters would really wear, not conspicuous through any meretricious beauty. Many of the suggestions came from Yeats, among whose theories were the beliefs that the use of only two or three colors in the setting of a poetic drama keeps it apart from daily commonplaces and in the life of untroubled emotion, and that outdoor settings, to be poetical, must be symbolic. Then many of the settings were the work of Robert Gregory, Lady Gregory's son, a young man of great promise, who lost his life in the World War. The theatre has discovered no one to take his place: each of several experimental theatres in Europe or America is making a greater contribution to the art of the stage in one year than the Abbey has made in all its history. Perhaps the situation will change. The poor cabin interior of many plays offered little opportunity for variety; new methods may develop,—the Abbey has entered a period which many critics believe will equal or surpass its early days.

In Glengariff on a summer evening I watched the fires of St. John flash from one hillside to another till every height from the Shrone to Bantry answered. So the National Theatre has kindled flames in other parts of Ireland.

The clearest of these sister beacons has been the Ulster Literary Theatre of Belfast. When word of the success of the Fay brothers reached the north in 1902, the Belfast Protestant National Society, up to that time a political organization, became greatly interested. With the help of the southern company, *Cathleen ni Houlihan* and *The Racing Lug* (by James Cousins, an Ulsterman) were produced in Belfast; later, *Deirdre* by George William Russell was given. In 1904 a group including Joseph Campbell and Gerald Macnamara, who called themselves the Ulster Literary Theatre, began producing the work of northern playwrights. "At this time the theatre was composed of very young men with very mature ideas in literature. Ten years later these young men became modest and 'blacked out' the word 'literary,'" writes Mr. Macnamara. Their early struggles at writing, painting scenery, and designing costumes parallel those of the Dublin group. The first program was Bulmer Hobson's *Brian of Banba,* a poetic drama, and Lewis Purcell's *The Reformers,* a municipal satire, both the work of beginners. Three playwrights soon established themselves: Lewis Purcell (*The Pagan* and *The Enthusiast*), Rutherford Mayne (*The Drone* and *The Turn of the Road*), and a satirist of unusual cleverness and unfailing good-nature, Gerald Macnamara, whose *Thompson in Tirna-n'Og,* the fancy of an Ulster Orangeman discovering himself in the Celtic Land of Youth, is one of the two most popular plays of the theatre; *The Drone* is the other. Joseph Campbell's *The Little Cowherd of Slainge* is also much liked. One of St. John Ervine's plays, *The Ship,* has been produced by the Ulster group, though Ervine has never allied himself with it.

By 1916 the northern theatre like the southern was losing vitality. The Ulster group did not possess a house of their own around which to center their activities; their publication, *Uladh,* had lived for only a short time, and their playwrights, with the exception of Mayne, were rarely able to publish their work as the writers of the Abbey had done. Several writers accordingly turned to commercial stages. Moreover, too ambitious a touring system hindered the building up of a loyal Belfast audience. Fortunately like the Abbey the Ulster has retrieved itself. In 1926 the Ulster Players were considered significant enough to be included with the Abbey Theatre, the Scottish National Theatre, and the Welsh drama in a series of articles on the leading little theatre groups in the dramatic section of the *London Daily Telegraph.* (A letter inadvertently addressed only to "the Ulster Players, Ulster, Ireland," was delivered promptly.)

The Ulster Players now have a room of their own,—"but nobody knows anything about it, except our landlord, the gas-meter man and the Poor-rate collector and even they sometimes find it difficult to find us"—and a repertory of more than fifty plays by Ulstermen, largely the work of members of the society. Most of these dramas are "folk" plays, though a minority deal with the legendary past. The actors perform annually in the Grand Opera House, Belfast, in the Gaiety Theatre or the Abbey, Dublin, in many towns of the Free State and of the Six Counties,—Londonderry, Dundalk, Newry, Ballymena; occasionally they go to Cork and to Liverpool. A few years ago they played for three weeks at the Scala in London, where their acting received much praise and Mayne's *Drone* favorable criticisms. *Dinkum Oil,* a play of the Irish in Australia by Purcell, has been accepted by the Royalty, London. Though the north may never equal the livelier imagination of the south,

Ulster drama has a note of its own in the study of its own people and a dialogue with a suggestion of Biblical rhythm.

To the south, as well, the influence of the Abbey Theatre spread. Besides enriching the Abbey Theatre with the work of the so-called "Cork realists" Cork has been the home of several busy dramatic associations. At one of these, the Cork Dramatic Society, T. C. Murray gained his first recognition with his *Wheel of Fortune,* 1909. Later—a split occurring —Parker K. Lynch, an actor, joined several of the members of the earlier group and founded the Munster Players; he was manager and producer during a year and a half till his work called him to England. Among the plays of Munster the best known are *Mary Margaret* by Maurice Dalton, *The Dark Vein* by John F. Lyons, and *The Yellow Bittern* by Daniel Corkery. Mr. Corkery, distinguished both in Gaelic scholarship and playwriting, has since been recognized by the Abbey. There are now three important amateur dramatic companies in Cork,—a Shakespearian society, which gave *King Lear* in the winter of 1928, well directed by a Catholic priest who is himself a fine actor, an opera company, which recently produced *The Mikado,* and the Cork Dramatic League, whose object is to stage unusual continental plays.

Meanwhile Dublin "little theatres" have multiplied: among the early are the Theatre of Ireland, with which Padraic Colum was identified for a time, and the Leinster Stage Society; among the more recent, the active Dublin Drama League, internationally minded, for which Lennox Robinson sometimes acts. The chief interest of several amateur groups has been the staging of Edward Martyn's plays. In 1904 The Players Club gave his *The Enchanted Sea* at the Ancient Concert Rooms, and in 1912 the Independent Theatre company, assuming the name and the ambitions of Grein's London theatre, gave *Grangecolman.* Count Markievicz produced this and his wife took the leading rôle. The Repertory Theatre and the Theatrical Club had the same ideals: the first was short-lived, but the second, of which Count Markievicz was a member, gave some artistic Ibsen performances in 1912 and 1913. The acting, particularly that of Elizabeth Young and Nell Bryne, was brilliant.

The next year, 1914, Edward Martyn, with Thomas MacDonagh, and Joseph Plunkett founded the Irish Theatre, a revival of the original Irish Literary Theatre. "Revival" may be used advisedly, for Martyn's ideals had not changed: he was still eager to advance the cause of intellectual drama, to complement not as "an adversary but as a sincere admirer," the work of the Abbey Theatre with the play of the cultivated upper classes, and, rather strangely, the Gaelic play.

Martyn wrote in the *Irish Review* for April, 1914:

What is my project, then? It is not original. It is simply to apply the methods of the Abbey Theatre to an organisation of the most talented amateurs for the encouragement and production of native Irish drama other than the peasant species, and thereby see if, by study and perseverance, we may similarly create a school of young dramatists who will devote themselves to this particular department. I feel that, however depressed and ruined we may have been by English government and our own inept acquiescence by often playing into the hands of the enemy, we have still some inhabitants left in Ireland besides peasants, and that a theatre which only treats of peasant life can never be considered, no matter how good it may be, more than a folk theatre. Consequently only partially representative of Ireland, it cannot be compared with those national theatres in Europe which represent so completely the minds of the various countries where they exist.

.   .   .   .

We can begin tentatively in the Abbey Theatre if they will let it to us; if not, in some hall. Our plays, both native and translations of foreign masterpieces, shall be those not usually acted by professionals. We will also act plays, co-operating with the Gaelic League players, in the Irish language, from which, of course, peasant subjects must not be excluded. Here they are fitting in every way. Above all, we will take the greatest pains, so that our performances may be intelligent and finished. We will not expect to make money; and in this respect we can be no worse off than we have been hitherto—nor than the Abbey Theatre was for many years when it had to bravely forge ahead before empty benches. But the Abbey plan was intellectually sound, and it triumphed by creating a thinking audience for itself, as I hope we may for ourselves in the end. To do this we must persevere. Well, we have now what the Abbey Theatre had not—namely, a successful example before us. I can hardly think that the more intelligent may not at least understand that this is the only possible way by which they may be taken seriously as artists. Ever since I helped to found the Irish dramatic movement in 1899, I have had this scheme in my mind, and made repeated efforts to carry it out. But owing to the blighting effect of the English stage on our giddy amateurs, I have met with disappointment, or even disaster.

The opening, the première of Martyn's *The Dream Physician,* was Monday, November 2, 1914, at the Little Theatre, 40 Upper O'Connell Street. John MacDonagh, brother of Thomas MacDonagh, was stage manager and one of the actors; Maire nic Shiubhlaigh, once of the Abbey Players, was in the cast. The second year opened with Chekhov's *Uncle Vanya* and included two short plays new to the stage —Eimar O'Duffy's *The Phoenix on the Roof* and *The Walls of Athens*—Martyn's *The Privilege of Place,* Thomas Mac-Donagh's *Pagans,* Villiers de l'Isle Adam's *The Revolt,* and Chekhov's *The Swan Song,* and Rutherford Mayne's *The Troth,* the last translated into Gaelic. In spite of the tragic loss of Thomas MacDonagh and Joseph Plunkett in the spring of 1916 as the directors were preparing Strindberg's *Easter* the work of the Irish theatre went on. Besides em-

phasizing foreign drama, producing an occasional Gaelic
play, and giving Edward Martyn a means of adequate production,—for a few years before his death,—the theatre
was able to develop the powers of two men of originality,
John MacDonagh, one of whose plays is the one-act, *Just
Like Shaw*, and Henry B. O'Hanlon, of *The All-Alone*. This
lovely play, though reminiscent of *The Lady from the Sea*
and Martyn's *The Enchanted Sea* and *The Heather Field*,
is no mere imitation. It is the story of a visionary:
O'Hanlon's dreamer finds his world of beauty the sea on
whose waves he was born; when materialism and intrigue
seem about to engulf him the spirit of the sea in the form of
a fairy maiden draws him back to her mysterious heart.
Idealism has never been long absent from the Irish drama.

A fascinating chapter on one aspect of the dramatic renaissance might be written by a student of modern Irish: the
history of Gaelic drama. As we have seen, one dream of
Martyn's later venture as of the early Irish Literary Theatre was its encouragement, though neither theatre made
much progress in this direction. Soon after Dr. Hyde's
Casadh an t-Sugáin, plays in modern Irish became rather
frequent, given under the auspices of branches of the Gaelic
League or such kindred organizations as Inghinidhe na
h-Eireann. Yeats, in the pages of *Samhain*, named the leading Gaelic playwrights of the first years of the century as
Douglas Hyde, Father O'Leary, Father Dineen, Mr.
MacGinlay and mentions performances of Gaelic plays at
Galway, Macroom, Letterkenny, and Dublin. Irish performances now are tremendously on the increase, given
regularly in Dublin, Galway, Cork, and occasionally in
many towns and villages, and the Gaelic Drama League has
become an enthusiastic and important institution; when the
Irish Free State Government granted the Abbey Theatre a
subsidy it also assisted the Gaelic organization to the extent
of £650. In 1927 it staged ten new plays to the nine which

the Abbey presented. (The Gaelic Drama League, however, gives only two performances a month, while the Abbey has, for ten months a year, a schedule as exacting as that of a commercial theatre.) Only time can show how vital this part of the Gaelic movement may become: its very existence is dependent upon the Irish Free State's encouragement of the traditional language.

New and daring is the Dublin Gate Theatre Studio. Since 1927, "in association with the Gate Theatre Studio, London," it has staged unusual plays at the Peacock Theatre under the direction of Michael MacLiammoir, Hilton Edwards, D. Bannard Cogley, and Gearoid O-Lochlainn. At the close of the second season, the Studio put on *The Old Lady Says, "No"*, "a romantic play with choral interludes," by E. W. Tocher, a young Dublin barrister. This is brilliant satire of the political and social life of Dublin today, as it appears in the dreams of the patriot, Robert Emmet, dead these many years. Through the drama moves not Cathleen ni Houlihan "with the walk of a queen," but an unpresentable old woman who disconcerts the many factions who are discussing Ireland's betterment. A thoughtfulness in presenting grave problems in a light vein, a richness of fancy, and an expressionistic technique make this satire long remembered.

"How many little theatres do you think there are in Ireland?" I asked a Cork bookseller who was in the audience at the first night of the Irish Literary Theatre over thirty years ago and has followed each development of the Irish renaissance since. I quoted the statement of a New York paper placing the number at six hundred.

"That's like the Kerry girl's fortune," the gentleman replied. "Divide it in two and take half of that. There's not room in Ireland for six hundred theatres, but there are a good many."

.   .   .   .

During the winter in which I have been writing this chapter two plays of the war have been the most discussed plays in English, *Journey's End* and *The Silver Tassie;* the future may decide that these are the most powerful plays inspired by the great struggle. Both are intimately connected with the "little theatre" movement. Sherriff's play, which in London was first produced by the Incorporated Stage Society, has been given around the world,—simultaneously in at least three languages. *The Silver Tassie,* the work of Sean O'Casey, until recently of the Abbey, was also given in London. The Abbey rejected this play,—the story of Harry Heegan, athlete and soldier, who on leave from France has won "the silver tassie" for his football club, and of how he returns from the war, paralyzed, to find his sweetheart, Jessie, ready to slip into the arms of his more fortunate comrade. The directors may have remembered the tumult over *The Plough and the Stars,* and been dubious over the frank acceptance of physical passion in the love of Harry and Jessie and later of Jessie and Barney; they were probably concerned also over the bitter rhapsody of the adoration of the cannon, parodying as it does, a ritual of the Christian church. The discussion centered over the apparent lack of unity of the play—O'Casey mingles his comedy and tragedy with an Elizabethan profusion—and the introduction of general ideas in an expressionistic way. *The Irish Statesman,* for June 9, 1928, published the controversy over the play. In this debate among the Olympians, Yeats defined his theory of drama, "Dramatic action is a fire that must burn up everything but itself; there should be no room in a play for anything that does not belong to it; the whole history of the world must be reduced to wallpaper in front of which the characters must pose and speak."

O'Casey parried, "What's the use of writing a play that's just as like a camel as a whale? And was there ever a play, worthy of the name of play, that did not contain one or two or three opinions of the author that wrote it?"

And so it was a London audience and not a Dublin which listened to this ghastly and tortured beauty:

> God, unchanging, heart-sicken'd, shuddering,
> Gathereth the darkness of the night sky
> To mask His paling countenance from
> The blood dance of His self-slaying children.
>
> .   .   .   .
>
> Squeals of hidden laughter run through
> The screaming medley of the wounded—
> Christ, who bore the cross, still weary,
> Now trails a rope tied to a field gun.[23]

Though the Abbey Theatre has disowned *The Silver Tassie,* O'Casey is its child and the inheritor of its genius by reason of the evenings when he observed its technique (his other models were the plays of Shakespeare), the early encouragement which Yeats and Lady Gregory gave him, and his own originality, bravery, and intimate knowledge of the need and the spirit of his land. Through his genius and that of her other dramatists, Ireland has been fortunate to an almost unique degree in merging national and general European influences in the creation of a great art.

[23] From *The Silver Tassie,* by Sean O'Casey, pp. 64, 65. Courtesy of The Macmillan Company, Publishers, New York.

VII

THE DRAMATIC AWAKENING OF SCOTLAND
AND WALES

> The Thespian light can never be said to have burned
> brightly in Scotland [writes the chronicler of *The Na-*
> *tional Theatre Movement in Scotland*]. Rather has it gut-
> tered fitfully at far-stationed intervals, like a dying candle,
> snuffed out viciously by Presbytery or Parliament when-
> ever its wavering flame showed a tendency to gather
> life.[1]

ALLAN RAMSAY and John Home in the eighteenth century
and Scott in the nineteenth felt any attempt at a national
drama preordained to failure; Burns voiced a longing rather
than an expectation in his prologue written for the Dumfries Theatre:

> Is ther nae poet, burning keen for fame,
> Will try to gie us sangs and plays at hame?
>
> .   .   .   .
>
> There's themes enow in Caledonian story
> Would show the tragic Muse in a' her glory.

Yet the Scotch have now the beginnings of a national
theatre which is attempting to do for Scotland what the
Abbey Theatre has done for Ireland.

The forerunner of the Scottish National Theatre was the
Scottish Repertory Theatre which flourished from 1909 till
the war, terminating only in 1922 at the founding of its
successor. This repertory theatre was "Scotland's own

[1] Denholm, Reah, *The Scots Magazine,* July, 1924.

theatre, financed by Scottish money, managed by Scotsmen," established to make Scotland independent of London. Its objects were, to quote the prospectus:

(1) To establish in Glasgow a Repertory Theatre which will afford playgoers and those interested in the drama an opportunity of witnessing such plays as are rarely presented under the present Touring Company system.

(2) To organize a Stock Company of first-class actors and actresses for the adequate representation of such plays.

(3) To conduct the business of Theatrical Managers and play producers in Glasgow and other places, so as to stimulate a popular interest in the more cultured, important and permanent forms of dramatic art.

(4) To encourage the initiative and development of a purely Scottish Drama by providing a stage and an acting company which will be peculiarly adapted for the production of plays national in character, written by Scottish men and women of letters.

This Glasgow theatre, like the Gaiety, Manchester, was a house of modified repertory, usually giving a new play a week and depending largely on season subscribers. For several years the theatre lost money steadily and only the faith of Glasgow men kept it alive. Later it was more firmly established. Alfred Wareing, who made his first stage appearance with the Elizabethan Stage Society in 1894 and had since been associated with many prominent London companies, was the director of a company which reached so high a standard that many of its members were called to the metropolitan stage. The theatre produced several distinguished English plays simultaneously with their premières in London or the provinces, gave Chekhov's *Seagull* in English for the first time, and was almost as closely associated with the work of the young playwrights, Harold Chapin and Harold Brighouse, as was the Manchester group. But truly native plays were few. One of the rare performances which carried the flavor of Scotland was a joint bill containing *Macpherson* by Neil Munro and an adaptation of J. J. Bell's *Wee Macgregor;* another was Wilfred Gibson's *Womenkind* and a one-act historical play, *Campbell of Kilmhor.* This last performed by native actors was so moving that several members of the Saint Andrew Society, including Mr. D. Glen MacKemmie and Mr. W. Ralph Purnell, began to draw up plans for a national theatre, to ask for the appointment of a sub-committee, and to advertise for players. Then came the Great War.

When life began to resume its old semblance, the supporters of a Scottish theatre again became active. In January, 1921, three one-act plays were given in the Royal Institute Hall,—*Châtelard*, by C. Stewart Black, *Cute M'Cheyne,* by Joseph Laing Waugh, and *Glenforsa*, by John Brandane and A. W. Yuill. Two other successful programs led to the appointment of Andrew Patrick Wilson, formerly of Miss Horniman's theatre, to the directorship of a company, amateur and native,—the Scottish National Players. This was to be supported by the Scottish National Theatre Society, destined to grow in the next two years to eight hundred members. Many of the influential backers of the Glasgow Repertory Theatre Society, Lord Howard de Walden, Sir James M. Barrie, John Galsworthy, and others, were willing to turn over their holdings to the new company.

The aims of the Scottish National Theatre Society are the same as those of the earlier group,—"(1) to develop Scottish National Drama, (2) to encourage in Scotland a taste for good drama of any type, (3) to found a Scottish National Theatre." The very efficient "play-selection committee" of the society deserves the attention of the students of little theatres:

Plays go, or should go, [writes Mr. Reah Denholm,] first of all to the Hon. Librarian of the Society, who acknowledges their receipt and files them for circulation among the Reading Committee. That committee is composed of six readers, each one of whom is chosen for his ability to pronounce judgment on one aspect of the work sent in—its stage value, its historical accuracy, the soundness of its dialect, its playing qualities, and so on—and each reader provides the librarian with a written criticism of all plays submitted to him. That custodian of manuscripts, in turn, produces the play with its six written criticisms to a meeting of the committee, when, if the opinions are not unanimous, a round-the-table discussion takes place. The method is a fair one, but it takes time; and a decision for or against a play can seldom be given under four or five months.

Like the Irish Theatre, the Scottish warns young writers against cheap conventions, and asserts its devotion to the best in the national life:

As every reader of this article, however, is a potential play-wright, [Mr. Denholm continues] it may be as well to state two facts at this point. This first. The Reading Committee of the Society is not seeking for plays of the kailyard school, nor for pieces modelled on "Rob Roy" or "Cramond Brig," nor for conventional caricatures of the "pawky" Scot such as we have all grown accustomed to see portrayed on the English stage; it does not hunger after dialect nor thirst particularly for "but-and-ben" atmosphere or room-and-kitchen squalor. Its aim is to present in dramatic form the real life of Scotland, past and present, of every grade and shade, from every angle. It is looking for plays national in essence and outlook and atmosphere, but free from exaggeration of any kind. Secondly, this. The Society is non-political. In its ranks the Conservative "lamb" lies down with the Socialist "lion," all shades of party feelings are merged in a nationalism and a patriotism that are entirely free from political or international arrogance. It seeks to create rather than to destroy. It is anxious to call forth a national spirit that, while keeping green the memory of its own greatness, will add its quota to the accumulative wealth of all the nations. At the same time the Society is quite willing to produce plays dealing with political life or any phase of it in Scotland, because political life is part of

Scotland; but these plays must have the red blood of drama in their veins, they must have stage value, historical accuracy, and literary merit.

In season and out of season the leaders of the Glasgow school have preached the lesson which the Irish theatre mastered, that is, the need for direct knowledge and observation, the loving, detailed study of what is near at hand, the approach not by cloud-engirdled road but "by the boreen" to Olympus.

If the Scottish National Theatre, which Lennox Robinson a few years ago called the most interesting group in the English theatre outside London, has been less fortunate than its Irish neighbor in the discovery of genius, it has plenty of talent, of workmanship increasingly firm and skillful, of penetrating dramatic delineation of the dourness and beauty, the gravity and humor, and the innate lovableness of Scotch character. And a genius may come.

Brandane, thus far, is the most copious writer, and his plays, *The Lifting* and *The Glen Is Mine,* are two of the great successes of the theatre. *The Lifting* is a moving story of the ill-fated love of Iain MacLean and Flora MacLeod, a crofter girl from Innis Fada, in the troublous days of Bonnie Prince Charley, and of the devotion of Iain to his comrade, Callum MacLean. Much of the play is concerned with Iain's plan to save Callum by "a lifting" in the accepted Highland manner. Some of the finest character-drawing is of the contrasted women, Flora MacLeod, gentle and apparently lacking in strength, but rising to courage and sincerity when she refuses to condemn her lover for an unintentional crime, and Seonaid MacLeod, her cousin, strong, high-hearted, outspoken. Her wooing by Callum, in its impetuosity and splendor of phrase, is Gaelic and beautiful, though somewhat reminiscent of the Irish school. *The Glen Is Mine* is more spontaneous, with a richness of humor and shrewdness of observation that draws Scotch men and women, Highland and Lowland, to the life. The story, itself thoroughly amusing, is of the entangling of the fortunes of the old crofter, Angus MacKinnon, bagpipe playing, hard-drinking, good-humored, and canny, with those of his benefactor, the Highland colonel, who, in his own lifetime, has turned over his property to his son to avoid "the death-duties" (the heavy inheritance tax which has existed since the war). The colonel's son, Captain Charlie, is eager to make Scotland an industrial nation and is willing to sacrifice any number of ancient forests and green mountains to that end. How Angus circumvents the young man and becomes many pounds richer in ways which seem to him providential, although they include deer-stalking, is a dramatic tale with many amusing moments. All the characters are well-drawn: Angus, the housewife, Mrs. Galletly, who is Angus' reluctant hostess, and the avaricious and soft-spoken merchant, Dugald MacPhedran.

I am certain [writes Lennox Robinson of Brandane] that in him Scotland has got a very fine dramatist—perhaps a very great dramatist. He has written a peasant comedy of the first water— "The Glen is Mine." I am told that it succeeds wherever it is played in Scotland, and I can well believe it. I predict for it a success wherever it is played outside Scotland. If the Society wanted to take one of those easy roads to success it would bring this play to London. An Irish comedy has run there for three hundred performances; Devonshire has beaten that record with "The Farmer's Wife"; it is Scotland's turn next. "The Glen Is Mine" might easily beat Mr. Eden Phillpotts' record.[2]

This play has been translated into Norwegian and announced for production by the Norske Teater, national in spirit, though not in name.

Gregarach, by James W. Barke, and *James the First of*

2 *The Scottish Player,* Vol. 3, No. 17, p. 3.

Scotland, by Robert Bain, are also important. The first is a milestone in the history of the Scotch theatre, the first play to escape from a close imitation of the Irish. The second, by a professor at Crieff, an historical play in blank verse, is one of the finest achievements of the movement. It had been published in 1921, but the playwright had given up hope of production, for the drama requires a large cast, an imaginative reproduction of a distant age, and in the king an unusual actor of historical parts. James I, who sought for national unity and declared that, in the face of all opposition, "he would make the bracken bush [Scotland] keep the cow" is, as one critic says, "a symbolic key to the whole range of Scottish history and psychology. All the passion for beauty, justice and truth, and all the stubborn selfishness and will-to-power that lie bolted within the Scottish soul were contained in the soul of James. His times, his career, were the battlefield of these traits." [3] The production was in all respects a success: in the beauty of the scenery and the costumes and in the dignity and truth of the acting. James was portrayed by Mr. William J. Rea, who had given a remarkably fine conception of Lincoln in Drinkwater's play, and Graham by R. B. Wharrie. The enthusiastic praise was a tribute to the manager, Frank D. Clewlow, and to the power generated by the national theatre group in the first four years of its organization.

Another writer of talent is George Reston Malloch, whose one-act allegory, *The House of the Queen,* and three-act tragedy, *Soutarness Water,* were acted in January, 1926. On this evening the theatre first experienced awe and terror at a blending of the beautiful with the sinister, and discussion over the place of naturalism raged in Scotland as it had done earlier in France, Germany, and England.

William Power wrote in the tiny magazine of the theatre:

[3] *Ibid.,* Vol. 4, No. 33, p. 33.

In all respects one of the most powerful dialect plays I have ever read. The language is direct and picturesque, and is never forced or unnatural. There is no padding, and the interest never flags—it steadily increases to the end. The theme might be said to be objectionable on account of its (*a*) abnormality and (*b*) unpleasantness. Precisely the same objection might be taken to almost any of the great tragedies in ancient or modern drama—to the Œdipus plays of Sophocles, to Racine's "Phèdre" and to Shakespeare's "Measure for Measure," and several of his other plays. There are two kinds of play: one in which broad and deep interest is given to a normal theme and ordinary characters; the other in which an abnormal theme and abnormal people are brought into the main line of probability—the apparently unnatural made to seem, as it was, natural. The latter kind of play is as legitimate and as necessary as the former; it is to this latter species that "Soutarness Water" belongs. . . .

If the Scottish National Players cannot present this play, it were better that they should disband forthwith; and a Society that can be kept together only by the support of the kind of people who object to this play is of no conceivable service to Scottish drama.

Two outstanding plays have been by dramatists who have only a slight connection with the movement but whose themes cry out for Scottish presentation, *Gruach,* by Gordon Bottomley and *Mary Stuart,* by John Drinkwater. The first saw fifteen performances and met with deeper appreciation than in London. For *Mary Stuart* Mr. Frank D. Clewlow paved the way by writing a little before the production:

The setting is one considered suitable for the play; that it is utterly unlike any known room in Holyrood seems to me as much beside the point as the fact that we do not know whether or not Mary ever used actually any of the words attributed to her.

As I see it, the point at issue should be—is this a good play rather than is this true history. If this point is kept clearly in mind I do not doubt the ultimate judgment.

·   ·   ·   ·

As Boyd says in the prologue of the play: "History never so entangled itself. All the witnesses lied, and nearly all who considered it have been absorbed in confirming this word, refuting that. And at the centre of it, obscured by our argument, is the one glowing reality, a passionate woman.

The Scottish National Theatre is really national not only because it represents the interests of the many rather than a cult, and draws its inspiration from Scotland, but also because it is trying to reach as much of Scotland as possible. (Tours are constantly being extended,—to Dumfries, to Edinburgh, to remote towns and villages, to Balmoral for a command performance, to the Coliseum, London, an engagement of several weeks.) Throughout the northern land it is bringing a realization of the beauty of Scottish life, in a way that is non-political and non-partisan and wholly consistent with the finer aspects of the spirit of internationalism. A poet has expressed its ideal:

> Mockers have been already eager and hot
> In our belittlement; yes, they have denied
> That our beginnings can be worth their pride.
> But, as an unknown girl, one Kate Barlass,
> Whom I act here, whose destiny it was
> That her bare arm should be the only thing
> Between dark Fate and Scotland's hope and King,
> For ever since shines out an eminent
> Jewel on Scotland's bosom; so our intent,
> Even if we fail like her, can, when the time
> Has been fulfilled and when that next sublime
> Hour and the man have come, be named by him
> As the first movement of the spirit, dim
> And partial, that could shape and understand
> His tools and set them ready to his hand.
> A nation's theatre—this, no less, we seek.
> If for the enterprise we are still thought weak,

Remember that but one way can swell our powers—
And that's for you to add your faith to ours.[4]

.   .   .   .

"Let's have a drama," said Lloyd George at the National
Eisteddfod of 1912. Why the Welsh, with their emotional
Celtic temperament, had not developed a drama of any importance before the twentieth century is difficult to explain.
A Welsh critic suggests that his countrymen had no drama
because they are "essentially a dramatic people," witness
Boadicea, Caractacus, and Maelgwn, King of Gwynedd, who
left a monastery "twice more the son of hell" than when he
entered. The Welshman is always an actor, he continues,
in his love-making, his football matches, his funerals.
"Having all the abundance of material, then, why have we
produced no drama? This is just one of our difficulties. The
pastrycook does not eat his own pastry. The last thing the
physician does is to heal himself. The people who live at
the foot of Snowdon very seldom climb it." [5]

The ancient Gorsedd, the eisteddfod or bardic congress
for fostering lyric poetry and ancient customs revived in
the nineteenth century, Welsh translations of English
miracle plays and other drama, and the emotional preaching
of the non-conformist chapel have largely satisfied a national
yearning. A hundred years ago there were native plays of a
kind; Arthur Jones, the great Methodist preacher, inveighed
against "the play-plague that had become second nature to
the Welsh people." This opposition of the church has very
nearly passed; indeed a large number of chapels in remote
towns and villages open their halls to companies of players.
There is still an indirect censorship frowning upon some
themes of modern drama, particularly "the sexual question

---

[4] Part of Prologue written by Gordon Bottomley for Robert Bain's
James the First of Scotland.

[5] Griffith, A. S., *Cymmrodorion Society Transactions 1912-1913*, pp. 129-
130.

in its most squalid aspects. . . . We are a simple folk who have not travelled so far on the road of modern civilization as to have forgotten that love is a natural instinct whose function is to perpetuate the race, not to make moral and social satyrs of men and women." [6]

The first significant attempt at Welsh drama was made by Beriah G. Evans in 1885 with *Glyndwr, the Welsh Prince* and *Llewellyn, the Last Prince of Wales,* both historical plays. They were produced by various amateur groups and met with a fair amount of success. *Rhys Lewis,* a dramatization of Daniel Owen's Welsh novel, and the offering of prizes by some of the eisteddfodau for original plays date from the same period. (Most of the manuscripts were too reminiscent of Shakespeare to have much significance.) The first important dramatic company, Y Ddraig Goch, or the Red Dragon, was founded by T. O. Jones in 1906 for the purpose of giving a revised version of Evans' two plays at the National Eisteddfod at Carnarvon. The same company repeated *Llewellyn* in 1907 at the Prince's Theatre at Llandudno, the first performance of a Welsh play in a theatre. Four years later it was played at the Carnarvon castle in honor of the investiture of the Prince of Wales. From the time of the Carnarvon Eisteddfod, 1906, there has always been a drama section of the national festival.

Meanwhile three of the leaders of present-day drama were becoming known, though at first only to a small circle of their college classmates,—John Oswald Francis, David Thomas Davies, and John Edwards, all graduates of Aberystwyth College in Wales. Each offered to write a one-act play to be given at the Easter reunion, 1905, and continued the custom until 1913, though the production was not always in Wales. In 1911, five years after the reunion programs of the Welsh college had begun, there appeared an influential and untiring patron of the Welsh drama, Lord

[6] *Ibid.,* p. 130.

Howard de Walden. He had noticed the activity of local playwrights and the amateurishness of their efforts. Feeling that the future of native drama required higher standards, a national company, organized competitions, he offered a prize of a hundred pounds for the best play dealing with Welsh life by a Welsh author. Part of this was won by an American of Welsh descent, Miss Jeannette Marks, Professor of English Literature, Mount Holyoke College, for adaptations of her already published stories, *The Merry, Merry Cuckoo* and *Welsh Honeymoon.* The next year the prize went to J. O Francis for his three-act play, *Change.* Adding one or two of his own plays under the pseudonym of T. E. Ellis, by 1914 Lord de Walden had collected enough material to form a dramatic company.

Five plays made up this repertory,—two in Welsh, *Ephraim Harris,* by D. T. Davies, and *On the Cross Roads,* by R. A. Beurry; and three in English, *Change,* by Francis, and *Path to the Forest* and *Pont Orewyn* by Lord de Walden. Accordingly, the Welsh National Drama Company with Lord de Walden as its chairman and director and most of the literary people of Wales as its sponsors, gave its first program in May, 1914, at Cardiff. The plays chosen were *Change* and a one-act comedy, *The Poacher,* also by Francis. This was the first performance of a Welsh play in Wales by a professional repertory company. Hopes ran high that Wales might be on the eve of a great dramatic burgeoning like that of Ireland. The company played at Swansea, Llannelly, and in many other districts. Life indeed went very smoothly at first, but some representatives of the chapels objected to the possibility of their young people being turned toward the professional stage, and a performance of *Ephraim Harris,* a finely sincere study of illegitimacy, increased the disapproval. (Since the war this play has often been given without arousing protest.) Nevertheless, Lord Howard de Walden continued his plans for a touring group to penetrate the agricultural districts of the north as well as the towns and cities of the industrial south. A travelling theatre, modern and beautiful in equipment, was about to be constructed, when the war interfered.

The next phase of development belonged to several local groups, of which there are now many: ten years ago there were said to be over a hundred. The schools frequently give plays. Mr. S. M. Powell of the County School, Tregaron, Cardiganshire, has for instance trained his students in plays, many of them his own, based upon the national legends and traditions. Interesting in this Protestant country is the attempt of the Benedictine monks of the Isle of Caldey, Tenby, South Wales, to revive a medieval passion play with the use of the adaptable screen settings designed by the American, Mr. Sam Hume. The Mardy Players from the little mining town near Cardiff are perhaps more representative; since 1919, with the exception of two years, they have worked regularly, giving productions in their own community and on tours, and with true Welsh democracy including people of the professional and leisure classes, shop clerks, and miners, in their group of actors. The tours are usually arranged for school holidays when teachers and college professors are free. Contributions pay their expenses and reimburse those who must be absent from their work.

The Eisteddfodau are also very active. The festival at Swansea in 1919 included their first competition in play producing. Seven companies from within fifteen miles played to audiences numbering thirty-five hundred people in one week,—this in spite of the fact that the prizes were small and that each company had to meet its own expenses. From this festival developed the Swansea Dramatic Company, later called The Welsh Drama Society, which rents a professional theatre annually for a week of performances. In 1920 the Swansea Company, under the leadership of Mr. Dan Matthews, took the prize at the Carnarvon Eisteddfod with a revival of *Ephraim Harris*. A year later, at the Ammanford festival, the League of Nations Union offered two prizes of seventy and thirty pounds for the best productions of Francis' *The Crowning of Peace;* Mr. Dan Matthews and his company were again victors.

The foremost Welsh group in enthusiasm, in the spirit of coöperation, and in actual accomplishment, is undoubtedly the Portmadoc Players of Portmadoc, near Criccieth, Lloyd George's home. The idea of the association came from the young playwrights, Richard Hughes and Arthur Roberts. Though they are no longer able to be in Portmadoc, their work seems securely established, for Lord Howard de Walden is president and Miss Gwladys Williams, one of the finest of Welsh actresses, is secretary.

The first program stated the purpose of the founders:

The Portmadoc Players, who give their first performance tonight, are not another local company formed in rivalry to the existing local dramatic companies in the district. Their aim is a new one; they want to provide a central organisation, a League of the companies already formed in the Glaslyn Valley and its neighbourhood, which shall be able to draw its actors from the best in each of them. The casts performing tonight are purely experimental ones; there is not one of us who will not gladly stand down as soon as we can find better actors to take our places; our sole ideal is to collect from the whole neighbourhood the best company we possibly can, because we believe that in this way, by the formation of companies from wider districts than is at present the custom, can the cause of Welsh Drama best be served. We believe that Wales contains the best material for a national company of actors in the world, if it could be discovered and organised; and we dare to hope that when many such larger companies exist, a National Theatre may grow from them which shall put even the fame of the Irish Players quite in the shade. We hope in time to establish a small dramatic library and a collection of scenery for the common use of local companies so that we do not want to interfere in any way with the independence of any company.

The Portmadoc Players hope also to encourage original writing in both languages, and they look towards the idea of a Welsh National Theatre.

Their opening program, a typical one, was a bill of one-acts,—Robert's *Cloudbreak,* Francis' *The Poacher,* and Hughes' *The Man Born to Be Hanged,*—three of the best-liked plays of the whole movement. *Cloudbreak* has the struggle between a woman's soul and the spirit of evil woven about the legend of Judas and his thirty pieces of silver. *The Man Born to Be Hanged* is the strongly realistic study of a number of tramps sheltering from a storm. In relief against this sombre background is *The Poacher,* with its mellow drawing of the old man lately turned from poaching to religion watching through the chapel window "Old Soldier," the rabbit who has long eluded him, and learning the place of its burrow. Later the directors bravely chose a two-act play by Gwylim Peris after it had been rejected by other companies for its naturalism. They are ready to defend any powerful work, but they "do not mean to make a practice of violating to too great an extent the racial prejudices and doubts." [7] In 1926 one of Molière's plays was rehearsed and Ibsen's *A Doll's House* has been translated into Welsh and played successfully. It is interesting to discover that Ibsen appeals particularly to the Welsh. There is something in common between the "God-haunted" soul of this Celtic people and the deep earnestness of the Scandinavian.

The company is seven,—Miss Williams, one other woman, and five men. The scenery consists of only black velvet fireproof curtains which can be adapted to any hall or stage. The enthusiasm and faithfulness of the group are untiring:

[7] Letter of the secretary.

In conclusion [writes the secretary] may I hope that you will not be too disappointed in us? I could wish that an outsider had given you our history. It would certainly appear more interesting, but I could bear anything rather than that our zeal should be doubted. Critics have no idea what we have to put up with. All our performances are mostly in aid of some cause or other so that every economy has to be practised. We arrive home in the early hours of the morning after many performances away; not once but many times have we been held up by mountain gales and snow-storms. At one time we had a break-down and had to walk six miles to the nearest town on a road hard with frost. On occasions we arrive at places an hour before the performance perhaps, and find that there are no properties or stage furniture prepared for us. This is a private side I know but I am merely proving our enthusiasm. The Portmadoc Players may not keep their flag flying for ever but they have certainly been the means of inspiring other companies and of rousing the spirit of drama in Wales.

The Portmadoc Players have received such flattering publicity as would have turned the heads of a less devoted group. Soon after their first performance, Sir Nigel Playfair of the Lyric Theatre, Hammersmith, who happened to be sojourning in North Wales, expressed his desire to see one of their plays. This was arranged in an old stone kitchen and brew house, the stage formed by a little section of raised floor,—a most quaint and appropriate background for the homely atmosphere of the little plays. Sir Nigel was so delighted that he offered the players the free use of the Lyric for a week during the winter. On their London evening (the plays could be given only once, as the actors and actresses are employed in the daytime) there was a very real appreciation: Lloyd George was in the audience, the Prince of Wales sent his greetings, and the critics did the Welsh actors the honor of comparing them with the Irish group, naming them "the potential nucleus of a national Welsh theatre."

The present phase of the Welsh dramatic movement is marked by a growing spirit of coöperation and the development of an organization that is nation-wide. A large number of people assisted in the performance of Ibsen's *Pretenders* in Welsh at Holyhead, August, 1927, and Barrie's *What Every Woman Knows,* also in Welsh, at the Treorchy National Eisteddfod, August, 1928. The Ibsen play in particular, an experiment of Lord de Walden, who hopes to raise the standards of play-writing by familiarizing the audiences with great models, was most carefully prepared: members of the cast were chosen from amateur organizations in North Wales, and Fyodor Kommisarjevsky, the Russian producer, was in charge.

The other great development of the last few years is the formation of the Welsh Drama League. Its aim is "the development of a native Welsh Drama and foundation of a National Theatre." The League plans to affiliate amateur companies whether playing in Welsh or English and all other workers, organizers, producers, playwrights, critics. Six principal means have been suggested for furthering its objectives:

1. Competitions for original plays (in Welsh or English) by young Welsh writers.

2. Movable "drama weeks" twice yearly at selected Welsh towns, for the production by composite companies of leading amateurs, or by chosen existing companies, of the winning and other suitable Welsh plays.

3. Drama competitions for the production of *original Welsh plays* by amateur companies.

4. Publication of original plays, when funds permit.

5. Formation of the nucleus of a Welsh Drama Library.

6. Collaboration between young writers and amateur companies wishing to produce original work.

The response to the rallying cry of the League has been so whole-hearted in both North and South Wales that one can only believe that a national Welsh drama is not merely an expectation but a reality, existent in the spirit of many a company of players in town or mountain hamlet and in the achievement of an increasing number of playwrights. In the clash of old and new, as an intensely religious people responds to a changing environment, there is potential drama and in the brooding spirit of the Celt there is the vision without which an art, like a people, perishes.

VIII

THE MOSCOW ART THEATRE AND THE SOVIET
THEATRE OF RUSSIA

"The best set of actors upon the European stage," said Gordon Craig of the Moscow Art Theatre in 1911, thus placing the centre of theatre activity far outside the bounds of the civilized earth as it appears to the average man, across the confines of the known and familiar, in that land which has something of the East and something of the West, and yet conforms to the laws of neither. Two Russian gentlemen, Stanislavsky and Nemirovich-Danchenko, one an amateur actor and producer, the other an author, dramatic critic, and teacher of dramatic art, are responsible for the reform of the modern Russian theatre, which in the late nineteenth century suffered from the same maladies as other European theatres. Much of the achievement of the last thirty years has been theirs: perseverance, unflagging enthusiasm, originality, idealism, a mastery of organization— the qualities of genius—have built up one of the world's greatest theatres. For a quarter of a century the Moscow Art Theatre was a storm centre, a challenge: much of the finest work of the Russian stage has been upon its boards. Of other significant developments both before the Revolution and after the establishment of the Soviet Republic, a large part has been the creation of its pupils and erstwhile disciples who have carried into their work, often in opposition to the theories of the older theatre, a fervor and thoroughness caught from it.

Of the two enthusiasts who, in the early summer of 1897,

met by appointment at a Moscow restaurant for a conference, which lasted eighteen hours and established the principles of their Art Theatre. Nemirovich-Danchenko is the
less known because much of his activity is behind the scenes
and before the performance. His is the literary insight which
has detected genius in plays which have marked an epoch
and his the organizing talent which has preserved the life
of his company into the troublous days of the Soviet. Vladimir Ivanovich Nemirovich-Danchenko at this time was
teacher and stage director of the school of the Moscow Phil-
harmonic Society. He was already a novelist and the most
prominent of the younger Russian playwrights, for his play,
The Price of Life, in 1895 had been awarded one-half of the
Griboyedov prize while the other half had gone to Chekhov's
The Seagull. His absorption in the drama had already led
him to accept the managing directorship of the Moscow
Imperial Dramatic Theatre, but he had become conscious of
the limitations imposed by the bureaucracy and was almost
ready to resign. His greatest delight was his school of acting. He brought to an experimental theatre the knowledge
of a trained and delicate literary observer, the discrimina-
tion of a critic, as well as actual experience in organizing
and management. "He was," Stanislavsky writes, "the director of whom one could dream."

Alexeiev, who early took the stage name Constantin
Stanislavsky, was born in 1863, the son of a wealthy manufacturer of Moscow. His boyhood and early manhood, as he
tells us in his delightful autobiography, coincided with the
days when the upper middle class was rapidly outdistancing
the aristocracy in power and in devotion to the common
good. A cousin of Stanislavsky's and later a brother were
mayors of Moscow; the friends of his family were the men
who were donating art collections to their city, publishing
books which were to bring Russia in touch with world culture, encouraging modern music. Mamontov, for instance,

who built the railroads which connect inland Russia with the ocean and with the coalfields to the south, was the patron of Moussorgsky and Rimsky-Korsakov, composers, and the artists Korovin, Vasnetsov, Polenov. Because of his social position and his own tastes, young Stanislavsky was a close observer of all the art movements of Moscow.

Stanislavsky was drawn toward the stage by inheritance from his maternal grandmother, the French actress Varley, and by the environment created by his theatre-and-opera-loving family. He made his first appearance at three when, lost in a big fur coat, he depicted the spirit of Winter and startled the spectators by departing from make-believe and bringing the stick which he held in his hand toward the candle flame. This incident impressed him lastingly. He says that it taught him the feelings of the actor in three typical situations,—disappointment when he realizes that he does not have his audience with him, relief when he discovers a natural stage action, and delight when he meets appreciation. Days with childish performances of circus and ballet followed. At fourteen the boy helped organize the Alexeiev Circle in which with his numerous brothers and sisters, friends of the family, and once or twice an invited professional, he appeared in Parisian farces and operettas. The devotion of this little amateur group was striking: during the study of a play Stanislavsky and the more fervent would attempt to live their parts off-stage, improvising appropriate action and dialogue. Before the performance of Gilbert and Sullivan's *Mikado,* Stanislavsky, then twenty-four, spurred the other members of the Circle to reproduce as completely as possible all the moods, gestures, and attitudes of life in Japan. Several Japanese acrobats were asked to live in the family to give instruction in Japanese drills and dancing, in methods of walking (the women practised with legs tied together as far as the knee), and the use of the fan. Stanislavsky succeeded in reproducing the true details of

Japanese life—something which the Western stage had never before done.

Meanwhile, in spite of the responsibilities of a young business man, Stanislavsky had continued his education for the theatre. (Through his many years of acting, until the time of the Soviet, he managed his share of his father's business.) He haunted the Moscow Imperial Little Theatre with other members of a small group who made an exhaustive study of each play as it was produced, studied the text, the stage history, records of different methods of presentation, analyzed it, and saw it a second time. He read Shtchepkin's letters trying to reach the secret of that realistic genius and talked with the actors and actresses who had been his pupils in their youth. Looking at first toward the opera stage rather than the dramatic, Stanislavsky studied with the well-known Russian tenor, Fyodor Kommisarjevsky, whose son is now one of the producers of the New York Theatre Guild and whose daughter was to become the best-loved of Russian actresses. The association with Kommisarjevsky brought the young man much knowledge of the stage, and a wider acquaintance with professionals. However, it was not long before he realized that his voice was unequal to a sustained singing rôle and that his genius was better adapted to the drama than to the opera.

For a few weeks, to enjoy the teaching of the well-known actress, Glikeria Fedotova, he entered the school of the Imperial Theatre. Here he was discouraged by the difficulty of regular attendance, when much of his time had to be spent in his father's office, and by the narrowness of several of the teachers. He learned infinitely more from a special performance for charity in which famous actresses of the Imperial Little Theatre, Fedotova, Olga Sadovskaya, and others came to help the Alexeiev group in producing Nemirovich-Danchenko's *The Lucky Man*. But the marriages of Stanislavsky's sisters were rapidly depleting this little home theatre, and the young actor was soon forced to find opportunities for performances where he could in all sorts of amateur groups throughout Moscow. These evenings were often of dubious value. After one particularly worthless play which several of Stanislavsky's family were unfortunate enough to see, his father remarked, "If you want to play on the side, found a decent dramatic circle and a decent repertoire, but for God's sake don't appear in such trash as the play last night." The Society of Art and Literature was the result.

This organization came about in the following way. At about this time the well-known Russian producer, Alexandr Fillipovich Fedotov, returned from Paris to direct a Moscow presentation of Racine's *Les Plaideurs* and Gogol's one-act play, *The Gamblers*. The artist, Count Fyodor Salogub, had the principal part in the first, Stanislavsky, in the second. Finding the group reluctant to disband, Fedotov suggested the forming of a large organization to bring actors and artists together. This was similar to a favorite plan of Stanislavsky's and Fyodor Kommisarjevsky's. Accordingly, the younger actor brought together Fedotov, who represented the "Society of Writers and Actors"; Kommisarjevsky, the musicians and the opera singers; and Count Salogub, the artists. Stanislavsky gave a large sum of money to reconstruct certain rooms for the society, including a large auditorium, a foyer, and a meeting place for the artists which they decorated in designs from early Russian art. Various changes came in the organization, particularly at moments of financial strain. When the rooms proved too expensive they were rented to the Hunting Club of Moscow on the understanding that the Society of Art and Literature was to produce a new play once a week for the guest evening of the club.

During the next ten years the society was often praised, sometimes for its acting, sometimes for its stage settings, and at triumphant moments for both. Here Stanislavsky and several of the actors and actresses of the later Art Theatre developed their art under the direction of Fedotov, his wife, Fedotova, and other artists of the Imperial Little Theatre. No influence for Stanislavsky, and indirectly for the company, was more powerful than that of Kronek, producer and director of the Meiningen court group, which at this time visited Russia. This same company, it will be remembered, had stimulated Antoine. Kronek was vigilant not to create mere stage types but the true spirit of the plays of Shake- speare, Schiller, Molière, and also to secure historic exact- ness by every means. Stanislavsky admired and learned. Soon the Russian group was becoming known for the same qualities. The weekly plays for the Hunting Club, which had to be licked hurriedly into shape, did not prevent Stan- islavsky from choosing each season one play to be given after many months of work in the most artistic manner possible. Among these plays into which Stanislavsky put his very soul were *Uriel Acosta, Othello, The Assumption of Hannele, The Sunken Bell,* and *The Fruits of Knowledge.* This society had the honor of introducing Hauptmann's plays to Russia and also of giving for the first time publicly Tolstoy's play, *The Fruits of Knowledge,* written for per- formance before his family and an invited group at Yasnaya Polyana. This production so delighted the author that he gave Stanislavsky the opportunity of producing *The Power of Darkness* also for the first time. Many of the actors and actresses of the society, among them Lilina, Stanislavsky's wife, later became part of the Art Theatre. Vera Kommisar- jevskaya made her début with this older company.

By 1896 the performances of the society had been so well received and its actors and actresses were so engrossed in their art that the logic of events pointed toward a perma- nent theatre with a stable organization and nightly perform- ances. Stanislavsky was searching for a manager with whom to combine forces, when he happened to meet Nemirovich-Danchenko, whom he had long known by reputation. The two were drawn together at once and during many evenings inspected both the school of acting and the dramatic group by which their respective energies were absorbed. On the memorable evening in the early summer of 1897 when by Nemirovich-Danchenko's suggestion they joined each other at "The Slavic Bazaar" they were ready to analyze their ideals and to see whether they were sufficiently in accord to found a theatre together.

In the long conference the two enthusiasts discussed many subjects, even the delicate question of the right of veto in the case of difference of opinion, agreeing that Nemirovich-Danchenko was to have the final decision in literary questions, Stanislavsky in artistic, such as problems of acting and stage producing. The theatre was to be revolutionary, to break with the old.

We protested [writes Stanislavsky] against the customary manner of acting, against theatricality, against bathos, against declamation, against overacting, against the bad manner of production, against the habitual scenery, against the star system which spoiled the ensemble, against the light and farcical repertoire which was being cultivated on the Russian stage at that time.

Stanislavsky and his partner expressed some of these preferences in epigrams:

There are no small parts, there are only small actors.
One must love art, and not one's self in art.
To-day Hamlet, to-morrow a supernumerary, but even as a supernumerary you must become an artist.
The poet, the actor, the artist, the tailor, the stage hand serve one goal, which is placed by the poet in the very basis of his play.
All disobedience to the creative life of the theatre is a crime.
Lateness, laziness, caprice, hysterics, bad character, ignorance

of the rôle, the necessity of repeating anything twice are all equally harmful to our enterprise and must be rooted out.[1]

In many other conferences the founders decided upon the membership of their troupe, actors and actresses drawn from the two Moscow organizations and from provincial companies, each individual weighed not only for his talents but for his ideals and personality, for the Art Theatre has always held a belief in the interrelationship of dramatic expression and daily living. Stanislavsky has always desired "to bring art into life and life into art," to get rid of the duality of existence, by fusing both the material and the spiritual. In the rehearsal room, a barn at Pushkino, a few miles from Moscow, lent by one of the members of the Society of Art and Literature, and in the temporary homes of the actors in the little village an almost apostolic fellowship and community of interest existed.

Throughout the summer, the company rehearsed ten or twelve hours a day while Nemirovich-Danchenko struggled with problems of administration, Stanislavsky with the acting, and the artist, Victor Simov, with the scenery. To combat old methods of declamation and artificiality in actors new to him, Stanislavsky had to call upon his tried actors for examples and to use many ingenious devices. The number of the plays was in itself exhausting, for knowing that the Moscow theatres gave frequent changes of bill and not realizing that a notable production could draw large audiences for half a season, the directors kept in reherasal *Tsar Fyodor, Antigone, The Merchant of Venice, The Seagull,* and *Hannele.*

These days were further complicated by anxiety over the barrage of criticism in periodicals and newspapers inspired by the hostility of theatrical managers or the desire of

[1] From *My Life in Art,* by Constantin Stanislavsky, p. 298. Courtesy of Little, Brown, and Company, Publishers, Boston.

editors to exploit a novelty. One magazine gave much of its space for weeks to the Art Theatre and its terrific naturalism: the directors were said to be taking advantage of their country residence to breed mosquitoes and crickets for adding realism to the play. These and other ridiculous exaggerations, though irritating to the champions of dramatic sincerity, were soon discovered to be exceedingly effective advertising.

In costume and the more important stage settings Stanislavsky was indeed striving for actual representation. His reasons were two: he had always, from his first boyish experimenting, delighted in the creation of the manners and customs of a life fascinatingly distant in time or space; in his years of acting and producing he had discovered, sometimes to his own chagrin, that audiences rarely distinguish between acting and stage decoration, and that beauty of costume is therefore the best protective coloring for the inexperienced actor. The play chosen to open the theatre on October 14, 1898, Alexey Tolstoy's *Tsar Fyodor,* one of the same historic trilogy as *The Death of Ivan the Terrible* and *Boris Godunov,* had never before been allowed performance except at court. In his devotion to historic accuracy and artistic beauty Stanislavsky, his wife, Simov, and others of the troupe traveled hundreds of miles into the interior of Russia collecting antiquities, visiting early palaces, among them the Kremlin of Rostov Yaroslavsky, in which Ivan the Terrible had once lived. The costumes were either originals of the time of Tsar Fyodor or exact copies; many were the spoils of bazaars and even of one monastery which had sold a great mass of material to Stainslavsky at the fair at Nijny Novgorod. But the play was more than a magnificent series of pictures of old Russia, for out of it rose clear and true the portrayal of Ivan the Terrible, Godunov, and Shuisky under the firm and delicate characterization of Stanislavsky and the more experienced of his lieutenants. The success of this play won a permanent audience for the new theatre.

During this first season at the old Hermitage Theatre, the Moscow Art and Popular Theatre (the name which Nemirovich-Danchenko had bestowed in desperation on the eve of the first performance was soon shortened to the Moscow Art Theatre) gave with the same care five foreign plays, *The Merchant of Venice, The Mistress of the Inn, Greta's Joy, Antigone, Hedda Gabler,* and one play of contemporary Russian life,—this last destined to shape very largely the history of the theatre. This was *The Seagull* by Anton Chekhov. Nemirovich-Danchenko had long admired the author, and risking the disapproval of his partner and the company, forced the play upon a group who at first were only half persuaded of its value.

The Seagull has qualities which thirty years ago might well have affrighted a director—slightness of plot, when Russian audiences had a taste for the exaggeration of French and German farces, a theme raised little above every day existence, yet subtle in emotion, with half moods of doubt, of wistfulness, of baffling and unexplained suffering, and of a groping for joy. Added to this are a dialogue of a peculiar key broken yet lyrical, constant slight movement of people on the stage, subdued tones almost without contrast. Finally, the previous history of *The Seagull* was an alarming one, for it had been a failure on the St. Petersburg stage. The playwright, ill and discouraged, was in such a condition that Nemirovich-Danchenko and his other friends realized that a second failure might easily kill him. The Art Theatre was forced, as it had not been in its other productions, to seek for inward emotion, the springs of character, living speech, and a shadowing forth of contemporary life. Producers and company rose to the challenge. The triumph, a great one, connected Chekhov and the Art Theatre inseparably in the minds of the public.

It would be idle to measure exactly [writes Efros, the Russian critic] whether Tchehoff did more for the Art Theatre or the Art Theatre more for Tchehoff. At any rate, the Art Theatre would not be what it is if it had not been for "The Sea Gull" and "Uncle Vanya" and the problems brought to the stage and to the actors. It is equally true that were it not for the Art Theatre, Tchehoff would not have written at least "The Three Sisters" and "The Cherry Orchard" in the form of dramas.

The theatre is now often called Chekhov's theatre or the Seagull Theatre and bears a seagull upon the brown stage curtain.

After the success of the play Chekhov's relations with the theatre were those of intimate friendliness. Though his ill health, the tuberculosis which made him a frequent exile from northern Russia, and moments of shyness drew him from many rehearsals and kept him from the first performances of *The Seagull* and *Uncle Vanya,* his other early play, his occasional laconic and cryptic suggestions for the interpretation of his characters were famous; Stanislavsky has recalled that sometimes months afterwards these baffling suggestions would flash into clearness and become the controlling force of his interpretation. Chekhov, on his part, drew much inspiration from the players. Artem, the unrivalled actor of very old men, was to become Chekhov's original for Chebutikin in *The Three Sisters* and Firs in *The Cherry Orchard,* and Moskvin's sublime fooling at one of the informal gatherings of the theatre people gave the hint for Yepikhodiv, in *The Cherry Orchard.* For Meierhold, the actor who played Treplev in *The Seagull* and Johannes in *Lonely Lives,* Chekhov had a great admiration. Olga Knipper, one of the most talented of the actresses of the company, became Chekhov's wife.

The Art Theatre testified to its adoration of Chekhov by a journey of several hundred miles, in the spring of 1900, to Yalta in the Crimea to give him an opportunity to see his own plays. The event was a festival, for many of the leaders of Russian art and literature were assembled there. Among them was Maxim Gorky, risen to sudden fame, though not yet a playwright. The performances proved a challenge to him and led directly to his first play, *Small People,* which was to be followed by *The Lower Depths* and *The Children of the Sun.* Chekhov, too, felt new courage and began work upon *The Three Sisters.*

Only four short years later the Art Theatre gave another gala performance—this time in Moscow, on Chekhov's birthday, the première of *The Cherry Orchard.* This delicate play, the swan song of a cultivated, visionary, but decaying aristocracy, was at first only a moderate success, its welcome hardly promising its hundreds of revivals in Europe and America. On the platform was the author, barely able to stand for coughing, yet wistfully disregarding his own approaching tragedy with a courage like that of his dream children, for whom an almost groundless hope arises from defeated lives:

The music plays so gaily, so boldly, and one wants to live! Time will pass and we shall go away forever. They will forget us; they will forget our faces, our voices, but our sufferings will pass into gladness for those who will live after us. Oh, my dear sisters, our lives are not yet finished. We shall live! The music plays so joyfully, so gaily, and it seems that yet a little while and we shall know for what we live, for what we suffer. If only we knew! If only we knew! [2]

The world of Gorky, the other great discovery of the theatre, is very different. In *The Lower Depths of Life,* shortened to *The Lower Depths* at Nemirovich-Danchenko's suggestion, Gorky wrote of those who can fear no fall, those "on the very bottom," unbelievably impoverished in body and soul. Some of these pitiable creatures have never known

[2] From *The Three Sisters,* Act IV.

anything but thievery and violence; some have slid through drink from a world many levels above their bestial present. To catch Gorky's mood several members of the Art Theatre managed to gain admittance to the Khitrov Market, a community of tramps and thieves, honeycombed with underground passages, in the very heart of which were those whom Stanislavsky calls "the local university and the intelligentsia," a group of men who had enough education to earn something by copying parts for actors. These people were childishly astonished that lives such as theirs could offer material for drama. Their ruling passion appeared to be a belief in their own freedom, freedom to remain in complete degradation. The performance, directed by Nemirovich-Danchenko, became one of the great successes of the theatre both in Russia and in western Europe. Incidentally, because the playwright was looked upon as very radical, the Art Theatre had to consider what its attitude should be toward all forms of propaganda. The decision, from which the managers have never wavered, is that art has nothing to do with special pleading of any kind: only as an idea, whatever its origin, takes on the emotional characteristics of drama does it become art.

Two other evenings important for contemporary drama were Tolstoy's *The Power of Darkness* in the early days of the theatre, and Andreiev's *Life of Man* in 1907. No two productions could be in greater contrast. Tolstoy's drama of Russian peasant life was prepared for by a visit to the distant Government of Tula, the section of Russia in which the story unfolds. Here actors and artists studied every detail of home and community life,—architecture, furniture, costuming, village festivals, the traditions of the wedding feast. Two old peasants, a man and a woman, were brought to Moscow to correct any variation from absolute fidelity in interpretation. On the contrary, the *Life of Man,* in the Art Theatre interpretation, was an extreme departure from

realism, a study in the abstract. The stage settings were of
black velvet with the doors, windows, and furniture outlined in rope, white in the first scene, rose in the brief moments of man's love and joy, gold in the realization of the
hollowness of wealth and achievement. Against this black,
moved the enigmatic, sinister figure of Some One in Gray.
Everything was done to portray Man and his wife as types,
not as individuals, to enact an acrid allegory of the fruit-
lessness of existence. The performance was a brilliant
pioneer example of stylization.

The founders of the Art Theatre were too cosmopolitan
to neglect the writings of great foreigners. Nemirovich-
Danchenko, in particular, was an admirer of Ibsen. Beginning with *Hedda Gabler* in its first season, the theatre has
presented many Ibsen plays in careful detail. According to
Stanislavsky, the national genius of the Norwegian is too
far from that of the Slav for a Russian actor to identify
himself with character that is distinctly national. *Brand,*
however, because of the abstraction and generalization of
the terms of its allegory, was very successful. Even more
popular was *The Enemy of the People:* the play fitted the
spirit of the time in Russia—the production was in the
autumn of 1900 not long before the first revolution—and
the rôle of Doctor Stockman touched the imagination of
Stanislavsky till he experienced that complete fusing of personality and rôle that comes but rarely in a lifetime. To him
Stockman was the embodiment of honesty and the search
for truth, not an abstract symbol, but a very human being
endeared by his peculiarities, with "the short-sighted eyes
which spoke so eloquently of his inner blindness to human
faults, the childlike and youthful manner of movement, the
friendly relations with his children and family, the happiness, the love of joking and play, the gregariousness and
attractiveness which forced all who came in touch with him
to become purer and better, and to show the best sides of

their natures in his presence." For years the actor needed only to think of Stockman and his own body assumed all the physical characteristics of Ibsen's hero. The directness of this acting always warmed his audience. In St. Petersburg, on the evening of the day of the Kazansky Square massacre, when Stanislavsky reached Dr. Stockman's line, "One must never put on a new coat when one goes to fight for freedom and truth," the audience rushed as one person toward him, leaping upon the stage to shake his hand or to embrace him.

The Art Theatre has found the plays of Hauptmann, in both his naturalistic and poetic moods, and of Maeterlinck particularly sympathetic. Three of Maeterlinck's one-act plays were given as early as 1904, and four years later this theatre was the first to attempt *The Blue Bird* in its lovely mingling of symbolism and phantasy. Though Maeterlinck's confidence in the Art Theatre was complete and he sent permission for any alterations in the text, Stanislavsky thought best to accept an invitation to Normandy, and spent several days in discussion with the author. The director was conscious of the difficulties of the play, what he calls its "balancing on the edge of a knife" between the conventional extravaganza and the mystic solemnity of high poetic vision, and hoped to avoid all theatricality: everything should be as simple as possible in accord with a child's imagination. Indeed later when he found that the scene in the forest (Act III, Scene 2) and the scene in the cemetery (Act IV, Scene 2) frightened his tiny patrons, he left these out, though the second is to the adult reader one of the finest in the play.

The production of "The Blue Bird" [Stanislavsky charged his players] must be made with the purity of fantasy of a ten-year-old child. It must be naïve, simple, light, full of the joy of life, cheerful and imaginative like the sleep of a child; as beautiful as a child's dream and at the same time as majestic as the ideal of a poetic genius and thinker. . . .

.　.　.　.

If man were always able to love, to understand, to delight in nature! If he contemplated more often, if he reflected on the mysteries of the world and took thought of the eternal! Then perhaps the Blue Bird would be flying freely among us. . . .

In order to make the public listen to the fine shades of your feelings, you have to live them through yourself intensely. To live through definite intelligible feelings is easier than to live through the subtle soul vibrations of a poetic nature. To search those experiences it is necessary to dig deep into the material which is handed to you for creation. To the study of the play we shall devote jointly a great deal of work and attention and love. But that is little. In addition, you have to prepare yourselves independently.

I speak of your personal life observation which will broaden your imagination and sensitiveness. Make friends of children. Enter into their world. Watch nature more and her manifestations surrounding us. Make friends of dogs and cats and look oftener into their eyes to see their souls. Thereby, you will be doing the same as Maeterlinck did before he wrote the play, and you will come close to the author.[3]

Though one of the most interesting experiments of the Art Theatre, this production was not the most widely praised or the most artistic. To some it seemed to present symbolism too heavily. The acting was uneven, on the whole inferior to that of the later American production in which Walter Hampden played Tyltyl, but the Dog and the Cat were declared inimitable. There were stage effects of great poetic beauty such as the home of the Fairy with its soaring roofs, bits of gay grotesquerie as the Cat's holding his hat with its waving feather to imitate a plumy tail, and deep

[3] From *The Russian Theatre under the Revolution*, by Oliver M. Sayler, pp. 34-36. Courtesy of Little, Brown, and Company, Publishers, Boston.

reverence in the strain of a Russian sacred song, composed by a noted musician, heard from without to announce the entrance of Light. Perhaps the most inspired detail of setting was the likeness of the grandparents' home in the Land of Memory to the home of the children themselves, for a child's pictures of another world would take their forms from the familiar things of this.

No two productions illustrate more strikingly the theatre's range than *Julius Cæsar*, which absorbed all the energies of the staff during the summer and fall of 1903, and the Craig *Hamlet*, which was given eight years later. The first meant a mobilization of the entire force with the creation of nine special groups to study and investigate everything even remotely connected with Shakespeare's drama,—the literary aspects of the play, the social conditions in Cæsar's Rome, the costumes, the weapons, the music, and many other subjects. All the information obtainable in Moscow—rare books and collections of antiquities—was put at the disposal of the directors, and Nemirovich-Danchenko went to Italy for more. To familiarize themselves with a distant time, the actors wore Roman costumes throughout the entire preparation, whether they were rehearsing or busy upon stage settings. The result was a meticulously realistic scene, with stores, armouries, barber-shop, steep Italian path down a hillside, roof garden thronged with characteristic figures, in fact, a cross section of Roman life. In the other Shakespearian production, the Craig *Hamlet*, realism was the last thing thought of.

The work of Gordon Craig was brought to the attention of Stanislavsky by Isadora Duncan, the American dancer, in whose search for the expression of inner truth through art Stanislavsky found something akin to his own. Miss Duncan spoke of Craig's work—of his revolutionary theories and of the drawings which were to bring something new and dynamic into the theatre. On her recommendation and with the approval of his company Stanislavsky decided to spend a large sum of money upon a production of *Hamlet*. Craig went to Russia, exhibited some of his earlier designs, explained his pet theories, and after forming warm friendships with Stanislavsky and Sulerjitsky, one of the Art Theatre's finest spirits, returned to his own studio. A year later he appeared with an extensive *Hamlet* library and many drawings. A model of the actual Moscow stage was constructed to scale, and before this Craig would sit explaining his ideas and pushing about with his cane the little wooden figures which represented the actors. In some moods he repined that all drama could not be played with marionettes free from the idiosyncrasies of living men and women; at other times he praised enthusiastically the acting of Stanislavsky's company.

Stanislavsky describes Craig's vision of Hamlet:

Craig widened to a great extent the inner contents of Hamlet. To Craig, Hamlet was the best of men, who passed like Christ across the earth and became the victim of a cleansing sacrifice. Hamlet was not a neurasthenic and even less a madman, but he had become different from other people because he had for a moment looked beyond the wall of life into the future world where his father was suffering. After he came to know the life of tortures and suffering on the other side, the actuality of life changed in Hamlet's mind.[4]

Every incident in the play was to be seen through Hamlet's eyes: it became a "monodrama of Hamlet." To disclose this intense personal life to the eyes of the audience Craig wished to use for his background large, gray, convex screens, which should move their positions noiselessly, mysteriously, and then become motionless for the spiritual drama to begin. He wanted these screens of some organic

---

[4] From *My Life in Art,* by Constantin Stanislavsky, p. 513. Courtesy of Little, Brown, and Company, Publishers, Boston.

substance, metal, stone, wood, or cork, but without completely rebuilding the stage all of these materials proved impossible. The wooden frames covered with theatrical canvas which were at last decided upon caused the workmen endless vexations and had to be shifted behind a protecting curtain. Their effect under changing lights was beautiful. Though not all Craig's other designs could be carried out as he intended them, there were scenes of powerful originality. Hamlet in his troubled musings spied upon by king and queen stood in a golden corridor with narrow walls rising beyond the audience's sight, trapping the hero in a golden cage. In the court scene an enormous mantle fell from the shoulders of the king and queen, almost engulfing the stage, a mantle likewise of sinister gold, with holes through which the heads of parasitic courtiers looked toward their sovereigns—a vision of corruption. In the closing scene the white folds of the banners of Fortinbras enshrouded all but the face of Hamlet.

This production created a furor in artistic circles, and other theatres began to take over its methods. Mingled with the general acclamation, there were references to a lack of complete union of method and ideal. Apparently, to quote Bakshy, Craig never did decide whether he was *"representing* a higher, supernatural world, for which he designs his cyclopic scenic effects," or *"presenting* his message to the audience on the Elizabethan apron stage." Again there must have been difficulties in the training of the actors: Craig believes in something above and beyond realism, while Stanislavsky, though he has entered many fields, has been unusually fortunate in directing realistic dramas in which the voices and gestures are individualized. Nevertheless, even great flaws would have been insignificant compared with the broad-mindedness and daring of the Art Theatre in welcoming Craig while the theatres of western Europe were still closed to him. He has left his tribute,—"It is quite enough to say that what these Russians do upon their stage they do to perfection. They waste time, money, labour, brains, and patience like emperors."

Another departure has been giving novels, or rather certain chapters, not in a conventional stage adaptation, but in the original text, with stage settings taking the place of descriptive passages and the author's analytical and philosophical comments read by a trained actor. The first of these experiments, Dostoyevsky's *The Brothers Karamazov*, in the program of 1910-1911, has been repeated many times, both in Europe and America. One reason for the use of this and other novels was the scarcity of new Russian plays after Chekhov's early death.

The whole subject of the attitude of the Art Theatre toward the War, the revolutions, and the present Soviet government is most interesting. For many theatres of Europe the war brought one volume of history to a close, but not the Art Theatre. "A performance of Pushkin in the scenery of Benois—that is how we expressed our patriotism," says Stanislavsky. It presented *The Cherry Orchard* to quiet, attentive spectators on the night before the Third Revolution. The audiences of the theatre have of course changed greatly: after the coming of war the characteristic figures of the old régime, the cultivated and wealthy members of the middle class, were nearly submerged, and, in their turn, have appeared the different groups which were thrown into the arena of war and upheaval. During a considerable period after the Third Revolution, the theatre came under government control, the actors were considered state employees, and tickets were distributed free to the poor. On account of the general poverty, the Art Theatre has had to confine itself largely to revivals, but under all sorts of handicaps it prepared *The Village of Stepanchikovo* (in a new adaptation), Byron's *Cain,* and Gogol's popular *Inspector General.* While it has naturally revived plays in which its audience might be expected to feel interest, its loyalty to art has never weakened. Stanislavsky has no belief in the theory that plays selected for one group should be entirely of the life of that group, for instance, that peasants are interested only in peasant drama. The unlettered men and women at the Art Theatre watched *Cain,* a philosophical and poetic drama, completely absorbed, and long after its withdrawal —because of the illness of some of the actors—sent inquiries about its possible revival.

In the mists that surround Russia the present status of the Art Theatre is difficult to ascertain. Radicals are inclined to condemn it to oblivion or to preserve it only as a curious relic of the past, as belonging to the extreme conservative "Right" in contrast to the Soviet "Left." (Everything in art or literature is classified in political nomenclature.) To the reader of its history and the spectator of its exquisitely modeled productions as they were seen on the American tours there seems too great and certain a life in this theatre for it to be relegated to any dramatic museum, however distinguished.

If the present is obscure and the future a matter of dubious prophecy, the record of the Art Theatre's past is deeply significant. Since 1898 the Moscow Art Theatre has given over seventy plays, half of them drawn from the national literature, the work of Pushkin, Gogol, Griboyedov, Ostrovsky, Tolstoy, Turgenev, Andreiev, Gorky. Of these, Chekhov and Gorky owe their success to the theatre and Turgenev, after forty years of oblivion as a dramatist, his fame. (His plays were found to possess much the same mood as Chekhov's.) Among foreign dramatists stand Ibsen, Sophocles, Shakespeare, Molière, Goldoni, Maeterlinck, Hauptmann, and Hamsun.

Early in its history the terms "extreme realism" and "naturalism" became affixed to the theatre and have clung. Certainly the inspiration of the directors, particularly in the early days, was often realism and archeological exactness, and the controlling mood was the desire to help the spectators glimpse a co-existent life, that of the imaginary characters. Famous examples of realistic setting besides *Julius Cæsar* were several of Hauptmann's plays, for which members of the company visited the dramatist's native Silesia, and *The Three Sisters* in which several rooms were displayed simultaneously upon the stage. Nevertheless, realism in setting and acting was only one of the moods of the theatre; *The Blue Bird, The Sunken Bell, The Life of Man,* the Craig *Hamlet* are illustrations of this fact. Hamsun's *The Drama of Life* departed so thoroughly and consciously from realism that half the audience applauded with "Death to realism!" while the other half countered with hisses and an appeal for the old. Stanislavsky refutes the charge that he was interested only in realism and refers to "having paid homage to the enthusiasm for all sorts of productions along all the lines of creativeness, those of history and manners, those of the symbol, those of fantasy, and so on; having learned the forms of production of all artistic tendencies, realistic, naturalistic, impressionistic, futuristic, statuary, schematized, exaggeratedly simple." It is not perhaps widely known that Meierhold, who is thought of as Stanislavsky's great opponent in matters of art, was encouraged by the older actor and put in charge of a short-lived experimental studio founded in 1905 to investigate non-realistic moods.

No originality of conception, no perfection of setting can be successful without creative acting. Long before the Art Theatre came to America travelers had told us that such acting is the rule in this Moscow house. Oliver M. Sayler, who has done much to popularize knowledge of the Russian theatre, several years ago declared that of fifty important members of the company at least seven would be recognized masters of the stage if they could be understood in western theatres. Granville Barker wrote of his visit to *The Three*

Sisters and *The Cherry Orchard,* "I had not believed till then that there could be perfection of achievement in the theatre." Now that we in America have had the experience of being part of an audience of which only a handful could understand a word of the text, and yet have forgotten ourselves completely in the actors' sincerity and matchless *ensemble,* we know that such judgments have not been exaggerations. The perfection of this *ensemble* is attained by the complete banning of the star system, by the round-table method of study, in which every actor learns the purpose of the drama, by the care and devotion lavished upon each play until it is as nearly ready as human effort can make it, and by the age of the theatre. Several of the actors have worked together since its foundation; a small group were co-workers in the earlier Society of Art and Literature.

The greatest actor is Stanislavsky, richly endowed intellectually and emotionally, of high ideals, and beauty of spirit. His variety of rôles is amazing—Cavaliere Rippafratta in *The Mistress of the Inn,* Ivan the Terrible in the play of the same name, Satin in *The Lower Depths,* Gaiev in *The Cherry Orchard,* Shuisky in *Tsar Fyodor,* Famussov in *Trouble from Reason,* and a score of others. Ivan Moskvin is also renowned for his range and his emotional power; the blundering Yepikhodov of *The Cherry Orchard* and the mystical pilgrim Luka of *The Lower Depths* show his contrasts, and he was the original Tsar Fyodor. Vassily Kachalov, who has lately taken over the part of Tsar Fyodor, is another widely loved actor of the more intellectual type. He was Hamlet in the Gordon Craig production and the Baron in *The Lower Depths.* A recent success has been his Ivan Karamazov in *The Brothers Karamazov.* Artem, remarkable for his interpretation of old men, died during the war. Vassily Luzhsky as the father in *The Brothers Karamazov* and Firs in *The Cherry Orchard* is one of the first group, as are Alexander Vishnevsky and Leonid M. Leonidov. From the studios have come Kolin whose Malvolio has a touch of both whimsicality and bitterness, and Mihail Alexandrovich Chekhov, nephew of the playwright. The actresses are scarcely the equals of the actors. The finest of the older generation and a distinguished actress is Madame Olga Leonardovna Knipper-Chekhova, widow of the playwright, who has been compared to Mrs. Fiske. Lilina, wife of Stanislavsky, is clear and delightful in the conception of her parts. Other actresses of power are Butova, Germanova, and Zhdanova. Olga Baklanova, who began her work in the Second Studio, has shown herself an emotional actress of unmistakable genius.

A home of great acting has always both historic and sentimental interest. During its more than thirty years, the Moscow Art Theatre has lived under two roofs only, with the exception of the rehearsal barn at Pushkino. The first playhouse was a dilapidated one, the Hermitage in Karetny Row. Years before, an energetic and ambitious manager, Lentovsky, had erected a large theatre for operetta and an outdoor amphitheatre for fairy plays and surrounded them with miniature gardens, lakes, and summer houses. Time had told upon the building and a less careful managership than Lentovsky's had allowed it to deteriorate. Stanislavsky and his friends did all in their power to restore the place to neatness and comfort, but the decay resisted their efforts. In the first four years, till October, 1902, they were constantly discouraged by the difficulties of heating, the wretchedness of old electric wiring, the lack of storing place for apparatus, and the limitations of the stage.

Salvation came through the munificence of a wealthy manufacturer, Savva Morozov. He had watched the performances of the theatre from the evening of *Tsar Fyodor*. Later, when the sinking fund of the theatre had been exhausted and the group who had financed it could not give more, Morozov appeared at the meeting with the proposition that he should buy out the shareholders; after this for many years its ownership was divided among Morozov and the founders. Morozov was also profoundly interested in every activity of the theatre, especially in experiments in the art of lighting as knowledge of electricity advanced. After constantly associating with the Art Theatre people and studying their needs, Morozov a second time came to their rescue and offered a suitable building to be designed by F. O. Schechtel, an intimate friend of Chekhov.

The Moscow Art Theatre is in the Kamergersky Pereulok, or, as it has been rechristened by the Soviet, the Street of the Moscow Art Theatre, close to the Theatre Place in which stand most of Moscow's dozen pre-war theatres. It has one of the most spacious stages in the world, larger than that of His Majesty's Theatre, London, one of the best equipped, also, for Morozov lavished his wealth upon everything which made for the good of play and players and merely redecorated the auditorium—an attitude diametrically opposed to that of many builders who cramp the actors for the sake of a larger audience. The stage, built when very few revolving stages were in existence, was the first of the double-decked type, with both stage segment and sub-stage revolving by electricity. Both these levels are divided into three platforms, by lowering or raising one of which a stage valley or mountain can be created. This model was copied by Reinhardt in Berlin and later by the directors of the New Theatre, now the Century Opera House, in New York. The Moscow theatre has, too, a concave horizon and complete apparatus for its lighting, the most modern for their time. The electrical room, indeed, is a research laboratory in which scientists, devotees of theatric art—Morozov often used to be among them—carry on investigations in the use of direct and diffused lighting and the manipulation of shadows. Behind the stage on three elevations are spacious dressing-rooms for the actors and actresses.

The comfort of the audience is provided for by large cloak rooms, roomy corridors in brown and white decorated with photographs of actors, artists, and literary men, smoking room, restaurant, and a small museum for the display of some of the many photographs and drawings which concern the history of the theatre. The twelve hundred seats are arranged for seeing, and the quiet oak paneling and white wall spaces with little decoration efface all irrelevant moods. That the spirit of the play may not be interrupted the theatre has banned the orchestra, any entering of the auditorium during the course of the performance, applause afterwards, and curtain calls. In the winter of 1917, when many not accustomed to play-going sought its doors, there was some attempt at conventional applause, but it was promptly frowned into silence by the regular patrons. To accommodate its new audiences, for a time after the Revolution, the company acted in the enormous Solodovnikovsky Theatre.

The Moscow Art Theatre has traveled far,—in 1900, both to the Crimea and to St. Petersburg; later to Kiev, Odessa, Warsaw, and other provincial cities; to Germany when the first Russian Revolution made Moscow untenable; to Paris; and to America.

The first St. Petersburg visit was undertaken with some fear that the rivalry betwen the two great cities might mean a cool welcome. Instead the enthusiasm was so great that a spring tour to the capital became an annual event and netted the directors a considerable part of their resources. The welcome everywhere was sincere and admiring.

Gentlemen of the jury [said a leading orator of St. Petersburg conducting a mock trial in honor of the visiting artists] you have before you two criminals [Stanislavsky and Nemirovich-Danchenko] who have committed a cruel deed. With forethought and malice they have killed the well-known, well-beloved, respected, honored, and ancient—(after a comic pause)—routine. (Again the serious tone of the attorney.) The murderers have mercilessly removed from it the ancient cloak of the clown; they have broken out the fourth wall and have shown the intimate life of men to the crowd; they have destroyed theatrical lies and have put in their stead truth, which, as it is well known to everybody, is like poison to old routine. . . . Sentence the two of them, and all of their artists, to life imprisonment—in our hearts.[5]

The American tours are too recent and have too large a literature of their own for more than a summary here. The first opened January 8, 1923, at Jolson's Fifty-Ninth Street Theatre with *Tsar Fyodor,* the historical tragedy which was the Moscow première twenty-five years before. This was followed by *The Lower Depths, The Cherry Orchard, The Three Sisters, The Brothers Karamazov,* and *The Lady from the Provinces.* After twelve weeks the company went for shorter stays to Chicago, Philadelphia, and Boston, then to New York again. Success, prepared for, to be sure, by an inspired advertising campaign, was phenomenal. The next year, with only normal advertising, the company played in the same cities and six or eight others. Oliver M. Sayler, the American authority upon the Moscow Art Theatre, ascribes its popularity here to "the essential humanity of Russian Art," the large Russian public in New York, American wealth, and America's approval of courage in sending a large group of very fine actors half across the world.

An integral part of the Art Theatre is the group of studio theatres which have sprung up about the original theatre, younger shoots from the same stock. For the future they may have more meaning than the parent organization. The idea of the studio theatre is a favorite on the continent. It

[5] From *My Life in Art,* by Constantin Stanislavsky, p. 377. Courtesy of Little, Brown and Company, Publishers, Boston.

might be defined as a training school of dramatic art either possessing an independent organization or connected with an established playhouse, from which its instructors are drawn. The pupils give performances of their own and appear as supernumeraries and occasionally in minor parts on the larger stage. As we have seen, one source of the Art Theatre was exactly this type of school. In the memory of Stanislavsky and Nemirovich-Danchenko the studio theatre remained a synonym for experimentation under as few as possible restrictions; Stanislavsky, in particular, as the years went on, came to feel that he might be able to depart more confidently from his early realism, if he were the leader of a smaller and more plastic group. In such a group he hoped to put into practise some of the new expressionist theories which absorbed Vrubel and other painters, and the freedom from bodily restrictions which marked the dancing of Pavlova and Isadora Duncan. With Meierhold, who had been one of the early actors in the Art Theatre, he organized a studio on Povarskaya in an old and beautiful house redecorated by painters of the modern school. From all parts of Russia the directors recruited folk singers, tellers of fairy tales, and performers on strange instruments. A company of young and inexperienced actors was assembled and placed in Meierhold's charge during a summer of rehearsing in the country. Several months later when the young actors were tried in Maeterlinck's *The Death of Tintagiles,* Hauptmann's *Schluck and Jau,* and other plays, though excellent in certain scenes, they proved unable to sustain the new impressionistic mood. The experiment discovered some new methods in directing and staging; otherwise it was abortive.

The First Studio, now the Moscow Art Theatre Second, began not long before the War when Stanislavsky, again despairing of any opportunity to install a new system of training at the Art Theatre, got together a group of young actors and supernumeraries. His chief helper was a most unusual man, Leopold Sulerjitsky, a friend and disciple of Tolstoy, of strong originality, high ideals, and great ingenuity in training and inspiring young people. Another assistant was Boleslavsky, who later established his own studio theatre in New York. Their Utopian plans included not only experimentation which should plumb emotion and its reproduction in art but the organization of a wholesome and rounded life for the actors, a communal life close to nature where exacting mental practise should be supplemented by physical. The second half of the plan was only partly carried out because of unsettled conditions; for two or three summers the members did enjoy a form of community living on a great tract of land purchased by Stanislavsky near Eupatoria in the Crimea.

The Moscow home of the First Studio was a section of the building which had contained the rooms of the Society of Art and Literature years before. In a spacious hall and a few anterooms were contained a stage level with the front row of the audience, seats for nearly a hundred and fifty spectators, and all equipment for an experimental theatre. Here enthusiastic young people worked till dawn after acting at the Art Theatre. The very nearness of actors and onlookers gave unusual intimacy, not so much perhaps in the early production of Heijermans' *The Loss of "The Hope"* as in *Twelfth Night,* played very gaily and spontaneously with the actors sometimes mingling with the audience or letting their voices float in through an open window, and in Sulerjitsky's dramatization of Dickens' *The Cricket on the Hearth.* This last has been immensely popular, given before nearly six hundred different audiences in the last few years, for into it Sulerjitsky has woven all his whimsicality, tenderness, and admiration for his beloved novelist. The Studio has also produced Strindberg's *Eric XIV*—influenced, doubtless, by the more radical theatres, with scenery composed of geometric masses, and the faces of the actors painted to appear like masks; *The Flood,* an adaptation of an American play by H. Berger; and *The Taming of the Shrew* with constructivist scenery composed of many platforms, cones, curved staircases, and an arrangement of screens of magenta, blue, yellow, and orange. The most discussed program of the First Studio has been a modern version of *Hamlet* with Mihail Chekhov, the nephew of the playwright, the prince of Denmark. He has received more applause than Kachalov of the Gordon Craig production.

The First Studio has accomplished much of the founder's ambition in essaying new moods and in bringing new life to the parent organization. From it Chekhov, now the director, frequently goes to the Art Theatre, and the Art Theatre in return sends its actors to the boards of the First Studio, now the Moscow Art Theatre Second, in its newer and larger building, the Nezlobin or Novy Theatre. Here decorations and customs remind the audience of the intimate relationship between the two houses.

"We trap them young," said Stanislavsky of his little seagulls, some hardly more than children. Besides the First, there were for a time three groups: the Second dating from 1916, the Third and the Fourth from 1921. They represent new adjustments in art and life caused by political upheavals of these years. A general reorganization has lately consolidated the Second and a large part of the Third Studio into a new Dramatic Studio and School for which Stanislavsky is the adviser, while part of the Third and most of the Fourth have shown themselves more concerned with problems of the newer stagecraft than the other group and have broken from it. Stanislavsky's school, to which not one in twenty of the many applicants is admitted, offers a three-year course of study. At infrequent intervals there are public performances. The Studio, made up largely of graduates from the School, now has its own repertory, *The Fairy Lady* by Calderon, *Youth* by Andreiev, and *Yelizaveta Petrovna* by Dmitry Smolin.

While the work of Studio and School is the province of Stanislavsky the Musical Studio of the Moscow Art Theatre is largely the creation and special interest of Nemirovich-Danchenko. This studio, child of its middle years, to many represents greater enthusiasm and spontaneity than the older theatre. It followed the older group to America, where it was received with much interest. By its very purpose, the elevation of the lyric stage, this studio is less tied to realism than any other of the related groups, for all opera is based upon the convention that men and women sing what in actual life they would either speak or leave unsaid. In the closing days of the War Nemirovich-Danchenko took his suggestion for this Studio from the request of the Great Moscow Opera for help in training its singers to act. Gradually a school developed to which young singers came from all parts of Russia to be trained not in singing alone, but in the expression of emotion through voice and acting.

If a wonderful singer is not first of all an actor, if he is not an artistic medium for the creation of a dramatic image, participating in the dynamics of an operatic production, if he is able only to sing wonderfully, then there is no reason for him to don one costume or another, to put on wigs, to paste on a beard, to take in his hand a sword, a banner, a cup or a rope, or in general to attempt to resemble a genuine dramatic actor, while he is not one. Such a singer needs a low platform, a dress suit or any other costume, just to make him *statuesque*. We should seek for an interesting oratorical or symphonic form for a group of such singers. It is a different matter if the singing-actor reanimates the drama. Only such a one as this can create a performance instead of a concert.[6]

[6] From *Inside the Moscow Art Theatre,* by Oliver M. Sayler, p. 54. Courtesy of Brentano's, Publishers, New York.

Drawing for his assistants Vladimir Bakaleynikov from the Theatre of Musical Drama at Petrograd, Constantin Shvedov from the Moscow Touring Opera Company, and the well-known Vassily Luzhsky, Nemirovich-Danchenko began work upon Lecocq's *The Daughter of Madame Angot*. The words of the original libretto were altered by Mihail Galperin and given more point and liveliness and an occasional light satiric thrust. The staging and costuming were suggested by French color prints of the eighteenth century and the lighting carried out the same idea. Olga Baklanova, once of the First Studio and now of both the Art Theatre and the Musical Studio, played the rôle of Lange. She is very popular. The whole performance caught the taste of its audience, playing in Russia nearly three hundred times.

In 1920 the Musical Studio continued its advance toward "a synthetic theatre" to unite music, acting, dancing, the work of the designer and of the producer. The second opera was Offenbach's *La Périchole*, story of tyranny and romance in old Peru, a tale which in somewhat different version has since become one of the threads of Thornton Wilder's novel, *The Bridge of San Luis Rey*. *La Périchole*, like *The Daughter of Madame Angot*, was freed from the wrappings of an unworthy libretto and given a new text by Galperin. Three years later Aristophanes' *Lysistrata*, a much more daring production, followed. In 1924 *Carmen* was transformed into *Carmencita and the Soldier*, with the original music of Bizet and the story taken directly from the novel of Mérimée. The 1925 performance was a group of three short operas connected by their common source in the work of Pushkin.

These productions have included fascinating experiments aligning the Musical Theatre with the advanced houses of Moscow, from which revolutionary developments may be expected at any time. The performance which has most attracted the critics is *Lysistrata*. This comedy of the "love strike" of the Athenian women until their mates consent to a treaty of peace with the nation against whom they are at war is universal in its interest and will continue to be till the problems of war and of the position of woman are more nearly solved. The drama had already been revived a few times in our generation: in a "decadent" adaptation by Maurice Donnay given first at a Parisian theatre in 1892 and repeated during several later seasons; in a strongly farcical version in Madrid, 1905; in a free translation by Laurence Housman, produced by Gertrude Kingston, at the Little Theatre, London, in 1911, and at Maxine Elliott's Theatre in New York, for the Women's Political Union, a year or so later. It has since had a long run in New York in 1930. Smolin's Russian text endeavors to keep the frankness, the virility, the wholesomeness of the original. The music by Reinhold Gliere took its suggestion from the Phrygian and Dorian models without any slavish attempt at imitation. Rabinovich, of the group of Kiev artists of whom Alexandra Exter, designer of the Kamerny *Salome,* is a leader, planned the constructivist setting, one of the most satisfying expressions of the new scenic ideal. Looked at from every angle the curves and uprights of the structures upon which and around which the acting took place were beautiful. Sayler writes:

The actual, tangible setting comprises merely a few columns, pediments, staircases and platforms—the sublimation of the Acropolis and the Parthenon in ivory white against a deep blue sky. The significant thing is the way this simple setting rules and molds the action, the way the action rules and molds the setting, the way they interact and react on each other with a precision and an economy of means that fill the eye without confusing it. Even so vast a production as "The Miracle" does not appeal more continuously to the visual sense. As presented on the Art Theatre's revolving stage, with the circular platform and the

spare but exquisite symbol of all that once was Greece now at
rest, now moving deliberately, now whirling madly and fran-
tically, the visual embodiment of this pungent and rocketing old
comedy is ever fresh, ever alive, ever stimulating.[7]

But this account of the children of the Art Theatre is
anticipating history by many years. Even in the period before the new régime, Stanislavsky's company did not dominate the Russian independent theatre to the exclusion of
all others. Vera Kommisarjevskaya, Meierhold, Evreinov,
Baliev, Tairov have been no mean rivals.

Child of the friend of Stanislavsky with whom he had
once drawn up plans for a dramatic school, Vera Kommisarjevskaya was nurtured amidst discussions of the theatre
and early drawn to it. By 1896 she was a popular favorite
alike for her charm, the range and loveliness of her voice,
and a spirituality which added depth and significance to any
part which she chose to portray. She was an interpreter of
Chekhov a few months before the Art Theatre was founded.
In 1904 she organized a company of her own, the Dramatic
Theatre, in which she played several of Ibsen's dramas, repeated *The Sea Gull,* and gave the première of *Uncle Vanya.*
Almost as important were her productions of S. Naydenov's dramas, the first of which had been given by the
Korsh theatre in 1901. Naydenov, whose genius has escaped
the attention of English translators, is highly rated by his
own countrymen: Professor Wiener, for example, believes
him technically superior to Chekhov. Within a few months
the Dramatic Theatre had shown the public Naydenov's
Avdotya's Life, No. 13, and *Vanyushin's Children.* Though
Kommisarjevskaya's theories had not yet been formulated, she was reaching toward other moods than extreme
realism.

One of the most original geniuses among Russian pro-

[7] From *Inside the Moscow Art Theatre,* by Oliver M. Sayler, p. 98.
Courtesy of Brentano's, Publishers, New York.

ducers joined Kommisarjevskaya in 1906 as her stage director. This was Vsevolod Emilyevich Meierhold, revolutionary in art, as in politics, a flaming figure throughout the years, now since the Bolshevist Revolution the most active of the pre-war managers, for he is an enthusiastic radical heartily in accord with his epoch, not trying in bewilderment to understand it. He had been one of Stanislavsky's gifted actors in realistic plays, then a seceder playing some of the Art Theatre repertory in the provinces. In 1905, the days of the revolution, he had returned to Stanislavsky, experimenting under the ægis of the Art Theatre in non-realistic moods. Meierhold's travels had led him over much of Europe: he knew remote parts of Russia as well as its cosmopolitan cities, Greece, Italy, and the traditions of their theatres. Critics emphasize his debt to the ancients whose non-naturalistic theatre contained something which he was seeking. He was also indebted to a chapter upon stylization in *The Theatre of the Future* by the German theorist, Georg Fuchs, as well as to the Russian Remizov, whose investigations antedated Meierhold's by two years. But unlike many imitators Meierhold possesses the ability to use the discoveries of others in a creative way.

When Meierhold, after working largely with Maeterlinck's plays at the Art Studio, came to Kommisarjevskaya, he was engrossed with "stylization." This term, which has meant many things to many people, was then almost new. Meierhold defines it as "the expression by all expressive means of the internal synthesis of a given epoch or phenomenon, the reproduction of their concealed characteristic features, such as are to be found in a deeply concealed style of any artistic production." This definition concerns atmosphere and purpose rather than method. Meierhold supplements this by emphasis upon color and design, which assume new importance in his theory:

The Theatre of Conventions does not seek variety in the *mise en scène,* as is the case in the Naturalistic Theatre, where the wealth of planes produces a kaleidoscope of rapidly changing poses. The Theatre of Conventions strives deftly to manage the line, the group association, and the color blending of the costumes, and in its immobility gives a thousand times more motion than the Naturalistic Theatre. The motion on the stage is produced not by motion in the verbal sense of the word, but by a distribution of lines and colors, and by the artistic crossing and vibrating of these lines and colors.[8]

For Meierhold and his followers stylization has always been in revolt against realism. One method in which he and the artists Sapunov and Sudeykin had collaborated was the use of a flat decorative surface for background and a narrowed stage which give the bodies of the actors the effect of animated sculpture. Symbolic plays appealed particularly to Meierhold and could be adapted to stylization. Since there was little Russian symbolism, the producers depended largely upon Ibsen and Maeterlinck, opening their theatre with *Hedda Gabler.* In the initial season, however, there was included one of the first plays of S. S. Yushkevich, *In the City,* which criticized the social order under which Jews in Russia were required to live. Meierhold's championship of this playwright probably led to the Moscow Art Theatre's producing *Miserere* in 1911, and encouraged a group of talented Jewish playwrights whose work began to appear soon after; Ansky (*Father and Son*), Sholom Ash (*The God of Vengeance*), and Dymov (*Nyu*) are known in America.

Another striking play was *The Booth* by Blok, well-known Russian poet. This production is referred to by historians of the theatre as one of the most harmonious and lovely of its creations. The story traces back to *King Harlequin* written by Lothar in 1899, and appeared before a

[8] From *The Contemporary Drama of Russia,* by Leo Wiener, p. 136. Courtesy of Little, Brown and Company, Publishers, Boston.

swarm of Pierrots and Pierrettes had settled upon the literatures of Europe. Andreiev, cynical, darkly pessimistic, symbolic, was another favorite of Meierhold's. *Savva,* in plot the most direct and consistent of the playwright's work, could also be stylized. In November, 1907, Sologub's *The Victory of Death* was played upon an "architectural" stage with an impressive staircase centralizing the action and suggesting the mood of the drama. In these innovations there were probably German influences and perhaps those of Craig and Appia.

Meanwhile, Kommisarjevskaya watched stage and audience, amazed and distressed, for the spectators of 1907 were less prepared for the new than those of 1927.

I saw [she wrote] that we were by degrees changing the stage into a laboratory for the stage manager's experiments; the spectators looked at us distractedly, in perplexity shrugged their shoulders and ultimately left us. The thread between the auditorium and us was persistently broken, and every meaning of our work was disappearing.

Finally she wrote to her manager:

What you are seeking is not what I am seeking. The road which leads to the puppet show, towards which you have been traveling all the time, with the exception of those presentations in which you have united the principles of the 'old' theatre with the principles of the marionettes, (for example, *The Comedy of Love* and *The Victory of Death*), is not mine. To my great regret this has come to me in full in just the last few days and after much thinking. I look the future straight in the face and I say that we cannot walk together upon this path.[9]

Meierhold was released to follow unhampered the dictates of his imagination.

[9] From *The Contemporary Drama of Russia,* by Leo Wiener, p. 156. Courtesy of Little, Brown and Company, Publishers, Boston.

For a few months Kommisarjevskaya continued her programs with her brother as stage manager and the artist, Dobuzhinsky. While the stage technique was no longer Meierhold's, the dominant mood was still that of symbolism, and St. Petersburg theatre-goers continued indifferent. A trip to America, undertaken to repair the actress's fortunes, was likewise disastrous. Plays by Ibsen, Gorky, Ostrovsky, Molière, Sudermann, given in Russian might be acclaimed by dramatic editors: the wider public thought them outlandish and suspect. Bitterly disappointed, the actress returned to Russia and chose a new manager for her St. Petersburg theatre.

In Nikolai Nikolaievich Evreinov, as in Meierhold, Kommisarjevskaya had the insight to select one of the vital figures among the men who were welcoming new influences from Western Europe and combining these with theories of their own. If the short-lived Dramatic Theatre had had no other achievement—historians tell us of the genius of Kommisarjevskaya's acting and the power and beauty of some productions, among them *Sister Beatrice*—the encouragement of two such radical producers in the days before they had won their spurs would have made the theatre famous.

Evreinov is an example of the tremendous energy and versatility of the Russian temperament and its unsurpassed ability in turning out work. He is sometimes accused of shallowness, a charge to which his amazing fertility lays him open, but he is always credited with brilliance and enthusiasm. At the time of his appointment to the Dramatic Theatre he was barely thirty, a lawyer by training, once a teacher by necessity, and now a public official under the Ministry of Ways and Communications. His interest in the theatre had appeared in his childish attempts at play-writing, in his delight in acting—as a young boy he joined a circus, and at fourteen was one of a troupe of actors playing at Pskoff—and in his activities within the Legal Dramatic Circle of the School of Law at St. Petersburg. Several of his dramas,—*The Handsome Despot, War,* and *Such a Woman* among them,—had been given in the northern capital. For a year he had been directing the *Starinny Teatr* (Old Theatre) which he had organized for reviving the earlier Russian plays. His career with Kommisarjevskaya lasted only a few months. The main programs were *Francesca da Rimini,* Andreiev's *The Black Masks,* and Sologub's *Vanka the Butler and Page Jean.* The last is an ingenious picture of contrasted French and Russian temperament. The tale of the love of a servant and his mistress and the husband's detection of their guilt is shown first in terms of one nationality and then of the other; the Russian husband, more generous, or more indifferent, forgives the erring wife. *Salome,* which was rehearsed and staged at a great expense, was forbidden by the police on the evening before the performance. Madame Kommisarjevskaya, once more defeated, found her only resource another tour, this time to the East. Her death from an oriental fever came almost twenty years before the general awakening of interest in new ideas of stage decoration and production.

The later history of these directors of the Dramatic Theatre is important. Meierhold's activities are nearly coextensive with the Russian theatre under the Revolution and the Soviet Republic, and will be discussed later. Evreinov, less radical in politics, continued his technical innovations and the formulation of theories. With Fyodor Kommisarjevsky, brother of the actress, he founded the Gay Theatre for Grown-up Children in St. Petersburg. Later he controlled the theatre *Krivoye Zerkalo* (the Crooked Looking-Glass). Upon these and other stages he saw his own *Gay Death,* a harlequinade; *The Rape of the Sabine Women, Sweet Cake,* and *The Fugitive,* each an opera of a different type; and *The Representation of Love* and *The Theatre of the Soul,* "monodramas." Incidentally he composed songs, wrote dissertations on subjects as remote from one another as Aubrey Beardsley, serf actors, and corporal punishment in Russia, exhibited a futuristic painting, studied folk drama in remote provinces of his own country, in southern Europe, Africa, and the Near East.

His critical theories are contained in several volumes, only one of which, *An Introduction to Monodrama*, has been translated into English. Monodrama, with which Evreinov's name is linked, derives in part from German theory and has curious affiliations with ancient drama as well as with the dreams and soul-states of ultra-modern expressionism. In a monodrama the interest is centered upon the soul, the inmost personality, of one central figure—Evreinov calls him the "acting character." The audience sees all the other characters as this central figure would see them, and they and anything in the universe around them may change shape and color as the emotions of the acting character determine. To quote Evreinov's explanation:

I call monodrama the kind of a dramatic representation which endeavors with the greatest fulness to communicate to the spectator the soul state of the acting character, and presents on the stage the world surrounding him as he conceives it at any moment in his stage experience. Instead of the old incomplete drama, I propose the architectonics of a drama based on the principle of identifying the stage with the representation of the acting character.

.   .   .   .

Monodrama forces every one of the spectators to enter the situation of the acting character, to live his life, that is to say, to feel as he does and through illusion to think as he does. Consequently, first of all, it is necessary for him to see and to hear the same as the acting character. The cornerstone of monodrama is the living experience of the acting character on the stage dependent on the identical coördinate living experience of the spectator who by this act of coördinate experience becomes a similar acting character. To convert the spectator into an illusory acting character is the important problem of monodrama. For this, there must be on the stage first of all only one subject of acting, and not only for the reasons that have been set forth in the beginning but also because monodrama has for its purpose to present such an external spectacle as will correspond to the inner spectacle of the subject of acting; for to be present at once at two spectacles is not within our weak powers.

.   .   .   .

The surrounding world seems to borrow its character from the subjective individual "I"; and we understand what Goethe meant in saying of Hebel that the latter gave nature a great deal of the "peasant quality." Nature can be peasant-like, when Hebel perceives it, but it can be chivalrously beautiful when Wolfram von Eschenbach perceives it. And it changes together with us, with our soul-mood. The cheerful meadow, field and forest which I admire, sitting free from care beside my sweetheart, will become a bright green spot, yellow furrows, and dark age, only if at that moment I be notified of a misfortune that has happened to some one near to me. And the author of the perfect drama in the sense I understand it will fix in a remark these two moments of the setting surrounding us; pedantically he will demand from the decorator an instantaneous change of the cheerful landscape to a stupid combination of tiresome green, disquieting yellow and gloomy olive colors, and he will be right in his pedantry.[10]

Against the seriousness, if not sombreness, of many of these Russian programs stands out the Chauve-Souris as it is best known in western Europe,—the Letutchaya Muish or Bat Theatre of Baliev. What lover of European art is not familiar with its gorgeous color, its gaiety, and its variety? Each playlet, tableau, or dance is stylized from a story of early Russia, a bit of Dresden china, Marie Antoinette's fan,

[10] From *The Russian Theatre under the Revolution,* by Oliver M. Sayler, pp. 232, 235, 237. Courtesy of Little, Brown and Company, Publishers, Boston.

a traditional ballad, the wooden soldiers adored of childhood, or other delectable trifle, unless it is in tragic contrast. Every part of the performance is infused with the amazing vitality of Baliev, the founder, whose comic face and brilliant repartee create an unusual intimacy between stage and audience. He began his stage life as a member of Stanislavsky's company, and his Chauve-Souris developed more than twenty years ago from the "cabbage-parties" of the Art Theatre, those gatherings of actors and actresses for an evening of half-impromptu merrymaking before the beginning of Lent. Baliev's theatre has now a Moscow playhouse of its own.

Almost all theatrical experiment in Russia, as I have said, seems to trace to Stanislavsky and Nemirovich-Danchenko. Amca Koonen, the foremost actress of the Kamerny Theatre, was a student in the early school attached to the Moscow Art Theatre, where very appropriately, for she is a Belgian, she was the first portrayer of Mytyl in the world première of Maeterlinck's *The Blue Bird;* Alexandr Tairov organized his progressive group to eschew realism in any form, but particularly the Moscow Art Theatre brand. Certain art tendencies may be distinguished at Tairov's playhouse, but they have not hardened into moulds, and, from its inception in 1914 till the mandates of the Soviet government have somewhat marred its lustre, it has been a powerful champion of independence and a delight to the theatregoers of Moscow. Tairov, the ruling spirit, like Evreinov a lawyer, when still a young man abandoned his profession for the theatre. In 1912 he became a manager of the cabaret, the Stray Dog, in St. Petersburg, and a few months later the director of the Theatre Mobile, which traveled to remote sections of Russia. Next he was in charge of a new organization, the Free Theatre, and when this broke into two factions he headed the more radical. His wife, Amca Koonen, a favorite of the Moscow public, was a co-founder, and Henri Forterre, gifted French musican who chooses to live in Russia, and Nikolai Mihailovich Tseretelli, chief actor of men's rôles, were on the governing board. These four staunchly favor stylization in the theatre and careful technique. Their methods change with each play; the only safe generalization which can be drawn from their work is the ideal of frank theatricality. The Kamerny probably received something of its inspiration from Meierhold's studied artificiality in Molière's *Don Juan*.

No theatre has hunted further for congenial material or been more original in ways of presenting it. Beginning with the Hindu *Sakuntala* the Kamerny has given Synge's *The Playboy of the Western World;* Calderon's *Life Is a Dream;* Goldoni's *The Fan;* Kuzmin's *The Pentecost at Toledo* (a pantomime); Beaumarchais' *The Marriage of Figaro;* Remy de Gourmont's *The Carnival of Life;* Rostand's *Cyrano de Bergerac;* Tor Herberg's *Two Worlds; The Merry Wives of Windsor;* Annyensky's *Thamira of the Cithern;* Donanhy's *The Veil of Pierrette* (pantomime); Benelli's *The Jest;* Labiche's *Un Chapeau de Paille d'Italie;* Stolitsa's *The Azure Carpet;* Wilde's *Salome;* Lothar's *King Harlequin;* Debussy's *The Box of Toys* (pantomime); Claudel's *L'Echange;* Racine's *Phèdre;* Scribe's *Adrienne Lecouvreur;* Hoffman's *Princess Brambilla;* Claudel's *The Tidings Brought to Mary; Romeo and Juliet; Giroflé-Girofla;* O'Neill's *Desire Under the Elms* (the title in Russian is *Love Under the Trees*). For *Sakuntala,* after a trip to India and much musing upon Yogi philosophy, Tairov selected a decorative scheme suggested by the miniatures of early Hindu manuscripts, and trained his actors to assume the poses of the figures in them. *The Box of Toys* took its keynote from the toys themselves. *Salome* was in cubist garb, not only in its conventionalized background but in its costumes, and cubist upon the stage as well as under the designer's pencil. The costumes of

Salome, Jokanaan, Herod, and the others of Herod's court were stiffened into folds which were enlarged and made impressive by artificial, painted shadows. The acting tried to portray the abstraction of emotions rather than their realistic exhibition. Koonen, as Salome, achieved this effect by a subtle mingling of the intimate and the impersonal, alike passionate. Both the designs for Wilde's play and the curtain of the Kamerny Theatre were designed by Alexandra Exter. Sudeykin, some of whose paintings have been exhibited in America, and other prominent artists have been designers for this theatre.

Startling as have been Tairov's experiments and admired as he is by the Moscow intelligentsia and the more discriminating of theatre-goers, a figure now towers far above him in popular estimation, a figure which also dwarfs Stanislavsky, the great innovator of a generation ago—Meierhold.

Meierhold's early days have been discussed. From the Dramatic Theatre he turned to the Alexandrinsky Theatre in St. Petersburg, an important state-endowed house. Here he devoted his art to the frank acceptance of the playhouse as a playhouse, an emphasis upon sheer theatricality. His repertory included Moussorgsky's *Boris Godunov*, Tolstoy's *The Living Corpse*, Byelyaiev's *The Red Tavern*, Sologub's *Hostages of Life*, Lyermontov and Glazunov's *Maskarad*, Pushkin and Dargomuizhsky's *The Stone Guest*, Rimsky-Korsakov's *The Snow Maiden*, and Ostrovsky's *The Thunderstorm*, and the operas, *Tristan and Isolde, Don Juan, Orpheus, Elektra*. Meierhold could approach all his technical problems in either the mood of the Greek theatre, which bound its audience in one festival spirit, or the gay and cynical unreality of the theatre of Western Europe in the seventeenth century. He says:

On the extreme west . . . in France and Italy, Spain and England, and on the extreme east in Japan, within the limits of one epoch (the second half of the sixteenth and the whole of the seventeenth century), the theatre resounds with the tambourines of pure theatricality. . . . The academic theatre of the Renaissance, unable to make use of the greatly extended forestage, removed the actor to a respectable distance from the public. . . . Molière is the first of the masters of the stage of the era of Louis XIV to bring the action forward from the back and the middle of the stage to the forestage, to the very edge of it.

The *Don Juan* production was the quintessence of this phase of Meierhold's art. With the curtain removed that it might not create even a momentary coldness between actors and spectators, with auditorium lights blazing to intensify the excitement and gaiety, but paling before the hundreds of wax candles in great chandeliers upon the stage, moved the splendid creatures of the age of Molière and Louis XIV, the personifications of luxury and extravagance. That these magnificent courtiers might never be required to tax their delicate strength, little negro servants flitted about moving a chair, retrieving a handkerchief, or tying the ribbon of a shoe. They also scattered perfumes that the audience might breathe luxury as well as behold it, rang a tiny silver bell to reassemble the spectators, and made necessary announcements.

An account of the training given to young actors in Meierhold's Studio at this time reiterates this deliberate artificiality:

The meaning of the "refusal"; the value of the gesture in itself; the self-admiration of the actor in the process of acting; the technique of using two stages, the stage and the forestage; the rôle of the outcry in the moment of strained acting; the elegant costume of the actor as a decorative ornament and not a utilitarian need; the headgear as a motive for the stage bow; little canes, lances, small rugs, lanterns, shawls, mantles, weapons, flowers, masks, noses, etc., as apparatus for the exercise of the hands; the appearance of objects on the platform and further destiny in the development of the subject dependent on these objects; large and small curtains (permanent and sliding, curtains in the sense of "sails") as the simplest method of changes; screens and transparencies as a means of theatrical expressiveness; gauzes in the hands of the servants of the forestage as a means of underlining the separate accents in the playing of the leading actors,—in their movements and conversations; parade as a necessary and independent part of the theatrical appearance; various forms of parade in conformity with the character of the general composition of the play; geometrization of the design into the *mise en scène*, created even *ex improviso;* the mutual relation of the word and gesture in existing theatres and in the theatre to which the Studio aspires.[11]

Perfumes, cobweb handkerchiefs, the tinkle of silver bells —and the October fighting in Moscow's Red Square. Little canes, mantles, small rugs, gauzes—and the marching of Red soldiers and the strains of the Third Internationale. Tairov is continuing his highly individual art under the sufferance of the existing powers, Stanislavsky is assuring himself that he is not averse to dramas of Revolution if they will only use propaganda as a spring-board towards art, but Meierhold is the leading man in the reorganization of the Russian theatre, the most powerful force in this field of popular education. His ideas are fermenting not alone in Leningrad and in Moscow but in every remote village throughout the great Soviet republic, and his influence is extending to western Europe and America. He is a born revolutionist, not an evolutionist: he would smash the old mould to release a new truth. He is heart and soul with the new government: why haggle over the relation of propaganda to art when there are millions of workmen, soldiers, and peasants illiterate or half-educated, seizing each bit of encouragement which the theatre can offer them in their advance toward the communistic ideal?

[11] From *The Russian Theatre under the Revolution*, by Oliver M. Sayler, p. 216. Courtesy of Little, Brown and Company, Publishers, Boston.

The theatre in Russia has passed through a first and a second period under the Soviet government, and is now living in a third. The first was one of occasional interference by the Soviet; the second, that of government ownership; and the third, after the sudden withdrawal of official financial support, is that of voluntary allegiance to the ideal of the government and of general governmental supervision. The managers, loyal, though sometimes rather befogged by the quick succession of events, will not dare to attack the Soviet by any play presenting it in any unfavorable light, though there have been some amusing and inoffensive satires upon officials. A conscientious and ambitious minister of education, M. Lunatcharsky, presides over the department of drama and believes thoroughly in its power as a means of education. He is broadminded: so conservative a playhouse as the Moscow Art Theatre has been encouraged to continue its work. Perhaps the recent founding of three theatres which are not revolutionary is due to his protective influence as well as to Meierhold's interest in many races. The Jewish Kamerny Theatre, playing in Yiddish, founded by a group of Petrograd Jews about 1920, has given *The Blind* by Maeterlinck, *Uriel Acosta* by Kail Gutzkoiv, *In the Winter* by Sholom Ash. Later, in Moscow, the group put on several short plays by Sholom Ash and *Before Dawn* by Veiter. The Studio Theatre Habima, whose actors refuse to speak anything but Hebrew, gave a beautiful interpretation of Ansky's *The Dybbuk,* instinct with the poetry and mysticism of his people. (The Yiddish Art Theatre, the Neighborhood Playhouse, and the Vagabonds repeated this.) A Children's Theatre, tickets for which reach each school child several times a year, has been able to command the leisure of a number of Russian artists, T. S. Fedotov, Forterre, and others, and illustrates the government's concern over juvenile welfare. Organizations to promote drama for children have often seemed fitful in enthusiasm and uncertain in policy, but this Russian theatre has a wisely chosen repertoire,—*Mowgli* (Kipling), *Nursery Rhymes* (Moussorgsky), *The Pasha and the Beau* (Scribe), *The Nightingale* (Hans Christian Andersen), *Tom Sawyer* (Mark Twain), and *The Color Box* (Alexei Remizov).

The plays which Meierhold himself produces are often on a gigantic scale,—the world through Soviet eyes with the marching of Soviet feet and the sound of the Third Internationale. *Richi, Kitai—Roar China,* Trettakov's dramatization of an actual incident, censures Anglo-Saxon cocksure arrogance in the Far East in contrast with the communistic ideal of brotherhood. *Mandat* has its fling at a respectability built over unsure foundations. Crommelynck's *Le Cocu Magnifique* is played with a directness and emphasis which are unlike the suggestiveness of the performances in Western Europe. Indeed sex seems too individual a thing for its manifestations to be of much interest: the problems of the workers, means of acquiring education, methods for the industrialization of a tremendous undeveloped land, plans for disseminating world culture, all take precedence over the individual reactions of one man and one woman.[12] Returning travelers consider *The Destruction of Europe* typical of the new spirit. It is a series of brief scenes in which the stupidity and vices of one nation after another are broadly satirized and the nation is eliminated from the map of the world, outlined on a motion picture screen, until only "the workers of the world" are left. Meierhold has also encouraged gigantic festival pageants on days sacred to the new order. On May Day, 1921, he was one of the two directors of the *Mysteria Bouffes,* by Vladimir Maiakovsky at the Zon Theatre in Moscow. This, like *The Destruction of Europe,* seeks to prove the ineffectualness of everything except communism, beginning its demonstration with Noah and the Flood and ending with a lesson for the Workers of

[12] Flanagan, Hallie, *Shifting Scenes in the European Theatre,* pp. 98-121.

the World themselves: the need for exhausting, self-effacing work and for tools which have long been in the hands of the so-called progressive nations.

The method of these spectacles is more important than their content for the theatre of Western Europe. Constructivism reigns on the Soviet stage. The origin of this method of stage arrangement, one hesitates to call it decoration, is obscure. There have certainly been German influences in Russia and expressionism, like stylization, has departed from realism. Constructivism is the arrangement of scenes, usually without backdrop or curtain, on one or more elevated surfaces which may be chosen from a myriad of forms, with the sole requirement that this acting space should be carpentered to hold the weight of the actors when they play upon it, and not to descend upon them, when they are stationed beneath it. These structures may be combinations of platforms and stairways, parts of ships, factory machines, masses of gymnasium apparatus. The grace of the setting of *Lysistrata,* of the Musical Studio, dependent upon the combination of curves and straight lines, Meierhold and his followers foreswear,—they dote, at least for the moment, upon an escape from the slavery of beauty. There are several conditions in Russia which have encouraged this new development: the ignorance of the peasants and workers of the lives and homes of the "bourgeois", the uselessness of the older setting for the type of play which the Soviet encourages, the ease of procuring wood and steel and the difficulty of procuring silk and gauze, materials of foreign manufacture, the suitability of the heavier materials to the new "biomechanical" acting in a country which is recommending universal physical training, and the insistence of the Russian leaders upon the power of western machinery. Many a play ends with a tableau in which an American harvester is more featured than the actor.

The influence of Meierhold is felt in the other theatres of

the Left,—The Workshop of Comedy and the Drama, for which he has mounted several productions, the First Theatre of the Russian Socialist Federated Soviet Republic, and Zalka's Revolutionary Theatre. The Workshop encourages authorship and has received an almost infinite number of would-be plays, many of them nearly illiterate. A committee takes the most promising ideas and reworks them with results which, far removed from art, at least have the virtue of being close to the workers' interests. Foreign plays at these and other radical theatres are of the new order,— Rolland's *Danton,* Toller's *Man and the Masses,*—or classics into which a revolutionary note can be forced.

No survey of the advanced playhouses of Moscow and Leningrad can give any conception of Soviet Russia's interest in the theatre. Everywhere in workers' organizations, in factories, in political clubs, are men, women, and children feeling their way through this world-old form toward the learning which they covet, toward fuller knowledge of themselves, and toward greater service for the state. The number of dramatic organizations in this country, which covers one-sixth of the globe, is impossible to calculate. Before the Great War, there were two hundred and ten theatres in all Russia; in 1920 the government was subsidizing ten times that number and estimated that there were almost four thousand others. In 1927, two provinces numbered jointly fifteen hundred theatres. In the cities, fifty thousand men, women, and children sometimes take part in historical pageants.

Art has often looked askance at propaganda and has never for any long period flouted beauty. There are rumors even now that Meierhold is proclaiming its return to the stage. Perhaps it has never been absent: who can deny that devotion to a great ideal, no matter how crudely expressed, has something of beauty? Once long ago, in a little city state for a few years actors and audiences were united in their devotion to a drama that was at one with their religion: today another people, of overwhelming numbers, join in a ritualistic drama of brotherhood.

IX

THE IMPORTANCE OF THE INDEPENDENT THEATRE

THE free theatre, as many of its supporters avow, is justified because of the opportunities for self-expression which it offers a world in which such opportunities for the average person are few. Though this fact is of social and ethical importance, it would not alone make the institution significant in the history of the drama as an art form. There are several ways in which the independent theatre has enriched it.

This type of theatre, in the first place, is the medium by which new literary and art movements go from country to country before they have any wide recognition on the larger stages. Realism, beginning at Antoine's Théâtre Libre, in two years led to the establishment of the Freie Bühne in Berlin, and in two years more to that of Grein's London theatre. Comparatively remote, Russia did not feel the next mood so quickly as the more western countries, and the Moscow Art Theatre was inspired by realism, though at the time of its founding, this was already on the ebb in France and Germany, and had never been extreme in England or Ireland. In England, George Bernard Shaw, at the Independent Theatre, the Incorporated Stage Society, the Court, and the Duke of York's, had promptly substituted the drama of discussion. The second mood of reaction against exaggerated realism was strengthened by the growing knowledge of Ibsen's poetic and symbolic dramas, and the appearance of Maeterlinck. Lugné-Poë in several of the little advanced theatres of Paris aided both these dramatists, as did the Stage Society and other English groups.

The Irish Literary Theatre and its successor, organized at the time of this new influence, through special conditions and the presence of strongly individual genius, was able to unite national and international elements in a highly original way. The Welsh and Scottish movements are in direct imitation of the Irish. Expressionism,—though with Russian affiliations,—originating principally in groups of young German radicals, for whom Reinhardt has sometimes been producer, has moved west: programs of the London Incorporated Stage Society and the Gate Theatre, Dublin, show its influence. Constructivism is also beginning to pass beyond Russia.

The hospitality of the independent theatres to foreign drama has been a great force in popularizing the knowledge of it. Interesting plays of the Russian free theatres are given in Paris and London independent theatres, in the English provinces, and by the New York Theatre Guild; von Hofmannsthal's *The Great World Theatre* has been played in a church at Salzburg and an English chapel. Foreign plays are read widely also, and people make an effort to see the ones they have enjoyed whether at the little theatres or at the larger houses. This growing spirit of internationalism in one art form may have a wholesome influence upon other provinces of thought.

The independent theatre movement has also had several profound influences upon the commercial stage, or rather that part of it which is interested in something besides the more obvious forms of entertainment. In the first place, the movement has trained audiences in both Europe and America to attend the theatre more appreciatively, alert to the merits of the play, rather than the adroitness of the leading man. It has also interested them in the allied arts of the stage, and thus encouraged producers to careful artistic endeavor.

Secondly, men and women trained in the free theatres

have often gone from them to the commercial stages of their own and sometimes of other countries, bringing with them higher standards and new ideals. The Théâtre Libre was the training school for realistic acting, losing many of its finest actors and actresses to the established theatres. Antoine and Gémier, after their days at this pioneer theatre, became two of the greatest actors and producers of Paris; both have been directors of the Odéon. Sir Edward Gordon Craig, one of whose few early productions was the Art Theatre *Hamlet,* has recently made the designs for a much-heralded American production of *Macbeth.* Many of the English little theatre actors and some of the Irish are now upon the regular stages.

Perhaps the greatest gift of the free theatre to the commercial houses has been plays and playwrights. The Théâtre Libre began early to send an occasional play to the Odéon or to the Comédie-Française. Chekhov's plays, from the Moscow Art Theatre, have traveled widely. Plays of Shaw's, originally presented by the Incorporated Stage Society, the Court Theatre, and the Duke of York's, have been given throughout the English-speaking world. *Hindle Wakes,* the opera *The Immortal Hour,* and *Journey's End* have had distinguished success. (The record of the last has been phenomenal.) More important than the plays which have opened on the free stages are later plays on the commercial stages, by "little theatre" playwrights, men who might never have turned to the drama, if they had not had the help of the experimental groups. Their names are some of the greatest in modern literature: Shaw, Galsworthy, Masefield, Brieux, Curel, Hauptmann, Toller, and many others. Moreover, in all the countries possessing free theatres, there have been a considerable number of men who have worked directly for the regular theatres whose plays would probably not have been accepted if the more radical authors had not prepared the way for them; Sudermann and Halbe in Germany are illustrations.

To say that the independent theatre in Europe is in a state of transition may be a truism when the same can be said of any organism possessing life. But there is apparently a change in emphasis. At a meeting of the Incorporated Stage Society a few months ago, the members discussed earnestly the question whether their organization and other theatres of "the advance guard" may not have served their purpose now that the commercial houses often welcome radical plays. The greatest vigor at present is not in the small experimental stage societies of the cities, but in the groups which have a strong community or national purpose: societies in remote towns and villages where there is no commercial theatre, the Irish, Scotch, Welsh organizations,—always national in purpose,—the people's theatres of Germany, and the Soviet theatres of Russia.

BIBLIOGRAPHY

A COMPLETE list of all books and periodicals discussing the dramatists and the plays of the European experimental theatres as well as
the organization and history of the theatres themselves would be
almost coextensive with a bibliography of modern drama. Since many
excellent published lists covering the drama of the different countries
are easily obtainable, it has seemed best to include here only titles of
books which deal with the spirit of the modern dramatic revival or
with the history of the theatres under discussion. As far as possible,
recent editions, as more accessible, are mentioned. Names of American
publishers are in abbreviated form.

The major part of the material upon the English and Scottish
theatre groups I owe to the thoughtfulness and generosity of their
organizers and leaders who have sent me many programs, announcements, leaflets, and personal accounts. Their names are in the preface.

GENERAL SURVEY

CANNAN, G. *The Joy of the Theatre.* New York, E. P. Dutton, 1913.
CARTER, HUNTLY. *The New Spirit in Drama and Art.* London, Ken-
nerley, 1912.
—— *The New Spirit in the European Theatre, 1914-1924.* New York,
Doran, 1926.
CHENEY, SHELDON. *Modern Art and the Theatre.* Scarborough-on-
Hudson, The Sleepy Hollow Press, 1921.
—— *Stage Decoration.* New York, Day, 1928.
—— *The Art Theatre.* New York, Knopf, 1925.
—— *The New Movement in the Theatre.* New York, Kennerley,
1914.
CLARK, BARRETT H. *A Study of the Modern Drama.* New York,
Appleton, 1928.
—— *European Theories of the Drama.* Cincinnati, Stewart, Kidd,
1918.
CRAIG, EDWARD GORDON, SIR. *Books and Theatres.* London, Dent,
1926.
—— *On the Art of the Theatre.* New York, Dodd, Mead, 1925.

CRAIG, EDWARD GORDON, SIR. *Scene.* With a foreword and an introductory poem by John Masefield. London, H. Milford, Oxford University Press, 1923.
—— *The Theatre—Advancing.* Boston, Little, Brown, 1919.
—— *Towards a New Theatre.* New York, Dutton, 1913.
DICKINSON, THOMAS HERBERT. *An Outline of Contemporary Drama.* Boston, Houghton Mifflin, 1927.
—— *The Insurgent Theatre.* New York, B. W. Huebsch, 1917.
DOLMAN, JOHN, JR. *The Art of Play Production.* New York, Harper, 1928.
DRINKWATER, JOHN. *Theater-Going.* Boston, Houghton, 1927.
DUKES, ASHLEY. *Drama.* New York, Henry Holt, 1927.
—— *Modern Dramatists.* Chicago, Sergel, 1912.
—— *The Youngest Drama.* Chicago, Sergel, 1924.
FUERST, WALTER RENÉ, and HUME, SAMUEL J. *Twentieth-Century Stage Decoration; with an Introduction by Adolph Appia.* 2 vols. New York, Knopf, 1928.
GOLDBERG, ISAAC. *The Drama of Transition.* Cincinnati, Stewart Kidd, 1922.
GOLDMAN, EMMA. *The Social Significance of Modern Drama.* Boston, R. G. Badger, 1914.
HALE, E. E. *Dramatists of To-Day.* New York, Holt, 1911.
HENDERSON, ARCHIBALD. *European Dramatists.* Revised Edition. Appleton, 1926.
—— *The Changing Drama.* New Edition. Cincinnati, Stewart & Kidd, 1919.
HUNEKER, JAMES G. *Iconoclasts: A Book of Dramatists.* New York, Scribner's, 1905.
—— *Pathos of Distance.* Scribner's, 1913.
ISAACS, EDITH J. R., editor. *Theatre.* Boston, Little, Brown, 1927.
JAMESON, M. STURM. *Modern Drama in Europe.* New York, Harcourt, 1920.
LEWISOHN, LUDWIG. *The Drama and the Stage.* New York, Harcourt, 1922.
—— *The Modern Drama.* New York, Viking, 1915.
MACGOWAN, KENNETH. *The Theater of To-Morrow.* New York, Boni and Liveright, 1921.
—— and JONES, ROBERT EDMOND. *Continental Stagecraft.* New York, Harcourt, 1922.
MODERWELL, H. K. *The Theatre of To-Day.* New York, Dodd, Mead, 1927.
NICOLL, ALLARDYCE. *The Development of the Theatre.* New York, Harcourt, 1927.

PALMER, JOHN LESLIE. *Studies in the Contemporary Theatre.* Boston, Little, Brown, 1927.
—— *The Future of the Theatre.* London, G. Bell and Sons, 1913.
PHELPS, WILLIAM LYON. *The Twentieth Century Theatre.* New York, Macmillan, 1918.
ROUCHÉ, JACQUES. *L'Art Théâtral Moderne.* Paris, Blond et Gay, 1924.
STRATTON, CLARENCE. *Theatron: An Illustrated Record.* New York, Holt, 1928.
VERNON, FRANK. *The Twentieth Century Theatre.* Boston, Houghton Mifflin, 1924.

FRANCE

A New French Theatre in America. The Theatre du Vieux Columbier. New York, The Oxford Printing Co., 1919.
ADERER, ADOLPHE. *Le Théâtre à Coté.* Préface par Fr. Sarcey. Librairies-imprimeries réunies, 1894.
ANTOINE, ANDRÉ. *"Mes Souvenirs" sur le Théâtre-Libre.* Paris, Fayard & Cⁱᵉ, 1921.
AYNARD, AUGUSTIN. *Almanach des Théâtres, Année 1922.* Paris, Librairie Stock, 1924.
BLUM, LÉON. *Au Théâtre.* Paris, Ollendorff, 1906.
BRISSON, ADOLPHE. *Le Théâtre Pendant la Guerre.* Paris, Hachette et Cⁱᵉ, 1918.
—— *Les Prophètes.* Paris, J. Tallandier, 1903.
—— *Portraits Intimes.* Paris, A. Colin et Cⁱᵉ, 1894-1904.
BRUNETIÈRE, FERDINAND. *Essais sur la Littérature Contemporaine.* C. Lévy, 1892.
CAPUS, ALFRED. *Notre Époque et le Théâtre.* Paris, Charpentier et Fasquelle, 1906.
CLARK, BARRETT H. *Contemporary French Dramatists.* Cincinnati, Stewart and Kidd, 1916.
—— *Four Plays of the Free Theatre.* New York, Appleton, 1915.
—— *The Continental Drama of To-Day.* New York, Holt, 1914.
DARZENS, RODOLPHE. *Le Théâtre Libre Illustré (1889-1890).* Paris, 1890.
DELPIT, LOUISE. *Paris—Théâtre Contemporain: Rôle Prépondérant des Scènes D'Avant-garde Depuis Trente Ans.* Northampton, Smith College, 1925.
DOUMIC, RENÉ. *De Scribe à Ibsen.* Paris, Delaplane, 1893.
—— *Essais sur le Théâtre Contemporain.* Paris, Perrin et Cⁱᵉ, 1896.
—— *Le Théâtre Nouveau.* Paris, Perrin et Cⁱᵉ, 1908.

DOUMIC, RENÉ. *Les Jeunes.* Paris, Perrin et Cie, 1895.

—— *Portraits D'Écrivains.* Paris, Delaplane, 1892.

ELLIS, HAVELOCK. *Affirmations.* New York, Houghton, 1922.

ERNEST-CHARLES, M. J. *Le Théâtre des Poètes, de 1850 à 1910.* Paris, P. Ollendorff, 1910.

FAGUET, EMILE. *Drame Ancien, Drame Modern.* Paris, Colin et Cie, 1898.

—— *Notes sur le Théâtre Contemporain.* 7 vols. Paris, Lecène et Oudin, 1889-1895.

—— *Propos Littéraires.* 5 vols. Société française d'imprimerie et de librairie, 1902-1910.

FILON, AUGUSTIN. *De Dumas à Rostand.* Paris, Colin et Cie, 1898. ("English version by J. E. Hogarth as Modern French Drama.")

FRANK, WALDO. *The Art of the Vieux Columbier. A Contribution of France to the Contemporary Stage.* Paris, Nouvelle Revue Française, 1918.

JULLIEN, JEAN. *Le Théâtre Vivant. Essai Théorique et Pratique (L'Echéance, la Sérénade, le Maître, la Mer, Vieille Histoire).* Vol. I, Charpentier et Fasquelle, 1892. Vol. II, *Théorie Critique,* Tresse et Stock, 1896.

LARROUMET, GUSTAVE. *Études d'Histoire et de Critique Dramatiques.* Paris, Hachette et Cie, 1892.

—— *Nouvelles Études d'Histoire et de Critique Dramatiques.* Paris, Hachette et Cie, 1899.

Le Théâtre Libre, 1890.

Le Vieux Columbier, 10me Année, Saison, 1923-1924. Fontenay-aux-Roses, L. Bellenand.

LECOMTE, L. HENRY. *Histoire des Théâtres de Paris.* Paris, Daragon, 1905.

LEMAÎTRE, JULES. *Impressions de Théâtre.* 10 vols. Paris, Lecène et Oudin, 1888-1898.

—— *Les Contemporains.* 7 vols. Paris, Lecène et Oudin, 1885-1899.

MÉLOTTE, PAUL. *Essai sur le Théâtre Futur.* Bruxelles, Dechenne et Cie, 1911.

MENDÈS, CATULLE. *L'Art au Théâtre.* 2 vols. Paris, Charpentier, 1895. Paris, 2e année, Fasquelle, 1896.

MODERWELL, HIRAM K. *The Theatre of To-Day.* Revised Edition. Dodd, Mead, 1927.

MOUSSINAC, LÉON C. *La Décoration Théâtrale.* Paris, F. Rieder et Cie, 1922.

NOËL, EDOUARD, and STOULLIG, EDMOND. *Annales du Théâtre et de la Musique.* 1900-1905.

PARIGOT, HIPPOLYTE. *Le Théâtre d'Hier.* Lecène et Oudin, 1893.

ROLLAND, ROMAIN. *The People's Theatre;* translated from the French by Barrett H. Clark. New York, Holt, 1918.

SARCEY, FRANCISQUE. *Quarantes ans de Théâtre.* 8 vols. Paris, Aux bureaux des Annales politiques et littéraires, 1900-1902.

SCHEIFLEY, W. H. *Brieux and Contemporary French Society.* New York, Putnam, 1917.

SÉCHÉ, A., and BERTRAUT, J. *L'Évolution de Théâtre Contemporain.* Paris, 1908.

SMITH, HUGH ALLISON. *Main Currents of Modern French Drama.* New York, Holt, 1925.

SOUBIES, ALBERT. *Almanach des Spectacles.* Librairie des bibliophiles, 1890-1892. Vol. 20, Flammarion, 1893. Le même. Nouvelle série, Années, 1893 à 1898. Flammarion.

—— *Le Théâtre en France de 1871-1892.* Flammarion, 1893.

STOULLIG, EDMOND, and NOËL, EDOUARD. *Les Annales du Théâtre et de la Musique.* 41 vols. Paris, Ollendorff, 1876-1918. Paris, Noël 1891-1895.

THALASSO, ADOLPHE. *Le Théâtre Libre.* Paris, Mercure de France, 1909.

VITOUX, GEORGES. *Le Théâtre de L'Avenir.* Paris, Schleicher frères, 1903.

WAXMAN, SAMUEL MONTEFIORE. *Antoine and the Théâtre-Libre.* Cambridge, Mass., Harvard University Press, 1924.

ZOLA, EMILE. *Le Naturalisme au Théâtre.* Nouv. éd. Paris, E. Fasquelle, 1923.

Several contemporary articles on the Théâtre Libre appeared in *Revue d'Art Dramatique, Revue des Deux-Mondes,* and *Revue des Libres et du Théâtre. Die Gegewart* for May 31, 1890, had a review of the French free theatre by Maximilian Harden.

Accounts of later theatres, particularly of the Vieux Colombier, have appeared in many periodicals. A brief list is the following:

COPEAU, JACQUES. "The Theatre du Vieu-Columbier," in *The Drama,* February, 1918, 29:69-75.

"Elaborate simplicity of Jacques Copeau's new theater," in *Current Opinion,* January, 1918, 64:29.

GILLIAM, F. "Pitoev and répertoire," in *Freeman,* September 12, 1923, 8:15-17.

HAMILTON, C. "Le Théâtre du Vieux Colombier," in *Bookman,* January, 1918, 46:534-7.

390   BIBLIOGRAPHY

"Jacques Copeau and the repertory theater," in the *Outlook*, February 21, 1917, 115:310.

LE BAYON, JOSEPH. "Le Théâtre Populaire de Sainte-Anne D'Auray," in *Revue Celtique*, Vol. XXXV-XXXVI, No. 4, 514-527.

LUTETIUS. "Le Mouvement Dramatique en France," in *Modern Languages*, London, June, 1924, Vol. V, No. 6.

ROEDER, RALPH. "Notes on the Stage in Paris," in *Theatre Arts Magazine*, July, 1922, VI, p. 209.

SPIERS, A. G. H. "Opening of the Vieux Colombier," in the *Nation*, December 6, 1917, 105:642-4.

"Vieux Colombier players (After the play)," in the *New Republic*, February 9, 1918, 14:60.

GERMANY

BOOKS

ARNOLD, ROBERT FRANZ. *Das Deutsche Drama*, in Verbindung mit Julius Bab, Albert Ludwig, Friedrich Michael, Max J. Wolff und Rudolf Wolkan. Herausgegeben von Robert F. Arnold. München, Beck, 1925.

—— *Das Moderne Drama.* Second edition. Strassburg, K. J. Trübner, 1912.

BAB, JULIUS. *Neue Wege Zum Drama.* Berlin, Oesterheld and Co., 1911.

—— *Wesen Und Weg der Berliner Volksbühnenbewegung.* Berlin, Ernst Wasmuth, 1919.

BANNER, MAX. *Das Französische Theater der Gegenwart.* Leipzig, Renger, 1898.

BENOIST-HANAPPIER, LOUIS. *Le Drame Naturaliste.* Paris, Félix Alcan, 1905.

BERG, LEO. *Der Naturalismus.* Munich, Pösal, 1892.

BULTHAUPT, H. A. *Dramaturgie des Schauspiel.* 4 vols. Oldenburg, Schulzesche Hofbuchdr., 1918-1924.

CARTER, HUNTLY. *The New Spirit in the European Theatre, 1914-1924.* New York, Doran, 1926.

—— *The Theatre of Max Reinhardt.* New York, Kennerley, 1914.

CONRAD, M. G. *Von Zola bis Hauptmann.* Leipzig, Berlin, H. Seemann, 1902.

DOELL, OTTO. *Die Entwicklung der Naturalistischen Form in Jungstdeutschen Drama.* Halle, H. Gesenius, 1910.

FRANCKE, KUNO. *A History of German Literature.* 4th ed. New York, Holt, 1901.

—— *German After-War Problems.* Cambridge, Harvard University Press, 1927.

—— *German Ideals of Today.* Boston and New York, Houghton Mifflin, 1907.

—— *Glimpses of Modern German Culture.* New York, Dodd, Mead, 1898.

—— *Social Forces in German Literature, a Study in the History of Civilization.* New York, Holt, 1896.

—— *The German Spirit.* New York, Holt, 1916.

FRIEDMANN, SIGISMUND. *Das Deutsche Drama des 19 Jahrhunderts.* Vol. 12. Leipzig, H. Seemann, 1900-1903.

HANSTEIN, ADALBERT VON. *Das Jungste Deutschland.* Leipzig, R. Voigtländer, 1905.

HELLER, OTTO. *Prophets of Dissent.* New York, Knopf, 1918.

—— *Studies in Modern German Literature.* Boston, New York, Ginn, 1905.

HOLZ, A. *Die Kunst, Ihr Wesen und Ihre Gesetze.* Berlin, G. Schuhr, Neue Folge, 1893.

KAISER, GEORG. *Gas,* Part I. Translated by Hermann Scheffauer. In Tucker, S. Marion, *Modern Continental Plays.* New York, Harper, 1929.

LEWISOHN, LUDWIG. *Dramatic Works of Gerhart Hauptmann.* New York, Viking Press, 1914-1924.

—— *The Modern Drama.* New York, Viking Press, 1915.

LITZMANN, B. *Das Deutsche Drama in den Litterarischen Bewegungen der Gegenwart.* Hamburg, L. Voss, 4 Afl., 1897.

LOTHAR, R. *Das Deutsche Drama der Gegenwart.* Munich, G. Müller, 1905.

POLLARD, PERCIVAL. *Masks and Minstrels of New Germany.* Boston, Luce, 1911.

ROBERTSON, JOHN G. *A History of German Literature.* New York, Putnam, 1902.

SAYLER, OLIVER M., ed. *Max Reinhardt and His Theatre.* New York, Brentano, 1924.

SCHEFFAUER, HERMAN GEORGE. *The New Vision in the German Arts.* New York, Huebsch, 1924.

SCHLENTHER, PAUL. *Gerhart Hauptmann, Leben und Werke.* Berlin, S. Fischer, 1912.

—— *Wozu der Lärm, Genesis der Freien Bühne.* Berlin, 1899.

STEIGER, EDGAR. *Das Werden des Neuen Dramas.* 2 vols. Berlin, F. Fontane and Co., 1898.

STERN, A. *Studien zur Litteratur der Gegenwart.* Dresden, Esche, 1895.

STOECKIUS, A. *Naturalism in Recent German Drama.* (Privately printed.) New York, 1903.

THOMAS, CALVIN. *A History of German Literature.* New York and London, Appleton, 1914.

TOLLER, ERNST. *Man and the Masses (Masse Mensch).* Translated by Louis Untermeyer. Garden City, New York, Doubleday, Page, 1924.

WITKOWSKI, GEORG. *German Drama of the Nineteenth Century.* Authorized translation from the 2nd German ed., by L. E. Horning. New York, Holt, 1909.

—— *Naturalism in Recent German Drama.* Translated by L. E. Horning. New York, 1909.

WOLFF, E. *Geschichte der Deutschen Litteratur in der Gegenwart.* Leipzig, S. Hirzel, 1896.

ZOLA, E. *Le Naturalisme au Théâtre.* Paris, Charpentier, 1881.

Many articles on naturalistic drama are in the following reviews: *Die Gesellschaft,* Munich, 1885; *Kunstwart,* Munich, 1887; *Die Freie Bühne,* Berlin, 1890-1894, which continued as *Neue deutsche Rundschau,* and 1903 as *Neue Rundschau; Das Litterarische Echo,* Berlin, 1898; *Bühne und Welt,* Berlin, 1898.

PERIODICALS

BARKER, A. GRANVILLE. "Two German Theatres," in *Fortnightly Review,* January, 1911, 95:60-70.

CARTER, HUNTLY. "The German Theatre in War-Time and After," in the *Fortnightly Review,* February, 1921, 115:284-294.

CLARK, B. "New trends in the theatre," in the *Forum,* November, 1924, 72:665-72.

CURTIN, D. T. "Footlight warfare in Germany," in *Bookman,* October, 1918, 48:155-60.

"Drama the forerunner of German defeat," in *Current Opinion,* June, 1919, 66:368.

"German stage," in the *Edinburgh Review,* October, 1906, 204:447-67.

KINGSTON, GERTRUDE. "Things theatrical in Germany and England," in *19th Century,* December, 1909, 66:990-1007.

LEWISOHN, L. "German theatre of Today," in the *Nation*, May 15, 1920, 110:663-64.

MACGOWAN, KENNETH. "An American Note-Book Abroad," in *Theatre Arts Magazine*, October, 1922, 6:299-312.

—— "The Theatre of Tomorrow," review in *Theatre Arts Magazine*, Vol. 6

MEYER, EDWARD STOCKTON. "The Modern German Drama," in *Critic*, July, 1905, 47:61-70.

RANDALL, A. W. G. "Drama of the German Revolution," in *Contemporary*, December, 1923, 124:755-62.

SAYLER, OLIVER M. "With Europe as Preceptor," in *Theatre Arts Magazine*, October, 1922, VI, 267.

SIMONSON, LEE. "Apologizing for America," in *Theatre Arts Magazine*, July, 1922, VI, 226.

—— "Down to the cellar," in *Theatre Arts Magazine*, April, 1922, 6:117-38.

SMITH, GARNET. "Contemporary German Drama," in the *Quarterly Review*, January, 1914, 220:69-95.

SOISSONS, COUNT DE. *Contemporary*, March, 89:370-79. Same, *Living Age*, May 12, 1906, 249:345-52.

—— "The recent dramatic movement in Germany," in *Contemporary*, February, 1914, 105:236-43.

"The Dominating figure in the new theatre of Germany," in *Current Opinion*, January, 1920, 68:56-57.

STEHLE, MARIE. "Art for the People," in *The Drama*, November, 1928, 19:40-43.

ENGLAND

BOOKS

A Short History of Bristol's Little Theatre—First and Second Seasons. Bristol, Partridge and Love, Ltd., 1925.

ARCHER, WILLIAM. *Study and Stage*, 1899.

—— *The Old Drama and the New; an Essay in Re-valuation.* Boston, Small, Maynard, 1923.

BORSA, MARIO. *The English Stage of To-Day.* Translated from original Italian by Selwyn Brinton. London and New York, J. Lane, 1908.

BOUGHTON, RUTLAND. *The Glastonbury Festival Movement.* London, Somerset Folk Press, 1922.

CLARK, BARRETT H. *British and American Dramatists of Today.* New York, Holt, 1915.

DICKINSON, THOMAS HERBERT. *The Contemporary Drama of England.* Boston, Little, Brown, 1917.

ERVINE, ST. JOHN. *The Organized Theatre.* New York, Macmillan, 1924.

FILON, A. *The English Stage.* Translated by Frederic Whyte. Introduction by Henry Arthur Jones. London, Milne, 1897.

FOWELL, F., and PALMER, F. *Censorship in England.* London, F. Palmer, 1913.

GRANVILLE-BARKER, HARLEY. *The Exemplary Theatre.* Boston, Little, Brown, 1922.

GREIN, JACOB THOMAS. *The New World of the Theatre,* 1923-24, with a preface by G. K. Chesterton. London, M. Hopkinson and Co., 1924.

—— *The World of the Theatre; Impressions and Memoirs, March 1920-1921.* London, W. Heinemann, 1921.

HAMILTON, CICELY MARY. *The Old Vic,* [by] Cicely Hamilton and Lilian Bayles. London, J. Cape, Ltd., 1926.

HENDERSON, ARCHIBALD. *George Bernard Shaw, His Life and Works.* London, Hurst and Blackett, 1911.

HOWE, PERCIVAL PRESLAND. *Dramatic Portraits.* New York, H. Kennerley, 1913.

—— *The Repertory Theatre: a Record and a Criticism.* New York, Kennerley, 1911.

JAGGARD, WILLIAM. *Shakespeare Memorial, Stratford-on-Avon; Fifty Years' Retrospect with Record of Plays and Players.* Stratford-on-Avon, Shakespeare Press, 1926.

JONES, HENRY ARTHUR. *Foundations of a National Drama.* London, Macmillan, 1912.

—— *The Renascence of the English Drama.* London, Macmillan, 1895.

LEE, SIDNEY. *Shakespeare and the Modern Stage.* New York, Scribner's, 1906.

LITTLEWOOD, S. R., and others. *Somerset and the Drama.* The Somerset Folk Series, Number 7. London, Somerset Folk Press, 1922.

MACCARTHY, DESMOND. *The Court Theatre, 1904-1907.* London, A. H. Bullen, 1907.

MACKINNON, A. *The Oxford Amateurs: A Short History of Theatricals of the University.* London, Chapman and Hall, Ltd., 1910.

MAUDE, CYRIL. *The Haymarket Theatre.* London, G. Richards, 1903.

MONTAGUE, C. E. *Dramatic Values.* Garden City, New York, 1925.

MOORE, G. *Impressions and Opinions.* New York, Scribner's, 1891.

MORGAN, ARTHUR E. *Tendencies of Modern English Drama.* New York, Scribner's, 1924.

NICOLL, ALLARDYCE. *British Drama.* New York, Thomas Y. Crowell, 1925.

—— *The Development of the Theatre.* New York, Harcourt, Brace, 1927.

OLIVER, D. E. *The English Stage: Its Origin and Modern Developments.* London, Ouseley, 1912.

PALMER, JOHN. *The Future of the Theatre.* London, G. Bell and Sons, Ltd., 1913.

PLAYFAIR, NIGEL, SIR. *The Story of the Lyric Theatre Hammersmith.* London, Chatto and Windus, 1925.

POEL, WILLIAM. *What is Wrong with the Stage?* London, G. Allen and Unwin, Ltd., 1920.

SCOTT, CLEMENT W. *The Drama of Yesterday and Today.* London, New York, Macmillan, 1899.

Shakespeare Memorial Association, Stratford-on-Avon. *A History of the Shakespeare Memorial, Stratford-on-Avon.* Published for the Council of the Shakespeare Memorial Association. London, Cassell, Peter and Galpin, 1880.

SHAW, GEORGE BERNARD. *Plays Pleasant and Unpleasant.* New York. Brentano, 1905.

The Drama in Adult Education. A Report by the Adult Education Committee of the Board of Education, being Paper No. 6 of the Committee. London, His Majesty's Stationery Office, 1926.

WALKLEY, A. B. *Drama and Life.* London, Methuen and Co., 1907.

—— *More Prejudice.* London, W. Heinemann, Ltd., 1923.

—— *Pastiche and Prejudice.* New York, Knopf, 1921.

—— *Still More Prejudice.* London, W. Heinemann, Ltd., 1925.

WESTWOOD, DORIS. *These Players; a Diary of the "Old Vic" with a Foreword by Lilian Bayles.* London, H. Cranton, Ltd., 1926.

PERIODICALS

ARCHER, WILLIAM. "The Free Stage and the New Drama," in *The Fortnightly Review,* Vol. 50 (New Series), November 1, 1891, pp. 663-672.

CRAIG, EDWARD GORDON, SIR. "Theatres for all. Notes on the new theatre at Welwyn," in *Mask,* 1929, Vol. 14: 51-53.

"Everyman theatre," in *Contemporary Review,* November, 1919, Vol. 116, pp. 577-80.

FORMAN, W. COURTHOPE. *Sadler's Wells*, Notes and queries, London, 1925, Vol. 148, pp. 273, 274.

GREVILLE, EDEN. "Bernard Shaw and his Plays," in *Munsey's Magazine*, March, 1906, Vol. xxxiv, no. 6, pp. 765-768.

MOORE, GEORGE. "Our Dramatists and their Literature," in *Fortnightly Review*, Vol. 76 (New Series), November 1, 1889, pp. 620-632.

—— "A Preface to *The Bending of the Bough*," in *Fortnightly Review*, Vol. LXVII (New Series), February 1, 1900, pp. 317-24.

POLLOCK, WILLIAM. "Norwich's apron-stage theatre," in *Landmark*, London, 1921, Vol. iii, pp. 729-731.

R. H. "The Maddermarket Theatre, Norwich," in *The Garrick Magazine*, October, 1926, Vol. 10, no. 1.

ROBINSON, LENNOX. "The Playhouse, Liverpool," in *The London Observer*, January 25, 1925.

"Shoreham Village Players," in *Kent Education Gazette*, August, 1926.

SMALTZ, ALFRED G. "The Old Vic Theatre," in *Drama*, 1929, Vol. XIX, pp. 197, 198.

The Shakespeare Journal—The Organ of the London Shakespeare League, June-August, 1925, Vol. XI, no. 2.

IRELAND

BOOKS

BICKLEY, FRANCIS. *J. M. Synge and the Irish Dramatic Movement.* Boston, Houghton Mifflin, 1912.

BITHELL, JETHRO. *W. B. Yeats.* Paris, 1913.

BORSA, MARIO. *The English Stage of To-Day.* Translated and edited with a prefatory note by Selwyn Brinton. New York, Lane, 1907.

BOURGEOIS, MAURICE. *John Millington Synge and the Irish Theatre.* London, Macmillan, 1913.

BOYD, ERNEST A. *Ireland's Literary Renaissance.* New York, Lane, 1916.

—— *The Contemporary Drama of Ireland.* Boston, Little, Brown, 1917.

BROWN, STEPHEN J. *A Guide to Books on Ireland, Part I.* Dublin, Longmans Green, 1912.

CARTER, HUNTLY. *The New Spirit in Drama and Art.* London, Kennerley, 1912.

CHANDLER, F. W. *Aspects of Modern Drama.* New York, Macmillan, 1914.

CHESTERTON, G. K. *Irish Impressions.* New York, John Lane, 1920.

CLARK, B. H. *British and American Drama of To-Day.* New York, Holt, 1915.

COLUM, PADRAIC. *The Road Round Ireland.* New York, Macmillan, 1926.

CORKERY, DANIEL. *The Hidden Ireland.* Dublin, M. H. Gill and Son, Ltd., 1925.

ELTON, OLIVER. *Modern Studies.* London, E. Arnold, 1907.

FIGGIS, DARRELL. *Studies and Appreciations.* London and New York, J. M. Dent and Son, 1912.

GREGORY, LADY. *Our Irish Theatre.* New York, Putnam, 1913.

—— ed. *Ideals in Ireland.* London, At the Unicorn, 1907.

—— *Poets and Dreamers.* Dublin, Hodges, Figgis and Co., Ltd., 1903.

GWYNN, STEPHEN. *The Irish Drama.* (In McCarthy, Justin, *Irish Literature,* vol. X, pp. XII-XXV.) Philadelphia, 1904.

—— *To-Day and To-Morrow in Ireland.* Dublin, 1903.

HAMILTON, CLAYTON. *Studies in Stagecraft.* New York, Holt, 1914.

HONE, JOSEPH MAUNSELL. *W. B. Yeats.* Dublin and London, Maunsel and Co., 1916.

HOWE, P. P. *The Repertory Theatre.* London, M. Secker, 1910.

—— *J. M. Synge. A Critical Study.* London and New York, Secker, 1912.

HUNEKER, JAMES. *The Pathos of Distance.* New York, Scribner's, 1913.

JACKSON, HOLBROOK. *All Manner of Folk.* New York, Kennerley, 1912.

—— *The Eighteen Nineties.* New York, Kennerley, 1913.

KENNEDY, J. M. *English Literature: 1880-1905.* London, Small, 1912.

KRANS, HORATIO SHEAFE. *W. B. Yeats and the Irish Literary Revival.* New York, Doubleday, 1904.

MALONE, ANDREW E. *Modern English Literature.* New York, Holt, 1914.

—— *The Irish Drama.* New York, Scribner's, 1929.

MARTYN, EDWARD. *The Heather Field.* New York, Brentano, 1917.

MASEFIELD, JOHN. *John M. Synge: A Few Personal Recollections.* New York, Macmillan, 1916.

MASON, EUGENE. *A Book of Preferences in Literature.* New York, Dutton, 1915.

MONAHAN, M. *Nova Hibernia.* New York, Kennerley, 1914.

MONTAGUE, C. E. *Dramatic Values.* New York, Doubleday, Page, 1925.

398 BIBLIOGRAPHY

Moore, George. *Hail and Farewell.* 3 vols. New York, Appleton, 1911-1914.
—— *The Bending of the Bough.* Chicago and New York, H. S. Stone 1900.
Morris, Lloyd R. *The Celtic Dawn; a Survey of the Renascence in Ireland, 1889-1916.* New York, Macmillan, 1917.
Nevinson, H. W. *Books and Personalities.* New York, Lane, 1905.
O'Casey, Sean. *The Silver Tassie.* New York, Macmillan, 1928.
O'Conor, Norreys Jephson. *Changing Ireland.* Cambridge, Harvard University Press, 1924.
Paul-Dubois, L. *Contemporary Ireland.* New York, The Baker and Taylor Co., 1908.
Reid, Forrest. *W. B. Yeats; a Critical Study.* New York, Dodd, Mead, 1915.
Wauchope, G. *A New Irish Drama.* University of South Carolina, 1925.
Weygandt, C. *Irish Plays and Playwrights.* Boston, Houghton Mifflin, 1913.
Yeats, William B. *Autobiographies: Reveries Over Childhood and Youth and the Trembling of the Veil.* New York, Macmillan, 1927.
—— *Dramatic Poems.* New York, Macmillan, 1924.
—— *Ideas of Good and Evil.* London, A. H. Bullen, 1903.
—— *Irish Fairy and Folk Tales.* New York, Boni and Liveright, 1918.
—— *Plays and Controversies.* New and rev. ed. New York, Macmillan, 1924.
—— *The Bounty of Sweden.* Dublin, Ireland, The Cuala Press, 1925.
—— *The Cutting of an Agate.* New York, Macmillan, 1912.

PERIODICALS

Beltaine. An Occasional Publication. The Organ of the Irish Literary Theatre. 1899-1900.
Bewley, Charles. "The Irish National Theatre," in the *Dublin Review,* January, 1913, and *Living Age,* February 15, 1913, 276:410-18.
Bickley, Francis. "Deirdre," in the *Irish Review,* July, 1912, pp. 252-254.
Birmingham, George. "The Literary Movement in Ireland," in the *Fortnightly Review,* December, 1907, 88:947-957.
Bourgeois, Maurice. "Synge and Loti," in the *Westminster Review,* May, 1913, 179:532-36.

BOYD, ERNEST A. "The Abbey Theatre," in the *Irish Review,* February, 1913, pp. 628-634.

COLUM, PADRAIC. "The Irish Literary Movement," in the *Forum,* January, 1915, Vol. 53, pp. 133-148.

—— "Youngest Ireland," in *The Seven Arts Magazine,* September, 1917, Vol. II, no. 11, pp. 608-623.

CONNELL, NORREYS. "John Millington Synge," in the *English Review,* June, 1909, 2:609-613.

COOPER, BRYAN. "The Drama in Ireland," in the *Irish Review,* May, 1913, pp. 140-43.

DUNCAN, E. M. "The Writings of W. B. Yeats," in the *Fortnightly Review,* February, 1909, 91:253-270.

DUNSANY, LORD. "Romance and the Modern Stage," in *National Review,* July, 1911, 57:827-836.

ERVINE, ST. JOHN. "The Irish Dramatist and the Irish People," in the *Forum,* June, 1914, Vol. 51, pp. 940-48.

GUNNING, G. HAMILTON. "The Decline of the Abbey Theatre Drama," in the *Irish Review,* February, 1912, pp. 606-609.

GWYNNE, STEPHEN. "The Irish Literary Theatre and its Affinities," in the *Fortnightly Review,* 1901, Vol. 70 (New Series), pp. 1050-62.

—— "The Uncommercial Theatre," in the *Fortnightly Review,* December, 1902, Vol. 72 (New Series), pp. 1044-1054.

HOARE, JOHN E. "Ireland's National Drama," in the *North American Review,* October, 1911, Vol. 1, 94:566-575.

JOHNSTON, DENIS. "Sean O'Casey: an appreciation," in *Living Age,* April 17, 1926, Vol. 329, p. 163.

MACGRATH, JOHN. "W. B. Yeats and Ireland," in *Westminster Review,* July, 1911, 176:1-11.

MAGUIRE, MARY C. "John Synge," in the *Irish Review,* March, 1911, pp. 39-43.

MARTYN, EDWARD. "A Plea for the Revival of the Irish Literary Theatre," in the *Irish Review,* April, 1914, pp. 79-84.

MENCKEN, H. L. "Synge and Others," in *Smart Set,* October, 1912.

MENNLOCK, WALTER. "Dramatic Values," in the *Irish Review,* September, 1911, pp. 325-329.

MONTGOMERY, K. L. "Some Writers of the Celtic Renaissance," in the *Fortnightly Review,* September, 1911, 96:545-61.

REID, FORREST. "The Early Work of W. B. Yeats," in the *Irish Review,* January, 1912, pp. 529-536.

Samhain, 1901-1907.

TENNYSON, CHARLES. "Irish Plays and Playwrights," in the *Quarterly Review*, July, 1911, 215:219-43.
—— "The Rise of the Irish Theatre," in the *Contemporary Review*, August, 1911, 100:240-7.
"The Abbey Directors and Mr. Sean O'Casey," in the *Irish Statesman*, June 9, 1928, Vol. 10, no. 14.
TOWNSHEND, GEORGE. "The Irish Drama," in the *Drama*, Chicago, August, 1911.
YEATS, WILLIAM BUTLER. "The Irish Drama," in *Twentieth Century Magazine*, Boston, 1911, Vol. 5, pp. 12-15.

An important series of articles appeared in the *Boston Evening Transcript*, September 19 to October 20, 1911, while the Abbey Players were in the United States.

SCOTLAND

BOOKS

Since the Scottish theatre is little known in the United States, the titles of some of its published plays are added.

BAIN, ROBERT. *James the First of Scotland.* Glasgow, Machhose, Jackson and Co., 1921.
BELL, JOHN JAY. *One-Act Plays of To-Day.* J. W. Marriott, compiler. London, 1924.
—— *The Laird's Lucky Number; a Farcical Comedy in One Act.* London, Gowans and Gray, Ltd., 1926. (Repertory farces, No. 4.)
—— *The Pie in the Oven, a Comedy in One Act.* London and Glasgow, Gowans and Gray, Ltd.; Boston, L. Phillips, 1922.
—— *Thead o' Scarlet; a Play in One Act.* In Marriott, J. W., *One-Act Plays of To-Day.*
BLAKE, GEORGE. *The Mother; a Play in Two Scenes.* Glasgow, W. Wilson and Co., Ltd., 1921. (Scottish national plays series, no. 1.)
BRONCH, JAMES H. *The Waefu' Bridal; a Play in One Act,* and *The Reekin' Lum; a Comedy in Three Scenes.* Two short Scots plays. Paisley, A. Gardner, 1927.
FERGUSON, J. A. *Campbell of Kilmhor; a Play in One Act.* London, Gowans and Gray, Ltd., 1915. (Repertory plays, no. 13.)
MALLOCH, GEORGE RESTON. *Thomas the Rhymer (a Play in One Act).* Montrose, The Scottish Poetry Bookshop.
WODEN, GRACE. *The Money's the Thing; a Play in Three Acts.* Glasgow, W. Wilson and Co., Ltd., 1921.

PERIODICAL

DENHOLM, REAH. "The National Theatre Movement," in *The Scots Magazine*, July, 1924. Reprinted in leaflet of theatre.

WALES

BOOKS

FRANCIS, J. O. *Change*. Drama League Series.
HART, OLIVE ELY. *The Drama in Modern Wales*. Philadelphia, University of Pennsylvania Press, 1928. (See bibliography for plays in Welsh and English.)

PERIODICAL

GRIFFITH, A. S. *Cymmrodorion Society Transactions 1912-1913*, pp. 129-130.

RUSSIA

BAKSHY, ALEXANDER. *The Path of the Modern Russian Stage and Other Essays*. London, Palmer and Hayward, 1916.
CARTER, HUNTLY. *The New Spirit in the European Theatre*. New York, Doran, 1926.
—— *The New Spirit in the Russian Theatre*, 1917-1928. New York, Brentano's, 1929.
CHEKHOV, ANTON PAVLOVICH. *Letters on the Short Story, the Drama and Other Literary Topics*. Selected and edited by Louis S. Friedland. New York, Minton, Balch, 1924.
CRAIG, EDWARD GORDON, SIR. *On the Art of the Theatre*. Chicago, Small, Maynard, 1925.
EVREINOV, NIKOLAI. *The Theatre of the Soul (The Foreword)*. Translated by Marie Potapenko and Christopher St. John. London, Hendersons, 1915.
FLANAGAN, HALLIE. *Shifting Scenes in the European Theatre*. New York, Coward-McCann, 1928.
FREEMAN, JOSEPH, KUNITZ, JOSHUA, and LOZOWICK, LOUIS. *Voices of October. Art and Literature in Soviet Russia*. New York, Vanguard, 1930.
FÜLÖP-MILLER, RENÉ. and GREGOR, JOSEPH. *The Russian Theatre*. Translated by England, Paul. Philadelphia, Lippincott [1929].
KITCHEN, KARL KINGSLEY. *The Night Side of Europe as Seen by a Broadwayite Abroad*. Cleveland, David Gibson, 1914.

KOMISARJEVSKY, THEODORE. *Myself and the Theatre.* New York, Dutton, 1930.

KORNILOV, ALEKSANDER. *History of Russia, Vol. II.* New York, Knopf, 1916-1917.

MASARYK, THOMAS GARRIGUE. *The Spirit of Russia, Vol. II.* New York, Macmillan, 1919.

OLGIN, MOISSAYE JOSEPH. *A Guide to Russian Literature.* New York, Harcourt Brace, 1920.

SAYLER, OLIVER M. *Inside the Moscow Art Theatre.* New York, Brentano, 1925.

—— *The Russian Theatre.* New York, Brentano's, 1922.

—— *The Russian Theatre Under the Revolution.* Boston, Little, Brown, 1920.

STANISLAVSKY, CONSTANTIN. *My Life in Art.* Boston, Little, Brown, 1927.

WIENER, LEO. *The Contemporary Drama of Russia.* Boston, Little, Brown, 1924.

WILLIAMS, HAROLD WHITMORE. *Russia of the Russians.* New York, Scribner's, 1914.

PERIODICALS

BAKSHY, ALEXANDER. "The Russian Dramatic Stage," in *The Drama,* February, 1919, 9:31-61.

BARKER, GRANVILLE. "The Moscow Art Theatre," in *The Seven Arts Magazine,* September, 1917, Vol. 2, pp. 659-667.

"Bolsheviki stamping out art," in the *Literary Digest,* April 22, 1922, 73:30-1.

BROWN, JOHN MASON. "The Russian Theatre," in the *Atlantic Monthly,* Vol. 143, January, 1929, pp. 83-94.

CALDERON, GEORGE. "The Russian Stage," in the *Quarterly Review,* Vol. 217, July, 1912, pp. 21-42.

CARTER, H. "Historical sketch of the theatre in Soviet Russia," in the *Fortnightly Review,* March, 1922, 117:498-508.

—— "Modern Polish and Russian theatres," in the *Living Age,* December 17, 1921, 311:727-31.

—— "Notes on the newest Russian theatre, the State children's theatre," in *Drama,* May, 1924, 14:248-50.

CHAMBERLAIN, W. H. "New trends in the theatre," in the *Forum,* October, 1924, 72:520-26.

"Climax of the Russian dramatic invasion," in *Current Opinion,* March, 1923, 74:329-30.

CRAWFORD, J. "Moscow to Broadway," in *Drama*, March, 1923, 13:212.

DOLE, E. M. "Most distinguished stock company in the world," in the *Mentor*, March, 1923, 11:38-9.

HARRISON, M. E. "Bolos and the arts," in the *Bookman*, December, 1923, 58:384-94.

KING, G. B. "Democratic drama in Russia," in the *Outlook*, November 10, 1915, 111:598.

MACGOWAN, K. "How a little theatre grew great," in *Collier's*, May 19, 1923, 71:18.

NABOKOFF, C. "Russian drama in the XIXth and XXth centuries," in *Contemporary Review*, May, 1922, 121, 636-644.

PARKER, R. A. "Moscow's Art Theatre visits New York," in *Independent*, February 3, 1923; 110:97-8.

PIERCE, LUCY FRANCE. "The Seagull Theatre of Moscow," in *The Drama*, February, 1913, 9:168-177.

"Playing to the Russian peasants," in the *Literary Digest*, May 31, 1924, 81:31.

"Punchless plays of Russia's most original theatre," in *Current Opinion*, September, 1917, 63:170-71.

SAYLER, OLIVER M. "The World's First Theatre: Moscow Art Theatre," in *The Drama*, June, 1919.

—— "Russian Theatre under the Revolution," in *The Drama*, December, 1918.

UZZELL, T. H. "Antique theatre," in *Harper's Weekly*, November 27, 1915, 61:526-27.

YARMOLINSKY, A. "The Moscow Art Theatre," in *The Russian Review*, January, 1917, 3:34-38.

YOUNG, S. "Many gods," in the *North American Review*, March, 1923, 217:343-352.

ZILBOORG, GREGORY. "The Theatre of the Past in Soviet Russia," in *The Drama*, March, 1927, Vol. 12, 195-196.

Almost innumerable articles in periodicals and newspapers appeared upon the Moscow Art Theatre during its seasons in America.

INDEX

405